BACKSTABBING FOR BEGINNERS

BACKSTABBING
FOR BEGINNERS

My Crash Course in International Diplomacy

MICHAEL SOUSSAN

NATION
BOOKS

A Member of the Perseus Books Group

Published by Nation Books, a member of the Perseus Books Group
116 East 16th Street, 8th Floor
New York, NY 10003

Nation Books is a co-publishing venture of The Nation Institute and the Perseus Books Group.

Books published by Nation Books are available at special discounts for bulk purchases in the United States by corporations, institutions, and other organizations. For more information, please contact the Special Markets Department at the Perseus Books Group, 2300 Chestnut Street, Suite 200, Philadelphia, PA 19103, or call (800) 810-4145, ext. 5000, or e-mail special.markets@perseusbooks.com.

Designed by Brent Wilcox
Text set in 11.25 point Adobe Garamond

Library of Congress Cataloging-in-Publication Data
Soussan, Michael.
    Backstabbing for beginners : my crash course in international diplomacy /
by Michael Soussan.
        p.   cm.
    Includes bibliographical references and index.
    ISBN 978-1-56858-397-6 (hardcover : alk. paper)
    1. United Nations. Oil-for-Food Program.   2. United Nations. Oil-for-Food Program—Corrupt practices.   3. Humanitarian assistance—Iraq.   4. Food relief—Iraq.   5. Economic sanctions—Iraq.   6. Petroleum industry and trade—Iraq.   7. Soussan, Michael.   I. Title.
JZ6373.S64 2008
363.8'8309567—dc22

                                                                    2008031698

10 9 8 7 6 5 4 3 2 1

This book is dedicated to my father, André Soussan.

CONTENTS

ACKNOWLEDGMENTS

I wish to thank my editors, Ruth Baldwin and Carl Bromley, and my agents, Jennifer Gates and Mary Beth Chappell, whose advice and direction helped guide this project to completion. A number of talented friends and colleagues also provided valuable feedback, advice, or encouragement at critical stages in my writer's journey. They include Audun Huslid, Jad Mouawad, Hedi Kim, Daniel Cruise, Liz Bowyer, Robert Whitcomb, Terry Collymore, Celeste Katz, David Guç, Web Stone, Robert McKee, Tamara Chalabi, Keith Fleming, Amir Afkhami, Chris Chappell, Megan Kingery, Joanne Dickow, Patrick Arfi, Jacques Baudouin, Denis Poncet, Hesi Carmel, Ami Horowitz, Matt Groff, Tanaz Esheghian, Inna Khavinson, Douglas Rogers, Paul Rothenberg, Shannon Godwin, Scott Anderson, and Judy Goldstein.

Afsane Bassir Pour, of *Le Monde,* and Richard Roth, of CNN, offered me my first opportunities to cover the United Nations for the media, when I was just out of college. One reason they considered me was that I had cofounded and edited *The Brown Journal of World Affairs*, at Brown University, thanks to the support offered by the Watson Institute and grants from Vartan Gregorian and Artemis Joukwosky. Together with my academic mentors, Terrence Hoppman, Jarat Chopra, Pierre Hassner, and Marie-Claude Smouts, they helped me develop a strong interest in world affairs, and the confidence necessary to think for myself.

I am grateful to the staff at The Writers' Room, where most of this book was written, for offering a productive space in which to work in New York. My students at New York University's Center for Global Affairs unwittingly helped me more than they can imagine with questions for which I am in their debt. Finally, I wish to thank the many UN staff whose dedication and competence may not be the focus of this tale, but whose example gave me hope that our world organization can in fact be held to higher standards.

AUTHOR'S NOTE

I wish I could say none of the events in this story ever happened. Unfortunately, they now form part of our collective history. Information pertaining to wrongdoing by particular individuals named herein is drawn from the publicly available findings of the Independent Inquiry Committee into the Oil-for-Food Program (www.iic-offp.org). It is important for the reader to understand that none of the persons referred to in this story should be considered guilty of criminal behavior unless they have been sentenced in a court of law.

Some names have been changed in order to protect the privacy of individuals who were not already in the public sphere. I took the liberty to describe the events and the attitudes that defined this critical era in world affairs without the pretense of cold objectivity. I was an emotional participant in this story. As I recall certain events from memory, I am also aware that others may disagree with details of how these unfolded. The characters who appear herein cannot be defined only by their mistakes, or by their portrayal in this or other written works. I too made mistakes, and had ample opportunity to change my mind about important issues throughout this story. And thus I hope that our collective misadventures, our moments of ridicule or tragedy, will not be judged too harshly, for we were merely ordinary, flawed individuals faced with extraordinary circumstances.

CHAPTER 1

Whistleblower

DELTA SHUTTLE, EN ROUTE FROM NEW YORK CITY
TO WASHINGTON, D.C., APRIL 28, 2004

I never imagined it would come to this. Yet here I was, sitting on a plane headed for Washington, D.C., where I was scheduled to testify before Congress in less than two hours. I would be speaking about a rather strange affair. Margaret Warner, of the PBS *NewsHour*, described it as the "largest financial scandal in UN history." Fred Barnes, of Fox News, went further, calling it the worst scandal in the history of mankind.

I fiddled with the ventilation knob. My armpits were drenched. I sat back, took a deep breath, and closed my eyes. How the hell had I landed myself in this mess?

"Should be a nice day, huh?"

I opened my eyes and looked at my neighbor. I knew from the instant he sat down that he was a compulsive airplane conversationalist, and I had tried my best to avoid his eager gaze.

"Not a cloud in the sky," he added, pointing out the window and encouraging me to check for myself.

"That's right," I said. "Should be a smooth flight."

I reached inside my bag, withdrawing my iPod and the speech I was supposed to give in a couple of hours. I needed to go over my remarks one last time.

"So!" he said. "What brings you to D.C.?"

Did he not see I had plugged in my earphones?

"I have to . . . give this speech," I said.

"Really? Where?"

"At the House International Relations Committee."

"Huh. . . . Are you like an expert or something?"

"No, not exactly. I used to work for the UN. I just need to focus on this for a bit, if you don't mind."

"Of course, of course. . . ."

I could feel his gaze over my shoulder as I tried to concentrate on my text. I took a deep breath and exhaled irritably.

"You feeling nervous?" he asked. He had a knowing grin on his chubby face.

"Yeah, a bit. But I'd feel much better if I could—"

"Have you seen the studies they did?"

"Who? What studies?"

"You know, about people's fears? Apparently, public speaking ranks number one."

"Really?"

"Yeah. You know what number two is?"

"No."

"Death! Ha ha ha ha!"

With that, he slipped out a copy of the *New York Post* and started flipping the pages noisily. I turned up the volume on my iPod and forced myself to concentrate. I was on the second page of my testimony when he poked me on the shoulder.

"*What?*"

"Is that you?" he asked, pointing at an article in his tabloid. It had a big fat title:

U.N. BIG WILL TELL ALL ON OILY SCAM

"Oh," I said. "No, that wouldn't be me. Nobody would call *me* a 'UN big' . . . do you mind if I have a look, though?"

To my knowledge, no senior UN official had agreed to testify yet, so I was curious to know whom the article was talking about. As I read the story, by Niles Lathem, I had a shock:

WASHINGTON—Michael Soussan, a former program coordinator for the $100 billion fund, is expected to be the star witness of a House International Relations Committee hearing looking into Saddam's gigantic $10.1 billion rip-off.

Committee sources said Soussan, now a New York–area writer, is expected to give the first, under oath, public account from an insider about how top U.N. officials were aware of Saddam's oil smuggling and kickback schemes. . . .

I put the paper down and stared blankly into space.

"Do you know this guy?" asked my neighbor.

"Um . . . yeah."

"Sounds like he's ready to spill the beans."

"Yeah. . . . Excuse me, I have to go to the bathroom."

As soon as I got up, a stewardess came running.

"Sir, please return to your seat. The pilot has put the seat belt sign on."

"But I really need to go, I—"

"I'm sorry, sir, please return to your seat."

"Come on, lady, let him go," my neighbor intervened. "He's testifying in Congress today. He's nervous."

I wanted to strangle him.

"I'm fine . . . it's *fine*!" I sat back down, turned up the music full blast, and looked out the window.

It had been seven years since I left Washington, D.C., to embark on this unusual journey. The UN Oil-for-Food operation had been set up in 1996 to provide for the humanitarian needs of Iraq's civilians who had suffered dramatic shortages of basic necessities under the stringent economic sanctions adopted in 1990, following Iraq's invasion of Kuwait.

While diplomats jousted for the moral high ground in New York, lecturing one another on international law, those same laws were being violated methodically behind the scenes through an ever-increasing flow of crooked deals that cheated Iraq's civilians out of an enormous share of their country's wealth. Billions had gone missing from right under our nose, and we weren't even sure how many. Soon, this collective fiasco would be investigated by a high-level anticorruption commission. France, the United States, and Russia would get embroiled in a mutual blame game. Bureaucrats at the United Nations would turn on one another. Hundreds of lobbyists would be called up to defend some 2,300 companies that had broken the law in order to gain favor with Saddam Hussein. The trickle of damning revelations would soon turn into a flood. A judge investigating the fraud in Iraq was killed in an explosion, and several sources used by investigators on the ground mysteriously disappeared. Some influential diplomats, politicians, and other power brokers would go to jail. It promised to be a political bloodbath.

Some people blamed me for helping set this whole debacle in motion after I became the first former employee of the UN operation to call for an independent investigation in an op-ed published in the *Wall Street Journal* the previous month. My intervention had snowballed, and I received myriad requests for interviews, including from CNN, Fox, ABC, the BBC, and many others—most of which I turned down. But when I received the invitation from Congress, I decided to accept.

My position, at the crossroads of pressing humanitarian concerns, big-power politics, and multibillion-dollar business interests, provided an un-usual vantage point on the Iraq conflict. While much of the international community was hypnotized by the "hunt" for Saddam's proscribed weapons, my colleagues and I had our eyes on the human dimension of the conflict.

In Iraq, we became familiar with a society in which youngsters had less ed-ucation than their parents, where the infrastructure was rotten beyond repair, where criminal gangs close to the regime ruled all the country's trade and smuggling routes, and where the only thing that held society together was fear. In 2003 the United States and its allies had set out to create a "new Iraq" on the ruins of the old one. This ambitious agenda underestimated the damage that had been done to the Iraqi people in the thirteen years since the Gulf War.

In New York, we saw the institution that was supposed to stand for inter-national order break its own laws for seven years. The UN Security Council operated much like a drug cartel, fighting over access to Iraq's oil and, in so doing, letting the Iraqi dictator cannibalize his own country in partnership with our most respectable international corporations.

A strange conspiracy of silence had prevailed for many years. The Clinton and Bush administrations had been intimately aware of the massive fraud. French and Russian government officials had directly participated in it, as had officials from all over Europe, South Africa, Australia, India, Lebanon, Jordan, and Syria, among others. Reuters, the Associated Press, and most news organizations with correspondents in Iraq had ample evidence as well. As did we, the humanitarian community of the United Nations.

I was determined to break that silence now. But I couldn't care less how the unfolding "scandal" ranked in the annals of history. It was merely the third act of a tragic story that highlighted some of the core flaws of our international system and the frightening, corrupting power of the black elixir that fuels the world economy. From the end of the cold war to the onset of the "war on ter-ror," the Iraq conflict can be looked at as a mirror reflecting the evolving na-ture of our global political power game.

In order to explain what happened, I would need to describe the events and the attitudes that prevailed at the United Nations during this critical era in international affairs—a time during which I came of age.

As I stepped out of the plane in Washington, D.C., my neighbor insisted we exchange business cards. When he read mine, he looked up at me.

"So it's you! The guy in the article. . . ."

Well, I can't say I recognized myself in the article's depiction. I had never thought of myself as a whistleblower. I had stayed loyal as long as I could.

I knew there would be no going back on this decision. But it was a lonely road. Between the UN-bashers who were hyping up my appearance and the UN-apologists who resented it, I felt everyone in this affair somehow fell into rank behind interest groups that could protect them—except me. What I had to say would not flatter any side in this conflict.

The choice, as I saw it, was between cynicism and candor. If all of us insisted that we really cared about the people of Iraq as much as we professed, then this story could only be described as a conspiracy of saints. Alternatively, we could accept that what made this episode in recent history possible was not so much the lies we told one another but the lies we told ourselves.

Part One

CHAPTER 2

Do-Gooder

Four hundred women crammed into a warehouse. The deafening sound of sewing machines. Ralph Lauren and Tommy Hilfiger shirts piling up in large bins at the far end of the factory floor, ready to be shipped out. The shirts were labeled "Made in the USA." But what the label did not specify was that the women working in this sweatshop—young Filipinas and Chinese girls, for the most part—were paid far less than the U.S. minimum wage. A loophole in the law allowed the U.S. commonwealth island of Saipan, located somewhere near nowhere in the Pacific Ocean, to import foreign workers and pay them dirt to make shirts.

The point of my presence at the scene was to help these factory owners get away with exploitation.

"See? Working conditions are not as horrible as the press would have us believe," said Pat, the team leader of the Congressional delegation that had come here to "witness conditions on the ground"—as well as to play golf, enjoy the amenities of a five-star luxury resort, take sightseeing tours, and stop over for two days in Hawaii on the flight back to Washington, D.C. The junket's only uncomfortable moment was the present one. Walking through the aisles of the sweatshop like noblemen from a different century, dressed in khakis and blue shirts, we observed the girls at work. I noticed that they did not look up at us. They could not afford a moment of reprieve. One girl was sewing zippers, and after I insisted on catching her eye, she paused—just long enough to acknowledge me but not long enough to cause a stoppage in the chain of events that made *shmattes* into clothes. By the time I managed a smile, she was back at work.

"It's clean, well lit," Pat continued. And the members of the Congressional junket nodded. We were all eager to get the hell out of there as quickly as possible. A special treat awaited us at the end of the tour: discounted clothes. A chance to shop *directly* from the sweatshop! And to distract us from any sinking feeling such direct sponsorship of exploitation might cause, we had a field trip planned for the afternoon. We were going to visit the neighboring island of Tinian, to see the airfield from which the United States launched the Enola Gay on its mission to drop an atomic bomb on Japan.

"Fact-finding missions." That's what these free, lobbyist-operated vacations were called in Congress. Our job was to drop little one-liners here and there: "These girls come from very poor families." "It's a lot of money for them here." "They work a few years, and when they go back they can buy houses for their entire family." "The stories of mistreatment are exaggerated." "If they had to be paid U.S. minimum wage, the factory would go out of business, and then what? The island's economy would collapse. Then what?"

But we knew, and our nodding counterparts knew, that this was exploitation. These girls lived in barracks, shopped at the company store, and could be kicked off the island anytime it pleased their owners. If they were abused, they could run to the authorities. But given that the governor of Saipan was in the factory owner's pocket, the girls knew better.

The pride I felt for my job at that moment made me want to put a bullet through my head. I had joined the Washington, D.C., law firm Preston Gates as an international research analyst in order to prepare myself for law school. My ambition, shaped by the words of Vartan Gregorian, president of Brown University, had been to "go out there and make a difference." Well, I was making a difference, all right—one I was so ashamed of I didn't share it with my closest friends. I'd couch the work I did in general terms, as PR work for corporate clients. But I knew I had to put in at least a year at this firm if I wanted my résumé to look halfway credible to a law school or my next employer. And I had to impress the head of our client group, Jack Abramoff.

The law firm's partners tended to be old-school Democrats, but after the Republicans took control of Congress in the mid-1990s, the firm hired Jack, a conservative lobbyist extraordinaire, who would guarantee the firm access to top Republican lawmakers. Jack would rise to become the number-one rainmaker on Capitol Hill, before his dealings became the center of a scandal that took Washington by storm. The debacle would bring down House majority leader Tom DeLay and threaten President Bush, who denied knowing Jack even though they had been caught on camera together at the White House. Frank Rich of the *New York Times* would refer to him as the "new Monica"; *Time* magazine plastered his face on its cover as "The Man Who Bought Washington."

I had told Jack early on that I held liberal political views.

"That's all right," he said. "You'll grow out of it."

In any case, Democrats were just as happy to go on his junkets as Republicans were, so he didn't mind having a young liberal around. The moment these Congressional staffers got on the plane and washed down their first bloody marys, they were "Republicrats" and "Demoblicans," out for a good time.

"Just make sure people like you," Jack had advised me. In retrospect, it was an ironic piece of advice to receive from him.

Yet back when he was a senior rainmaker at Preston Gates (the firm started by Bill Gates's father), Jack was a very popular guy in Washington, including among many Democrats, who took about a third of his political contributions.

Jack's one-liner advice was all I got by way of a job description. Whether it meant staying late at the office or working the D.C. cocktail circuit, picking up golf so I could lose to clients or taking Congressional staffers to strip clubs during a "fact-finding mission" in Puerto Rico, I usually found ways to follow his advice.

After six months at the law firm, I received a big raise. I went out with my girlfriend to celebrate. We got a table at Sequoia, a trendy seafood restaurant overlooking the Potomac River and the Watergate Hotel. As I held her hand after dessert, she told me how proud she was of me.

I believe that is when I realized how fully I had come to hate myself. Not knowing how to share this discovery with the woman I longed to impress, I simply hailed the waiter for another glass of wine. We moved on to a party, where a friend of mine insisted on toasting with whiskey shots to celebrate my promotion. A colleague from work was there. He offered me a cigar and congratulated me for being "right on track for six figures."

Much later—after a one-way conversation with a toilet bowl—I reached a drunken epiphany. Out of disgust, I abandoned my plan to study law. And in the following weeks, I began sending out résumés to humanitarian organizations.

Weeks went by without an answer. I turned twenty-four. I broke up with my girlfriend. And I continued to help my bosses pervert the democratic process in Washington with increasing skill, even as I was sinking deeper and deeper into depression. All I could do to compensate for my chronic self-loathing was purchase flashy yellow ties. One morning, as I was tying one on, I pulled on the fabric to check how sturdy it was. Would it hold my weight if I tied it around the fan and stepped off a stool?

Then, one afternoon, my phone rang. It was Daniel, a friend from Brown University. Together, we had founded a publication called *The Brown Journal of World Affairs,* which, we felt certain at the time, would prepare the ground for illustrious careers in international affairs. Instead, Daniel had landed in banking, and I in lobbying. But the tide was about to turn.

Daniel had heard of an immediate opening at the United Nations. In fact, he had been offered the job but had decided to turn it down in favor of a post in the Clinton administration.

"Ever heard of Oil-for-Food?"

"Oil for *what*?"

"It's this new UN program. Just got started. But you might have to travel to Iraq."

"I'll go anywhere. I need to get out of here."

"Children are dying over there, you know, because of the sanctions. It's a pretty bad situation. The UN is starting this huge humanitarian operation. They need a coordinator type. . . . I gave them your name. They're waiting for your call."

I tried to remain calm, but my cubicle shook as I frantically looked around for my résumé. I got on the phone with the recruitment woman, Mira, who had a sensual Eastern European accent. She confirmed that they needed someone right away.

"Would you like to have a look at my résumé?"

"Sure. Send it over. And feel free to add any details. You know, like your height, the color of your eyes."

"Um . . . sure."

"Just kidding, darling."

Daniel had told me the woman was flirtatious. So I decided to push my luck. I improvised and said that I would be visiting New York for work that Friday and would be happy to drop in for a chat. The interview date was set.

Three years. That's how long I had tried to get an interview at the UN. Finally, a door had creaked open.

A few days later, I was flying through the streets of New York in a yellow cab piloted by a man who seemed as worried about crashing as a kid playing

Grand Theft Auto. The car came to a screeching halt in front of One UN Plaza. I stood there for a moment, looking up at the tall blue skyscraper. I readjusted my suit, checked my watch, and took a deep breath.

I had learned from experience not to appear too eager. The worst thing I could do was try to promote myself. *Boast and you're toast. Just listen to these guys. Figure out what they want before you say anything.*

So I did some active listening as Yohannes Mengesha, a jovial Ethiopian man I assumed was the head of the budding UN operation, explained to me that "Oil-for-Food" was a misleading nickname for what they did. There was no barter of oil in exchange for food. Iraq sold oil, and the UN took the money to pay for a range of "humanitarian" goods, including food, medicine, and industrial equipment. The UN then observed how these goods were used inside the country to ensure that they were helping Iraq's civilians rather than the regime. It was an unprecedented experiment that could be halted at any time if Saddam was seen to be cheating, he added, so there would be no guarantee of job security. He waited for a reaction to this, but all he got was a nod.

"What are your needs?" I asked.

He explained that he needed a person who could write speeches and official correspondence, coordinate trips and briefings, deal with the press—in short, someone who could hit the ground running in a highly political environment.

I treated him like one of Jack's clients, seeking to make sure I understood his concerns, occasionally jotting down notes on a pad, and adjusting my glasses—a move I hoped made me look older than my twenty-four years. When the time came for him to ask me if I had any questions, I said, "Yes. Is there a strategy in place for dealing with the media?"

"Erm . . . we have a public information officer, but we're still a new operation. That aspect definitely needs to be developed further as the program expands."

"Right."

"Why?" he asked.

"Well, I did some research before coming here. There seems to be some opposition to this operation in Congress. Quite vehement, in fact. I believe this is an issue to handle with great care."

The man nodded, and soon, the question I had been waiting for came: "When would you be able to start?"

I had pulled a Jack Abramoff on him. If potential clients walked into Jack's office thinking they had a small problem, he'd make sure they walked out thinking they had a huge one—and that Jack was the only person who could fix it for them.

A few days later, I was back at the firm waiting by the fax machine for my letter of employment. It was a beautiful thing: "On behalf of the Secretary-General, I am pleased to inform you. . . ."

As I read on, I had a shock. I'd be making $5,200 a month! More than double my current salary! Plus rent subsidy, full medical insurance, and daily allowances when I went "on mission." Sweet Lord, I would have *paid* to go "on mission" for the UN!

But still, I had to call up and ask, "Um . . . the $5,200 . . . is that tax free?"

"*Oui, absolument!*"

I would not only be making a positive difference in the world; I'd get paid enough to party my ass off in New York!

My skin was tingling from my scalp to my feet. No amount of dancing around could possibly release the overflow of energy that was unleashed by this sudden turn of events. As I sought to regain my composure, the words "tax free" stopped bouncing around in my head and a sense of great responsibility seeped in. I was deeply grateful for this chance to become an official do-gooder. But I would be a civil servant now. And I had just seen how easily such people could be bought with trips and concert tickets, manipulated and finessed into inaction, even when serious moral issues were at stake. The line between serving the public interest and serving one's personal interest was an easy one to cross. I would be on the other side of the fence now.

Standing before the bathroom mirror, I made a solemn promise to myself: "No matter what happens, you will *never, ever* deviate from your mandate!" I looked into my eyes until my reflection appeared to understand how serious I was about this.

A few minutes later, I walked into Jack's office. I waited for him to get off the Dictaphone and then broke the news.

"Good for you!" he said. And as I explained the nature of the Oil-for-Food deal to him, a devilish smile appeared on his face. "Let's definitely keep in touch! You never know what might come up."

CHAPTER **3**

Welcome to the Game

"They've been to your apartment," said Trevor Philips after the foam on his Guinness had settled.

"Who's been to my apartment?" I asked as I stared, wild-eyed, at the UN's senior Iraq analyst.

A quaint smile formed on Trevor's lips, even as his eyes remained dead serious.

"The Iraqis," he said, as if it were obvious.

"The Iraqis! When? How did they . . . why?"

Trevor made big eyes and raised his chin, quelling my eruption. He took a slow sip of beer and lay down his pint, rebooting our conversation. We had just sat down at an Irish pub located a stone's throw away from the United Nations. It was happy hour, and I had wanted to sit up front, next to a group of tipsy girls, but Trevor had insisted on a darkly lit booth in the back.

I took an amateurish peek over my shoulder, checking for unwanted ears, then leaned in toward Trevor. I asked my questions slowly this time.

"You're telling me that the Iraqis have broken into my apartment?"

Trevor nodded.

"When?"

Silence.

"And how do you know this?"

"They're very thorough," said Trevor. "*Very* thorough. They like to know who they're dealing with, especially someone in your position, Michael."

"My position? I don't even have a job description yet!"

"They know you're drafting the director's communications, assigning work in the office. . . . Naturally, they want to know if you're a plant."

"A plant?" I was thinking green leaves.

"A *plant*," said Trevor, dropping an imaginary parachutist onto the table.

"Like a spy?"

Trevor barely nodded, closing his eyelids in quiet frustration, the way my sixth-grade math teacher used to do.

"And . . . who would I be spying for?"

"That's the question," said Trevor. "They probably suspect it's either the French—"

"Trevor, I told you already, I'm not French!"

"Or the Americans."

"But I'm not American, either! I'm Danish!"

Trevor sat back and crossed his arms.

"Don't give me Danish. You've lived most of your life in France and the United States. You earned a bachelor's at Brown and a master's in Paris. Your last job was in Washington, working for a quote-unquote law firm. You're hardly old enough to be in this job, yet you've been recruited in less than two weeks. Next thing we know, the new big boss picks *you* to go to Iraq with him. . . . Who are you, Michael? Some people are wondering."

"Who's wondering? *You* don't think I'm a spy, do you?"

"It wouldn't be the first time the U.S. or France recruited a foreign national to collect information for them. But that's not the point. I'll have you figured out soon enough. Now, if *I'm* trying to figure out who you are, you can bet the Iraqis are, too."

Trevor took his time sipping his beer, then looked at me deadpan, studying my face and waiting for me to say something. I pondered my next move. Anything I said, any question I asked, might give away my real identity, that of a complete amateur, which was the last impression I wanted to leave on my new colleague.

"OK," I said, "let's just backtrack here for a second. How do the Iraqis even know where I live? Are you saying they broke into the United Nations and stole my file or something?"

"Our security is lax enough," said Trevor. "I know they have visited us on occasion. But I suspect they didn't need to steal your file. Someone could simply have followed you home from work."

"But my building has a doorman. They can't just walk in there!"

"Oh, yes they can," said Trevor, enjoying the sight of my panicked expression. "They'll do what it takes. They've got a lot of money invested in this operation of ours. They'll want to know about everyone they have to deal with . . . as would I."

Trevor's suspicion was beginning to get on my nerves. But in all fairness, I was equally interested in his background as he was in mine. Trevor had attended Oxford University. He was the son of a small shop owner, had grown up in the modest outskirts of London, and had risen through the ranks on the force of his stunning ability to digest huge amounts of information in record time and then dispense it selectively, as required. Every one of his words was consciously chosen and properly pronounced for intended effect. Each sentence was weighed. Between the need to communicate and the need to say as little as possible, Trevor had found a balance that always left one convinced he knew more than he was letting on.

"You better go on home," said Trevor after a long silence. "Get some sleep. You've got a big day tomorrow."

I washed down my beer and looked into my empty glass, trying to collect my thoughts. The vision of an Iraqi operative going through my things sent a shiver down my spine. My apartment was in such a mess that I might not have noticed. I had moved to New York only weeks ago to take up my new job and had yet to unpack my boxes.

"I need another drink," I said. "You can't just drop this bombshell on me without offering some kind of evidence."

Trevor declined to get into specifics, other than to share the fact that "they"—the Iraqis—had visited his own apartment several times when he was away and purposely left behind "signs" that they had been there.

"Signs? Like what?" I asked.

Trevor told me that one visitor had left behind some poo in his toilet and put out a cigarette in his teacup, which he interpreted as a willful effort to insult his British identity and, by extension, Her Majesty's Government.

Was this guy out of his mind? Or was he playing some kind of hazing joke on me? I was the youngest guy in the office *and* the "new guy." An ideal target for a prank. Especially on the eve of my first mission to Baghdad. I was sufficiently nervous as it was. Trevor's innuendoes were more than I could bear.

"All right, Trevor. Time out," I said. "An Iraqi agent went into your apartment and took a dump? You've got to be kidding me."

"You don't believe me?"

"No, of course I don't believe you! Do you think I'm some kind of idiot?"

Trevor's smile disappeared. He was now fixing me with small eyes and a truly bitter, almost dangerous expression.

"You're the one who asked for this briefing," he said. He took out his wallet and sought the waitress's attention. In an instant his face had flushed bright red. His ears were beaming.

If he was playing me for a fool, he was a damned fine actor. Not even Dustin Hoffman can get his ears to turn scarlet on command. Adding to my sudden doubts was the fact that Trevor was too important a player in the office to alienate.

"Why would they leave, um, 'signs' on purpose like that?" I backtracked.

Trevor hesitated but decided to answer anyway.

"Intimidation," he said. "They also send me a card each year on my birthday, just to let me know they have an eye on me."

"Why don't you alert the authorities?" I asked.

"What authorities?"

"I don't know. . . . The FBI?"

"The U.K. mission doesn't expect me to be speaking to the FBI. Nor does the UN itself. Our loyalty is to the UN Secretariat. And they have no means to do anything about these sorts of incidents, so we're basically on our own."

"There's got to be some authority to report this to."

"It's not how the game is played," said Trevor.

"The *game*? What game?"

"Watch your back!" It was the Irish barmaid leaning over my shoulder to lay two dripping pints of beer on the table.

"These are on the house," she added, with a cheery wink. It took a moment for my nerves to relax from the sudden shock of her unexpected arrival. When I looked back at Trevor, he was smiling.

"Like she said, Michael, watch your back. But don't worry too much about the Iraqis. The worst blows usually come from your own side . . . whatever your side is, Mr. Soussan. That's not a Danish name, is it?"

Leaving that last question hanging, he excused himself for the restroom. Time to collect my thoughts. What the hell was Trevor driving at? Two possible answers. Either he was on the verge of a major paranoia attack, of the kind that lands people in straitjackets, or this was serious and we were being watched and intimidated by shadowy Iraqi operatives in New York. And all this was supposed to be part of some "game," where the most dangerous blows came from one's "own side."

What, I wondered, was *my* side?

Of all my new colleagues, Trevor had been the last one to give me face time. I had received mixed messages about the guy from day one. Some people even said he was a spy himself. "He reports to the British," said one colleague, conspiratorially, after Trevor passed us in the corridor. But another colleague warned me not to take anything coming out of *her* mouth too seriously. Trevor was on loan to the United Nations from the British Ministry of Defense. There was no secret about that. What could he possibly have to report to the British that we, at the United Nations, should be hiding from them? Britain has a seat on the Security Council, and the Security Council was like our Board of Directors.

Besides, Trevor didn't fit the (Hollywood-inspired) image I had of a spy. He was no gadget-wielding, slick-haired, martini-guzzling macho type. Before I had seen him get intense, just earlier, I had considered him a nice, rather low-key fellow. He looked a bit like Elton John, without the wig or the colored glasses. He dressed plainly, in gray suits, sober ties, and gum-sole shoes, which allowed him to slip in and out of someone's line of vision without leaving a distinct impression. Not that this helped him very much in an office where half the employees were calling him a spook behind his back.

I had worked hard at getting Trevor to sit down with me. He was the first person I had wanted a briefing from because of his background at the Defense Ministry. My meetings with some of the other colleagues in the office had quickly turned into venting sessions. They all seemed highly frustrated at someone or something, but it was hard to understand who, or what, because they referred to everything in acronyms.

"The MDOU are offended that the UNOHCI report includes only inputs from the UNGOU. UNICEF [OK, I knew that one] thinks WFP and UNCHS should have a seat at the UNSECOORD meetings."

Wuah?

Complaints about other coworkers were frequent and varied from the substantive to the menial. One reason Trevor was intensely disliked by a large and combative woman named Maria (leaving aside the fact that he was British Anglican and she was Irish Catholic) was that he refused to contribute money to the common coffeepot. The thing was, Trevor was a tea drinker, and he made his own brew using a rusty old electric boiler he kept in his office.

In contrast to my other colleagues' digs, which were as nicely appointed as the décor allowed, with family pictures and souvenirs from various parts of the world where their UN careers had taken them, Trevor's office was spartan and dimly lit. His blinds were always down, and he preferred to use a small desk lamp rather than the fluorescent ceiling lights. The only ornaments on his wall were a large map of Iraq and a small blurry picture, which revealed its contents only upon close examination. It had been taken sometime in the late 1980s. Trevor was in it, standing reverently next to a stiff, gray, tall, and bespectacled person who simply *had* to be an English diplomat. Across from them was a tall, dark, mustached figure.

"Is that who I think it is?" I had asked.

"The man himself," Trevor had replied.

If the British government trusted Trevor enough to send him to meetings with Saddam Hussein, maybe I could take him at his word when he said some Iraqi operative had crept into his apartment. Still, it was not the kind of briefing I had expected.

As an analyst in the British Defense Ministry, Trevor was by far the most knowledgeable person about Iraq at the United Nations. He understood how that country's electrical grid was set up; the state of its telephone networks and its water and sanitation infrastructure (presumably because all these installations had been targeted by allied bombings during Operation Desert Storm); and, most important, he knew in great detail how the Iraqi regime functioned politically. As an analyst, Trevor had little authority over other staff. But all data and information collected by our UN observers in Iraq came directly to him, and in an environment where exclusive information yields power, Trevor had carved out an influential role for himself. He was not the type who sought to please his superiors, nor did he really need to, because they depended on him entirely when it came to getting the facts straight. But getting the facts straight was one thing. Translating them into UN-speak was another. And that's where I was expected to come in, to edit Trevor's straightforward reports under the guidance of our common director, a career UN official from Ethiopia who had a clear idea of what could and could not be said in a UN document.

Given the need for me to work closely with Trevor, I had sought him out early on. Problem was, the man who had previously briefed Margaret Thatcher about Iraq clearly saw it as a waste of his time to speak to the kid who had knocked on his door one afternoon and attempted to start a conversation by asking him why he kept the lights in his office off all the time. I finally managed to corner him one day, after he had evaded all my previous attempts. His office was filled with mounds of reports and looked alarmingly disorganized. Yet Trevor appeared serene and in control of his little universe. Every time I had knocked on his door he had looked up from his pile of papers with a pleading expression, and I had agreed to reschedule. But not this time. I had just been tapped to accompany the new big boss of the operation on his first mission to the field, and I needed to pick Trevor's brain before heading to Baghdad.

So I invited myself to a cup of Trevor's tea. He was tight-lipped with me at first, and after a half-hour during which I felt like I was trying to open a can of beans with a plastic fork, I decided on a more direct approach.

"Look, Trevor, I need your help. I talked to all of our colleagues. They speak a language I hardly understand."

"Ah, yes," said Trevor. "UN-speak. Or UN-ese, if you prefer."

"Right. It's like they're stuck in their own little clusters, bitching about stuff that's all in acronyms, and I'm not getting the political perspective here. I understand you worked at the British Defense Ministry during the Gulf War."

Trevor's ears perked up at the mention of his former employer.

"If you brief me now, I promise you a debriefing when I come back from Iraq."

Trevor had so far been prohibited from traveling to Baghdad because of his nationality (and, of course, the widely shared assumption that he had been planted inside the UN by the British government in order to spy on Saddam's regime). I knew that he would find a firsthand account of the situation on the ground invaluable. I had to bargain for it, but I finally got his attention.

"All right," he said. "But not here."

"Why not?"

Trevor glanced at the wall, suggestively, then back at me. Was he implying the place was bugged? I glanced at the wall, then back at him, and said, "What's wrong with your office? I'm leaving early tomorrow morning. I need to know what I'm walking into here."

Trevor looked up at me for a moment.

"Let's have a beer, you and I," he said. "I'll swing by your office at seven."

As soon as we stepped out of the building at One UN Plaza, Trevor removed his UN badge from around his neck and slipped it into his coat pocket, urging me, with a discreet nod, to do the same. I was reluctant to do so. I felt incredibly proud to have this badge dangling around my neck. It gave me access to places where normal people would never set foot, and I was kind of enjoying feeling like an international VIP. Like the young medical students who refuse to take off their green scrubs when they go to lunch, I wanted the whole city to know I was a diplomat. But Trevor found the right words: "Come on, you look like a freshman."

With that, I slipped my badge into my pocket. At the end of our little talk at the Irish bar, I decided to cast aside my doubts. Whatever the truth of Trevor's assertions, his would be the last advice I would get before I zipped my suitcase shut.

"So what does all this mean for my trip tomorrow?" I asked him when he returned from the bathroom. "I mean, so the Iraqis are watching us. I got that. But I am who I am. Can't change that, and if they don't like it, too bad. We have a mandate from the Security Council, and I intend to help execu—"

"What's our mandate?" asked Trevor. "Do you even understand it?"

"Sure! I mean, I've read the Security Council resolutions. We're supposed to help the Iraqi people survive the sanctions."

"So why doesn't the UN just lift those sanctions?" Trevor asked, rhetorically.

He had a point. There was something rather awkward about a mandate that asked us to save the Iraqi people from, well, our own policy of sanctions.

"The whole idea here is to prevent any money from flowing into Saddam's pockets. As you can imagine, Saddam will try everything in his power to make sure we fail. And he's not our only problem. We're sitting on a big pot of money, Michael. Billions of dollars. It's more cash than the UN has ever handled. And all sides want to get their paws on it."

Trevor waited for me to nod before continuing.

"So just be aware, Michael. They know who you are, and they'll be watching you. This program is enormously important to them. Saddam is counting on this operation to erode the sanctions, rebuild his military machine, and break out of his international isolation. He used to be the most powerful man in the Middle East. He intends to become so again. And he has no intention of letting a bunch of UN bureaucrats stand in his way. Do you understand?"

He had spoken calmly, like an educator, without breaking eye contact.

"I understand."

"So keep your eyes open. Be aware of what goes on around you. And most important, be your own man."

My own man? Trevor saw the question mark on my face. His stone face melted into a smile as he waited for me to formulate my thought.

"How can I be *my own man,* Trevor? I have a boss. My job is to represent *his* interests."

"Yes, well, I'm afraid your life is about to get a bit more complicated than that," said Trevor. "Think for yourself, Michael. You'll be glad you did when the game is up."

CHAPTER 4

Fasten Your Seat Belts

NEW YORK CITY, NOVEMBER 12, 1997, 5:30 A.M.

I shut off my alarm clock, sat up in my bed, and turned on CNN. Blaring trumpets accompanied footage of F-15s taking off from an aircraft carrier in the Persian Gulf. *Showdown with Iraq* was on. The longest-running reality show in "infotainment" history. The anchorwoman frowned as if to contain her excitement. The United States was on the verge of bombing Saddam Hussein (again) for blocking the work of the UN weapons inspectors.

On a normal day, the prospect of bombings in Iraq would not have fazed me. We all knew the drill: night-vision fireworks over Baghdad, Pentagon videos shot from the tip of a diving missile, nondescript buildings blowing up, and Saddam declaring victory from a bunker while his people sorted through the rubble outside. But this was not a normal day. In eighteen hours, I would be on the ground in Iraq. Surely, the view from there would be different.

As I stepped into the shower, I wondered what it would feel like to be on the receiving end of a Tomahawk cruise missile attack. Would we hear it coming? Would there be some kind of siren warning? And if so, what should I do? Jump under a desk?

I made a note to pack some aspirin.

I was shaving when the intercom buzzer sent me into a panic. The under secretary general was downstairs, ten minutes early, waiting to pick me up on his way to JFK Airport.

His name was Benon Sevan, but the staff had nicknamed him Pasha in reference to his reputation as a Byzantine manager. Pasha was the boss of my boss. His appointment had been announced suddenly, a few weeks after I started work, when it occurred to Kofi Annan that the Oil-for-Food operation might soon be handling sums of money that dwarfed the UN's own yearly budget. The program needed to be helmed by a high-level official, and Pasha was a UN heavyweight, in both rank and appearance.

Yohannes, my Ethiopian director, was not exactly jumping for joy at the prospect of having Pasha as a boss. Yohannes was a guy I had taken an instant liking to during my job interview. He had hired me "off the street," so to speak, which meant he didn't mind investing the time necessary to render me functional within the UN system. Yohannes was normally pretty relaxed and confident, but after his first encounter with Pasha he came back to the office visibly shaken. When I asked how he liked our new overlord, he hesitated before venturing, "He's a bit . . . unusual."

"How so?" I asked.

"You'll see for yourself," he said. "We're seeing him this afternoon. He wants to go to Iraq immediately, despite the crisis. . . . I'm just glad he's not taking me with him."

"Really. Is he planning to go all by himself?"

"No. I think you're going to have to go with him."

"Oh."

When we showed up at the doorstep of Pasha's large corner office on the fifteenth floor of the UN Secretariat, the under secretary general sprang up from his seat, walked toward us threateningly, slapped Yohannes on the neck surprisingly hard, nodded at me, and popped his head out his door to yell, "Coffee!" before inviting us to sit on a large leather couch that offered a spectacular view of the East River.

What followed was a strange briefing in which my director endeavored to outline the complexities of the UN's responsibilities in Iraq amid constant interruption from Pasha, who appeared highly volatile and prone to unforeseeable mood swings. His elocution was somewhere between a mumble and a blurt, and it got worse when he had a cigar in his mouth. I can't say I understood much of what he said, except for the word "fack," which he used often. "I don't give a fack about Stephanides," he had kept saying. Joseph Stephanides was one of the UN officials who had helped lay the groundwork for the Oil-for-Food operation, and Pasha, it seemed, wanted him out of his way. Apart from that, I caught zilch of what he said. And I couldn't even figure out why.

Was it his accent? He was an Armenian from Cyprus, but I had never had any trouble understanding either Armenians or Cypriots before, so I considered the possibility that the under secretary general might suffer from some kind of speech impediment.

Despite his highly unusual speech pattern, Pasha exerted a powerful charm on the people around him. A heavyset man, he was the center of gravity of whatever room he was in. Everybody seemed slightly off balance in his presence. His burly demeanor was tempered by his elegant taste in clothing. His smartly tailored suit was perfectly matched by his Hermès tie and Italian moccasins. He carried his imposing frame with surprising grace, gliding along the UN's corridors at a fast pace, in a manner that kept his upper body at a constant height. When he wasn't greeting the many UN employees who stopped and bowed at his passage with the kind of reverence normally reserved for royalty, his hands would be flapping at his sides, facing backward, as if paddling through the air as he whisked by.

His eyes were sharp. They were everywhere at once. Nothing seemed to escape him. When he wasn't in the midst of a blurry outburst, he observed other people's body language with keen interest, occasionally raising and lowering his bushy eyebrows behind drifts of smoke from his puffed cigar. He appeared generally suspicious of people, especially if they worked for him. Perhaps this explained why, of all the people Pasha could have chosen to accompany him on his first mission to Iraq, he had picked me, the greenest apple in the shop. His decision caught everyone by surprise. I had been recruited only a month earlier and had yet to settle into the UN bureaucracy. I was twenty-four, enthusiastic as a puppy dog, and fully devoted to the United Nations Charter, a miniature copy of which I kept in my pocket at all times in case a legal question came up and I needed to look up the answer.

My colleagues immediately nicknamed me "The Kid." Given the age difference between us, they could have easily nicknamed me The Toddler, so I took to it graciously. And the nickname actually worked in my favor, because it cast me as a nonthreatening character in an office fraught with personal rivalries. This would not last. But in these early days, it made me an attractive candidate to accompany Pasha on his first mission to Iraq.

Before leaving, I had three days to compile a massive briefing book on Iraq, get my vaccination shots, finalize our itinerary, and conduct a flash survey of where the players in the UN Security Council stood on the issues we were expected to raise with the Iraqi government. I had been so busy with my preparations that I even forgot to get anxious—until the night before our trip, when Trevor freaked me out with his ominous warning that my apartment had been "visited."

When I got home, after a few too many drinks with Trevor, I thought of ways I could detect if a visitor had been through my things. Suddenly, everything seemed out of place, but as I foraged through my possessions, I found no clear signs to feed my paranoia. I remembered a trick from a James Bond movie: in one scene, Sean Connery had removed a hair from his scalp, licked it, and placed it on his hotel door. When he came back and the hair was gone, he knew someone had been there in his absence. I experimented with that for a bit. If Trevor was right, and my apartment had been visited, I needed a system to alert me to any recurrences. But my hair, unlike Sean Connery's, wouldn't stick to my door, so I abandoned the effort and tried to get some sleep.

No luck there either. I tossed and turned for hours, growing increasingly tense. So much so that the next morning, when I exited my building and saw Pasha's stretch limousine parked at the curb, engine running, my nervous system laid siege on my senses. With sweaty palms and a lump in my throat, I walked up to the car, opened the door, and peeked inside.

Pasha sat in the rear, looking like someone had pissed in his cornflakes that morning.

"Good morning, Sir!"

Pasha responded with a grunt and pointed his finger at his chin, which was his way of saying that I had something stuck on mine. I had indeed cut myself shaving when he buzzed me, and I had applied a small piece of cigarette paper to stop the bleeding. Embarrassed, I quickly wiped it off.

Pasha motioned for me to sit across from him, some five feet away. I had never ridden in a stretch limousine before, and the distance between us made me feel awkward. So I leaned forward, elbows on my knees, and ventured something about the weather being chilly this morning. The driver stepped on the gas and caused me to nearly slide off my seat.

Grabbing the handle above the window, I adjusted myself and smiled at Pasha, who just looked at me, perplexed.

After a few awkward beats, Pasha asked me if "mumble blurt Yohannes blah?"

"I'm sorry, what?" I cringed.

Pasha shook his head, and repeated his question.

"Sorry, I . . . I'm much sharper when I've had coffee, ha, ha . . . ahem . . ." As my laughter turned into a cough, Pasha asked his mysterious question for the third time.

Sounded like Albanian.

Since I couldn't ask him to repeat himself a *fourth* time, I simply froze in a silly expression that must have looked something like "Please don't throw me out of the car."

"Rumble bumble facking vacation, can you believe it?" Pasha said finally, allowing me (miraculously) to catch his drift. Yohannes had asked Pasha for a
vacation to go visit his family back in Ethiopia. He hadn't taken leave for more
than two years, and so I thought I would point that out, in my boss's defense.
This prompted Pasha to look at me suspiciously. Clearly, he would have preferred if I had agreed with him that my director was a flake. An awkward silence followed, during which I racked my brain for something smart to say.

"Mumble blurt mumble," said Pasha, after a few beats.

"Um . . . I'm sorry, what?"

"*Mumble blurt mumble!*"

"Oh . . . yeah. . . ."

I shook my head knowingly and raised an eyebrow to signal empathy with
Pasha's point of view. And so it went all the way to the airport. I agreed with
him on a lot of issues and he seemed to like that. I soon developed an arsenal
of jujitsu answers, like "Really?" "Interesting," "Is that so?" "I see," just to
keep the conversation going.

At university, I had been taught that diplomats like to keep talking until
they agree, or agree to keep talking. In this case, Pasha just kept talking and I
kept agreeing.

I managed to survive the trip to the airport, though my neck was starting
to hurt from all the nodding. Through some act of divine intervention, I was
not seated next to Pasha on the first leg of our flight, which meant I had seven
hours to figure out a strategy for surviving the next two weeks with a boss I
couldn't understand. I concluded that my best bet was to initiate conversations so that I would at least know what the topic was. Perhaps he would be
easier to understand if we spoke French? Or maybe I should try reading his
lips? Or, better, his mind? If only I could catch a few hours of sleep, I would
be able to figure it out.

"Mumble blurt facking Halliday will like it?"

After six hours of adjusting my pillow, I was finally about to doze off when
Pasha woke me with a statement, or a question, or something, which included the word "Halliday" in it. He was also waving a case containing a bottle of cologne, which allowed me to put two and two together.

"Facking Halliday" referred to Mr. Denis Halliday, the United Nations humanitarian coordinator in Iraq, the number-two man in the operation, after
Pasha. As for the bottle of cologne, I guessed it was a token gift from Pasha
to Halliday. Would Halliday like it?

"Um . . . sure!" I said. In truth, I felt that a bottle of cologne was a strange
gift to give a man stationed in an international crisis zone. But I was pleasantly

surprised that Pasha would bring "facking Halliday" a present, for I had heard through the grapevine that Pasha and Denis had been bitter enemies since before I was born. Had the animosity between the two men been exaggerated? I hoped so. In any case, it was good to see that two adults with the kind of responsibilities they had didn't let personal conflict interfere with their work.

The problem, as it turned out, was not so much that their personal conflict interfered with their work; it was more that the work interfered with their personal conflict, which would eventually grow into a full-blown showdown that would take on international proportions. But for the time being, Pasha came bearing a gift. I was still years from understanding how Pasha really functioned. I would later learn that the nicer he was to a fellow colleague, the more worried that person should be.

Changing the subject, Pasha pointed his chin at a young stewardess.

"Cute, huh?" he said, his eyes suddenly sparkling.

"Um . . . yeah!" I said, with too much emphasis. "Pretty hot!"

The stewardess wasn't *all that,* but who cared? I understood what Pasha was saying, and we were now bonding.

"*Elle a du chien!*" said Pasha, which in French means she has a doglike quality. This was supposed to be a compliment, I think. I returned his wink and shook my head, communicating a false desire to copulate with the poor unsuspecting stewardess. This was great. Pasha and I would get along now. Two horny bastards on their way to Baghdad.

"Hamabla itinerary!" said Pasha.

Got it. The man wants to see his itinerary. I had scheduled appointments for him with every Iraqi minister, every Kurdish rebel leader, and every UN agency head working in Iraq. Pasha looked at it for a bit and suddenly began to laugh.

"Who's this Nasredin?" he asked.

"Erm . . ." I looked at my own copy of the itinerary for a guy called Nasredin. Ideally his title should be there too.

"I had a friend called Nasredin, you know, when I was young, in Cyprus."

"Really?" I said.

"Yeah. We caught him facking a donkey, ha ha ha!"

"Rrr . . . really?"

Somebody please tell me there's a hidden camera somewhere.

It would take me years to accurately describe how I perceived Pasha at that moment. Then I saw the movie *Borat.*

Pasha was laughing to tears as he recounted how his donkey-fucking friend Nasredin had been caught with his pants down, standing on a stool behind the animal. This whole bonding thing was getting a bit out of control. So after pretending to laugh along for a bit, I tried to get Pasha to focus back on his itinerary. But Pasha cast it aside.

"Rumble mumble report?" he asked, suddenly serious. He had this way of changing moods all the time, which is not something people from my native Scandinavia do unless they've had a lot to drink. This would be stop and go, I realized, as I endeavored once again to decrypt Pasha's thoughts. Let's see, what could he mean by "rumble mumble report?"

"Yes, I've read it twice, actually," I said, betting that he was referring to Halliday's draft report on the humanitarian conditions in Iraq, which I knew Pasha wanted to rewrite completely during our trip. "You mumble the recommendations and give to me," he said.

He went back to his seat, and I proceeded to go through the report and highlight important passages with a yellow marker as the plane began its shaky descent to Heathrow Airport.

As we waited for our connecting flight to Kuwait in the British Airways lounge, Pasha read through the report, from time to time shaking his head with an expression of disagreement or frustration with something, or someone. Occasionally, he would point to a passage and mumble something, and I would agree in a tentative sort of way, since I couldn't see what he was talking about from where I was sitting.

CNN kept showing the same images over and over. U.S. planes taking off from aircraft carriers. Iraqi citizens chanting defiantly on their way into one of Saddam's palaces in their excitement to serve as human shields for their beloved leader. Incredibly, CNN had no comment on whether the Iraqis in question really were so eager to stand in harm's way or whether, as seemed evident to me, they had been forced into that role by Saddam's henchmen. Here was footage epitomizing the moral blackmail to which the international community was subjected by the regime of Saddam Hussein, and the twenty-four-hour newspeople had no comment.

The way I read it, Saddam was holding his people hostage. And we were in the role of the hostage negotiators, flying in to make sure his people could be fed while the whole ordeal lasted. But how long would this permanent state of crisis last? Nobody seemed to have an answer, least of all Pasha and I.

But there we were. The United States was about to bomb Iraq for impeding the work of the UN weapons inspectors. As nonessential UN personnel were being pulled out of Baghdad, we were going in.

Secretary of State Madeleine Albright and Iraqi chief diplomat Tariq Aziz were both touring the Arab world in separate attempts to drum up support for their respective positions. Wherever Albright went, her host would call on Iraq to "cooperate with the UN Security Council," and wherever Aziz went, his host would call for "a peaceful resolution to the crisis." In essence, a poll was being conducted to see how many countries would support a U.S. strike against Iraq and how many would oppose it. Albright was adamant that, one way or another, Saddam Hussein would be "kept in his box." It was a great one-liner, but unfortunately, Saddam was not alone in his box. More than twenty-three million people had to live in that box with him, hence the reason for our mission.*

The strict economic sanctions kept in place since the 1991 Persian Gulf War had been devastating for the population. Originally the sanctions had been imposed in 1990 to force Saddam to withdraw his forces from Kuwait. After the UN-mandated international coalition kicked him out by force, the sanctions were left in place to ensure that the Iraqi dictator complied with the terms of the cease-fire. In the immediate aftermath of the war, the UN weapons inspectors quarantined and blew up a significant chunk of Iraq's weapons of mass destruction, but lately the Iraqi dictator had begun to impede their work. According to the inspectors' records of what had been sold to Iraq before the war, there were still some weapons missing, particularly in the biological field. Regular finds kept confirming suspicions that Saddam was lying and evading the inspection teams at every turn, so quite logically, the UN concluded that the Iraqi dictator must still be up to something on the WMD front.

Meanwhile, it wasn't Saddam's WMDs that were killing most Iraqis. The Iraqi dictator was content to kill most of his subjects the old-fashioned way: the lack of food, clean water, and electricity was decimating the poorest layers of Iraq's population. The Oil-for-Food program was meant to alleviate the humanitarian situation, but it had gotten off to a very slow start. More than a year had gone by since the UN and the government of Iraq had signed on to the Oil-for-Food deal, and the UN was still scrambling to get it up and running.

The process of pumping oil, signing contracts, and getting UN approval to import food and medicine and spare parts had met with delays at every turn. The need in Iraq was enormous, not just for the food and medicine the program promised to bring but also for electricity, clean water, education materials,

---

*Twenty-three million was the figure we used in 1997. It was based on an outdated and proba-bly erroneous census, but it was the best figure available then. By the time of the invasion in 2003, Iraq's population was estimated at twenty-four to twenty-five million.

vaccination campaigns, farming tools, hospital equipment, transportation—all the things societies need to function at a basic level.

In response to those needs, Denis Halliday and his UN observers in the field had written a report advocating a massive increase in the size of the Oil-for-Food program. The problem was that we were still in a trial phase. The United States had threatened not to renew the program if there were any signs that the Iraqi government was diverting humanitarian goods to serve the needs of the elite or the military. And at this early stage, the Clinton administration meant business. The program was to be renewed every six months. We had no idea that it would go on for years and grow into the largest humanitarian operation in UN history. Washington's threat to nix the next phase had credibility, because the Clinton administration was under siege from Newt Gingrich and Jesse Helms on Capitol Hill and could not afford to look weak on Iraq.

In Washington's view, the job of our observers was to monitor the distribution of goods throughout Iraq, not to advocate for more supplies. Of course, if they wanted that kind of reporting, they should never have put humanitarian workers in charge of it. Most of our people had made a career out of advocating for more aid wherever they went. Never before had they been asked to hold a totalitarian regime accountable for distributing humanitarian goods to its population. In essence, we were struggling to respond to two contradictory demands: on the one hand, the UN was asked to enforce sanctions on Iraq, and on the other, it was asked to alleviate them. It was a twisted mandate, which bore within it a seed of contradiction that allowed Saddam Hussein to use his oil wealth to play nations against one another, further dividing the international community for years until finally he succeeded in shattering the unity of the coalition that had evicted him from Kuwait in 1991.

But the program had its deliverables: food and medicine going to people in need. My conviction was that in order to ask for more humanitarian imports, we had to provide assurances to the Security Council that we were on top of our observation duties. The whole point of the program was to help Iraq's civilians without letting a cent of Iraq's oil money go into Saddam's pocket. Our UN observers in Iraq were supposed to make sure that the goods were not diverted to serve the needs of the regime. The problem was that our guys were not free to go where they wanted. They were always escorted by Iraqi security personnel, and their ability to cross-check information was extremely limited. The civilians they interviewed seemed to speak from a script drafted by Saddam himself, and that script ended up in our report, unsupported by reliable information. We would read that five thousand children were dying every month, but no solid source or methodology for coming up with that statistic could be cited. My college newspaper had a better fact-checking mechanism than our UN observers in Iraq. When I ventured to say as much to Pasha, he looked up at me with an expression that clarified his vision of my duties. I was there to take orders, not to emit opinions. But to the extent that my remark could be used to undermine his archenemy and second-in-command, Denis Halliday, he made a mental note of it.

Upon landing in Kuwait, we were escorted into a special lounge for government officials by a fellow from the Kuwaiti protocol. The lounge was equipped with a human coffee dispenser. He stood in a corner of the room with a silver platter, and once in a while he stepped up to serve us another coffee shot. It was no ordinary espresso. It wasn't even like Turkish coffee, which is pasty and black. It was a yellowish, hyperconcentrated caffeine brew, the smell of which could wake up a hibernating bear a mile away.

The human coffee dispenser kept serving me shots because I did the wrong hand movement when trying to return my cup. I had noticed the Kuwaiti minister shake his hand before putting his cup back on the tray and figured the move was a gesture of politeness. In fact, it meant "Fill me up again"; I must have drunk a few too many of those coffee shots, because when we got to the airplane I had a pressing urge to visit the men's room. Of course, the sight of the old UN-emblazoned, Russian-built albatross of a propeller plane that was supposed to take us into Iraq didn't help. But we had left the lounge and were now in a remote part of the airport under military control, with no bathrooms in sight.

We were greeted by a red-faced Ukrainian fellow who reeked of vodka. Apparently, he was the pilot. He handed us a pair of large bright-orange ear mufflers, similar to those worn by airport workers in the 1970s, and showed us in through the cargo door at the back of the plane.

If the exterior appearance of the aircraft was disconcerting, its interior was downright frightening. Who in their right mind would fly into Iraq in the middle of a crisis in a Khrushchev-era propeller machine equipped with half-bolted cardboard seats and defective, toylike seat belts? The question hovered in my mind as I tried to settle in.

I looked at Pasha. He seemed just as uneasy.

"Mumble facking should have gone by road," he said.

Yeah, no kidding! Soon, the plane's rotors started spinning, prompting us to put on our ear mufflers. After a minute Pasha poked me on the shoulder and began to talk.

Had the plane's engines not been so loud, and had we not been wearing ear mufflers, I might conceivably have stood a chance of deciphering part of his mumble, inasmuch as I was beginning to develop the ability to read his lips. But even so, he wouldn't have been able to hear my answer even if I'd screamed it at the top of my lungs. So I calmly began moving my lips in reply, at which point it finally occurred to him that it was impossible for us to talk. He sat back, and I resumed trying to buckle my seat belt.

Then Pasha poked me on the shoulder again. This time, he had a smile on his face. He pointed toward the cockpit and began to imitate the drunken pilot at the controls. Pasha, it turned out, was a fantastic mimic, and we both needed a good laugh to calm our nerves.

We were the only passengers on the plane. Behind us, covered by a net, was a large shipment of spaghetti and canned tomatoes. This was somewhat reassuring. If we survived the crash that now appeared inevitable to me, we'd have enough food to sustain ourselves in the desert for weeks. I tried for a second time to buckle my seat belt, but nothing clicked, so I tied the strips together and took a deep breath. I would have killed for a Xanax.

The plane took off over Kuwait City, and within minutes we were flying at a low altitude over the no-man's-land that separates Kuwait from Iraq. The city I had woken up in was experiencing something akin to a modern-day gold rush: a bubble of prosperity and unbridled optimism, fueled by the colonization of cyberspace. The country I was flying into had been left to rot for more than six years under a combination of repression and deprivation. As we flew over the no-man's-land, I saw that the sand was littered with craters of all sizes, courtesy of Operation Desert Storm.

The sun was scorching, but the inside of the plane was beginning to cool off as we gained altitude. I kept looking out the window, taking refuge in the purity of the desolate sight down below. Not a man or an animal. Not a house, not a tree. Just sand craters, as far as the eye could see. It was unreal—like flying over the surface of the moon on a sunny day.

Looking at the vast landscape made me feel insignificant, which in turn helped me relax a bit. What good did it serve to worry? I had zero control. It suddenly dawned on me why people in the region kept saying "*inshallah*" (God willing) at the end of almost every sentence. It had irritated me at first. Sentences like "We hope to send over the memo shortly, *inshallah*" struck me as useless invocations of the will of the Almighty. Now, I was just hoping to land in Iraq safely, *inshallah*.

I checked my UN *Laissez Passer*—a light-blue diplomatic passport that affords UN employees immunity while on mission. Would it protect me if suddenly hostilities broke out between the United States and Iraq? I sure hoped so. But I couldn't bank on it. The image of UN peacekeepers chained to allied bombing targets in the former Yugoslavia came to mind. Surely Saddam Hussein had no more respect for the UN than Slobodan Milosevic did. He had kept international workers as hostages for months before the Gulf War. He eventually released them, right before hostilities started, but given the pounding he took thereafter, I thought he would act differently next time. And news reports had increasingly indicated that "next time" might be *this* time.

Back at the airport lounge, I had asked Pasha if this was really the best moment for us to visit Iraq. He didn't look so sure himself, but he thought it would send "the wrong signal" if he backed out of his trip. It would mean that the UN was anticipating the outbreak of violence.

But wasn't it legitimate for the UN to read the writing on the wall and protect its personnel? Would our *acting* as if violence wasn't about to break out *stop* it from breaking out? The Iraqis had insisted that Pasha stick to his schedule, because they calculated that a high-level visit by a UN official might complicate Washington's plans. I personally saw little reason why we should play into their hands. But other considerations had come into play as well. Kofi Annan felt that the humanitarian program should not be held hostage to the politics of the conflict. His instinct was noble, it seemed to me, but was it realistic?

Hell, what did I know? Kofi Annan and Pasha had been through major crises before. Afghanistan. Bosnia. Somalia. Surely, they knew what they were doing. In fact, Pasha, in addition to being the head of the Oil-for-Food program, was also the UN's security coordinator, the highest-level official in charge of staff security within the organization. I wasn't sure how he could be expected to handle both of these functions at the same time, since they were both full-time jobs, but if I added up everything that I didn't understand at that stage, I'd have had a nervous breakdown before touchdown and would have needed a medevac out of Iraq on day one. Perhaps this was not the best way to jump-start my UN career.

I had to pull it together. I had strived to get myself into just this type of situation ever since I graduated from college, and it hadn't come easy. This wasn't the time to freak out. International politics had been part of my life since I was a kid. Sitting on my father's shoulders, at age six, I attended protests in front of the Soviet Embassy, demanding the release of political refugees. My parents were international journalists and, because they couldn't afford a nanny, they often took my brother or me along to work. Sometimes, it meant we got to shake hands with heads of state. Other times, it meant we were gassed by police as they broke up street protests my parents were covering.

I was born in Denmark, grew up mostly in Paris, and immigrated to the United States at eighteen. After graduating from Brown University, I hitched a ride to New York. Most of my friends went for banking jobs in the city. I just went to the city and banked that I would find a job.

After being called "human spam" by a busy pedestrian as I was trying to collect donations for an environmental NGO one day, I went about looking for a real job. That same day I decided to find a way to break into the United Nations. After roaming around the UN building for a whole day, during which I took the tourist tour twice, I managed to find out about a job opening— for the position of messenger. I was actually pretty excited about the prospect of being a messenger at the UN. The "help wanted" pages of the *New York Times* had been most uninspiring. It seemed most firms wanted accountants or receptionists, and I had not exactly been a hit at the interviews I had managed to line up. At the Sierra Club, an environmental advocacy group, I had shown up wearing a suit. Everybody else was in shorts and Birkenstocks. A temp agency gave me a typing test, which I failed miserably, leading them to conclude that I would not make a good secretary. I had interviewed for a paralegal position at a law firm, but I believe I hurt my chances when they asked me if I was "detail oriented" and I casually admitted that I "wasn't exactly the anal type."

So I went to the interview for the position of UN messenger, assuming that if only I could get my foot in the door I would soon be able to move up the ladder. Unfortunately, the United Nations is not a place where people start in the mailroom and end up in management. Myriad rules are there to prevent support staff from moving to higher levels of professional responsibility. We're not talking about a glass ceiling here. More like reinforced concrete with armored plates. Thankfully, the recruiter turned me down.

"You're overqualified," she said. "You should be a professional, not general-service staff." At the UN, they have an apartheid-like system to separate people in support functions from those in policy functions. The latter are called the "professionals," even though they are no more professional than the former.

"So do you have any openings for professional staff?" I asked.

"Sure," she said, "but you need a master's degree to apply."

I walked out of the UN thoroughly depressed. How could I be both overqualified and underqualified to work there? I cursed at myself for not having secured some kind of banking job during my last semester in college. At the same time, I knew that I wouldn't necessarily excel in that environment. But what kind of environment would I be a fit for if I couldn't even land a messenger gig?

"Journalism!" I said to myself, out loud, on Forty-Second Street, like someone on the verge of a nervous breakdown.

When I got home to the dingy little apartment I shared near Times Square with a good friend from college (and, occasionally, a big fat rat), I opened the Yellow Pages and called *Le Monde,* the French daily that I had grown up reading when I lived in Paris. I figured it would have a correspondent in New York, and that since I spoke French and was right here and wanted to be a journalist, I could perhaps be of service.

Incredibly, my assumption proved correct. Afsane, the charming Persian woman who served as UN correspondent for *Le Monde,* was going on vacation, and she needed an intern to be in the office in her absence.

Afsane saved my professional life. And she gave me my first glimpse of the inner workings of the United Nations. From one day to the next I was wandering around, wide-eyed, on the second and third floors of the UN Secretariat, which hosts the Security Council and the UN correspondents' offices. In addition to working for *Le Monde,* Afsane was a weekly guest on the CNN talk show *Diplomatic License,* anchored by the channel's UN correspondent, Richard Roth. At the start of the UN General Assembly, in September, CNN needed a production assistant to help Richard cover the event, and by that time I was hungry enough to walk up to his producer and make a pitch for myself. It worked, and soon I was hired by CNN and ordered to chase after ministers and UN ambassadors with a camera crew angling to ambush them with sound-bite-provoking questions.

The General Assembly is to the United Nations what Oscar is to Hollywood—except the climax comes at the beginning, not at the end. The only day the General Assembly hall is full is when the U.S. president makes his address, opening two weeks of speeches by heads of state from around the world. The Russians and the Chinese used to speak to a full house during the cold war, but since then they have had to contend with a lot of empty seats.

The American president's arrival at the General Assembly has an imperial quality to it. Every year, the entire UN building is cordoned off with cement trucks. Helicopters hover in the air, sharpshooters are positioned on every rooftop, and a warship stands watch on the East River. The president rolls in like a Roman emperor. His twenty-car motorcade is preceded by dozens of state troopers on Harley Davidson motorcycles, who rumble into the UN compound ahead of him like a Praetorian Guard. When the president walks up to the General Assembly, jaws drop and eyebrows rise all around. A strange giddiness follows his passage. Murmurs of "Did you see?" trail in his footsteps. Then the president speaks and everybody claps, even though many of those in attendance represent governments that revile all that the American president has just said.

The General Assembly is a largely ceremonial forum. It is open to all members of the United Nations and operated on the basis of "one nation, one vote." Its greatest achievement is to approve its own budget. The other resolutions it passes are "nonbinding," which means that they have the same weight as a poll—an opinion survey of what governments think at a given time.

The action, insofar as war and peace are concerned, takes place in the Security Council—a sort of VIP lounge where governments get down to business. The Security Council is composed of five veto-wielding permanent members (the United States, Britain, France, the Russian Federation, and China) and ten rotating members. Assuming no veto is used, it takes nine out of fifteen votes for a resolution to pass.

At the entrance to the Security Council chamber hangs a large woven replica of Picasso's famous *Guernica* painting, a cubist depiction of the Fascist aerial bombing of the Spanish village of Guernica on April 26, 1937. The picture hangs there as a reminder to all of the horrors of war. To political doves, the lesson of Picasso's *Guernica* is that war should be avoided at all costs. To political hawks, the lesson is that Fascist dictators must be confronted before they can do more harm. The same picture conjures up completely opposite lessons, depending on one's intellectual predisposition. But beyond the moral grandstanding, members also have concrete interests at play in Security Council deliberations. This explains why hawks and doves sometimes switch roles, depending on what issue is under discussion.

Covering international news was fascinating to me. But when the action at the UN died down, I was sent on local news shoots, for which I displayed little talent. Covering the Macy's Thanksgiving Day Parade, for example, was not exactly my kind of gig. Neither was trespassing on the lawn of a mother who had just lost her son to ask her to share her feelings with the rest of the world. As soon as I stepped out of the international news realm, I felt rather inadequate. Besides, I had developed a jealousy of the people I saw walking in and out of the Security Council chambers. Some meetings there are public, but the most interesting ones—where the real negotiations take place—are closed to the media. I wanted to be on the other side of the fence—making a difference!

It took me almost three years to get an interview at the UN. The queries I sent after getting my master's degree seemed to vanish into a bureaucratic black hole, and when I called to follow up, it was like trying to get through to a customer service representative at the phone company. In the end, I took the job at Preston Gates with Jack Abramoff, learning how to manipulate the democratic process in favor of the special-interest groups.

The call that shook me out of my cubicle job and landed me my first interview at the UN had electrified me. I hadn't quite expected to find myself on a plane heading for Baghdad so soon. But I had gotten what I wished for: a chance to make a difference in the lives of millions of destitute civilians.

The further north we got, the more the landscape began to look like the idea I had of Mesopotamia ("the land between the rivers," the ancient name for Iraq). Patches of green would appear sporadically along the banks of the Tigris River, and the density of towns and villages grew steadily, indicating we were approaching the Iraqi capital. The ride on the flying carcass of UN Airlines had turned out to be surprisingly smooth. Unfortunately, this was not a sign of things to come.

CHAPTER **5**

Cowboys and Bunny Huggers

HABANIYA AIRPORT, IRAQ, NOVEMBER 13, 1997

We landed at the Iraqi military airport of Habaniya, an hour outside Baghdad. MIG-29 airplanes were stationed along the runway, engines running, ready for takeoff, in anticipation of an imminent U.S.-led airstrike. Some of them were covered in green nets, in what seemed an absurd attempt at camouflage, given the observation powers of U.S. satellites.

As we waited for the cargo door to lower, Pasha turned to me and made a boxing motion. I was unsure whom exactly Pasha was planning to punch upon arrival in Baghdad, but before the day was over, I would understand the meaning of his gesture. Right then, I just nodded, giving him carte blanche to punch anybody he felt like as long as it wasn't me.

A few minutes later, we were met by Denis Halliday—a.k.a. "Facking Halliday"—the UN's number-one man in Iraq. He greeted us with a certain Irish cool—a demeanor I had not expected of the character my colleagues at headquarters had described as a political hothead. He introduced me to his assistant, a finely dressed young Lebanese fellow whom everybody seemed to call Habibi, an Arabic term of endearment. Habibi was about my age and had an equally confused smile on his face. Some friendships take a long time to establish. Under the circumstances, this one took about the time of a handshake.

Several other UN staffers were huddling around us, and in the commotion I suddenly couldn't find my bag containing all of Pasha's briefing notes. Habibi told me that one of the drivers had probably put it in the trunk of one

38

of the cars, and since the motorcade was about to leave, I would probably wait till we arrived at the hotel to retrieve it. It didn't immediately occur to me that our UN drivers were part of the Iraqi intelligence machine, and so I placed my hope in Habibi's theory and stepped into one of the white air-conditioned SUVs that formed our motorcade.

As I did, my eyes briefly met those of an Iraqi guard. He stood there in military fatigues, clutching an AK-47 rifle and staring directly at me with eyes that seemed glossy with hate. Perhaps he had singled me out because, of all the people there, I looked most like a Yankee. Or maybe he was simply jealous, seeing me step into an air-conditioned vehicle while he had to stand there in the scorching heat waiting for a Tomahawk cruise missile to fall from the sky. I would never find out. But the hostile look in his eyes stayed with me.

The drive to Baghdad took us through several military roadblocks. The country, it appeared, lived in a state of permanent self-occupation. We eventually arrived at the Al-Rasheed Hotel, where a horde of photographers awaited. They were strategically positioned at the entrance of the hotel, so as to catch a snapshot of my boss stepping onto the famous mosaic featuring George H.W. Bush looking like a bloodthirsty vampire. Under his face, the Iraqi artist had added the words "Bush is criminal" in big letters. The flashes were blinding, and the pictures published in the papers the next day had us stepping over Bush's face with what looked like a smile.

The Al-Rasheed Hotel, made famous by CNN's reporting during the Gulf War, is a claustrophobic construction designed with the intent of spying on its occupants. Rumor had it that while Peter Arnett was reporting from the rooftops during Desert Storm, Saddam Hussein was hiding somewhere in its basement, knowing America would not bomb its own journalists, no matter how irreverent they were. A Finnish architect who had been involved in the hotel's construction later told me that there were cameras behind some of the mirrors. And apparently the many sprinklers on the ceiling had little to do with Iraq's fire-code regulations. Saddam's ears were everywhere.

Thankfully, Habibi had managed to get my bag back from one of the drivers. It looked like someone had thrown a party inside, but none of my things had been removed. I checked out our itinerary for the day. We had an important meeting with all the heads of the UN agencies working for our humanitarian operation in Iraq. The UN agencies, all of which had to work with Saddam's regime on a daily basis, had essentially gone "native." They were, for the most part, in full agreement with their counterparts in the Iraqi ministries: they felt the sanctions on Iraq should be lifted immediately.

Knowing such a move was not in the cards, we considered it our job to re-mind them that their bosses sat in New York, not in Baghdad. It promised to be a fight.

In a few days, Kofi Annan was scheduled to submit his report to the Secu-rity Council about the humanitarian conditions in Iraq and the impact of the Oil-for-Food program. The Iraqis were calling our operation the "Oil-for-Nothing" program, and the Americans were calling it the "Oil-for-Palaces" program. The UN was as polarized as the larger international community, and it would be a challenge to come up with an internal consensus on what the objective reality of the program really was.

Some of the assertions in the report sounded just like the propaganda of the Iraqi regime and contained very few verifiable facts. Scattered reports of malnutrition and rampant disease had been lumped together by Halliday's of-fice into a draft report that recommended a massive overhaul of the Oil-for-Food program. There was no question that the situation in Iraq was dire, but in order to persuade the most skeptical members of the Security Council of the need to improve the program, we needed hard facts. The field mission had already warned that it would not stand for any changes, and yet they would have to be made.

Suffice it to say that the situation was tense when Halliday came by the hotel to pick us up. My first faux pas in Baghdad helped clear the air. Pro-tocol usually demands that the most important person sit in the rear right seat of the car. Unaware of that, I left Pasha and Halliday to chat, entered the air-conditioned vehicle, and sat in what I generally consider to be my favorite seat. Suddenly, I noticed both of them bending down to look at me with incredulous smiles on their faces. I smiled back, unsure what they were smiling about, and then Pasha pointed his finger at the shotgun seat, my rightful place.

The car took off with both of them sitting in the back (Pasha in the rear right). Pasha and Halliday dabbled in generalities and exchanged vague complaints about the "system." At the UN, complaining about the system was like complaining about the weather—a frequent subject of conversa-tion for people who don't really feel like talking to one another. Since tak-ing up my duties at the UN, I had heard so many employees complain about the system that I first assumed we were on the verge of some kind of staff rebellion.

At first, I was shocked by the criticism I heard from UN staff. I thought it reflected a lack of loyalty to the organization. But then I saw people at higher levels of management doing the same. Even Kofi Annan, in his speeches to the staff, rarely failed to mention that he was "aware of all the frustration" involved in working for the organization. So I figured that being critical of the system was like a skill you needed to acquire in order to be part of any discussion.

Picking up on Pasha and Halliday's conversation, I decided to share my recent insights with them on the organization's managerial problems.

"The thing about the UN," I ventured, "is that it can't seem to staff itself properly and it's desperately inept at buying the things it needs. If you can't hire and you can't buy, how are you supposed to manage?"

Silence in the car.

Unknown to me, Halliday had previously served as the head of human resources. And Pasha had extensive experience in UN procurement. Mr. Hiring and Mr. Buying shifted in their seats.

"Cute kid, huh?" Pasha said, finally. I looked back and saw Halliday rolling his eyes in agreement.

The UN compound in Iraq was known as the Canal Hotel. It had been occupied by the UN since 1991, when the weapons inspections began. I had seen the entrance to it on TV, because that is where the media filmed the weapons inspectors before they went out to "hunt" for WMDs. Back then, they were actually finding stuff. They destroyed tons of chemical and biological weapons—more than had been hit during the Gulf War. It felt strange being there, in their midst. It was like being inside the TV.

It was easy to tell the weapons inspectors apart from the humanitarian workers. The inspectors were mostly former military people from the United States, Britain, France, and Russia. The humanitarians were mostly from the developing world, especially the Arab world and Africa. In the cafeteria, where we made a quick stop for lunch, the humanitarians and the inspectors sat separately. I realized this when I tried to sit down at one end of the cafeteria and was called by Halliday to come sit at the other end.

"That's the inspectors sitting over there," Halliday whispered, as one of them walked by us with a T-shirt that read, "Bunny Huggers kiss my ass!"

I didn't understand the meaning of the message until Halliday explained to us that the humanitarian observers called the weapons inspectors Cowboys and that the weapons inspectors called the humanitarian observers Bunny Huggers. Right there, in the UN cafeteria in Baghdad, we had the physical representation of the division that plagued the international community—and the contradiction that was at the heart of the UN's own mandate. The sanctions *enforcers* and the sanctions *alleviators* couldn't stand to sit down at a table with one another. Like the jocks and the nerds in a high school cafeteria, they eyed one another suspiciously. I spotted another T-shirt, this one worn by a Bunny Hugger. It read, "UN-SCUM," a play on the acronym UNSCOM (the United Nations Special Commission), meaning the UN weapons inspectors.

Pasha and Halliday agreed that it was all pretty childish. But then, when we got up, Pasha said to me, "Take your walkie-talkie off your belt. You look like a facking Cowboy!" We had been issued walkie-talkies because of raised security concerns. The UN used code names for its high-level officials. Halliday was Eagle One. I wonder how long it took the Iraqis listening in to figure that one out. Halliday had a huge freaking pet eagle in his backyard, for which he had asked us to bring along special gourmet seeds.

As we were finishing up lunch, I was surprised when a guy came up and spoke to me in Danish. He skipped the niceties and asked to speak with me in private. He looked deeply worried, so I agreed. I excused myself from the table and went to meet him in the TV lounge, next door.

Torben had been a member of our UN guards in Iraqi Kurdistan—a region outside Saddam's control. There, he had accidentally run over and killed a child some two months earlier. The UN had paid compensation to the family in a Kurdish court, and the legal proceedings looked to be over as far as the local Kurdish authorities were concerned, when the Iraqi government asked that the UN guard be brought down to Baghdad to face Saddam Hussein's tribunal. Halliday, instead of letting Torben leave the country through Turkey, had ordered him down to Baghdad in compliance with the Iraqi order. Now the guy sat there, unable to leave the country and facing the prospect of prison time at Abu Ghraib. He was freaking out, and he wanted my boss to plead for him with the Iraqi authorities.

"I want to go back to Denmark," he said. "My family would go crazy if I had to spend time in an Iraqi prison. And so would I."

I shook his hand firmly and promised I'd do everything I could to ensure a safe exit for him. Why had Halliday caved to the Iraqi regime on this? If the Kurds were comfortable with the settlement, why subject one of our own to possible prison time in Baghdad?

When I went back to the table, Halliday asked me what my compatriot had wanted to talk to me about.

"He wants to get out of the country," I said. "As would I."

"You know, he's a bit unstable," said Halliday.

"Unstable how? Is his story not true?"

His story was true, but apparently he kept talking about seeing his comrades getting killed when he served in Bosnia. All the more reason to get him out, I thought. In any case, I'd add his case to Pasha's talking points and make sure to remind him before his meeting with the foreign minister.

But first, we had a mutiny to quell. Before walking into the meeting with the UN agency heads, Pasha did his boxing move again and winked at me. Only problem was, there were eight of them and one of him.

The United Nations had eight agencies working to implement the Oil-for-Food program in Iraq. UNICEF dealt with children, FAO with agriculture, WFP with food distribution, WHO with health, UNESCO with education, UNCHS (Habitat) with construction, UNOPS with demining, and UNDP with electricity. They all wanted a piece of the Oil-for-Food cake, and as a consequence the entire UN system was represented in that conference room in Baghdad.

The UN agency heads were a fiercely independent bunch. Technically they were supposed to be part of the UN, but in reality they considered themselves to be as sovereign as nation-states.

Meetings at the United Nations rarely begin on time. The rule of thumb is that the first ten minutes are reserved for coffee and small talk. In this case, there was coffee but not much talk. There was too much tension in the air. The interagency meeting was about to start when the representative from the World Food Program, an African fellow named Holbrooke Arthur, threw out his arm at lightning speed and caught an Iraqi fly with his fist.

"Nice catch," I said, truly impressed.

"What?" It was Pasha, sitting to my left. He had just cleared his throat and was about to start talking when I made my comment. Everybody had fallen silent.

"No, I just. . . . Arthur here caught a fly and, well, he was pretty quick."

"Shadap!" said Pasha, causing the room to smile.

"And my first name is Holbrooke, not Arthur," said Holbrooke Arthur.

Pasha proceeded to open the meeting. The niceties lasted about twenty minutes. Then the brawl began. One after the other, the agency heads lashed out at U.S. and British policies toward Iraq. Their position had the advantage of being clear: sanctions amounted to genocide and needed to be lifted immediately. With few exceptions, the agency heads categorically refused to change a word in the text of the report they had sent to UN headquarters. On grammar grounds alone it needed a complete rewrite.

The agency heads, for the most part, were not interested in the politics of peace and security. They were trained in issues relating to economic development. They usually considered their counterparts in the host countries' ministries to be their bosses and functioned more or less according to the government's wishes. But this was not Bangladesh. This was Iraq. And part of our mission was to observe and report on the government's equitable distribution of the goods it bought under the program. Were medicines going only to friends of the regime, or did everybody have access to them? Did certain ethnic groups get cheated out of the food ration? If the program was to be renewed by the UN Security Council, not to mention improved, that type of information needed to be included in our reports. To that effect, the UN had established an "observation mechanism," which at that stage was barely up and running. If the secretary general had presented that draft of the report to the Security Council, the United States and Britain would have lost all confidence in the UN's ability to oversee the Oil-for-Food program, and the pipeline of goods flowing into Iraq would likely have been held up for at least several months. As Secretary of State Madeleine Albright had warned, the "continuation" of the humanitarian program was "not automatic."

The agency heads either did not understand or did not care about that equation. They wanted sanctions lifted. Feeding on one another's rhetoric, they grew more arrogant with every speaker. As far as they were concerned, it was their way or the highway. Pasha was cornered. Halliday, who was supposed to be working for him, had in fact set up a trap on the first day of his visit.

Incredibly, Pasha stood his ground. When all of them were done, he began speaking. His voice was calm, and his elocution was much clearer than usual. Not BBC-clear, but still I was able to take notes, and some of the agency heads looked like they caught some glimpses of what he was saying as well, though the strain was clear from the creases in their eyes. Somewhat theatrically, Pasha whipped out a text that had been written at UN headquarters and reflected more closely the tone, style, and content of what was expected in a secretary general's report to the Security Council. The agency heads twitched, fidgeted in their seats, or scratched various parts of their bodies, but they remained silent. The Pasha was speaking, and they didn't yet know if they could get away with interrupting him. His proposal was simple: to use the headquarters draft as a boilerplate and incorporate into it those agency inputs that were factual as opposed to opinionated. Any recommendations would be up to the secretary general to decide on, based on the facts.

When Pasha was done, Halliday ventured a loaded question: who had actually written the headquarters draft? Pasha turned to me. He had only recently been appointed to head the program, and the name of the drafter escaped him. I knew who had drafted it. It was Trevor, the man who had warned me on the eve of my trip that I was being observed by Iraqi operatives. I understood that Trevor was disliked by some of our humanitarian colleagues, because of his affiliation with the British Defense Ministry, but I did not expect the room to explode at the mention of his name.

Some people threw their hands in the air; others cursed. The agency heads were literally "up in arms," and it was quite a sight. Halliday stood up, knocking over his chair. His job was to keep the agencies in line, but instead he led the mutiny. In a fit of rage, he accused Trevor of being a spook, working "for the MI5 or the MI6 or whatever!" (He wasn't sure which actual service, foreign or domestic, the accused spy was working for.)

Spooky, as Pasha nicknamed Trevor thereafter, had his views about the Iraqi regime. While they were not those of Halliday or the agency heads, he did, in my opinion, care deeply about helping the Iraqi people. To my knowledge, nothing he ever did was inconsistent with Security Council resolutions. And his work proved very useful in shaping proposals for improving the program in a way that made them acceptable to the United States and Britain, both veto-wielding members of the Security Council.

Part of the reason the agency heads hated Spooky so much was that he was constantly sending faxes asking them to verify this or clarify that with their Iraqi counterparts, in an effort to bring consistency to the UN's observation effort. Agency heads didn't like receiving those faxes. They were reluctant to go to the Iraqi ministries to ask intrusive questions because if the Iraqis refused to answer (which they did nine times out of ten), the agency heads would be forced to report that the government was "not cooperating." This they would not do, in part because they felt that any report charging poor cooperation by the Iraqi regime would play into the much-hated policies of the United States and Britain, and in part because they feared retribution from the Iraqis themselves. If the government kicked them out of the country, chances were they would need to look for another job. Some of these agency heads had it good in Baghdad, living in large villas with pools and helpers, and racking up huge savings from mission premiums. None of them were eager to get transferred to Khartoum. So most often they simply ignored Spooky's requests and rationalized their behavior by labeling him a spy.

Nonetheless, the accusation was serious, and I couldn't believe it had been made openly in this forum. The row lasted a few minutes, with agency heads interrupting one another to lash out at the absent Spooky and at UN headquarters in general. They sounded exactly like Iraqi government officials. Veins were protruding from their throats, and fingers were being wagged. Lifetimes of frustration from working in the UN system were being voiced, and for a moment it looked like the entire Oil-for-Food program was about to implode.

Then it happened. Pasha slammed his fist on the table, picked up his things, and stood up. Shouting, he informed the mutineers that he was going back to New York immediately, cutting short his two-week mission, and that he would report directly to Kofi Annan about their behavior. As for the report to the Security Council, he would write it himself; and if agencies refused to cooperate, then he would hold them to account. He reminded everybody in the room that their salaries were paid out of the Oil-for-Food program and that failure to live up to their responsibilities under Chapter VII of the UN Charter carried serious consequences.

Of course, with all the excitement, Pasha had reverted to "mumble-blurt" mode, and many of the agency heads who weren't used to his accent probably understood only a few words, like "don't give a fack . . . going back . . . write report alone . . . your salaries . . . facking consequences." But the meaning was clear to all. They had overstepped their authority and Pasha was bringing down the hammer.

The agencies cowered. Not since middle school had I seen anybody assert authority so effectively. After a long, painful silence, Halliday sighed and proposed that the meeting be reconvened in an hour, to give everybody a chance to calm their nerves and read the headquarters draft—or something to that effect. Before he finished his sentence, Pasha got up and made for the door. I followed in his trail, trying, as best I could, to keep a poker face. There was no plane out of Iraq that day or the next. So I figured Pasha was bluffing when he threatened to go straight back to New York. At least that's how I managed to keep the image of Pasha and me on camelback out of my head.

We walked upstairs, and Pasha installed himself in Halliday's office. He pointed to the large no-smoking sign on the wall, winked at me, and lit up a cigar. Halliday was the man who had led the campaign to impose a smoking ban throughout all UN buildings in the world. Our UN compound in Baghdad was plastered with absurdly large no-smoking signs everywhere. Halliday hated smoking with a vengeance, and his crusade to ban smoking at the UN was one of his pet projects. His own assistants were not allowed to smoke, even out of his presence. So when Halliday finally entered his office and saw Pasha sitting with his feet up on his desk, blowing thick Cohiba puffs at the ceiling fan while talking on the telephone, I seriously thought he was going to lose it.

Impressively, Halliday managed to remain somewhat composed. But his face was very red, and his lips were trembling with anger as he stuttered: "*Dih*-did . . . didn't you see the no-smoking signs?" Pasha ignored him and continued to speak on the phone.

"Excuse me," Halliday insisted.

Pasha raised a finger putting Halliday on hold.

Effectively "on hold," Halliday turned to me, exasperated. I didn't know what to tell him, so I just shrugged, trying to look understanding and hoping he hadn't seen the cigarette I was hiding behind my back. Halliday exhaled, shook his head, and informed me that the agency heads were ready to reconvene if Pasha was still interested.

Pasha let them wait a bit, but eventually we went back. When the meeting reconvened, everything was back to normal. In a reverent tone, the agency heads took turns issuing apologies. The report would be written according to Pasha's wishes. In exchange, Pasha agreed to recommend a review of the program to identify the unmet humanitarian needs of the Iraqi population. That review would eventually force the Security Council to more than double the amount of oil Iraq would be allowed to sell through the Oil-for-Food program (boosting its annual revenue from $4 billion to more than $10 billion).

This approach made sense from a humanitarian point of view, but it would also strengthen Saddam's ability to enrich himself and bribe his allies around the world. It would push the UN into an expanded business relationship with his regime—one that would come under intense investigation years later by the new Iraqi government as well as by the CIA, the FBI, the New York District Attorney's Office, the U.S. Congress, the UN itself, and the judicial authorities of just about every country involved in buying oil and selling humanitarian goods to Iraq under the UN's flag. Billions of dollars would go missing. Thousands of criminal acts would be committed. And the revelations that would emerge from the dozens of international investigations into the UN's "deal with the devil" would force unprecedented changes on the world organization.

Unbeknownst to all of us in the room, the compromise we had reached over how to redraft a report would set in motion a chain of events that would change the course of history—and affect our individual lives in a most dramatic way.

But all we saw, all that really mattered to us that morning, was that Denis Halliday had taken a wild stab at Pasha's back and missed. His followers had deserted him at the last moment and renewed their allegiance to Pasha. "Denis the Menace" (as Pasha now nicknamed him) had no choice but to fall back into rank. For now.

CHAPTER 6

Coffee With Criminals

Before they became faces on a deck of cards, Saddam Hussein's cronies were powerful men, feared throughout Iraq and the Middle East and treated with utmost respect by much of the international community. I did not look forward to shaking their hands. But sitting down with them was part of our job as the liaisons between the Iraqi government and the rest of the world.

Before our meetings with the Iraqi ministers, I tried my best to feed Pasha the contents of the briefing notes my colleagues had prepared for him at headquarters. But every time I whipped them out, Pasha would roll his eyes and plead to do it later. As a result, Pasha met with several Iraqi ministers without much in the way of a prior briefing. This didn't matter so much with the ministers of agriculture or education, for the nature of our discussions was technical, but when it came to the minister of foreign affairs and the vice president, I had to make sure Pasha brought up certain points or my colleagues back at headquarters would strangle me upon my return. So on the day of our first meeting with the foreign minister, I decided to ambush Pasha at breakfast.

Strangely, the Al-Rasheed Hotel cafeteria was teeming with Asians—I assumed they were North Koreans, since Iraq maintained excellent relations with that country. There were about a hundred of them. We had no idea what they were doing there. They weren't there for tourism, I figured, for they had not brought any wives. Still, they added an unexpected, almost festive ambiance to the cafeteria, and they completely filled up the buffet area. I looked around and saw Pasha sitting down over coffee, sticking out like an elephant in a birdcage.

He saw me approach with my briefing notes in hand, rolled his eyes, and asked me for a cigarette. I asked him how the food was, and he explained that he hadn't had an opportunity to sample it because of "all these facking people." I volunteered to get some food for us, and eventually, over eggs that tasted like they had been cooked in Jiffy Lube oil, we went through Pasha's talking points in a somewhat orderly fashion. After a few mouthfuls, we looked at each other with a grimace. We were literally having oil for food.

The Al-Rasheed Hotel was once the pride of Baghdad. Now they couldn't scramble together enough butter to cook eggs. That fact alone spoke volumes more than our briefing notes. With little more than black coffee in our stomachs, we set off to meet with some of Saddam's top henchmen.

By order of the Iraqi dictator, the cabinet ministers were required to wear their green military fatigues and black berets every time there was a crisis, and this was one of those times. Most of them were long past fighting age and looked rather awkward dressed like would-be commandos. Especially when wearing Gucci shoes instead of boots.

The minister of foreign affairs at the time was Mohammed Said al-Sahaf, the man who would draw something of a cult following a few years later in his capacity as Saddam's spokesman during Operation Iraqi Freedom. Sahaf was a fantastic liar. Minutes before making his final escape in April 2003, he gave TV interviews denying that U.S. troops had taken Saddam International Airport in Baghdad and arguing that Iraq was winning the war—all with that signature winning smile of his, which was strangely absent from his face when he was picked up by U.S. forces a few days later.

The staff in the Foreign Ministry looked tense. They had good reason to be. The news that day made it appear as if U.S. bombings were imminent.

We were led into a red meeting room adjacent to the minister's office, which looked like the only well-kept space in the building. After a few minutes, Sahaf came in to greet us. Short, square-framed, and thick-necked, he gave the impression of a bulldog with glasses. He sat down, invited Pasha to speak, and lit up the first of a dozen Marlboro Reds. He seemed agitated, like someone itching to go to the bathroom. He almost jumped up from his seat when one of his aides suddenly walked in with a printout.

Pasha and I looked at each other as the foreign minister read the dispatch. Something was happening. I grabbed on to my bag. I had argued that we should fax Pasha's itinerary over to the Pentagon, to avoid being in the line of fire in any initial strike, but no one thought it would be a good idea to display any level of cooperation between the UN and the Pentagon, lest we be seen as vassals of the United States. One day, after the fall of the Iraqi regime, that same attitude would cost us many lives.

Politics aside, it struck me that sitting in an Iraqi government building at the onset of a U.S. bombing campaign might be a terribly bad idea. Would we have to make a run for it if we heard sirens? After a few tense beats Sahaf looked up at us with a smile. The United States had announced that it would postpone any immediate military action against Iraq.

The news cleared the air of palpable tension. Pasha wiped his forehead, and I rubbed my sweaty palms on the pants of my suit. Sahaf sat back and ordered some coffee for us all. Then, pointing to the ceiling, the minister said, "They know we are meeting." By "they" he meant the Americans. Since most of his contacts with America had come in the form of bombs raining down from above, it was perhaps not surprising that he would point to the ceiling when referring to the United States. In fact, the following year, when America finally launched Operation Desert Fox, Sahaf and several other members of Saddam's Revolutionary Command Council narrowly escaped certain death when they rushed out of the Social Affairs Ministry, in which they had taken refuge, seconds before a Tomahawk cruise missile slammed into it.

Sahaf, like other Iraqi ministers, lived in a world where every word he uttered was liable to make its way to Saddam Hussein's ear—and, on occasion, to a translator at the U.S. National Security Agency. So he wasn't only talking to us. He was talking to the walls as well. Saddam would get a full report on this meeting. It was like having him in the room.

The rest of the meeting proceeded in a more relaxed atmosphere. Once Sahaf was done criticizing the United States and its lackeys (as was customary in any meeting), he began to complain about something he called "the chock points." Pasha wasn't sure what the minister meant by "chock points," and so by way of explanation, Sahaf squeezed his fist as if he had just caught a little tweety bird and was choking it, after which we understood that he meant to say "choke," not "chock." He was referring to the choke points, the hurdles that were holding up the importation of civilian goods into Iraq under the Oil-for-Food program.

Here is how the system worked. Iraq would sign a contract for the sale of oil and send the contract to the UN in New York, where a UN "oil overseer" would check that the price corresponded to the market rate, which ranged from $18 a barrel to about $40 throughout the period. Oddly enough, prices would rise higher and higher even as more Iraqi oil was made available to the market. After the UN approved the price of oil, a tanker would show up at the loading dock of the Iraqi port Mina al-Bakr and fill up with Iraqi crude. A UN inspector would be present to make sure that the quantity of oil that was loaded corresponded to the amount that the buyer had paid for. The payment would be made in U.S. dollars into a UN-controlled account in the New York branch of the Banque Nationale de Paris (BNP), a French bank that had been selected in consultation with the Iraqi government. One-third of the proceeds from the sale of Iraqi oil would go toward compensation for the destruction Iraq had created during the Gulf War, and the remaining two-thirds would pay for humanitarian goods.

In order to buy food, medicine, and other goods, Iraq had to sign contracts with foreign suppliers, then send those contracts to the UN in New York, where they would be scrutinized by our office—again, to check if the price was market rate and to avoid a situation in which the Iraqi government could get kickbacks from the business it offered foreign companies. After our office checked the contract, we would forward it to the UN sanctions committee, a subsidiary of the UN Security Council also known as the 661 Committee, in reference to Resolution 661, which imposed sanctions on Iraq four days after Saddam invaded Kuwait. The 661 Committee had ultimate authority to approve or block any Iraqi contract. If it was approved, the seller would be authorized to export goods to Iraq. At the Iraqi border, a UN inspector would check the shipment and, with a copy of the bill of lading, send a message to the UN in New York to authorize payment to the foreign company out of the UN's BNP account. Once the goods were inside Iraq, the UN was in charge of observing their distribution. For food, the UN had the World Food Program set up a network of distribution points throughout the country. For medicine, we relied on observations from the World Health Organization. For construction equipment, Habitat was in charge. And so on. The job of these UN agencies was to make sure the goods went to the people and were not just hoarded by Saddam Hussein's regime.

On paper, it was an airtight system. On the ground, it was a logistical nightmare.

The mechanism for the importation of goods into Iraq was indeed inefficient, which, as far as the United States and Britain were concerned, was the whole point. Iraqis were familiar with bureaucracy, as their own totalitarian system of controls carried its cumbersome paper flow, too. Nonetheless, the rules set out in the UN resolutions drove them mad. For every piece of equipment they wanted to import—including, say, a water pump—they had to fill out an application stating where and how they intended to use it. It was like asking a grocery shopper which department of his fridge he intended to store a given piece of produce in, and when he intended to eat it, before letting him buy it.

Understandably, the Iraqis were irritated by the system and often failed to fill out their applications thoroughly enough for the U.S. diplomats sitting in New York, who then put their application "on hold pending further information." This made the Iraqis even more frustrated. Since they did not have any direct contact with the United States, their only opportunity to blow off steam was with the UN. They rarely missed their chance, and in the case of Sahaf, the steam came accompanied with spit-filled cigarette breath, which made him particularly unpleasant to sit across from.

In response, Pasha did his job, which consisted of giving his counterpart the runaround. At this, Pasha was a Jedi master. He had honed his technique over many years, and his incomprehensible accent came in surprisingly handy. First, he made a very convincing show of empathy for Sahaf's point of view, which had the Iraqi minister glimmering with hope that he could turn the UN diplomat to his cause. Then, Pasha embarked on a long mumble about the UN rules and regulations, taking the Iraqi foreign minister through the detailed procedures outlined on the following page.

At the end of Pasha's explanation, the Iraqi minister had the same look on his face as a traveler who's been standing far too long before a luggage conveyor belt.

I rather enjoyed seeing this paranoid bully being so completely disoriented by Pasha's bureaucratic mumble. But when it came to the effectiveness of our rules, Sahaf and his friends would have the last laugh. They had yet to find a way around them, but they would. It was just a matter of time before every one of the "choke points" Sahaf was referring to would be lubricated by the lure of profit. So far, the system was at a test-run stage, and most of the participants involved were still in the process of figuring out how to tinker with it.

When he understood there was no way around Pasha's mumbo jumbo, Sahaf changed the subject. Determined to get something out of us before the meeting ended, he brought up the issue of the "snake."

Apparently, a snake had infiltrated the United Nations. It took Pasha and me a moment to understand what he was talking about, but when the minister eventually mentioned that the "snake" was an "Englishman" it became obvious that he was talking about Trevor, or Spooky, as Pasha now called him. The minister wanted Spooky fired. Pasha said he was in control of his staff and that if there was a snake among them, it would always be possible to "defang" it. The minister clearly didn't know what the term "defang" meant, so

SCR 1409 - 986 APPLICATIONS PROCESSING CHART   PAGE 1

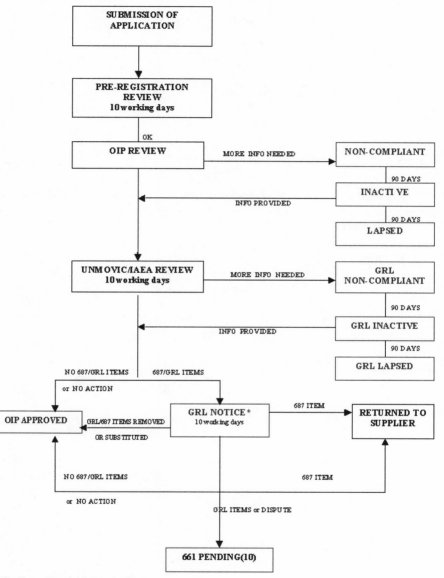

* See Reconsideration Processing Chart

54

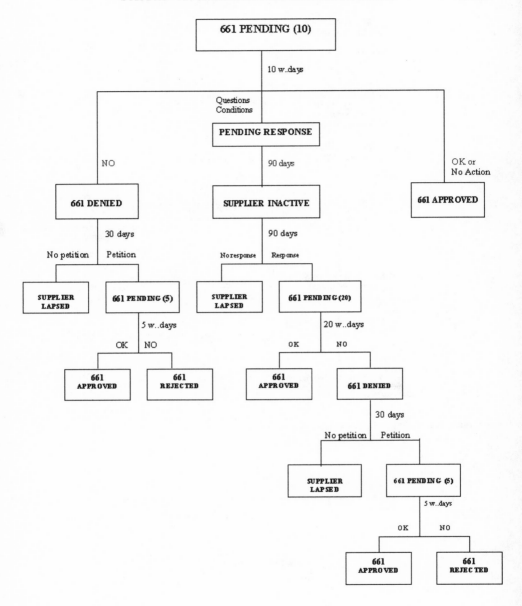

Pasha felt obliged to make a wild gesture to illustrate his point. The minister was a bit startled by Pasha's sudden arm movement, but he appeared satisfied that the snake had a nasty thing coming its way.

When I eventually told Spooky about this episode, he beamed with pride. Having the foreign minister of Iraq call him a snake was like a medal of honor for him. I didn't mention that Pasha had told the Iraqi minister he intended to have the snake defanged, though, because I assumed Pasha had not been serious. Assumptions were really all I had to work with when it came to Pasha.

Before leaving, Pasha raised the issue of our Danish colleague, who sat in our UN compound awaiting possible trial in a Baghdad court. "Please, Mr. Foreign Minister. Let me take him home with me when I leave the country." He pleaded. I was relieved that he had finally brought up the subject I had been pestering him with for days.

"The Danish citizen is now in Iraq," said Sahaf, "and he will have to be tried according to Iraqi law."

Iraqi law. Right.

That evening, upon returning to headquarters, I saw the Danish guard waiting for us in the cafeteria. He came toward us, and I quickly made a sign saying, "Not now." I didn't want Halliday, who was right there, to see us talking. He walked over to the bathroom, and a minute later, I excused myself to join him. I found him there washing his hands, waiting for an Iraqi driver to exit. I decided to wash my hands too, should someone else walk in on us. I told him in whispers what had happened. He stood no chance of getting out of Iraq without a trial. At least not with the approval of the Iraqi government. His face dropped.

"Do you have a plan B?" I asked.

"Maybe," he said. "But it's dangerous."

"How would it work?"

"We have other Danish guys up north. They can drive down, hide me in their car, and smuggle me past the checkpoints. We can't go out through Jordan, but if we can make it up to the Kurdish mountains, I can cross over to Turkey."

"All right, buddy. My advice is to go for plan B," I said.

"Shit."

"I know."

"We'll have to organize it," he said. "I can't communicate with them from here. Our lines are bugged!"

I had assumed they would be. But what had surprised me was that even our fax and copy room was manned by an Iraqi national. Every fax and every report we ever handled went through this room, and the Iraqi guy in charge could easily make doubles of everything.

"I'm going up to Kurdistan with my boss in a few days. There I will make contact with the Danish guards and explain your situation. I can then take a message back to you."

"Why don't you guys just take me with you to Kurdistan?"

"Our drivers are Iraqis. We'd have to convince Pasha or Halliday to hide you."

"Too dangerous."

"I agree. Halliday doesn't like you for some reason."

"He thinks I'm crazy! I'd like to see his face if he had to do jail time in Iraq!"

"I'll talk to the Danes. We'll make it work."

We looked into each other's eyes for a beat, then he shook my hand firmly, holding me to my promise.

"Only talk to the Danes. Nobody else."

"Got it. We'll talk when I get back."

The vice president of Iraq, Taha Yassin Ramadan, was next on our schedule. The meeting was to take place at one of the presidential palaces to which the arms inspectors had been refused access when they searched for weapons of mass destruction.

The contention that economic sanctions would somehow lead to the overthrow of the Iraqi regime crumbled in front of my eyes as we drove into the palace. The level of security was staggering. Our convoy of white vehicles was stopped twice by heavily armed guards—these elite troops looked nothing like the soldiers we could see manning roadblocks around Baghdad. They bore no resemblance to the famished, shoeless troops who had given themselves up in droves as U.S.-led forces pushed into Iraq and Kuwait in 1990. They were extremely well equipped and moved with fierce discipline. Two separate rows of guarded fences separated the palace grounds from the outside world, with heavy weaponry positioned throughout.

Had a group of hungry, fed-up Iraqis tried to storm such a place, they would have been mowed down mercilessly in a matter of seconds, and that's only if they were lucky. Prison and torture were far worse prospects for Iraqis suspected of rebellious activity. I had read up on how Saddam's regime dealt with its political opponents.

A 2001 Amnesty International report specifically noted that "victims of torture in Iraq [were] subjected to a wide range of forms of torture, including the gouging out of eyes, severe beatings and electric shocks. . . . Some victims have died as a result and many have been left with permanent physical and psychological damage." The total number of torture subjects may never be available, but the terror these methods spread reached all strata of the Iraqi population, including members of Saddam's own family, forty of whom were killed by the Iraqi dictator.

Ramadan, the man we were here to meet, had been in charge of suppressing the Shiites of southern Iraq during that time. He had without question been one of Saddam's top honchos on a number of dirty jobs. He was openly referred to as one of Saddam's "enforcers." He was at Saddam's side from the very beginning and was so zealously loyal to him that he had managed never to be purged. Of the original band of criminals who executed the 1968 coup that put the Baath Party in power, he was the only one to have survived at Saddam's side.

Born to a family of farmers in the region of Mosul in northeast Iraq, Ramadan began his career as a bank clerk after completing his secondary education. From 1968 onward, he remained on the Revolutionary Command Council, which ruled until 2003. Among his known exploits that earned him Saddam Hussein's trust, he headed a kangaroo court in 1970 that sentenced forty-four officers to death for plotting to overthrow the regime. He also led the People's Army, a large paramilitary force at the service of the regime. It was disbanded in 1991 when he became vice president. Ramadan was accused by Iraqi exiles of crimes against humanity for his role in crushing the Shiite uprising in southern Iraq in 1991 (estimated to have caused anywhere from 30,000 to 60,000 deaths) and for his involvement in the killing of thousands of Kurds in the north in 1988. Ramadan followed every one of Saddam's orders to the letter and often went overboard just to please his boss. Once, after Saddam had jokingly criticized his ministers for putting on too much weight, the guy went on a diet and lost twenty-seven kilograms. That's almost sixty pounds! Now that's motivation. I suppose he didn't want to end up on the wrong side of the torture chambers he was overseeing.

As I stepped out of the car, I noticed that our driver, an Iraqi intelligence officer, was sweating profusely. Just setting foot inside the palace grounds made him horribly nervous. We had another Iraqi government official with us from the protocol, whom we called by his first name, Adnan, because he had this apologetic way about him that made me think he was an easygoing man who had been born in the wrong country at the wrong time.

Walking into the palace, seven UN officials led by Pasha and me passed a life-size picture of young Saddam Hussein in a Rambo-like pose, clutching a heavy-duty machine gun and smiling to the camera from atop a pickup truck. He looked really happy—like he had just been shooting at people. This was not a picture I had seen in the media before, and I would have loved to take a photo, but we were forbidden to carry anything other than pen and paper into the meeting. Vice President Ramadan had escaped two assassination attempts that year alone, so even though we were visiting UN officials, the security check was rigorous. After passing metal detectors and getting patted down, felt up, and forced to empty our pockets, we were led into a vast rectangular room furnished in gold, pink, and cream Louis XIV furniture and opulent crystal chandeliers. The Iraqi protocol officer accompanying us from the Foreign Ministry was pale with fear at the thought of being in the vice president's presence, and the rest of us were on edge, too. We sat silently for several minutes. I spotted a large mirror stuck to the wall at one end of the room. Was the meeting being videotaped?

Finally, the vice president walked in. His handshake was feeble and fleeing, which suited me just fine. I could rationalize that I was doing my job, but my intrinsic hatred for men of his kind made me wonder what we were doing here to begin with. Why was the UN engaged in talks with this government? Had it not violated every principle our organization stood for? And could we sit here and talk shop with Ramadan without even mentioning his regime's crimes against humanity, against the UN Charter?

The answer would have to be yes. Talking to criminals like Taha Yassin Ramadan was a necessary component of making the Oil-for-Food program work. The minister of foreign affairs did not have a tenth of Ramadan's power. Saddam had trusted this former bank teller and torturer with running the humanitarian program for the Iraqi side. I suppose this should have tipped us off as to Saddam's intentions.

An expression of disdain was pasted onto Ramadan's face. A gun holster hung from his hip. Inside was a silver .45 Magnum with an ivory handle. The gun's barrel pointed forward (toward us) when he sat down, which was not exactly a comfortable feeling. He remained silent for a few moments, which Pasha interpreted as an invitation to speak.

It was not. Pasha had hardly uttered a sentence when the vice president cut him off. The contempt on Ramadan's face was unmistakable. He began to speak through an interpreter, blasting the United States, Britain, and the UN for what seemed an eternity, occasionally raising his voice in a threatening manner, causing his interpreter, a scrawny little mouse of a man, to try to do the same. Evidently, they were a practiced duo.

The VP would occasionally pause and fiddle with his gun holster, making it abundantly clear that Pasha wasn't invited to talk. In fact, the vice president barely looked at Pasha the whole meeting, and so Pasha had the opportunity to throw some glances around the room. At one point, he did something incredible. Looking at Adnan, the protocol officer and the only Iraqi official we had sort of befriended, Pasha did an imitation of the vice president fiddling with his gun holster. This almost caused us to explode in laughter. I was able to contain myself only by looking down at my notes, but when I glanced at the Iraqi protocol officer, I saw that his face was painfully contorted. His jaw was trembling. Poor Adnan had tears in his eyes. I figured his only possible escape route, if Ramadan suddenly looked at him, was to pretend to be crying.

Ramadan's soliloquy lasted about thirty minutes. During that time, he complained that the Oil-for-Food program had stripped Iraq of its sovereignty and that our very presence in Iraq was insulting. Having basically accused us of being a bunch of spies (Spooky was not alone now), the VP finally stopped talking. Pasha didn't even try to give him the runaround. After all, the man had a gun, and there were pretty good chances it was loaded. So he said a few polite words about how we would do our best to help the people of Iraq. Pasha then tried to extend an invitation for the vice president to visit New York, but Ramadan replied that the last time he had set foot in UN headquarters, he had met only liars and traitors who were at the beck and call of manipulative Zionists. Nice try, Pasha. Now we had the vice president going off on a rant again, complaining about the imperialist/Zionist conspiracy to undermine Iraq's sovereignty, which, he reminded us, was protected by international law.

It's an interesting thing about international law: even those who trample it most violently and most often can occasionally be caught touting its merits.

Ramadan let a beat pass to let that last point sink in, then he ordered Pasha to finish his coffee. Pasha picked up his cup with a grateful nod and a side glance at me, urging me to imitate him.

To sit there and be lectured about international law by this criminal, and to hear my boss address him as "Your Excellency," was nauseating. I had to ask myself what we were doing there drinking coffee with him. What service were we rendering to the Iraqi people by treating this monster with the highest respect? Sure, we needed the Iraqi government's cooperation to make the humanitarian program work. But why were we acting as if we had no bargaining power?

I imagined what would happen if, in the middle of Ramadan's delirious and hateful rant, Pasha had gotten up, said he'd had enough, that he had gotten the clear impression that the Iraqi government was not interested in extending sincere cooperation to the UN, and that he would go back to New York and report this to the UN Security Council. Then what?

Ramadan would probably have taken it down a notch and started treating us with a minimum amount of respect. For his alternative would have been to go tell his boss—the man for whom he had recently lost sixty pounds over a passing remark—that he had just screwed up their biggest opportunity to make money since the end of the Gulf War.

Of course, Pasha couldn't do this. He had to think about the Iraqi people. Any interruption in our operation would hurt them before it hurt the Iraqi regime. And second, such behavior likely would have cost Pasha his job. When Richard Butler, the chief UN weapons inspector, confronted the Iraqi regime too zealously in 1998, Russia and France demanded that he be fired (and fired he was). It would have been a different situation if the UN Security Council were united in confronting Saddam's regime. Then UN diplomats would have been able to hold Iraqi leaders to their word and to judge their deeds exactly as the resolutions intended. But the world we had created for ourselves with this unusual program forced us to compromise at every turn. Did it mean we were on our way to compromising ourselves?

Pasha put his cup down, and the vice president nodded to his interpreter, signaling the end of the meeting. From our point of view, the encounter had been useless. From theirs, it had probably meant to serve as an intimidation session. Our failure to stand up to this kind of bullying would eventually cause us, and the organization we worked for, great harm. But as we exited the vice president's palace, we couldn't quite envisage a world in which the man we had just met with would be sitting behind bars and put on trial by the people he had oppressed.

We got to meet some of these people and witness their suffering firsthand. But this only played to the regime's advantage, because the more suffering we witnessed the more we wanted to help, and the more we wanted to help the easier it would be for Saddam and his cronies to manipulate our humanitarian efforts for their personal gain.

In the years to come, the Iraqi dictator would prove more successful than any world leader at playing the game of UN politics. Not only would he use our program to fill his own pockets with billions of dollars; he would also use it to buy support in the UN Security Council. In the end, this multiple violator of international law would succeed in turning the UN into a defensive shield against the world's largest superpower. That one of the world's vicious human rights abusers finally succeeded in turning international law to his advantage remains an astounding achievement, in the grand scheme of history. Woodrow Wilson had led America into the very unpopular First World War and launched the League of Nations in order, he said, to make the world "safe for democracy." What we were doing through this masquerade of a humanitarian mission was making the world safer for Saddam's dictatorship. So safe, in fact, that America would once again perceive him (rightly or wrongly) as a threat, years later, when the onset of the "war on terror" reshaped the Bush administration's strategic outlook. By that time, our mission had become tragically distorted, and our reputations—in some cases our lives—had been destroyed.

But far from imagining what the future held in store for us, as we left Vice President Ramadan's palace, our thoughts were with Adnan, who had almost lost his composure to a frightening fit of laughter.

"Poor Adnan," said Pasha, as we got back in the car.

"I know! How did he keep it together?" I wondered. "I thought he was going to explode."

"If he had laughed . . ." Pasha started. Then, instead of finishing his sentence, he looked at me and sliced his own throat with his thumb.

Adnan joined us in the car, riding shotgun. We stayed silent for a moment, each of us looking out of our respective windows. When our eyes connected again, Pasha blinked at me, then tapped on Adnan's shoulder and repeated his move, imitating the vice president fidgeting with his gun. This time Adnan exploded in laughter. The chauffeur was observing us with suspicion. Only after we passed the first public poster of Saddam was Adnan able to regain control.

The freedom to laugh, I realized, had never been mentioned in any text of human rights law. We hear about freedom of expression or of association. But at heart, can either of those freedoms truly exist if the people don't have the right to laugh at their leaders?

As I pondered the question, I wondered how much "freedom of expression" I might have within the UN itself. Was this an organization that could withstand ridicule? Or would all the compromises we made with tyrants, and hence with our own declared principles, restrict my ability to tell the truth as I saw it?

CHAPTER 7

The Great Misunderstanding

"Let there be no misunderstanding: we have no quarrel with the people of Iraq."

PRESIDENT GEORGE H.W. BUSH,
in his prewar radio address to the Iraqi people,
September 17, 1990

She was a beautiful six-year-old girl with sparkling hazelnut eyes and flowing brown hair. When we entered her room, she looked up from her coloring book and gave us a radiant smile.

Our tour of the Baghdad hospital had been gruesome. The facility lacked everything from painkillers to antiseptics. The contrast between the plush vice presidential palace and the smelly green halls of the hospital located in the Shiite slum of Baghdad was striking. The tour was a beaten path, offered to all visiting journalists and foreign dignitaries. Halliday had visited several times and was highlighting the facility's worst deficiencies as we walked through. Some of the patients were in such pain that they were hardly able to acknowledge us when we entered their room. The doctor said they had no painkillers. There were patients waiting to be cut open with dirty scalpels in operating rooms that had no electric light. There were emaciated kids, too. But this little girl looked healthy. She was excited to see visitors. Her eyes were playful, vibrant, and alert. She was so full of life that we forgot, for a brief moment, why we were there.

"She is going to die," said the minister of health.

It seemed absurd. But the bright-eyed little girl, we were told, had a form of leukemia that was treatable in prewar Iraq but too expensive to cure in a country under economic sanctions. Before the Gulf War, and the ensuing sanctions, Iraq was known to have one of the best-performing health-care systems in the Middle East. Clearly, the Sunnis received better treatment than the Shiites or the Kurds, and many government statistics from the time were unreliable and somewhat pumped up to reflect the glories of the totalitarian state. But when asked to compare the current conditions with their former work environment, the doctors had merely to grimace to make the tragic gap evident. And the girl before us was a clear victim of this decadence.

The girl's mother sat silently at her side. She showed no surprise at our presence. Surely we were not the first international visitors to be paraded through her daughter's room. She avoided eye contact with us, trying as best she could to maintain some dignity, even as her government put her private pain on public display.

The little girl had made a drawing, and she held it up proudly for all to see. That's when Pasha broke down in tears. The under secretary general cried uncontrollably, in plain sight of the child and her mother. The tensions of the day had been extreme, and to see such a beautiful child condemned to death was just unbearable. The emaciated kids we could deal with, for some reason. But not her.

Seeing his guest cry, the minister of health began to cry as well, followed by his deputy and the Iraqi protocol officer who acted as our minder. All the crying made the mother start weeping too. Soon the whole room was crying, except for the little girl, who was unaware of her fate, and me, who couldn't accept it.

I walked over and sat on her bed, in an attempt to shield her from the spectacle. Her smile had disappeared, leaving only an innocent question mark on her face. Pasha was wailing—unstoppable—and the Iraqi health minister was struggling to keep up with him. About a year later, Spooky told me Saddam had thrown his health minister in jail. Perhaps he had failed to cut Saddam in on his business, which consisted in reselling medicine purchased through the UN to pharmacies in Jordan. Media reports eventually surfaced, starting in 1998, citing anecdotes of customers walking into pharmacies in Jordan and being asked if they wanted to purchase legitimate painkillers or secondhand "Oil-for-Food pills." To us it was just a rumor that never got checked out by our own UN observers. As similar rumors grew in the years that followed, nobody inside the UN moved a finger to confirm them or report them to the UN

Security Council in New York. We would learn to live with them for reasons, and with justifications, that can only be comprehended by people who were more familiar with the UN's culture of incompetence than I was at the time.

At this early stage the questions in my mind were simply accumulating, taking an increasing toll on my mental faculties. It would take me years to see clearly, to relearn a skill I had mastered perfectly well by age four—namely, that of simply describing the obvious. The diversion of goods within Iraq was systematic in most ministries and would grow with time, as our observers failed to catch on to the scheme or neglected to mention it in their reports. In total, the diversion would be valued at $1.9 billion. Enough to cure lots of little girls from lots of diseases.

Here's what we didn't know, as we stood there weeping (or, in my case, holding back tears for fear of frightening the little girl): Saddam Hussein's Ministry of Defense, his Ministry of Military Industrialization, and his General Security Directorate, all of which were obviously not allowed to sign contracts under the UN's humanitarian program, simply ordered other ministries like Health or Agriculture to sign contracts for them. Or, for efficiency's sake, they just borrowed another ministry's letterhead and wrote up the contracts themselves. Evidence later emerged showing that a great number of trucks (in particular, models that could be used to pull artillery) had been ordered, along with tires, batteries, forklifts, and even date palm excavators, which were used to uproot palm trees and transport them to presidential palaces. We thought all of this was being used to transport food and medicine, and we couldn't understand why the humanitarian situation failed to improve at a more rapid pace. Records eventually showed that Taha Yassin Ramadan, who had just been lecturing us on international law, illegally contracted for $29 million worth of equipment to refurbish his palatial offices. But such records were not available to us then. All we had to judge the situation by was what we saw and what the Iraqi ministers were telling us. Here was a little girl who was going to die because of UN sanctions.

The girl dropped her drawing on the floor, which was not surprising, given the terrible impact it seemed to have on her visitors. I picked it up and made a face like I was very impressed. I pinched her cheek and smiled at her to get her attention away from all the drama. She looked a bit like one of my nieces, so I just behaved as I would with her. I didn't speak Arabic, so I spoke to her in English, using sign language as best I could to clown around with her, in the hope that the weeping delegation would soon leave the room.

But the girl was obsessed with all the crying men behind me. She asked her mother a question, which I assumed was "Why is everybody crying?" But she got no answer. She looked at the table next to her and picked up a doll, and made a movement to suggest she wanted someone to take it. Maybe if she gave them her doll, all the big men would stop crying?

The minister of health was just about done pretending to cry. His performance would not have gotten him into the Actors Studio, but he had managed to produce real tears, which, given his lack of formal training, was pretty impressive. Acting was not so much a starving artist's occupation in Iraq as a survival skill for most public office holders. Anybody who joined the Baath Party had to develop some skills on the acting front, if only to look convincing while lying to foreigners like us. When he finished he peeked at his gold watch and invited us over to his office.

Before exiting, Halliday gave the girl's mother some money. In the following months, he did his best to raise funds to buy the chemotherapy drugs for her treatment. Halliday was someone with whom I would have intense political disagreements about how to deal with the regime of Saddam Hussein, but he was a true humanitarian—one who actually dipped into his own pockets to help these and other destitute people. Unfortunately, it did not always make a difference. On Christmas Day, I was in my office at UN headquarters in New York when I received an e-mail from Denis. The little angel had passed away, he said, and he hoped that her tragic fate would persuade me to support lifting the UN sanctions.

The tears I had held back for months welled up. She wasn't the first or the last Iraqi child to die from a curable disease during the sanctions. Contaminated water alone had claimed thousands of young lives since 1991—about a quarter of a million, according to the most conservative estimates available. But statistics were statistics. This was a little girl I had met.

Her memory stayed with me during countless hours spent in the UN Security Council in New York, listening to ambassadors jousting for the moral high ground, even as they maneuvered to squeeze the most out of Iraq's resources. My memory of her always came accompanied by the question her mother had asked as we exited the room, and which we would hear again and again from the Iraqi civilians we met: "Why are you doing this to us?"

It was all they could ask. They weren't allowed to have a real discussion with us, because we were accompanied by minders from the Iraqi government who were immediately recognized as Mukhabarat, Saddam's secret police. They couldn't ask us why we left Saddam in power after destroying their entire infrastructure in 1991, effectively condemning them to a future of despair. They could only ask why we were doing "this" to them. Be it in a hospital, or a dilapidated water station, or a slum overrun by sewage from a bombed-out water pipe, there were no lack of visuals to illustrate what they meant by "this." In the words of the first international envoy to visit Iraq after the Gulf War, Iraq had been bombed back "to the pre-industrial age."

This statement, by the former president of Finland, was not an exaggeration. The problem was not with the precision of the so-called smart bombs. They flew in and out of windows and chimneys all right. The problem was with the actual targets selected by the Pentagon. Unlike the planners of the 2003 Iraq War, who focused their fire primarily on government facilities and military installations, the planners of the 1991 campaign actually targeted the entire civilian infrastructure of Iraq for destruction. Secretary of State James Baker had sent a letter to Saddam explicitly promising that Iraq would have no economy to speak of after the war. That was a promise America kept by systematically bombing every bridge, every water station, and anything that looked remotely like a factory. It was part and parcel of the strategy to deprive Saddam of a functional society, rather than to deprive that society from a dysfunctional Saddam.

After a month of bombing and a hundred-hour ground campaign, the United States signed a cease-fire agreement with the man George H.W. Bush had previously compared to Adolf Hitler.

"Let there be no misunderstanding," Bush had said in his radio address to the Iraqi people before Desert Storm. "We have no quarrel with the people of Iraq."

And yet it was Iraq's people, not Saddam and his henchmen, who suffered the most from the war and the policy of sanctions that followed. Pentagon planners had detailed projections showing that the bombing of Iraq's water and sanitation network would cause outbreaks of waterborne diseases. They knew that the obliteration of the country's electrical grid would incapacitate hospitals, prevent cold storage of medicine, black out operating rooms, and cause most economic activity to cease. What they hadn't planned for was how the Iraqi population was supposed to cope with this damage in the aftermath of the war, especially with sanctions still in place.

If we didn't have a quarrel with the people of Iraq, why were they the primary victims of our policies?

Surely there had been some kind of misunderstanding. Or had we simply lied to them?

On May 7, 1991, Deputy National Security Adviser Robert M. Gates (the current defense secretary) helped clear the misunderstanding when he declared, "Saddam is discredited and cannot be redeemed. His leadership will never be accepted by the world community. Therefore, Iraqis will pay the price while he remains in power."*

Iraqis would pay the price. It was a far cry from the promise of international justice announced in Bush's "New World Order" speech. But it may survive in the history books as the only honest statement the international community ever made to the Iraqi people during the entire span of the conflict.

Carl von Clausewitz, the architect of modern warfare doctrine, once described war as "the continuation of politics by other means." By maintaining Iraq in a state of limbo after the war, we had turned Clausewitz's mantra on its head. Our policy toward Iraq was a continuation of war through other means. But the primary victims of our policy were not our declared targets. Until we met the victims of this silent war face to face, I believe we thought of them as "collateral damage." Only that label didn't fit. We were hardly causing enough harm to Saddam Hussein and his clique to call the rest of the damage we inflicted on Iraq's civilians "collateral."

Sure enough, we were there to help minimize this damage now. But one thing was becoming clear. Then and in the future, we would be working with a population that had every reason to mistrust our declared best intentions.

---

*Andrew and Patrick Cockburn, *Out of the Ashes: The Resurrection of Saddam Hussein* (New York: HarperCollins, 1999), p. 43.

CHAPTER 8

From Russia With Love

A claustrophobic panic room with beige, soundproof padded walls. Saddam's ears could not reach us here. The Russians had made sure of that. Their Soviet-era embassy was built to sustain a siege. Merely penetrating into this room had involved passing through a series of thick doors with key codes and strange beeping locks.

The Russian envoy was tall, fit, and surprisingly young, with a crew cut of white hair and a wide wolflike grin on his face. He didn't look like an ambassador at all. He looked like a karate instructor. And his assistant looked like he could bend metal bars over his knee. I decided these guys were from the KGB school of international diplomacy.

The ambassador offered us some tea and encouraged us to grab a cookie. The man had initially offered us vodka, but much to my regret, Pasha had declined.

I took out my notepad, and the ambassador's eyes zoomed in on it. His smile dropped. Pasha saw that, and he told me that it was all right, I didn't need to take notes.

"This is informal," said Pasha, and the Russians nodded enthusiastically. The ambassador was smiling again. He leaned forward on his seat and said, "So!"

And that was it. He didn't add anything. He just nodded, wringing his hands together, tapping his foot, and waiting for Pasha to speak. So Pasha eventually spoke, outlining various aspects of the program as he munched on his cookie, which didn't make him too easy to understand. Eventually the Russian seized on a key word. Pasha had mentioned that there was a chance the Oil-for-Food program might be expanded.

"Expanded!" the ambassador repeated, leaning even further toward us, all ears, and still doing that nod of his to urge Pasha to elaborate.

"Well, obviously the Security Council has to approve it, but we're going to do a review of the situation . . . with recommendations, you know, from the secretary general."

"When will you submit this report?" asked the ambassador.

Pasha looked at me. We hadn't thought that far ahead. But Pasha ventured that it might be ready in three to four months. The ambassador's eyes went into REM mode for a few seconds, as he calculated his way to the date when an eventual expansion would come into force, then they settled, like dollar signs on a slot machine.

"So perhaps in the spring!" said the ambassador avidly, scanning Pasha for a reaction.

"Maybe," said Pasha. "*Inshallah!*"

"Yes, *inshallah*, yes!" said the ambassador, with a nod to his deputy, who instead of saying "*inshallah*," like the others, just blinked. An awkward silence ensued, during which Pasha opted to seize another cookie.

"The humanitarian situation here is very bad," said the Russian, trying not to smile for just one second. It seemed hard for him. I think he was genuinely excited. His smile was not that of a selfless humanitarian, relieved at the prospect that a child might get more to eat. His smile was that of a guy who was about to eat a big fat juicy steak all by himself.

"What do you think of the security situation?" asked Pasha. He had just given the Russian some high-value information to report to his superiors in Moscow. So the least the Russian could do was throw us a bone. Since our meeting with Foreign Minister Sahaf we assumed the U.S. bombing campaign was off, for now. But with nothing other than news reports to work with, we had no idea what the future held in store.

The Russian told us with some assurance that the crisis would probably not reignite before a year's time. His confidence surprised me. I had never thought of international crises as moments scheduled well in advance. I wondered how a Russian diplomat would know anything about future U.S. plans to strike Iraq. But in retrospect, it is not difficult to figure out how the ambassador arrived at this conclusion. He didn't necessarily know about U.S. plans *per se*. But he knew what America's policy was. It had been stated again and again on the Sunday morning talk shows. If Saddam blocked the work of the UN weapons inspectors, the United States would act militarily. The policy was clear, but it carried the disadvantage of giving Saddam the initiative in deciding when to produce a crisis. The challenge, from Saddam's point of view, was to gauge correctly what types of actions would tip the scales, causing the United States to cease playing the diplomatic game and go into countdown mode for military action.

Saddam had a range of options at his disposal for sabotaging the work of the UN inspectors, and he was always testing how much he could get away with. From blocking UN convoys with sheep herds to actually expelling inspectors from the country, Saddam could pick and choose and then watch the reaction of the international community on CNN. While ambassadors would call for concerted action in New York, Saddam had various ways of wrecking the harmony in the UN Security Council. His latest test had involved singling out U.S. members of the inspection team for expulsion, while maintaining Russian, French, and Chinese inspectors in Iraq. The result was that all UN inspectors had withdrawn right before we had flown in. They would be allowed back in February 1998 under a deal brokered by Kofi Annan, then expelled again in August of that same year, sparking Operation Desert Fox some four months later. The whole process would indeed take a year, just as the Russian Ambassador had predicted.

Ultimately, all sides understood that a clash was inevitable, because Saddam's bottom line and Washington's bottom line were not compatible. Saddam wanted the inspectors out of Iraq; Washington wanted them inside his palaces. The only question was when the next showdown would take place.

With the prospect of a massive expansion of the Oil-for-Food program, Saddam decided to wait about a year before halting cooperation with the inspectors completely.

Once UNSCOM was definitely out of the country (December 1998), the Russian Federation moved to secure this gain by making sure the inspection team wouldn't return to Iraq anytime soon. Citing evidence that the United States had used UNSCOM to spy on Saddam (wasn't that the whole point?), Russia moved to have Richard Butler, the chief UN inspector, removed from his position. UNSCOM was temporarily dismantled, only to be renamed UNMOVIC, a more Slavic-sounding name for a tamer organization that would remain barred from entering Iraq until right before the war, when Washington suddenly adopted a more aggressive stance toward Iraq, citing the four-year interruption in UN inspections as proof that Saddam had something to hide. Throughout what we might call a five-year "perma-crisis," Moscow and Baghdad acted in collusion to prevent UN inspectors from resuming their work. As the years of sanctions wore on and the Oil-for-Food program expanded, what motivated Moscow to offer such dedicated support to Saddam's policies?

Let's follow the money. In total, Iraq would sell $19.1 billion worth of oil to Russian companies. Why is this significant? After all, oil is traded on the international market, and Russia could well have bought it from Venezuela. Only here's what we didn't know as we sat there chatting with Russia's ambassador in Baghdad: Iraq was planning to sell its oil at below-market prices. And Saddam Hussein explicitly allocated a third of Iraq's underpriced oil to Russia's political leaders, meaning only they, or a company they approved of, had a right to purchase the below-market oil and resell it to an actual oil company at a profit. This would later become known as the "oil-voucher" system.

Saddam understood a thing or two about bribing people. In the case of Russia, he went right to the top. President Vladimir Putin's chief of staff, Alexander Voloshin, was allocated millions of barrels of oil throughout the life of the program to do with as he pleased. According to the U.S. Senate's Permanent Subcommittee on Investigations, the oil allocations to Putin's chief of staff amounted to a total value of $2,982,984.28, which was paid directly to the benefit of the Russian Presidential Council, headed by Alexander Voloshin. Everybody won, except of course the Iraqi people.

As we would observe in coming years, one way Vladimir Putin consolidated absolute power in his own hands was by buying off other parties in the Russian Duma. Here, too, Saddam and our Oil-for-Food program would come in handy.

In addition to the bribes offered to the Kremlin, the Iraqis allocated oil to various Russian political parties, including seventy-three million barrels to the fascist (and misnamed) Liberal Democratic Party, headed by Vladimir Zhirinovsky, and 121.1 million barrels to the Communist Party, in the name of its leader, Gennady Zyuganov (who came in second during the Russian presidential elections of 1996 and 2000). Both men would often travel to Iraq and swear their allegiance to Saddam Hussein. In February 2003, Zyuganov met with Saddam, and when he returned to Moscow, he called on Russia to use its veto in the UN Security Council in order to avoid a war.

Not that the government of Vladimir Putin needed any encouragement from Zyuganov to protect the regime of Saddam Hussein. Iraq had done much better than distribute underpriced oil allocations to various political parties in Russia. It had handed over responsibility to the Russian government itself to choose which Russian *private* companies would be given allocations. This meant that Victor Kalyuzhky, the minister of fuel and energy, was enlisted to hand out Saddam's bribes in Russia *for him.*

Here's how this worked. Kalyuzhky would draw up a list, copies of which were subsequently found in the Iraqi Oil Ministry. This list would name the companies the Russian government felt should receive allocations of oil from Iraq. The Iraqis then sold the underpriced oil to these companies (which included Lukoil, Yukos, Sibneft—basically, all the companies owned by Russia's Putin-friendly oligarchs).

For the price of $19.1 billion, Saddam Hussein had, essentially, bought himself Russia's seat on the UN Security Council. It guaranteed that the United States would never again be able to attack Iraq with the approval of the UN.

Putin was allowed to use Saddam's underpriced oil to dole out cash favors to Russia's oligarchs and political parties, and Saddam was allowed to buy (mostly) Russian- or Chinese-made weapons on the black market.

In addition to benefiting illicitly from oil sales, Iraq's trading partners also poured cash into Saddam's pockets through the sale of humanitarian goods. Here's how that worked. Companies that sold products to Iraq through the Oil-for-Food program would send a 10 percent kickback to Saddam. (On some occasions, it went as high as 30 percent, but on average 10 percent was the rule.) In the case of Russian companies, they would literally send the money in cash. An employee would head over to the Iraqi Embassy in Moscow with a sports bag (or several) filled with money—mostly dollars, though toward the end of his reign Saddam seemed to prefer euros. Three Iraqi Embassy employees were in charge of taking receipt of the cash. Because Saddam liked to have his own people keep an eye on one another, these three employees included the embassy's commercial counselor, its accountant, and a third staffer who would change every couple of months, to make sure the other two didn't get any funny ideas.

This was classic Saddam Hussein School of Management. The trio of embassy staff formed what the Iraqis called a "payment committee." Such committees would be replicated in other countries as the Oil-for-Food program grew, including Greece, Egypt, Switzerland, Italy, Malaysia, Turkey, Austria, Yemen, and Syria. In France and other countries, further creative solutions would be found, but the Russian cash-transfer model had the clear advantage of staying out of the international banking system entirely, operating without a trace. Well, almost.

After they counted the cash, the Iraqis on the payment committee would issue a receipt in three copies, which each of them would have to sign. The receipts would contain a serial number, the amount of the payment, the name of the company depositing the money, and the names of the Iraqis who had counted it. Sometimes the receipts even contained the names of the individuals bringing cash to the embassy. International investigators would eventually find some of these receipts.

After the money was taken in, the Iraqi ambassador would sign and stamp each receipt. One copy would go to the company (which probably sent it straight to the shredder); one copy was placed with the cash in a safe, for future shipment to Iraq; and the last copy stayed in the embassy books.

The Iraqi Embassy staff were then charged with transporting the money to Iraq in red canvas diplomatic bags that were immune from search by airport authorities. Each diplomatic bag could hold up to $1.5 million in $100 bills. The bags were numbered and sealed with wax before the trip. Problem was, flying into Iraq was illegal under the sanctions. But this didn't stop one very entrepreneurial airline operator, A.V.M. Air, from scheduling regular Moscow-Baghdad flights, which operated from 1999 to 2003 with the full accord of the Russian government. The trick was to avoid flying through the U.S.-operated no-fly zones over northern and southern Iraq. Flying in through Iran would usually do the trick. A.V.M. are the initials of the company's owner (Al-Dzhilaui) and pilot (Vladimir Malyugin). It was basically a two-person shop, and one has to imagine that ticket prices on the A.V.M. flights were pretty steep—not only because the flights were illegal but also because a piloting error could cause the plane to get shot down by patrolling F-16 fighter jets. Bringing the cash into Iraq by road was not an option either; even under Saddam Hussein, the unruly tribes of western Iraq regularly ambushed travelers coming into the country from Jordan or Syria. Our own staff never took that road by night. In addition to running a profitable air route, the owners of A.V.M. Air eventually solicited an oil allocation from the Iraqis for themselves.

Once the plane full of cash landed in Baghdad, the Iraqi diplomat who had been charged with transporting it usually began to sweat, and not just because of the temperature. Upon arrival, he would be met at the airport by one of Saddam's henchmen and transported to the Ministry of Foreign Affairs, where the money was to be counted once again. The Iraqi diplomat had better pray that every bill was still in there, or he'd be in for a particularly unpleasant time. From the Ministry of Foreign Affairs they would call the embassy in Moscow and double-check that the sum matched the receipt that had been left behind. They would then draw up new receipts, just in case Saddam decided to throw an audit on his little business, and then the money would simply be deposited into Saddam's bank to do with as he pleased, just as in the old days, when there were no sanctions on Iraq.

At the time of our first trip to Iraq, in November 1997, there was still a cap on how much oil Iraq could sell. So in terms of volume, Saddam was not yet receiving as much cash in kickbacks as he might have before the Gulf War. Iraq was allowed to sell only $2.2 billion worth of oil every six months, or $4.4 billion per year. But in light of the conditions we had seen on the ground, and UNICEF's alarming studies on child mortality rates due to continuing problems with water and sanitation, food transportation, and other basic services that Iraqi civilians depended on to survive, Pasha and I were becoming convinced that the solution was to expand our operation. What we didn't understand then, because we did not know for sure why the Russian ambassador in Baghdad was smiling at us like a hungry wolf, was that lifting the cap on Iraq's oil sales was basically equivalent to lifting the sanctions on Saddam. For every Russian contract that went through our complex system of bureaucratic controls, red bags filled with cash flew directly into Saddam's pockets.

From Russia With Love,
Vladimir & Friends.

CHAPTER 9

Never Say Kurdistan!

"Our only true friends are the mountains."
KURDISH SAYING

UN HEADQUARTERS, BAGHDAD, NOVEMBER 17, 1997

"**What do you mean** there's no fuel?" I asked, exasperated. "We're in Iraq! The world's second-largest oil reserves! How can there be no fuel?"

I was furious. Some idiot from UN logistics had just announced that we'd be unable to stop at a gas tank and refuel on our way from Baghdad to Iraqi Kurdistan. He said that the only way we could make the trip was if we carried huge plastic jerry cans of gas inside the cars with us. The things leaked and had to be patched up with electrical tape. The cans emitted fumes even when the top was on. With Pasha and his cigars, we'd be lucky if we drove a mile before torching up.

"Forget it," I said. "I'm not having the fuel cans inside the car. Go back to the Iraqi government and tell them to find a solution. We're going to Kurdistan, and we'll need to refuel on the way. Surely they can arrange something!"

"But—"

"No buts! I don't want to hear from you until you've got a solution!"

The next morning, our convoy of about ten white SUVs departed as planned. I was sitting shotgun, with a jerry can of gas located between my legs. All I could do was enjoy the high from the fumes and pray that Pasha wouldn't light a Cuban.

Iraq had no fuel? I couldn't get over it. I initially thought it was a ploy by the Iraqi government to prevent us from traveling to the Kurdish areas. The largest part of our UN operation was there, because in the autonomous Kurdish zones, we (not the Iraqi government) were responsible for buying humanitarian goods and distributing them to the people.

Vice President Ramadan had asked us specifically not to visit the area. He didn't want a high-level UN official to meet with the Kurdish rebels who ruled this mountainous patch, and I figured that since Pasha had failed to comply with this request, the Iraqis had come up with this fable about there being no fuel to prevent us from traveling. But in fact, we saw the empty gas stations for ourselves on our way up north. Normally there would be lines of cars leading up to the pumps, but people didn't even bother. There wasn't a drop of fuel to be had on the way. And yet we also saw many trucks driving by. Something didn't add up.

Our first glimpse of the Kurdish mountain range was magical. It appeared all of a sudden through the morning mist, a blurry lavender wall on the horizon that grew increasingly defined as we approached the crossing point into the no-man's-land that separated Iraqi Kurdistan from the rest of the country.

We stopped for a few minutes at the last checkpoint manned by the Iraqi army. While we waited there for the Iraqi guard to go over our diplomatic papers, I figured I would find a spot to relieve myself. I walked out into the field, on the side of the road, and was about to let nature take its course when a shout caused me to freeze.

"Careful! The mines!"

Stafford Clarry, an olive-skinned and blue-eyed American from Hawaii, had come to meet us at the border. He was Halliday's deputy in the region, and he knew Kurdistan intimately. Some people even said he was a spy. But I was getting used to Anglo Saxons being called spies by now. I even considered myself a sort of spy—intent on helping the Danish guard facing the prospect of possible jail time in Iraq flee the country.

Of course, my spying career would not be off to an especially glorious start if I pissed on a mine. It took extreme Zen concentration, but I was eventually able to turn around and retrace my steps. Very, very carefully. Iraqi Kurdistan was estimated to be one of the most heavily mined areas of the world, on par with some areas of Afghanistan and Cambodia. By the time I got back to the car, the convoy was cleared for passage and ready to go. "Oh, well," I said, getting back into the vehicle. "I'll wait till we get to Kurdistan."

"Never say Kurdistan!" thundered Pasha, insisting to all present that we refer to the region only as the "three northern governorates" of Iraq. The region was not only a physical minefield; it was a political one as well.

Dohuk, Erbil, and Sulaymaniyah were the three predominantly Kurdish governorates of northern Iraq that gained autonomy from Saddam Hussein in 1991 after a costly rebellion in which the Kurds lost thousands of men before the United States and Britain imposed a no-fly zone on the Iraqi army. Without air support, the Iraqi army was forced to withdraw to dug-in positions in the plains south of the mountain range.

The Kurds are the largest nation of people without a state of their own. Up to twenty-five million Kurds are estimated to live in a swath of territory that stretches from Iran through northern Iraq and into Turkey and Syria. They stem from an ancient, non-Arabic tribe that predates Islam. Today, most of them are Sunni Muslims, but Christian, Bahai, and Zoroastrian minorities remain in the region as well. Most of the Jewish Kurds left in the 1950s and early '60s. Some Kurds have light hair and blue eyes, which, historians speculate, could date back to the time when the Vikings descended on Baghdad. But opportunities for ethnic mixing were plentiful during the Crusades, and in recent centuries as well, given that the Silk Road, used by merchants from all over Europe and Asia, ran straight through the region.

The fact that the Kurds' homeland is mountainous and difficult of access has been both a blessing and a curse. On the one hand, it has afforded them occasional refuge from their enemies. On the other hand, it made their region a natural frontier between the Byzantine Empire to the east, the Persian empires to the west, the Russian Orthodox Empire to the north, and the Arab tribes to the south. The quasi-perpetual state of conflict among these empires meant that the Kurds almost never experienced a time when a proxy war wasn't being fought in their backyard.

In principle, the international community had promised the Kurds a state in the Treaty of Sèvres, signed after World War I. In carving up the Ottoman Empire, the Treaty of Sèvres recognized the Kurds' right to statehood, but no Kurdish state was ever established. The first problem was that the Kurds themselves disagreed on how to delineate their territory. And a country called Kurdistan, which would cut into a large chunk of eastern Turkey, northwestern Iran, Syria, and, of course, Iraq, was not appealing to the Allies, who were establishing their own respective protectorates in these countries. For the sake of "stability," every member of the international community had therefore agreed to act as if the Treaty of Sèvres had never been signed into international law. By 1923, Kemal Atatürk had led an uprising that reclaimed the entire Turkish peninsula and established the modern Republic of Turkey. The ensuing peace deal, the Treaty of Lausanne, superseded the Treaty of Sèvres and made no mention of a Kurdish nation or Kurdish rights. But the dream of a Kurdish nation remained in the hearts and minds of succeeding generations.

"Welcome to Kurdistan" came the many greetings on the Kurdish side of the no-man's-land. The guards were smiling at us. Didn't they know they were supposed to say, "Welcome to the three northern governorates?"

"You see?" said Pasha. "We can't let them think they're going to get independence. We work here *on behalf of the government of Iraq.*"

True enough, it was theoretically our mandate to be operating the program in the north "on behalf of the government of Iraq," but it seemed to me that if we were truly working on Saddam's behalf, we would be in the business of gassing the Kurds, not helping them rebuild their homes. And so I said.

I knew, by the silence in the car, that I had committed another faux pas. Pasha shook his head, incredulous yet wordless. The driver, an Iraqi intelligence agent, didn't flinch. I must admit I had forgotten about him. It felt great to be out of Baghdad, away from all the oppressive pictures and statues of Saddam Hussein. Freedom may be a political concept, but it is first and foremost a feeling. A breath of fresh air. A smile on people's faces. The absence of fear in their eyes. The difference between the north and the south was palpable.

Iraq's sovereignty and territorial integrity, which were enshrined in every UN resolution dealing with that country, were a concept, not a reality. Saddam was not in control of Iraqi Kurdistan, and he was unable to exercise many of the rights that normally come with sovereignty in the rest of his country. He couldn't fly around in much of his own airspace, and he had no right either to export or import anything unless it was cleared by the UN. And yet every resolution the UN passed on Iraq insisted on pretending that the Kurds remained subjects of Saddam Hussein.

The idea of Kurdish independence seemed an especially frightening prospect for much of the international community, principally because it would upset Turkey, a major NATO ally. So frightening was the prospect of a Kurdish state that the world stayed largely silent when Saddam gassed the Kurdish village of Halabja with a cocktail of sarin and VX gas in 1988. Few countries other than the United States have agreed to classify Saddam's systematic massacre of an estimated 180,000 Kurds in the 1986–1988 campaign as a genocide. More were killed after the Gulf War, but even then the prospect of Kurdish autonomy within Iraq remained so taboo that the no-fly zone imposed by the United States and Britain to protect the Kurds against Saddam's air force after the Gulf War was never approved by the UN Security Council and was thus considered "illegal" by the United Nations. So frightened were we of Kurdish claims to self-rule that we were not even allowed to call the region by its name.

If Iraqi Kurdistan was to be called "the three northern governorates," what were we to call the Kurds themselves? The "three-northern-governorakians"?

If Saddam Hussein had failed to eradicate their identity, the notion that a bunch of perfume-wearing diplomats could tell the Kurds what they could or could not call themselves was laughable. If we had only accepted this simple reality, it could have been a love story between the UN and the Kurds. After all, the Oil-for-Food program was an economic boon for them. Thanks to the UN, they were finally getting a fair share of Iraq's oil revenues to rebuild their villages and repair their infrastructure. So why did they grow to resent the UN so much? Why did they maneuver to keep the UN out of Iraq after the war? And why did they fan the flames of the scandal that would eventually bring us down?

The Kurds bit the hand that had fed them not because they were ungrateful but because we behaved arrogantly toward them. We sought to keep them down. When they arrogated to themselves the titles of ministers, we would refuse to acknowledge them as such. They had established a beginning of democratic governance, but our own protocol (owing to our respect for that illusion we called Iraq's sovereignty, by which we actually meant Saddam's sovereignty) prevented us from acknowledging their titles. The Kurds exploited their first shot at autonomy by trying to prove to the world they could take care of themselves. Sure, they lacked a bit of elegance for us international sophisticates. But they were bubbling with energy. You could see it everywhere. They would engage us enthusiastically with their fancy business cards. "Hey, color copies, five Swiss dinars!"

Swiss dinars? Yes, they had started printing their own money outside the country. They didn't care much for seeing Saddam's face on their bills. Who could blame them? They had set up their own TV stations, their own Internet links, and they were building the foundations of an independent future.

I asked myself, what was so frightening about these people being free to rule themselves? They were not a threat and were still very much in the act of rekindling a sense of normalcy, which they hadn't been able to enjoy for generations.

Evidence of the Iraqi army's destruction was everywhere. And the small village of Mamand, where we stopped on our second day, was a case in point. The UN was helping the villagers rebuild their homes after they had been destroyed seven times by Saddam's forces.

Seven times. And every time the Iraqi army had its back turned, survivors of the village returned on donkey back and started rebuilding. To avoid this (Saddam was trying to collectivize the Kurds) the Iraqi army would actually mine the villages after it razed every building to the ground. And the army would mine the surrounding fields, too, to ensure that farm boys would lose a leg, or worse, as soon as they started cultivating their ancestral land again. Kurdistan was teeming with people who had been disabled by mines; one of the UN's most useful services to the Kurds involved demining, mine awareness campaigns, and the provision of prosthetic limbs to the injured.

In the village of Mamand, an old tribal chief walked up to us to thank the UN for its help. But he hastened to add that they would be perfectly capable of rebuilding their village without us.

We were a bit taken aback by this statement. But these guys had rebuilt their village seven times already. They did not need our charity. What they needed most from the international community was security. He repeated the word "security" more times than our interpreter cared to translate it. And all we could do was nod, knowing that the only thing guaranteeing this village's security—the no-fly zone—was considered illegal by the UN.

Just as it was considered illegal to depose Saddam Hussein after the Gulf War, so it was considered illegal to keep the Kurds autonomous from Saddam's rule. Minds that could bend around such absurdities still prevailed in the UN Security Council and in the upper management of the UN Secretariat. But their rationale never prevailed upon the Kurds. The village elder we spoke to did not have a doctorate in international law, but he knew a thing or two about survival. And when his community had been the subject of massive human rights violations, there had been no international lawyers around to protect them. So none of us were about to lecture him with a "legal" explanation for why the UN was unable to offer protection to the Kurds, or even to offer legal backing to the no-fly zone.

We did have guys with guns—the United Nations Guards Contingent for Iraq (UNGCI)—driving around. But the UNGCI guards were mostly there to protect *us*, not them. With greater freedom in the Kurdish zones came greater insecurity for foreigners, and so as we traveled through the region, we were escorted by this contingent of blue guards, who were outfitted with handguns and walkie-talkies. Given that local farm boys walked around with

AK-47s, the UNGCI looked about as fierce as a one-legged man in an ass-kicking contest. But they offered valuable logistical support to the mission, and they were popular with the children.

I quickly identified the Danes among them and took two of them aside. I explained the situation of our man in Baghdad, awaiting trial in an Iraqi court for an accident the Kurdish courts had already settled. They knew about him and had made plans to exfiltrate him, if need be. They had hoped another solution could be found, for if they were caught, all might face prison time in Iraq. I broke the bad news: the UN's leaders were not going to move a finger to get our colleague out.

"Fuck," said the taller guard. And then the smaller guard said "fuck," too. They would need to take the matter into their own hands.

The key to exfiltrating the Danish guard was timing. The Iraqis probably suspected that his pals would try to get him out. In addition to deceiving the Iraqis, the guards knew they would have to hoodwink their own UN supervisors. If managers found out about their plans, they would throw a wrench in them. Disobeying the Iraqi government, even when it illegally threatened the life of a UN staff member, was not something the UN establishment had the guts for. The worst that could happen, if the exfiltration was successful, was that the Iraqi government would send a letter of complaint to the United Nations. Yet none of the UN's managers were willing to do anything that risked provoking such a letter.

"What are they so afraid of?" asked the taller guard. "The weapons inspectors never have to deal with this crap! The Iraqis would never dare hold one of *their* guys! It's against international conventions! This man has a *right* to leave!"

While always reluctant to play hardball with the Iraqi government, the UN's leaders had no problems frustrating the Kurds. Pasha set the wrong tone for our relations with them right from the start with his "three northern governorates" nonsense. In his first interview on Kurdish TV, Pasha appeared to threaten the Kurds with being returned to Baghdad's rule once the sanctions on Iraq were lifted. And his contempt for them came out clearly from his media statements. In May 2002, he would eventually be quoted by Jeffrey Goldberg in *The New Yorker* as saying that he was "unmoved" by the demands of the Kurds.

"If they had a theme song," he added, "it would be 'Give Me, Give Me, Give Me!' I am getting fed up with their complaints. You can tell them that!" Pasha would come to regret those words after the war, when the Kurds took up leading positions in the first free Iraqi government and pushed to hire the consulting firm KPMG to investigate his actions as head of the UN Oil-for-Food program.

The UN paid a severe price for underestimating the Kurds. They had wrestled with the greatest empires in history, survived genocide, and sprung back from the abyss. Without a country they could call their own, the Kurds were oppressed by the states that administered their lands throughout the twentieth century—Turkey and Iraq. During the cold war, the region was a hotbed of conflict, with frequent interventions by the KGB, the CIA, and the Mossad. While each of these entities pretended to support Kurdish national aspirations, they all had agendas of their own. The KGB supported the PKK, a Communist terrorist group that aimed to destabilize Turkey, a key member of the NATO alliance. The PKK would remain a thorn in the side of Iraqi Kurdistan for many years, leading to countless Turkish military incursions into Iraq both before and after the Iraq War. The Mossad helped the Kurds rise up against Baghdad way back in the 1950s, in return for assistance in exfiltrating Iraqi and Kurdish Jews from the country through the Turkish border. In the aftermath of the Gulf War, the CIA established a presence that it used to foment, and then abort, a coup against Saddam Hussein. In his book *See No Evil*, Robert Baer, a former CIA agent posted to Kurdistan in 1995, recounts how, with the help of top Kurdish politician Jalal Talabani and notorious Iraqi Shiite exile Ahmad Chalabi, the Kurds had counted on U.S. support for an attack on Saddam's forces stationed at the border of the Kurdish provinces.

The Kurds had survived centuries of brutal repression. No diplomat was going to decide their future for them. Baghdad would never rule them again. If anything, they would help rule Baghdad.

In any case, they turned out to be far smarter at the PR game than the UN was. The Kurds would make plays against the UN on Capitol Hill, inflicting severe damage to our already tarnished reputation there. They would be present in cyberspace, with websites dedicated to criticizing the UN; they had the most complete collection of critical articles on the Oil-for-Food program on the web, and when journalists started digging into the scandals that emerged after the war, they found this archive quite useful. Finally, they had an ace. They knew what was going on in Baghdad better than we did. They had communication lines that we were not aware of. One of the two factions, the Kurdistan Democratic Party (KDP), ruled over the zone that borders Turkey—an essential smuggling route for Saddam Hussein during the sanctions. We got to see the system they had established with our own eyes when we drove up to the Turkish border.

"See those trucks over there?" said Stafford Clarry, pointing at one of three lines of trucks—two coming into Iraq, and one going out.

"Yeah?"

"They're the trucks coming in under the Oil-for-Food program."

"Oh, great," I said, snapping a picture. "So what's the other line coming in?"

"That's all the trucks that are not part of Oil-for-Food," said Stafford.

"But I thought. . . . I mean, are they allowed to import stuff outside of the program? Aren't they supposed to be under sanctions?"

Stafford had this bright smile.

"Well, yeah, but they import whatever people want to sell them. It's up to other countries to decide if they want to enforce the sanctions. There's no actual checks here at the border."

"Huh . . . but with what money do they buy all this stuff?" I asked.

"Well, see the line of trucks driving out of Iraq?"

"Yeah?"

"They're filled with fuel. They sell it in Turkey."

"So *that's* why there's no fuel in Iraq?"

Stafford nodded. "And that's not the worst part. Our program is part of the system."

"How is that?"

"Well, forget the trucks coming in with illegal goods for a moment."

"OK. . . ."

"The trucks that come in under the Oil-for-Food program—their transportation is paid for under the contracts we approve in New York, right?"

"Aha. . . ."

"So when these same trucks drive out again, they pick up the illegal fuel shipments. Thanks to the UN, their smuggling is essentially free of charge."

"But that's . . . that's sanctions-busting!" I said, then raised my camera to take some pictures, expecting these would be part of our report to the Security Council when we went back.

"Sure is," said Stafford. "But the Kurds take a cut, of course. A big cut, in fact. The trade can't happen without them. And the Turkish military profits from it too. These are all U.S. allies. So everybody wins. I just thought I'd show it to you," Stafford said to Pasha, "in case anybody cares back in New York."

Pasha stayed silent until we got back in the car.

"This is not our responsibility," Pasha concluded once we had left the area. "If members of the UN Security Council don't care, why should we?"

There was some logic in his statement. But it was not a legal logic; it was a political one. The violation was a clear breach of international law. As I was beginning to understand, the law concerned the UN's top brass only when it suited their bosses on the Security Council.

The Security Council eventually pretended to care, once, when the United States and Britain forced a briefing on the issue, on March 24, 2000, inviting U.S. Vice Admiral Charles Moore to brief UN diplomats behind closed doors. He explained that, in addition to smuggling through the Turkish border, oil was being smuggled by pipeline to Syria, by trucks to Jordan, and by ships along the Iranian coastline. In all, Saddam Hussein made an estimated $13 billion from this smuggling. After hearing all the evidence, the UN Security Council decided to remain "seized" of the matter. And they looked very seized indeed at the end of that meeting, as they sat down for cappuccinos in the Delegates' Lounge.

Even on the eve of war, the Bush administration was still ignoring the phenomenon. E-mails from the Treasury department, disclosed by Senator Carl Levin in 2005, were very clear about that policy. No measures would be taken against U.S. allies (meaning Turkey and Jordan) that profited from Saddam's sanctions-busting. In a March 2003 e-mail recovered from the (U.S.-based) broker that handled some shipping for the illicit trade between Iraq and Jordan, an employee who had specifically sought an opinion from the U.S. Office of Foreign Asset Control on whether they could go ahead with what, on paper, was an illegal sanctions-busting trade stated that he got a call back from a U.S. government employee who responded that "her office was 'aware of the shipments and has determined not to take action.'" This was weeks before Operation Iraqi Freedom, and the United States seemed to be fine with illegal oil sales from Iraq to Jordan, an ally. The routes going through Syria and Iranian territorial waters were of greater concern. But ultimately, business was business, and some of that smuggled Iraqi oil even ended up as fuel in U.S. gas pumps, after it was resold on the international market to American oil companies.

I was surprised that the Kurds, of all people, would be in business with Saddam, after everything he had done to them. But this smuggling route was their only major source of ready cash—except for the drug trade, specifically heroin, from Iran and Afghanistan, which also passed through Kurdish territory. The money made available under the Oil-for-Food program could only be spent by UN agencies, so the Kurds had to stand aside as foreigners made decisions about what kind of garbage trucks to buy, what types of construction materials they could build their houses with, and what sort of agricultural equipment they would use to cultivate their fields. This only added to their frustration with the UN and kept them dependent on Saddam's smuggling for the cash they needed to run their autonomous government and arm their troops.

We stopped to refuel. The gas pumps were open for business around here. Though the rebels participated in Saddam's illicit fuel-smuggling operation, they never got as greedy as to deny their own people access to gas. The difference between the Kurdish rebels and the man we considered their sovereign leader could not have been made any clearer to us. But the mania of not calling things by their names would allow our top brass to ignore certain basic realities. And ultimately, it would allow them to make the wrong moral choice. Between the aspirations of a free people and those of an oppressive dictator, the UN would manage to find itself on the wrong side of the fence. At least that is how the Kurdish leaders would perceive it.

CHAPTER 10

The Rebels

Massoud Barzani and Jalal Talabani were the two competing rebel leaders of Iraqi Kurdistan. Barzani wore a turban and traditional Kurdish baggy pants that became tight around the ankles. Talabani wore suits. Barzani's guys had yellow flags, and Talabani's guys had green flags. That's how we knew which zone we were in.

On our way up to visit Barzani, the tribal leader of western Iraqi Kurdistan, we were met by two 4x4 pickup trucks filled with *peshmergas* ("those who face death") armed to the teeth. Their weapons included heavy machine guns and rocket-propelled grenades. Much to Pasha's displeasure, they escorted us up the mountain of Salahuddin, named after Saladin, the great warrior to whom Saddam Hussein often liked to compare himself despite the fact that the former was an ethnic Kurd. Saladin is probably the greatest hero of Sunni Islam. He expelled the crusaders from Jerusalem in 1187 and set up his own ruling dynasty in Egypt called the Ayyubids, who, through the centuries, worked to expand Sunni Islam in the Arab world at the expense of Shiite Islam.

If Saddam's forays into war and bloodshed seem senseless to many Western observers, it is probably because they don't understand his wish to be recognized as a modern-day Saladin. The name of Saladin resonates as widely in the Middle East as that of King Arthur in the Western world. The difference, of course, is that if Tony Blair started comparing himself to King Arthur, everybody would laugh, which was not a luxury available to Iraqis living under Saddam.

From the security of his fort perched atop the mountain of Salahuddin, Massoud Barzani received us with a suspicious smile on his face. Massoud is the son of the notorious Mustapha Barzani, who led the first organized rebellion against Baghdad. Massoud was born in 1946 on the day his father founded the Kurdistan Democratic Party (KDP), the first and most widely recognized political movement for Kurdish independence, and he eventually succeeded his father at the helm of the KDP. Mustapha was the military chief of the Soviet-backed, Kurdish-dominated Republic of Mahaban, in northern Iran. This attempt at an autonomous Kurdish state, erected after World War II as Stalin tried to retain control of Iraq, failed within a few months, and Mustapha had to flee. He took his young son and five hundred followers with him into refuge in the USSR. In 1958 the Barzanis were invited back to Iraq, but in 1961, when the Kurdish region suffered renewed repression, Mustapha took up arms and once again was condemned to the life of a guerrilla warrior. Massoud joined the fight at sixteen, often spending his time in exile. He survived an assassination attempt in 1978 as he was making his way back to Iraq once again. By the time Massoud succeeded his father at the head of the KDP, one of his father's generals, Jalal Talabani, had founded a rival Kurdish faction, the Patriotic Union of Kurdistan (PUK). In the year before we arrived in the area, Barzani and Talabani had been fighting a bitter civil war for control of the region's trade routes.

There was construction going on at Barzani's mountaintop headquarters, for it had recently been hit by a missile, courtesy of his archrival Talabani. Foremost on our agenda was the goal of consolidating the recent truce between the KDP and the PUK. The humanitarian program had been slow in getting up and running, and we didn't want more skirmishes between the two sides to further impede our work or put our staff in danger. Even though we were in way over our heads trying to reconcile these old foes (something even the CIA had failed to do), we did have one advantage: we were in control of the money—more money than the region had ever seen.

The interior of Barzani's housing complex was lined with snowy white carpeting.

Unfortunately, I had managed to muddy my shoes during an earlier visit to a sewage project. When positioning myself to take a photograph of Pasha greeting the mayor of the town, I had somehow managed to step into the actual sewer. So before stepping onto Barzani's pristine carpet, I tried to wipe off my shoes. What I needed was a big roll of Bounty, but under the circumstances, I was lucky to get my hands on a Kleenex. Having managed to dirty my hands and sleeve with mud as well, I finally stepped in to catch up with Pasha and Barzani and a massive delegation of

UN and Kurdish officials. The room where the meeting was to take place was also lined with white carpeting.

I walked in, trying as best I could to keep a low profile as I strolled into the meeting room, leaving heavy tracks of mud in my wake. I sat down and surveyed the damage. Incriminating brown footprints led straight to where I was sitting. I looked guilty as a raccoon atop a trash can. Since I didn't know what the repercussions could be for walking into a Kurdish rebel leader's house and messing up his carpet, I decided to cover my tracks. In the commotion that preceded the meeting, I did something truly shameful. I stood up and got hold of Stafford Clarry, gave him some random document, and politely offered to let him sit in my place, saying he needed to be close to Pasha "just in case."

"In case what?" asked Stafford.

I nodded at the document I had just given him as if it contained the answer. Stafford looked slightly confused but accepted my offer to sit. I tiptoed a few seats away and sat down, innocent as a firstborn. The room settled down and coffee was brought in. The protocol officer was now looking straight at Stafford, who was nervously checking the soles of his shoes. Thankfully, the cameras were invited in and everybody put on their best official smiles.

The Kurds insisted on filming every meeting we attended. Their recently acquired autonomy was not quite the independent Kurdistan of their dreams, but in all aspects of protocol they behaved as if they were at the head of a little state. This irritated the Iraqis tremendously, of course, and I think that was partly the point. Showing their leaders holding bilateral talks with the United Nations strengthened their claim to independence. After the cameramen were whisked out, the meeting began in earnest.

Barzani, speaking through an interpreter, thanked the UN for its work in Iraqi Kurdistan, then ran through a litany of complaints about the inefficiencies of the humanitarian program. Essentially, he wanted a larger share of the pie, direct control over funds, and greater autonomy from the Iraqi government, which, under the Oil-for-Food deal, remained responsible for purchasing food and medicine for the whole country. The Kurds were convinced the Iraqis were cheating them out of their share by dumping expired drugs on them. That might well have been so, but the UN's World Health Organization (WHO) was denying it, so all we could do was promise to monitor the situation more closely in the future. The head of the WHO in Iraq turned out to be a Saddam Hussein apologist who avoided setting foot in Iraqi Kurdistan so as not to upset the regime, despite the fact that his greatest managerial responsibilities were there, not in Baghdad. While our working-level staff seemed to get along just great with the local population, a majority of our leaders appeared bent on snubbing their Kurdish counterparts, creating an atmosphere of undue suspicion that permeated the entire mission and sabotaged the work of the midlevel managers.

Barzani raised several issues that challenged my preconceptions. I had never imagined, for example, that Iraq had a rich potential for agriculture. But the region around Erbil, under Barzani's control, produced vast amounts of wheat. Before the onset of Oil-for-Food, Kurdish farmers used to make a killing selling their crop to the food-strapped Iraqi government. But now, with all the wheat being imported from France and Australia, the Kurdish farmers were losing out. So Barzani wanted the UN to buy his farmers' wheat.

It was clearly an issue of significant domestic concern for Barzani, and he got visibly angry when Pasha explained that the sanctions did not allow the UN to buy food locally from the Kurds. Barzani didn't understand why the sanctions had to apply to the Kurdish region, and indeed, he had a point. There was no moral reason the sanctions should have applied to Iraqi Kurdistan, since the Kurds were not under Saddam's control. The only reason they applied was that the international community felt a need to perpetuate the illusion that Iraq was one entity. Therefore, the UN found itself breaking one of the basic precepts of economic development, overseeing the dumping of foreign wheat on a wheat-producing region.

Most of Barzani's complaints concerned issues that Pasha felt he couldn't really do anything about. Unfortunately, the Kurds were not very good at being given the runaround, because they would simply repeat their question again and again and again until they got some sort of answer. They had four times the patience we had. Not to be outdone, Pasha developed new techniques that helped him sidestep their complaints. Pasha often described the limitations of the humanitarian program with colorful metaphors. On this occasion, he compared the Oil-for-Food program to a coconut, for a reason that escaped just about everyone.

The poor interpreter, who had done his best to make sense of Pasha's elocution, stalled at this one and looked around nervously, as if asking for help. Since nobody in the room had understood what a coconut had to do with anything, the interpreter was on his own. With every second of silence, the pressure on him mounted. Pasha tried to help him by repeating the word "coconut" several times, but clearly the interpreter had no idea what he was talking about. Some members of Barzani's delegation then came to his rescue, offering a translation for "coconut," but that didn't help either, because by that time, the context of Pasha's image was long lost. The confusion aroused Barzani's suspicion, and he pressed his interpreter for a translation. The latter turned to Pasha, apologized profusely, and asked him to please repeat himself.

"Coconut! You know what is a coconut?" Pasha said, as if speaking to a retarded person.

"Yes, Excellency," said the interpreter, after which he turned to Barzani, coughed, wiped the sweat off his forehead, and said something about a coconut.

Barzani creased his foxlike eyes. *Had Pasha just called him a coconut?* Thankfully, another member of Barzani's staff intervened, offering a lengthy explanation in Kurdish. I have no idea what the man said, but I could tell that he, too, was struggling to find meaning in Pasha's words. He spoke apologetically, and after a while Barzani nodded impatiently. He had heard enough about coconuts.

Changing the subject, Barzani went on to discuss the most pressing issue facing the region under his control: the lack of electrical power.

The Dokan Dam, then under Talabani's control, used to produce electricity for the city of Erbil. As a result of recent fighting between Barzani and Talabani, the electricity supply from the Dokan Dam to Erbil had been cut off. Bilateral negotiations had been initiated to resolve the problem, and the broad outline of an agreement had been reached. However, Talabani seemed to enjoy antagonizing his nemesis too much to follow through on the deal, so instead of adhering to the established schedule of power supply, the PUK authorities switched the electricity on and off at will, following an erratic pattern based on the daily mood swings of their leader.

By way of retaliation, Barzani blocked commercial vehicles from traveling to his enemy's territory. This unending game of tit for tat hindered our work. It needed to be resolved immediately. Hence, I was delighted when Pasha agreed to offer the United Nations' good offices to help resolve the dispute. Finally, there was something concrete—an actual achievement to point to when we came back from our mission!

When I found myself unable to take a hot shower that same evening, I became even more strongly convinced of the need to get electricity to Erbil. After a glacial scrubbing, I took a moment to admire the majestic view from my hotel window. The fortified city glowed like a jewel in the late afternoon sun. Surrounded by the walls of an old castle, the ancient city of Urbillum was founded sometime before 2300 B.C. by the Sumerians. It is known as the oldest continuously inhabited city in the world. Its strategic location near some of the few fertile plains in an otherwise mountainous region had made it a coveted stronghold for centuries, and the city had seen many battles throughout the ages—including, most notoriously, the battle between the Persian King Dara and Alexander the Great in 330 B.C. Anywhere else in the world, such a location would be swarming with tourists. I earnestly hoped it would one day attract visitors intent on admiring the place rather than destroying it, but for the moment I savored the rare sight of this golden fort-city at sundown.

The next day we drove over to Sulaymaniyah, the city under Talabani's control. In contrast to Barzani, who came across as suspicious and calculating, Talabani was a world-class charmer. A jovial bon vivant, he never said no to a good cigar. His Michelin Man proportions testified to a love of good food. He received us in an informal setting, without pomp or circumstance. Jalal, as one felt like calling him, was sociable and easygoing, but unlike many of his compatriots, he was rather impatient and didn't like to sweat details. If he felt he was getting the runaround, he would immediately change the subject with a wave of the hand. He wasn't interested in talking technicalities. He spoke English perfectly and came across as well educated, especially when it came to history. Born in 1933 in the Kurdish village of Kelkan near Lake Dokan, Talabani has spent most of his life in Iraq (unlike Barzani). A true son of the land, he received his elementary and intermediate school education in Koya (Koysanjak) and his high school education in Erbil and Kirkuk. In 1946, when Barzani was born, Talabani was already 13 and in the process of forming a secret Kurdish student association. The following year he became a member of the Kurdistan Democratic Party, and in 1951, at eighteen, he was elected to the KDP's central committee, under the leadership of Mustapha Barzani, Massoud's father. Upon finishing his secondary education, he sought admission to medical school but was denied it by authorities of the then-ruling Hashemite monarchy because of his political activities. In 1953 he was allowed to enter law school, but he was obliged to go into hiding in 1956 to escape arrest for his activities as founder and secretary general of the Kurdistan Student Union. Following the July 1958 overthrow of the Hashemite monarchy, Talabani returned to law school, at the same time pursuing a career as a journalist and editor of two publications, *Khabat* and *Kurdistan*. After graduating in 1959, he served in the Iraqi army, where he held positions in artillery and armor units and as a commander of a tank unit. By the time of Mustapha Barzani's death, Talabani felt he was the rightful heir to the KDP, but because of the tribal nature of the region, Massoud took over—hence the rivalry that endured for years between Mustapha Barzani's son and his top field commander.

Despite having spent more time inside Iraq than Barzani, Talabani appeared more worldly than his rival. He was interested in talking about big-picture politics. He shared with us his vision of how Saddam Hussein could be confronted and defeated, which was a subject on which Pasha had very little to say. Talabani then provided us with an analysis of the region's challenges and of the road ahead for the establishment of an autonomous Kurdistan within a democratic and federal Iraq.

In terms of a vision for the future, Talabani was light-years ahead of Pasha, who was still working on the basic premise that, one day, sanctions would be lifted and the Kurds would again come under Saddam's control, which would make the man he was talking to a future fugitive in his own country. Talabani was already a marked man, as far as Saddam was concerned, partly because a few years earlier he had actually attacked (and temporarily routed) the Iraqi army V Corps. He did so using no more than two thousand lightly armed *peshmergas*, which testified to his audacity and skill as a military commander.

After outlining his vision of the future, Talabani paused to finish his coffee. Pasha sat there nodding, unsure of what, if anything, to say. The visionary rebel commander and the UN bureaucrat had little in common, and I was afraid Talabani would wrap up the meeting before we had a chance to broach the subject of electricity. So I wrote down "ELECTRICITY" in bold letters and placed it in Pasha's line of vision.

"On the subject of electricity," Pasha began, before being interrupted.

"I know, I know," said Talabani, smiling like a naughty boy who had gotten caught with his hand in the cookie jar. "We'll turn the power back on. But . . ." and he launched into a litany of complaints he had about his rival Barzani. Chief among them was that the KDP was not sharing the revenue it was raking in from its cut of the illegal fuel trade that was going on between Iraq and Turkey. We weren't in a position to help him on that one, because to begin with, the fuel trade was a breach of the sanctions. Everybody knew it was taking place, but we did not have any power of enforcement, and the United States seemed to sleep perfectly well at night knowing that its great ally Turkey was busting the sanctions and putting cash into Saddam's pockets. The only one who never got to see a dime from the fuel trade was Talabani—and that drove him mad! So mad, in fact, that it had caused him to launch his most recent round of attacks against Barzani.

Talabani's recent bid to control Erbil by force failed when, in August 1996, the KDP invited Saddam's army to come in and kick Talabani's forces out. Saddam's lightning strike happened so fast that the Clinton administration failed to intervene from the air. Clinton dispatched four B-52 bombers to

Guam to signify that the United States would not stand for continued progress by Saddam's forces. Saddam knew that he could not hold Erbil for long without control of the airspace over the region, so he was soon forced to withdraw his troops from their exposed position. Officially, Saddam said he had assisted Barzani in this Kurdish factional fighting because Talabani had been working with Iran. In fact, Saddam had a business agreement with Barzani. The latter allowed the Iraqi dictator to use eastern Iraqi Kurdistan as a smuggling trade route.

The factional fighting in and around the city of Erbil had initially delayed the start of the UN humanitarian operation. The prospect of increased trade helped calm the rivalry between the two Kurdish factions. Now that goods were flowing into the region at a higher rate than ever before, Talabani had an interest in resolving the disputes with his nemesis peacefully. During our meeting he had effectively admitted as much by saying that the time for Kurdish infighting had passed. And so we left with a commitment from Talabani that he would abide by the terms of a negotiated settlement for electrical power-sharing.

The negotiations were held on November 20, 1997, at the site of the magnificent Dokan Lake, where the famous dam was located. The water was bright turquoise, and I wanted nothing more than to jump in it. Instead, we drove directly to the entrance to the dam, where we were met by two negotiating teams, one from the KDP and one from the PUK. At the onset of the meeting, each side spoke for about twenty minutes, accusing the other of bad faith in implementing previous electricity-sharing agreements. The idea was simply that Talabani's side should offer a reliable time schedule for supplying Erbil with electricity from the dam. It's a lot easier to run a city when you know in advance the times when electricity will be available. After many back-and-forth accusations, I saw Pasha getting antsy. How would he resolve this one?

Finally, he put his hand up and nodded, as if to say, "I get it." Then, instead of addressing the issue at hand, Pasha came up with one of his stories about his time spent as a UN envoy in Afghanistan—something about flying between two mountains in a Cessna plane, being shot down, and crash-landing in a minefield. Unrelated as it was to the negotiations under way, Pasha's story threw both parties off the track of confrontation. They just listened to him, wondering what the hell he was talking about. Once he was done with his story, Pasha picked up the document containing the outlines of a new agreement between the parties and asked, "So, should we sign this thing or what?"

Caught completely off guard, both parties looked at each other and realized this was a yes-or-no situation. Confused, they agreed to sign.

That's how it was with Pasha. One moment, he would appear the hopeless bureaucrat, and the next, he'd pull a rabbit out of a hat. Brokering the agreement on electricity sharing was one of many ways the UN helped promote reconciliation between Barzani and Talabani. But Pasha held little hope that these agreements would last.

"They're like the Afghans," he said of the Kurds. He was pretty sure that the KDP and PUK factions would resume fighting at the first opportunity. And as for Talabani's vision of an autonomous Kurdistan within a federal and democratic Iraq, Pasha was downright dismissive: "This guy is dreaming," Pasha said to a group of snickering colleagues, as we drove away from his residence.

Talabani was dreaming, all right. But one day, this dreamer would become the first president of a democratic, federal Iraq. Sadly, it would not be the Iraq of his dreams.

CHAPTER 11

On the Edge

The humanitarian community's favorite watering hole in Iraqi Kurdistan was a bar that was operated on a part-time basis by a buxom blond Finnish woman named Yanna. She had named it The Edge, which accurately described the mental state we were in when we arrived there.

After a week spent drinking coffee with mustached men, it was a pleasure to step into a "co-ed" bar in the Christian zone of Erbil. Hours earlier we had visited another massively dysfunctional electrical dam. The Derbandikhan Dam was located in a lush green valley. The trip had begun with picturesque views of remnants of the old Silk Road carved into the Kurdish mountain ranges. I was so busy looking out at the beautiful landscape that I forgot to read up on the problems affecting the structure we were about to view. And so when we were informed that we would be taken all the way to the bottom of the dam, I initially felt excited. I always marvel at great feats of structural engineering, and I was genuinely curious to see how this massive structure actually worked.

As we walked down several flights of stairs to reach the bottom of the dam, we had the opportunity to observe a lot of incomprehensible machinery. Pasha and I tried to look as if we knew what we were looking at. All I could really say was there were many tubes and control panels that looked like they were built at the time that the TV show *Star Trek* was filmed. With lots more dust.

Since the departure of the highly trained government engineers following the Gulf War, the dam had been managed by local Kurds with scant experience in electrical power generation. They had done their best to keep it going on a shoestring budget, but as we were about to find out, their ability to keep the dam running came at the expense of basic safety regulations. The further down we went, the more we felt like we were deep in the bowels of a submerged Soviet submarine.

After an endless descent into the belly of the beast, Pasha and I were met by two Kurdish engineers in dirty white shirts, sporting pencils in their ears. One was a bucktoothed man with curly hair and a psychotic grin on his face. I think he was the boss of the pair. He informed us that "UNDP no work," by which he meant to say that the United Nations Development Program, which had been charged with improving the dam, had not delivered any results. He repeated "UNDP no work" several times as he fiddled with some levers, apparently trying to set some machine in motion.

A question began forming in the back of my mind: if "UNDP no work," how could the dam work?

"What's the facking problem?" asked Pasha, already exasperated by our claustrophobic surroundings. The UNDP representative in Iraq had told us that all repairs were on track, and we had expected our visit to confirm progress, not problems. As usual, the Kurds saw things differently. And they soon made sure we saw things their way.

The engineer walked us over to the dam's floodgate, which, as its name suggests, is critical for the stability of the entire damned structure. This floodgate had a big crack in it, out of which pressurized water was gushing out. That is, water from the lake now situated . . . above our heads.

I swallowed hard and looked at Pasha, who was livid. We needed no further convincing. There was indeed a major facking problem, and it was about to get us all killed. Before we could stop him, the chief engineer proceeded to turn on the dam's turbines. Slowly, the rusty turbines began to rotate. The whole dam began to rattle and hum. The ground began to shake, and the noise level shot up dramatically. The Kurdish engineer was smiling at us, as if to say, "See the problem?"

Yes, we did. The damned dam was about to collapse. Since the noise level was far too high for us to communicate, there was no way for us to tell him to switch the whole thing off again except with random hand signs, which didn't seem to have any effect on our guide. Instead of turning the turbines off, he directed our attention to various parts of the machinery that were rattling but weren't supposed to. We nodded abundantly in an exaggerated effort to show the self-declared engineer that we had seen more of the problem than we needed to see. Again, we had little impact on him. The engineer appeared to enjoy watching the dam get more and more unstable.

I decided that the guy had gone suicidal on us and began, unilaterally, to walk back up the stairs. Pasha saw me leave and immediately followed suit. The mad engineer waved for us to come back down, and we responded by waving "bye, bye."

Our escape from the Derbandikhan Dam was not our most heroic hour, but then again, on our way back, a (real) engineer confirmed to us that the threat of complete collapse was very real indeed. A U.S. bomb had exploded on its edge during Operation Desert Storm, damaging its underlying structure.

It was all I needed to hear before ordering my first beer at The Edge once we got back to Erbil. It felt rather nice being in a Western-style bar, and furthermore, it was an opportunity to take the pulse of our humanitarian community in a less formal setting. The Edge was not the kind of place where people came for wine tastings. Beer and liquor flowed nonstop, and old pop tunes from the 1980s forced the crowd to make loud conversation. Yanna welcomed us warmly. She wore a deep décolleté for the occasion of our visit. Partly as a result, Pasha and I were riveted by what she had to say.

Yanna was one of an extremely diverse group of people who, for whatever reason, had come to work in Iraqi Kurdistan either with the UN or with NGOs. To see this smiling sunshiny thirty-year-old Finnish woman after ten days of meetings with men was incredibly refreshing. After my second beer, I started wondering "what a woman like her was doing in a place like this." I shared my question with my friend Habibi, who reminded me that Yanna was not Ingrid Bergman, that I was not Humphrey Bogart, and that this was not exactly Rick's Café. He took me by the arm, yanked me away (leaving Pasha to extol on his many merits), and introduced me to other colleagues. They were all eager to vent to me about the frustrations of working in the field while people at UN headquarters (i.e., my bosses) rolled their thumbs and messed up their initiatives with red tape. To apologize on behalf of UN headquarters I kept buying them rounds of drinks.

The more lubed up we all got, the more interesting the conversations became. Someone who had traveled with us from Baghdad told me that he and some colleagues were sitting in their hotel room chatting one night when suddenly they heard their conversation replayed from some kind of recording device located on the other side of the wall. An Iraqi intelligence agent must have pressed the wrong button and rewound his tape recorder.

The incident did not surprise me. I had seen enough evidence that, in the region under Saddam's control, we were under constant surveillance. But I was shocked to learn that no official complaint about the incident had been made to the Iraqi authorities. The staffers had told their boss about it, but all he did was shrug it off. It seemed to me we should have made a scandal of it. But I suppose the UN was so used to getting spied on by all sides that there was no desire, at the top of our bureaucracy, to challenge Baghdad (or Washington or London or Moscow or Paris or Beijing) about their nasty spying habits.

In Baghdad, rumor had it that some of our staff had been blackmailed into collaborating with the Iraqi authorities after being caught in a "Kodak moment" with Iraqi prostitutes. Others were accused of taking bribes or being intimidated into inappropriate collaboration with their Iraqi counterparts. There were many ways the Iraqi authorities could make life hell for our staff, and now that my colleagues were in Kurdistan, they were pouring their hearts out. They spoke of how they had been forced to hire local Iraqi staff who were cousins of power figures of the regime. These staff members did very little productive work other than to report back to the Iraqi security services on our activities. They could not be fired. Sometimes, they would even threaten their UN bosses directly. Was this scandalous? Yes. But this was not the time for me to throw a fit. I needed to listen and gain all the information I could.

Threats against UN personnel could not be taken lightly. Occasionally, there had been direct attacks against our staff. A couple sitting in a field had been shot at close range by two armed assailants, seemingly without reason. The man was killed and the woman rolled over, down a hillside, and played dead, miraculously sparing her own life. The UN didn't have the capacity to investigate whether this was a random crime, but clearly none of the victims were robbed. And we knew Saddam Hussein had operatives working in the region. Other "random attacks" included shooting sprees at some of our agency headquarters, extreme cases of food poisoning, and mysterious car accidents. So when our staff received a veiled threat from an Iraqi intelligence officer/local employee, they were well advised to take it seriously—especially since they had no recourse inside the UN, given the nonchalance of our successive humanitarian coordinators in Iraq, whose policy it was to just cave in to pressure from the Iraqi government on all questions concerning the security of their staff.

On some occasions we had to evacuate people the government explicitly designated as those whose "security could no longer be guaranteed." Given the government's ability to kill some of our staff without any consequences, one might consider such warnings generous on their part. My sense was that we should have alerted the press to any threats made against our staff and seized the UN Security Council with such matters every time they came up. But this went against all UN traditions. The people this organization sends to the field are clearly on their own. In a dictatorship such as Iraq, this meant they lived in fear just like the rest of the population. No wonder we weren't getting any written reports of fraud or corruption from our staff in the field.

Before speaking to my colleagues that night, I had not fully realized how much pressure they were under from the Iraqi authorities. I don't know if I would have been better than any of them at withstanding such pressure. But one thing was clear: in the Kurdish areas they felt freer to speak their mind— not quite free enough to do so sober, but with the addition of an uncountable number of shots the picture became clear. The information I was collecting was evidently worth the investment in my own (declining) sobriety. That said, by the time I had gotten an earful, the room was beginning to spin.

I glanced over at Pasha. He looked like he was boasting about something to Yanna. She must have poured him one too many drinks, because at some point, when traditional Greek music came on, he got up and started clapping his hands and tapping his right foot. Seeing the under secretary general clap, others in the room started clapping too, and Pasha got it into his head to put on a traditional Greek dance show. With the floor to himself, he launched into a dramatic range of movements that involved bouncing unexpectedly from one foot to the other, turning his head like a matador, and sliding around the floor on one knee.

For a moment I admired him in all his ridiculousness. I hoped I would be just as capable as he of taking myself unseriously if and when I became under secretary general. But then Pasha's momentum began to wane unmercifully. He tried to invite Yanna onto the dance floor with him, but the poor woman was laughing way too hard to make a move. So he grabbed someone else, an older woman whose erratic movements indicated she had had more than just water to drink. They danced wildly, making do with uncoordinated missteps until, ten minutes into the song, Pasha let his improvised partner go rather inconsiderately and sat back down, out of breath and drenched in sweat. He had put on a fantastic show, but if his intention had been to impress Yanna, it was the wrong approach. After catching his breath, he examined the knees of his suit, which he had ruined by sliding on a dirty floor, and decided it was time to go home. As he left, he muttered something about Yanna being a "facking tease."

Habibi and I decided to have another round of shots. Beyond that, my recollection is a blurry series of snapshots. The images involved me kissing Yanna somewhere outside the bar; Habibi and I jumping into a swimming pool with our clothes on to fish up someone's shoe; and a wild scene in the lobby of our hotel, where I had to climb over two heavily armed *peshmerga* guards, who were sleeping on the floor under the front desk, in order to reach for our room keys. The final image I have of that night is of a woman named Rubina making her own run for the front desk to get her key and falling down on the Kurdish guards. They were startled and almost shot us all; but seeing that we were foreigners, they soon went back to sleep. Before we reached our rooms, I saw Rubina writing her name and room number on Habibi's forehead with a Bic pen, so he would remember to "knock on her door in the morning."

All these images slowly came back to me the next day when I was walking along a narrow marked path in a village that had been riddled with mines during the Iran-Iraq war. I was wearing a helmet and a flak jacket, even though the temperature exceeded that of the hottest sauna I had ever set foot in. I can safely say it was the mother of all hangovers.

The minefield was located in a village that had been so thoroughly decimated it looked like nothing more than a heap of rubble with only a few random walls left standing. The former village of Mahmoud Quajar was located a few hundred yards from the border with Iran. It was being demined by a bunch of former British and Australian soldiers—people I regarded as true heroes for coming this far and risking their lives to save people they had never met before.

Demining appeared to be one of the most tedious and nerve-racking jobs on earth. Inch by inch, the deminers had worked through the small patch of land on which we were standing, as they pointed out other unexploded ordnance only a few feet away. I was really grateful for the close look the deminers offered us, but I wished I was standing just about anywhere else.

Mines come in all shapes and sizes. Some are designed to kill; some, merely to wound viciously. There are devices specially fabricated to castrate the victim, by springing up from the ground and exploding right below the waistline. This was why our flak jackets were specially outfitted with an uncomfortable metal-plated strap that I had tied around my crotch area.

While sweating bullets, we tried to concentrate on the explanations being fed to us regarding the actual demining process. We learned that on flat terrain certain specially adapted vehicles can be used to clear minefields, but that in mountainous terrain the best method involves the use of dogs. Once trained, demining dogs never step on a mine. Their sense of smell is more reliable than any detection machine. Our dogs would occasionally get killed, not by mines but by people. In one instance, unidentified armed men killed nine of our dogs. The attackers broke into the place where the UN kept the dogs at night, aimed at the cages, and gunned them down at point-blank range with AK-47s. These were puppy dogs in training, killed before they could be deployed to the field. Seeing photographs of them lying in a pool of blood inside their cages was hard for all of us. And few of us had any doubts about who might have ordered the attack. The Iraqi regime had warned us on several occasions that our deminers were operating against their will.

Did the UN make a fuss? Of course not. Just another inconclusive investigation, as if there could be any doubt, in anyone's mind, about who could order such an act. In a region where 10,000 people had been killed or maimed by mines in the past decade, our operation had great support among the local population.

When the attack occurred, I felt we would have a good chance of making the front page of tabloid newspapers if we shared the pictures, and would thereby dissuade Baghdad from conducting further such operations in the future. But I was not able to persuade the bureaucracy to do so and was not yet ready to operate as "my own man."

The expression had planted itself in my brain since my first briefing with Trevor (a.k.a. Spooky), and I was slowly beginning to understand the stakes involved in deciding whether I should follow my conscience or choose the easier, safer route of bureaucratic discipline and inertia. Deep inside I knew how this internal struggle would end. But I also knew that my time to rock the boat had not yet come. I had enough trouble trying to figure out how this gigantic operation stayed afloat despite all the dysfunctions I kept witnessing. I assumed I was missing a major piece of the puzzle—something that would explain why the UN never seemed to stand up for its own staff, its own mission, and its own principles. Perhaps the compromises we made allowed us to do more good than harm? After all, the demining operation was going ahead despite Baghdad's attempts to undermine it . . . more slowly than we'd like, but moving forward nonetheless.

But something in my gut made me want to either yell or throw up. Since neither action was particularly diplomatic, or even an effective form of expression, I kept telling myself, through this and other heart-wrenching moments, that my time to speak my mind would come.

Meanwhile, the Iraqi government did everything it could to sabotage our demining efforts in Kurdistan. It blocked the importation of much-needed equipment, like GPS devices and metal detectors, and refused to give us maps of the mines its army had littered throughout the countryside to prevent the return of Kurds to their ancestral homes. Unfortunately, our deminers received far too little support from our successive humanitarian coordinators. Denis Halliday, in particular, was not very supportive of the demining program. None of his successors, or Pasha himself, ever went to bat for this part of the operation. But insofar as I knew Denis to be an honest humanitarian, his attitude was particularly frustrating to me. I felt like it was worth challenging him on that front, and the occasion came soon after our (rather awkward) visit to the minefield.

On the car ride back from the village of Mahmoud Quajar, Denis spoke of scaling back the deminers' activities, saying that their work was "provoking" the Iraqi government.

"I think these guys are heroes," I shot back. I could ill afford to get in the face of an assistant secretary general, but I was hungover, dehydrated, and overcaffeinated, and his stupid remark got on my nerves.

"It's irresponsible for the UN to be conducting demining operations so close to the Iranian border," Denis continued.

I was shocked. And confused. And I forgot my place in the power pyramid.

"Maybe we should go back and *remine* the place?" I said, sort of to myself but loud enough to spark an uncomfortable silence.

Denis had no response to my comment, nor was it clear that I expected one. If I didn't have some admiration for the man, I would never have expressed myself so directly, in violation of basic protocol. But it felt good to speak my mind. And I knew that Denis was not the kind of person who would take vengeance on someone for merely disagreeing with him. So I just sat back and, for the first time since my arrival in Iraq, began to enjoy the tense silence my remarks had caused.

Too bad my first mission was nearing an end. A few more weeks, and the reports from the Iraqi drivers might have earned me an official expulsion from the country.

Saying what you mean—bluntly—to senior managers is not exactly a recipe for a successful UN career. But Denis Halliday was a rare type of UN bureaucrat, in that he actually enjoyed heated political debates. After recuperating from my rhetorical question on the mines, he engaged me on the wider issue of the sanctions, which he wanted the UN Security Council to lift altogether.

My own opinion of the sanctions had entered a state of flux. Not to say schizophrenia. There was indeed something absurd about punishing Iraqi civilians for the sins of their dictator. At the same time, that dictator had repeatedly demonstrated the need for his containment. His wars, at home and abroad, had killed and maimed millions. But the sanctions had been harmful too, especially to the weakest elements of Iraq's society. A silent war was being waged on the Iraqi people. The old, the sick, the widows, and the orphans were the hardest hit by the ongoing decrepitude of Iraq's civilian infrastructure. But what was the alternative? To lift all sanctions and let Saddam rebuild his army, reoccupy Kurdistan, and get back to the business of destroying villages and spreading mines?

Not an option. The United States and Britain would never agree to lifting the sanctions on Saddam, even if Denis Halliday set himself on fire in Times Square to protest their policy. Deepening the Oil-for-Food compromise was the only way forward. Any improvement in the Iraqi people's lives would have to come from us.

The challenge before us was to put our politics aside and draw up a realistic plan to expand our operation. The aim, as defined by our initial mandate, would be to provide more help to Iraq's civilians *without* strengthening Saddam's regime. The assumption that such a delicate mission was achievable was obviously naïve, as should have been evident to us by now. Had we consulted any businesspeople involved in international trade with dictatorial regimes on the viability of our mission, they might have died of strangulation induced by uncontrollable laughter. But our PhDs and our master's degrees in international affairs did not equip us, or the diplomats sitting on the UN Security Council, for the realities that awaited us and that would, inevitably, draw us closer than any of us expected to the underworld of international corruption that makes our world economy go around.

But ignorance was bliss, as it offered a common ground on which Pasha, Denis, and other UN leaders could agree. Our program needed to be expanded. How, exactly, and with what focus, would be the subject of heated internal turf wars in coming months. After seeing the demining operation in action, I hoped to lobby for its continued expansion. Insofar as I understood the nature of the relationship between Pasha and Denis, I was rather optimistic that the mere mention of Denis's reluctance about the operation would automatically get Pasha to strengthen his support for it.

Gee, was I beginning to figure out how to get things done inside the UN bureaucracy? I felt both optimistic and devious, righteous and manipulative. A truly strange combination of emotions. . . . I wondered if it had something to do with what they call the "gray zone" of politics.

Who was I becoming? The question lingered in my mind for as long as it could, despite my devout attempts to clear my head and concentrate on the landscape. If Kurdistan became stable enough to attract tourism one day, it would have just about every variety of climate to offer. The day before, we had been in a lush, green, mountainous area. Now we were in flat desert terrain, heading for some soft Tuscany-like hills that promised yet another variety of climate. I yearned for cooler air. Unfortunately, our convoy made an abrupt turn and headed for what looked like a very ugly fort.

We stopped for lunch at a former military prison, which the deminers were now using as a forward operating base. We were given sandwiches that had sand in them and, to drink, some Iraqi version of Tang. After spitting out the sand, using the Tang as mouthwash, we all sat there in silence for a bit, waiting to see if we were about to get sick or what, before resuming our voyage. The courtyard of the prison camp was a perfect place to hang oneself.

I fantasized about getting home. In forty-eight hours, I'd be back in New York. I could be sitting at Pastis, eating a delicious *steak au poivre* and enjoying a nice glass of Bordeaux in sexy company. . . .

Pasha interrupted my mouth-watering daydream.

"So, Kid, I've decided to leave you here in Iraq for a few months."

"What? Why?"

"Halliday needs help writing the report."

My face decomposed, and my throat grew tight.

"But . . . ah . . ."

"Ha! You should see your face!" Pasha slapped my cheek and laughed some more before turning serious again. "Give me a facking cigarette. Let's get the hell outta here."

That was *not* funny.

Part Two

CHAPTER **12**

The Baghdad Diet

"**How did you lose** all that weight?" a curious colleague asked upon my return from Iraq. We were having lunch at the best cafeteria in New York, on the ground floor of the UN Secretariat building, speaking in half-hushed voices for fear that a group of interns might catch us in the act of having a male-diet talk. My friend had tried the Zone diet and the "eat all you want but only once a day" diet, and had recently abandoned the Atkins™ diet, on which he had gained five pounds and acquired the gift of high blood pressure. He now exercised three times a week, never cooked with butter, forced broccoli down his throat at lunch, and had low-fat sugar-free frozen yogurt for dinner. Two weeks of that and he had lost only two miserable pounds.

"You should try the Baghdad diet," I said.

I had lost a good fifteen pounds in Iraq.

"Really? How does it work?"

I advised my colleague that he might achieve similar results if he used laxatives irresponsibly. The weight I had lost was due to my stomach's stubborn refusal to cooperate with the bacteria found in most foods available in Iraq. Oh, well. At least I had gained a clear firsthand understanding of how our UN sanctions affected that country's sanitary standards.

If one thing was abundantly clear from our first mission to Iraq, it was that the population needed more, better-quality food, and more effective and clean means to distribute it. The UN ration consisted of a bucket of flour, some rice, some cooking oil, some chickpeas, salt, tea, sugar, powdered milk, and soap. We called it the "food basket," as if it was a gift from Citarella. But in reality Iraqis had to queue for hours with old plastic containers to get their monthly grub. There were more than three thousand distribution centers around the country, and the government required people in line to show ID, because there were no second servings.

With that, we had the nerve to send our "UN observers" out to the villages to ask people how they felt about the menu. It would have been a death mission were it not for the Iraqi government minders who accompanied them on every trip.

Who in this world would want the UN to decide what they get to eat? Those who didn't throw stones at our white SUVs, or insult our observers, informed us that they wouldn't mind more variety in their diet. As for quality, they would plead with us for servings of chickpeas that didn't contain stones in them, soap that didn't create rashes, and oil that didn't taste like petrol.

The Iraqi government was in charge of contracting for these commodities, so the UN was not in a position to affect the quality of the food that was ordered. Saddam Hussein consistently spent as little as possible on food and as much as possible on industrial goods that might be diverted to his security apparatus. From a technical standpoint, all the food that was distributed to Iraq's civilians had been declared fit for human consumption by the Iraqi authorities. But according to the consumers, it was fit for dogs. Personally, I wouldn't wish to be the owner of a dog afflicted with the condition I developed in Iraq.

The unsafe drinking water, mixed with the powdered milk, provoked life-threatening diarrhea in young children. There was an urgent need to pump more money into the water sector. And the electricity sector. And the agricultural sector. And the transportation sector. The "food basket" often lacked key ingredients, because there were not enough trucks to transport the food or because the truckers weren't getting paid by the government—or, as we later learned, because the trucks had been repainted green and were pulling cannons for Iraq's army.

In the case of severely malnourished children, staple foods were not sufficient to bring them back to health. They needed special medical care and high-protein foods with vitamin supplements in order to survive. So we'd have to think of equipping hospitals with special child-nutrition units. But the challenges quickly compounded as we considered them in detail. For example, most hospitals did not even have reliable electricity and couldn't store certain foods and medicines, so even when we focused narrowly on saving malnourished kids, we were also forced to consider wider challenges, like how to repair Iraq's bombed-out electrical grid, its water supply, and so on.

Iraq didn't need an Oil-for-Food program. It needed an Oil-for-Everything-Except Weapons program. But of course, Iraq's needs were one thing. What mattered, in the final analysis, was what the UN Security Council would allow through. Our ability to get more goods into Iraq was linked to progress on the weapons front. The UN inspectors continued to make discoveries that were far from reassuring to Western powers. UNSCOM had recently reported that it had uncovered the existence of an active "offensive biological warfare programme." In addition, UNSCOM inspectors had found samples and traces of the chemical nerve agent VX and other advanced chemical weapons capabilities; they had also dismantled Iraq's indigenous production of long-range-missile engines. Following these discoveries, UNSCOM directed and supervised the destruction or dismantling of several facilities and large quantities of equipment used to produce chemical and biological weapons as well as proscribed long-range missiles.

If the U.S. Army had found only half as many WMD materials when it eventually invaded Iraq, the Bush administration might have preserved a modicum of credibility. Ironically, it turned out that UNSCOM had done a better job than most observers ever expected. Saddam probably also got rid of any and all WMD-related materials that remained unaccounted for before the war—which may explain why the man kept laughing every time his face appeared on television. But back in 1998, he wasn't laughing as much. His grip on power had been weakened, and his only chance of strengthening his regime again was to abuse our humanitarian program and keep the world guessing about his potential WMD capacity, should any of his neighbors or his own people be tempted to repay him for the harm he had caused them in the past. Of course, we will never know the inner workings of the dictator's mind, but back in 1998, as we considered how to improve our humanitarian operation, UNSCOM and Baghdad were averaging a new crisis every couple of months. So if we wanted the Security Council to allow more goods into Iraq, we would need to make a convincing pitch on behalf of the Iraqi people.

Job number one was to establish what the humanitarian needs of the Iraqi people were. This assumed we could come up with a clear definition of what constituted a "humanitarian need," as opposed to any other needs humans have as they struggle to make their way through life and provide for their offspring. Job number two was to assure the members of the Security Council that they could let us meet those needs without screwing up their sanctions against Saddam. This, of course, was a highly unrealistic proposition.

Thus began the process of designing a new UN humanitarian program for Iraq. The Security Council drafts its laws based on reports presented by the UN Secretariat. So it is rather critical that those reports be clear and factually correct, and that they propose options that might help the Security Council adopt "resolutions" that result in concrete, helpful action.

The laws passed by the Security Council are called "resolutions" perhaps in part to preempt the public from questioning that body's actual *resolve* in dealing with certain problems. Every year it adopts dozens of such "resolutions," and it may be said that the institution's members are about as good at following through on their resolutions as most people are at sticking to their own New Year's resolutions come February.

In order to consider resolutions, the Security Council must be "seized" with a particular matter. To seize the ambassadors' attention, the UN Secretariat submits reports about given situations with suggestions that might, if Security Council members can agree, be adopted into laws that are supposed to be binding on all states.

Now, how do such reports, which are also written by committee, come to life inside an organization riddled with internal turf wars, petty office politics, dramatic personal rivalries, and, in our case, a shameless competition for control over more money than the UN system had ever seen?

It was easy to see how the process might quickly degenerate. So I was somewhat relieved when I was informed that all sides of our UN operation had agreed to approach the drafting process in a "scientific" manner. Science implies orderly procedures, factual assumptions, and technical method.

The technical term for what we were doing was a "bottom-up review" of Iraq's humanitarian needs, and it was highly scientific indeed, as the episode concerning the proposed inclusion of canned cheese in the Iraqi people's diet illustrates.

The idea had come from Denis Halliday, who, quite justifiably, had concluded that the Iraqi people needed more animal protein. East Village nutritionists will argue that "you can find all the proteins you need in soy," but an Iraqi mother cooking for her family wouldn't know what to do with soy. And when dealing with stunted, underweight children, the best way to help them is actually to provide them with nutrients rich in animal protein and calcium. The problem, of course, was that the powdered milk we were providing was more dangerous than helpful when mixed with bad water. Other forms of animal protein are very expensive and need to be transported and stored in a cold chain, which Iraq did not have the electricity to maintain. Canned cheese, though an acquired taste, did not require refrigeration and provided a cheaper source of protein than meat or fish.

Halliday therefore made a proposal for a multimillion-dollar purchase of canned cheese. Fifteen minutes after we had submitted the proposal to Pasha for clearance, I heard a ruckus in his office. I ran over to check if he was all right.

"Facking Halliday!" said Pasha, holding up Halliday's fax in one hand and slapping it with the other.

"What's the problem?" I asked.

"Why da fack do they need all this canned cheese?" he thundered.

"Um . . . protein, sir?"

"Protein my ass! Who eats cheese out of a can? Show me *one* facking Iraqi who'll eat cheese out of a can!"

As we didn't have such a "facking Iraqi" on hand to give us his opinion on the matter, out went the canned cheese. It soon became evident that Pasha and Halliday had radically different views as to what constituted a "bottom-up review" of Iraq's humanitarian needs. In devising his proposals with nutrition experts in the field, Halliday had not foreseen that some of the ideas would be shot down in New York with comments like "protein my ass."

From the onset of the exercise, Pasha had been reticent about the whole "bottom-up" thing. "It's *my* ass on the line," he would insist. "Not Halliday's! So I'll tell you where he can shove his bottom-up review . . ."

Say no more, Pasha . . . say no . . .

"Up his bottom!"

After the canned cheese episode, Pasha took to calling Halliday's report the "Up-the-Bottom" review rather than the bottom-up review. The new name of the report became such common usage that I worried Pasha might mistakenly use the wrong term when addressing the Security Council.

We had serious concerns about how our proposals would be received by the Security Council, and in particular by the United States. In advocating for a massive expansion of the humanitarian program, we were threatening America's containment policy.

The United States was not against the importation of more food per se. But Washington was reticent to allow for the rehabilitation of Iraq's heavy industry, for it saw every nut and bolt as a potential component in the fabrication of weapons of mass destruction. Fertilizers for agriculture could be used to make explosives. Centrifuges for Iraq's pharmaceutical plants could be used to produce deadly biological toxins, chlorine gas for water purification could also be (and had been) used to spray chemical weapons at Kurdish villages.

A long list of products were thus branded as "dual-use items." The dilemma, when it came to such products as chlorine gas, was that unsafe water had killed far more Iraqis since the Gulf War than Saddam Hussein's proscribed chemical weapons. In the balancing act between containing Saddam and saving Iraq's civilians, we, at the UN Secretariat, chose the civilians.

As we toiled to find the right formula to persuade the UN Security Council to expand the Oil-for-Food program, the infighting grew. The canned cheese battle was merely the first of many. Everyone, it seemed, had their own ideas as to what the Iraqi people should eat, how much money should go into water purification, transportation, agriculture, and so on. UNICEF, the children's health agency, sought funding for breastfeeding campaigns; FAO, the agricultural agency, was fighting for animal vaccinations (some strange malady called "foot-and-mouth disease" had spread through Iraq's ruminant herds); and UNESCO, the cultural branch, was whipping up a storm about education (the children needed school desks, schoolbooks, etc.).

An avalanche of projects landed on our desks. Our photocopier went on strike and our fax machine was making pleading noises. I arranged the projects into paper skyscrapers in the conference room and told Pasha it was time for him to assemble his crisis team, composed of Spooky; a guy whose nickname was Dracula (for reasons that shall become clear); a woman called Cindy (Pasha's special assistant, who didn't yet have a bizarre nickname); and me, The Kid.

"So, what do we do with all this shit?" wondered Pasha, looking at all the unstable paper piles on the table.

It was a good question. We couldn't just dump $50 billion worth of projects on the Security Council's doorstep and say, "Here, you deal with it."

"We'll probably need to set priorities," said Spooky.

"Who are *we* to set priorities?" asked Dracula.

"We can ask the field mission to do it—again," said Spooky. We had asked Halliday to prioritize the projects to begin with, but he chose to drown us instead.

"We'll need to set a ceiling," I said.

"What ceiling?" said Pasha.

"Well, if we want to prioritize projects, we need to know how much money Iraq can spend. Meaning how much oil they can pump."

"That's no longer a bottom-up approach," said Dracula.

"Fuck the bottom-up approach!" said Pasha. "The Kid is right. If the Iraqis can only pump $5 billion, it's no use coming up with projects for $10 billion!"

Dracula had to agree.

Pasha turned to his special assistant. "Bring in the oil overseers!" he said, and then headed back to his office. A few minutes later, in came the strange individuals known as "the oil overseers." A tall, gawky Russian and a high-strung little Frenchman appeared at the door and were invited to sit on Pasha's couch.

"How much oil money can Iraq generate every six months?" asked Pasha.

"Zat is impossible to predict," said the Frenchman. "It depends on ze price of ze euil!"

"I know that the price, it flucturates," said Pasha, doing a wave with his hand.

"Fluc-tu-*ates*," the Frenchman corrected.

"What?"

"Ze price. . . . It fluc-tu-*ates*," insisted the Frenchman.

"You think I'm a facking idiot?" growled Pasha.

"Euh . . . neuh, of curse nut."

"I'm getting fed up with you guys, OK? You sit there all day long facking picking your nose while we're working our ass off here, so don't get me started!"

Pasha was right. The oil overseers, whom we took to calling the Double-O's, in part because they were secretive as spies and in part because they had twice times nothing to do all day long, were tasked with a job that required about half a day of real work per month. But it was an important half-day, so important that the Security Council would fight for months on end each time a new overseer had to be appointed. Their job was to check that the price of Iraqi oil matched market prices, in order to prevent Saddam from receiving kickbacks from oil traders. In this task, the Double-O's would ultimately fail by a margin of billions of dollars. But at this stage, we merely had to get a number out of them: how much money could Iraq generate from its oil sales? And just doing that wasn't easy, because they would have to decide whether to include in their projection the oil Iraq was smuggling out of the country illegally—a political hot potato, which the oil overseers were not willing to touch. As all oil professionals understood from the very beginning of this operation, we were dealing with two sets of numbers when it came to oil transactions: official numbers and real numbers (most deals with oil-producing dictatorships leave room for bribes and kickbacks). Having quickly figured out that neither Pasha nor I was aware of this practice, they found it awkwardly hard to explain the challenge they faced in coming up with a projection of how much oil revenue Iraq might generate during any given six-month phase of the program.

"So just give me a facking projection!" said Pasha. "How much money do you think they can make in six months?"

"Mmmaybeee around four . . . four or five billiuns, some sing like zat," said the Frenchman, sounding extremely unsure of himself.

Pasha turned to the Russian.

"And you . . . why you never talk? Do you agree?"

"It dipiends vuot about dzia price, but I siyenk my kholieg is corriect."

To which the Frenchman added, "But pleeze dun't queute us. We cannut be ze source for zis number."

Pasha nodded and did that thing with his bushy eyebrows that meant the Double-O's could leave his office now before he got any angrier. If we couldn't quote our own UN oil overseers, who could we quote? The fact is, these guys did not really see Pasha as their boss. Their posts were so political that they felt loyalty only to their home countries.

"Can you believe these guys?" said Pasha.

Well, at least we had some kind of estimate, a number to work with: $4 billion to $5 billion per six months. So we decided to aim for the midpoint between the two numbers and settled on a budget of about $4.5 billion every six months. Cutting right through the middle seemed like a safe bet. The British colonial authorities employed the same logic when they designed the borders of the region, often cutting lines right through the midpoint between capitals, which is how maps of the Middle East contain so many straight (and continuously contested) lines. In a sense, not much had changed since colonial times. Today we, a group of UN bureaucrats, had become the czars of Iraq's economy; and based on the vague advice of the Double-O's, Iraq's budget would be $4.5 billion per semester, or $9 billion a year.

After further negotiations with Halliday, who raged that we had sabotaged his "bottom-up approach" and stabbed the Iraqi people in the back, we ended up raising the budget to $5.2 billion every six months, or $10.4 billion per year. The UN's own annual budget was around $2.2 billion. Syria's annual budget revenues were less than $7 billion. We were essentially lifting all civilian sanctions on Iraq.

"This is never going to fly," said Dracula. "The Americans will never agree to it."

We looked at one another in silence. It was around Christmastime. We were sitting around in the conference room, exhausted by a month of constant disputes, waiting for a pizza to be delivered to the office. It was around 10:30 at night and pissing rain outside.

Pasha returned from the restrooms with the pizza. He had intercepted the delivery man en route and slapped him on the neck by surprise, causing him to drop the pizzas in the corridor, so the opened box looked a bit chaotic, with some slices overturned and others missing the cheese, which had slid off and stuck to the carton lid.

"Here . . . eat!" said Pasha, as if speaking to famished sled dogs. Not that we felt very different. Pasha had driven us hard through the past two months, keeping us in the office late and throwing fits every time "facking Halliday" sent in a new project.

As we munched, Pasha looked at each of us quizzically; at some point he popped the question. "So that's it? $5.2 billion?"

Everybody nodded except Dracula.

"What?" said Pasha.

"It's never going to fly," said Dracula, as he had all week.

"So you have a better number for me?" asked Pasha.

"No," said Dracula. "I think it's the right number, but it might not pass the Council."

"Unless anybody has a better idea, that's it. That's the magic number," said Pasha.

"*Inshallah*," said Dracula.

"Spooky?" asked Pasha.

"It's a tough one. Her Majesty's Government might buy it, but the Americans, I don't know . . ."

"Kid?"

"Maybe we can . . ."

"Shadap!"

All right, I could bear being the object of comic relief, but the fact was, I was an integral part of a small team that had very limited competence on the matter to begin with, so after a round of laughter, Pasha nodded at me again to share my thought.

"Maybe we could sound out the Americans?" I said. "I mean, we'd have to share the same info with all the big five, but if the U.S. doesn't challenge us, who else will?"

"They're called the P5, Michael, not the big five," Spooky whispered in my ear as Pasha considered the option of sharing the magic number with the five permanent, veto-wielding members of the Security Council. The practice is often used, mainly to shield the Secretariat from the embarrassment of making proposals that are immediately trashed by a veto. But Pasha was shaking his head.

"No," he said, firmly. "Nobody speaks to anybody outside this room."

"But they've already called and asked," said Spooky.

"Nobody talks," said Pasha, looking each of us in the eye, one after the other, the way Tony Soprano does when he needs everyone in his gang to be on the same page. Pasha then threw his napkin back on the table and stood up.

"Nobody talks," he repeated as he walked out. "Let me handle this."

Pasha liked to play his cards close to his chest. He knew that if he announced the magic number in advance, the United States would raise hell. It would be far easier for the United States to challenge us face-to-face than in front of the entire Security Council. So I concluded that Pasha was smart to reject my proposal. His plan was to drop a bombshell on the Security Council and let the states fight it out amongst themselves. The French and the Russians and the Chinese would welcome our proposals, for sure. And the United States and Britain would find themselves on the defensive, having to come up with arguments for why Iraq should not benefit from this or that humanitarian project. They would inevitably look heartless, something any government prefers to do in private rather than in public.

"The Americans have other ways of finding out," said Spooky, eyeing the wall.

"Sure," said Pasha, "but as long as they don't hear it from us directly, they can't discuss it with us, can they?"

Logical. The United States was not supposed to be listening in on UN staff.

But sure enough, the next day, the U.S. deputy ambassador and an aide came storming into our office all red in the face, demanding to be told the magic number. Pasha played dumb, saying he couldn't tell them since he didn't yet know it himself.

The U.S. diplomats walked out even more furious than when they walked in. They went to the secretary general's office, only to get the runaround again. So they sent less important officials to try to get us to speak to them one-on-one. But we had our marching orders. Officially, they were told that we were still identifying which projects to include in our proposals, and in a very real sense we were. We just knew what number these proposals were supposed to add up to.

Hours before submitting the report to the printer, I got it into my head to run a check on the numbers to see if they added up to the total figure we were about to recommend. It turned out they did not. I barged into Pasha's office in a state of absolute panic. Either we were missing a project or we had taken one out without changing the total. Pasha went absolutely bonkers. There was obviously a limit to how much incompetence the UN could get away with, and having Kofi Annan appear in front of the Security Council with a report that didn't add up just about crossed that line.

With the clock ticking furiously loud, I sat down at my desk to try to resolve the problem. Unfortunately, I was a Microsoft Excel virgin. Besides, numbers have never been my forte. I could hardly trust myself with figuring out the tip on a bar check, and here I was trying to fix the annual budget for an entire country. Having Pasha, Cindy, Dracula, and Spooky breathing down my neck while I tried to manipulate the spreadsheet didn't make my work any easier. But I was the only young person around, and everybody always assumes young people are better with computers. I finally got the UN treasurer on the phone and conferenced in our office in Baghdad to cross-check some of the information. An hour before our deadline, I thought all was lost. I had identified the problem, but I couldn't get the spreadsheet to do what I wanted it to do—and the little Microsoft "paper-clip guy" in the corner of my screen kept distracting me with viciously useless and doubt-provoking questions. I made a mental note to track down the programmer who had conceived that spineless little paper-clip motherfucker and assassinate him.

I finally called a friend of mine who worked at a bank. Letting a private-sector friend in on numbers that some firms would pay lots of money to get their paws on was a risk I took only as a last resort. After he finished laughing at how clueless I was in operating a rather basic spreadsheet, he guided me through to completion in a New York minute.

The spreadsheet was the most important page in the report. It outlined how the money would be distributed among the different Iraqi ministries, which operated in the south and center of Iraq, and among the nine UN agencies that were in charge of buying goods for the Kurdish regions in the north. The rest of the report contained lengthy descriptions of the state of each of Iraq's economic sectors, the needs identified by our observers, and the kinds of projects that needed to take priority if Iraq was to regain the semblance of a functioning economy. There was much more information than the ambassadors sitting on the Security Council cared to read, and even their assistants would complain to us that we had swamped them with too much text. This, of course, was the crux of Pasha's old-school reporting strategy. By muddying the big picture with an abundance of tiresome and awkwardly committee-drafted technical details, we had significantly reduced the chances of being challenged on the substance or the "science" that helped us finally divide the pie. Most missions would have had to hire troops of specialized PhD holders to sift through all of our statements adequately and prepare focused talking points for debate. Nobody had time for that. As for the numerous promises we made about how we would strengthen our capacity to capably oversee the enormous increase in transactions and shipments, all the United States and Britain could really do was take us at our word. One thing would be certain: there would be no unemployment within the UN system as long as this operation ran. And since all new posts would be paid for by Iraqi money, none of the ambassadors felt the need to question our operational costs or how efficiently our new resources would be used.

When the report finally went to press, and the magic figure was divulged, U.S. diplomats did little, privately, to hide their anger at what they saw as an act of UN defiance. But what would their response be? How would they vote in the Security Council? The U.S. government now needed to develop an actual policy on how to respond. In the couple of days leading up to the crucial meeting at which Kofi Annan would present the report to the Security Council, the United States scrambled to come up with one. Now it was our turn to invite them out to lunch to try to find out what their government's reaction would be—and their turn to play their cards close to their chest.

The meeting was closed to the media and held in the informal chamber of the Security Council. The Iraqis were sitting outside, smoking cigarettes. The media was out in full force, including a special breed of reporters who cover the oil markets. Every member state of the UN wanted to know what would happen, because it meant potential business openings with the oil giant, so the crowd outside the Security Council was filled with smiling information mercenaries.

On the way in, I passed my former boss, CNN's Richard Roth. We joked about my crossing over to the "other side." He asked if I thought our proposals would "fly." I said I hoped they would but that it all depended on the United States at that point. "Doesn't it always?" came a quip from the aide to the U.S. ambassador, who enjoyed creeping up on people when they spoke about his country. Poker smiles all around, we entered the little room where Security Council ambassadors hash out deals before going public.

There was a lot of tension in the air. To my knowledge, the Security Council had never before been involved in decisions that would have such direct commercial repercussions, so the types of pressures its members were under from their domestic constituencies were of a completely different nature from usual. Australian wheat farmers, French pharmaceutical companies, Russian energy giants—all of these powerful lobbying groups had been talking to their governments.

Ambassadors took turns welcoming the secretary general's report. Many of them called it "comprehensive," by which they meant it was too long and convoluted. As often happens in such meetings, the ambassador from the most insignificant country in relation to the issue at hand will launch into long tirades about the moral authority of the United Nations, then trail so far off the subject that others at the table will start taking cellphone calls and exchanging jokes on little pieces of folded paper. In this case, the culprit was assaulted with coughs and nervous tics. Everybody was eager to hear what the United States had to say. There were billions at stake.

Finally, U.S. Ambassador Bill Richardson took the floor. Somewhat angrily, he "welcomed" the "comprehensive" report of the secretary general and said his government looked forward to studying it in more detail. They would have many questions for us. Like how we planned to guarantee that all these new goods actually got to the people instead of the regime. How we would strengthen all the financial controls to deal with the increased cash flow. All perfectly good questions, for which we had only the vaguest answers, leaving them with nothing to sink their teeth into.

After weeks of backroom negotiations, the Security Council reached a verdict. Our recommendations were adopted unanimously, on February 20, 1998, in Resolution 1153.

Champagne!

We had successfully steered the largest humanitarian operation in UN history out of port. We had made our case on the force of argument and pushed it through to adoption by making wild promises to the Security Council. Forget that Saddam Hussein had remained defiant in the face of allied bombings. We, the bureaucrats of the United Nations, promised we'd keep an eye on him, even as he was now free to sign contracts for dozens of billions of dollars a year.

Stepping away from the bustle of the cocktail party that night, I stood facing Gotham's skyline. We would now be in command of a formidable machine. Our program paid for the work of the UN arms inspectors and had signed contracts with nine UN agencies, each in charge of monitoring one of Iraq's economic sectors. We had hired Saybolt S.A., a Dutch company, to monitor Iraq's oil sales, and Lloyd's Register of London to check the humanitarian imports at the border. Soon, we'd give that monitoring contract to a new company, Cotecna, based in Switzerland. The fact that Kofi Annan's son Kojo worked at the company that stood to make millions overseeing the imports of goods into Iraq did not seem to faze those who knew about it. Pasha had not deemed it necessary to mention this potentially grave conflict of interest to us, so we'd have to learn about it through the newspapers some time later. Oh, we'd learn a lot of things about our own operation from news reports as time went by. But right now, the media were presenting our expansion as a successful diplomatic solution to a difficult political situation. The positive media coverage had us walking on air as we prepared to supersize our office, both in New York and in Iraq.

We had some 400 internationals on staff in Iraq and thousands of local employees. Those numbers would grow, as would our office space in New York. We would gobble up entire new floors and monitor billions of dollars in cash flowing through the Banque Nationale de Paris to thousands of companies across the world. There was something strangely exhilarating about it all.

Spooky stepped out onto the balcony.

"To making history!" he said, raising his glass to me in cheers. I took a big sip of the warm Champagne and paused for a moment as I tried to formulate the question that had formed in my mind over the past few weeks.

"Trevor, tell me something . . . and be honest," I said as we looked out over New York's bright lights.

"Honest? I don't know. If it's about your tie—"

"No, seriously."

"Yes, Michael?"

"We're in way, way over our heads, aren't we?"

He replied without looking at me. "Oh, yes. Most definitely."

CHAPTER **13**

A Can of Worms

VOLCKER COMMITTEE INTERROGATION ROOM,
MIDTOWN MANHATTAN, NOVEMBER 19, 2004

"**Do you remember** this e-mail exchange?" asked the investigator as he handed me a printout of an e-mail I had written years ago.

Seven years after we had launched the largest humanitarian enterprise in UN history, I was sitting in a cold conference room high up in a New York City skyscraper being interrogated by members of the Volcker Committee, named after Paul Volcker, the former chairman of the U.S. Federal Reserve, whom the Security Council had appointed to investigate what amounted to a mammoth train wreck. Billions of dollars entrusted to the Oil-for-Food program had vanished, from right under our nose, and suddenly the world had decided to hold us accountable. As one character said to George Clooney in the movie *Syriana*, in politics, you're "innocent until investigated." That movie was based in part on the experience of Robert Baer, a CIA case officer who ended up under investigation in Washington after he helped Jalal Talabani of northern Iraq foment a coup attempt against Saddam Hussein.

So there I was, feeling less than innocent and wondering what e-mail exchange my interrogator was referring to. As part of its investigation, the Volcker Committee had conducted computer forensics, extracting all of our e-mail communications from the UN database. They were in the process of examining those e-mails meticulously when they suddenly gave me a call. I had already testified with them once. Why were they calling me back?

I felt like a suspect in an old Columbo episode. *Just one last question. . . .*

Given the choice, many of us (especially those with a social life) would rather have submitted to a colonoscopy than have strangers peer through our most intimate, silly, ranting e-mails. Especially with *my* group of friends, who never hesitated to recount a night of debauchery in every detail the next day or to send around pornographic attachments just for the hell of it.

The investigator—a sharp-looking woman with strict hair and an impeccable business suit—was flanked by two silent aides, who took notes with electronic pens directly on the screens of their laptops whenever I opened my mouth. It was quite unnerving. The woman had an air of competence about her. She was looking at a printout, which she had whipped out of her file just as I thought the interview was about to end. She took her time to review its contents as I sat at the edge of my seat.

"In all fairness, I should probably let you read this first." She slid the sheet of paper across the table.

In all fairness? Why is she saying "in all fairness"? That's something you say to a GUILTY PERSON!

I grabbed the e-mail and started reading through it. As I did, my mind went back to that morning, that horribly embarrassing morning. . . .

I knew it would be a bad day as soon as I woke up. My neck was painfully contorted. I swallowed two Excedrin and looked at myself in the mirror. My tongue was white, dry as sandpaper. I was shaving when I noticed it: a huge hickey on my neck.

The New York dating scene had its dangers. The woman who had found it necessary to leave this gory-looking suction mark on my neck the night before had seemed like a perfectly reasonable person at the beginning of the evening. She *had* mentioned something about her medication not reacting so well with alcohol, but I hadn't really paid attention because her foot had already begun to play games under the table. When I heard the word "medication" I inquired if she was sick, and she replied, "No, it's for my brain. I have a chemical imbalance in my brain."

This was before the Sambuca shots she ordered after our second bottle of Pinot Grigio. She then went to the bathroom and came back with what seemed like a completely new personality. Her eyes were wide open, her fingers often rubbed up against her nose, and her speech had accelerated to the point where I found it hard to grasp when she was switching topics. When we walked out, she had a brilliant idea.

"Let's go sing karaoke! Come on, just for one song!"

When we finally walked out of our private singing booth, it was 4:30 a.m. and I had fingernail scratch marks on my back. It was there, on the street, that she pulled away from a kiss, gave me a strange look, and suddenly bit into my neck. The blue mark I noticed the next morning was only slightly smaller than a hockey puck.

My secretary was the first to notice it. I noticed her noticing it, and she noticed me noticing her noticing it. So she controlled her smile. But as soon as she left my office, the word started spreading.

"Mickey has a hickey!" And it rhymed.

I did not think it was funny. I was hungover and paranoid and nauseous. I settled in at my desk and tried to draft a press release, a rather difficult task for the one neuron I had left in my brain. One by one, my office mates found reasons to come into my office to check out my stupid hickey. It was a zero-credibility day.

Then the call came from Pasha's office, which I let slide directly to voice-mail. Fortunately, he left a clear message.

"Where the fack are you? Come to my office, *right now!*"

Uh-oh . . .

I immediately called back and got his secretary.

"Hey, I just got a call from—"

"Yes, Michael, he's expecting you."

"He didn't sound in a good mood," I probed.

"You can say *that* again," said Pasha's secretary.

Shit. I hung up, picked up a notebook, and ran down the stairs of my building. *Shit, shit, shit.* I crossed First Avenue in the rain, passed the security checkpoint of the UN Secretariat building, and ran toward the elevator yelling, "Hold it!" but failing to inspire anybody inside to press a button, much less stick out a hand between the sliding doors.

The checkered black-and-white floor of the UN lobby is quite slippery when wet, and I was forced to hold on to a stranger's shoulder in order to avoid losing my balance at the end of my run.

"Sorry," I said, not knowing quite what to add, as the stranger readjusted his shoulder pad, which now had a wet handprint on it. He didn't reply. Just glanced at me condescendingly, then looked away. Then he did a double take to reexamine my neck. I must have pressed the elevator call button twenty times before we finally got a *ding!*

On my way up to Pasha's fifteenth-floor office, I tried to organize my defense. Clearly, I had done something to anger him. The question was: what?

It could have been lots of things. We had recently been informed that the Danish guard the Iraqis wanted to throw in jail had escaped. He had done so exactly as we had planned. His Danish colleagues from Iraqi Kurdistan had driven down to Baghdad under the pretext that they were about to go on vacation, and in the middle of the night they had rolled him up in a carpet and loaded him into their trunk. After hiding their rolled-up pal in a hole they had carved out under the back seat of their SUV, they drove north, got past the military checkpoints without getting searched, and dropped their friend off in Turkey before anybody noticed he was gone.

Did Pasha find out I had been in on this plan? Who could possibly have told him? No, it had to be something else. . . .

Then it hit me. A few days ago, a Swiss magistrate had written to us revealing that a company doing business under the Oil-for-Food program was in fact a front (a legal entity set up for the sole purpose of doing a particular transaction while shielding the people behind the deal). Whoever sets up a front company wants to make sure the public will never be aware of their business. In his fax, the Swiss magistrate had asked us if it was legal, under the UN guidelines, to disguise the origins of the companies exporting goods to Iraq using ghost fronts.

It was a simple question, but somehow nobody could give me a straight answer, and the UN's Office of Legal Affairs (OLA) did not respond to my requests for advice. How was I to write a reply for Pasha to send to the Swiss magistrate? I decided to dive into the complex regulations governing the Oil-for-Food operation in search of an answer. Not surprisingly, I found it was absolutely illegal for a company to use fronts to export goods to Iraq, especially if these shell structures were not based in the country where the company operated. With that, I drafted a reply and sent it to OLA for clearance before I would submit it to Pasha for signature.

"Don't open that can of worms!" came the e-mail reply from one colleague.

Vladimir Golytsin, the Russian lawyer assigned to Oil-for-Food issues, agreed. He argued that the best course of action was not to reply at all. According to him, the Swiss magistrate had no business addressing such a query to the UN. Golytsin even suggested that the Swiss magistrate had political motives for his query.

Political motives? I thought the Swiss were the neutral guys. It sounded like I needed to consult Spooky.

"This is very serious stuff, Michael," said Spooky. "This should be handled at the highest level! The secretary general should be informed immediately!"

"Why, what's the big deal?" I asked. "This Swiss guy is asking us what our rules say, and I'm telling him what the rules say. Why does this have to get complicated?" I was getting increasingly confused.

"Because this is the first time we've been officially notified of this phenomenon," said Spooky.

"What phenomenon?" I asked.

"The Iraqis are using front companies in order to get kickbacks," said Spooky.

"How does that work?"

"Well, it's pretty simple," said Spooky. "The Iraqi Health Ministry will sign a contract with Company A to import medicines."

"Right. . . ."

"But Company A is not a pharmaceutical company."

"Then what is it?"

"Company A is, say, a Jordanian friend of the Iraqi health minister."

"OK. . . ."

"So Company A buys medicines from Company B, a real pharmaceutical company, then sells the goods to Iraq at inflated prices, yields a profit, and splits the money with the Iraqi minister."

"Holy shit!"

"Yes. I knew this was going on," said Spooky, "but now we have something tangible to work with. An official letter from the Swiss authorities."

"OK," I said, "but here's the problem. Legal Affairs won't sign off on my draft, and Pasha won't sign the letter unless Legal signs off on it. So we're stuck!"

Spooky nodded his head in quiet frustration. He had obviously been aware of this problem for quite some time, and I felt mounting resentment that he had not let me in on this issue. Why did I have to stumble on it like that? I thought he and I had a deal to keep each other in the loop!

Trevor knew as well as I did that our fundamental mandate required us to report any diversions of cash from the humanitarian program. Trevor was not one to dissuade me from that. He had briefed me on this aspect of our mission from the very beginning and had put his career at risk several times in the past by pushing for exactly this kind of reporting. Only he had been ignored. And his scheduled promotion had been delayed more than once. Trevor had to pick his battles, and from the look on his face, this had not come at an opportune time.

He looked at me apologetically. I nodded my acceptance. But what were we to do now? Trevor's eyes converged on a fixed point above my head; he took a deep breath and made a decision.

"I'll call Pasha right now," said Trevor, picking up his phone.

I breathed a sigh of relief.

A few seconds later, Trevor had Pasha on the line. "Yes . . . it's . . . ha, ha, ha . . . yes, sir! . . . yes . . . I'm sorry? . . . aha . . . well, sir, it's about the issue with the Swiss magistrate . . . right . . . but it's rather important, because you see . . . yes . . . but, sir . . . yes . . . yes . . . right . . . bye-bye now."

Spooky, as Pasha had no doubt called him, hung up with a desperate look on his face.

"He never listens to me anymore," he said.

Had Trevor been "defanged," as Pasha had promised the Iraqi foreign minister he might be? The thought crossed my mind, but I had no time to deconstruct Pasha's pattern of behavior toward his chief analyst.

It was beginning to look like the Swiss magistrate was not going to get a reply. If Pasha didn't take Spooky's advice on this one, it meant he was in no mood to make a fuss. We would hide behind procedure, which allowed us not to answer questions unless they came directly from a government, through official channels. In other words, the Swiss magistrate would be asked to direct his question toward his own government, which, at the time, was not a member of the UN (Switzerland joined the UN in 2002).

In essence, we would be telling the Swiss magistrate to "get lost" in polite UN-speak. And it would be my job to do so.

I went back to my office and shot an angry e-mail off to the lawyers at OLA, pointing out that many days had now gone by and we needed a clear answer from them.

"IS THE USE OF FRONT COMPANIES LEGAL OR ILLEGAL?" I asked, in all caps. The Russian lawyer I was speaking to had about seven grades of seniority over me and didn't appreciate being addressed in caps. So he simply didn't reply.

I didn't expect I would be reading a printout of this e-mail exchange while under questioning years later. But I would never regret putting my question to the UN's lawyer in caps. It was a simple yet fundamental question that had a yes or no answer. If my superiors could not get themselves to answer it, I thought, I might as well do this myself. I decided simply to pick up the phone and call the Swiss magistrate directly. I dialed and reached some kind of legal aide, to whom I explained the answer to the magistrate's question. The use of front companies was illegal, but I couldn't get my boss to put it on paper. Why not? Because, um, we had protocol issues, and they would probably get a letter explaining that. But in any case, the answer was already on paper, so to speak, since it was written into the UN resolution documents that made up our mandate, and these documents were public—even available on the web.

"Oh, and don't quote me," I added.

My interlocutor was somewhat puzzled that a UN official would worry about getting on record to confirm the UN's own publicly available laws. But he was nice enough not to insist.

I had answered the query in Pasha's place, sidetracked the UN Office of Legal Affairs, and communicated with an "outside entity" about a subject that Spooky himself thought should be handled at "the highest level." I had broken the chain of command.

I did this for two very contradictory reasons. The first was related to my conscience; the second, to my sense of loyalty. On the one hand, I would have hated myself if a Swiss court case concluded that the UN was uncooperative in answering a simple, straightforward question. On the other hand, I sensed that Pasha would be perfectly glad to avoid expressing himself on this issue, so as to maintain plausible deniability.

But offering a superior the option of deniability also means taking the fall if things go wrong. As I racked my brain trying to figure out why an angry Pasha had suddenly called me to his office that morning, the Swiss episode ranked number one on my list of possibilities. The nightmare scenario quickly took shape in my mind. Surely, the Swiss magistrate must have initiated some kind of probe, and now it was all coming back to bite me in the ass before the UN even had time to send an official reply. The UN Security Council would take up the matter, the United States would go bonkers, and the whole program would grind to a halt—all because of me!

When I reached Pasha's office, I bit my lip before knocking on his door. "Yes!"

I opened the door and stayed at the entrance instead of walking in. Pasha was shaking his head. *Uh-oh, here it comes. . . .*

"You're dressed like a clown!" said Pasha.

He had a point. I had chosen my shirt based not on how well it matched my suit but on how high the collar was—hoping it would help conceal my hickey. It was yellow, and the left tip of the collar kept flapping upward because it lacked that little piece of plastic that would have kept it straight. I wore it with a blue tie, which would have been fine with a blue suit. But my blue suit was at the dry cleaners, and as I had been running late after my night of debauchery with the chemically imbalanced vampire girl, I had thrown on a thick gray suit I purchased back when I was fifteen pounds fatter.

Pasha's taste in clothes was really impeccable, and it visibly pained him to see me looking like a clown. He got up, walked toward me, and snapped my collar back down before proceeding to adjust my tie.

"Let's go! And get yourself a new suit. I can't take you to the thirty-eighth floor looking like this!"

"The . . . the thirty-eighth floor?"

We were going to Kofi Annan's office. *Oh, God.* . . . I walked with my head tilted slightly to the left, in an attempt to hide the mark on my neck. But in the elevator ride up, Pasha noticed it.

"What the fack is this?" he asked, pressing his finger into my neck.

"Aw! . . . I don't know," I answered.

"Who did you fack?"

"Well, I . . . erm . . . you don't know her."

"Tsk . . . tsk . . . tsk . . ." Pasha shook his head, then added, "You should have put some powder on it!"

I nodded, feeling truly idiotic.

It was my first time setting foot on the thirty-eighth floor. An eerie silence prevailed there. People moved stiffly and spoke in hushed tones. Well, except for Pasha, who slapped people on the shoulder and called them "fackers."

How many UN secretary generals had Pasha worked for? He had joined the organization before I was born, in 1965. He was part of the building, and even Kofi Annan's aides appeared a little scared of him.

The top floor of the UN building is a rather impractical location for the secretary general's office. If the UN were a ship (which is how it looks from the angle that journalists often pick as background to their stand-ups), the secretary general's office would be all the way up in the mast. The building is so flat that the wind actually causes it to bend, as evidenced by the subtle creaking sounds that permeate the structure on stormy days.

The security guard saluted Pasha with extra stiffness. As UN security co-ordinator, my boss was also this man's boss. We proceeded to take a left, walking down the corridor to Kofi Annan's office. We arrived before the desk of Elisabeth Lindenmayer, Annan's executive assistant (and his former French teacher), who lit up on command as we approached. I assumed she always did this with visitors coming to see her boss, but I didn't expect that she would start grilling me with questions as we waited for Annan to be disposed. She seemed like a very charming and intelligent lady, but I was a bit confused by her line of questioning. I felt like she was profiling me. And it got pretty intimate, too, when she started asking me where I was from, where I had studied, and why I had a French-sounding name if I was from Denmark.

Pasha wagged his finger at her and said, "Don't steal this one from me. He's not trained yet!" For the first time that morning, I began to entertain the possibility that I might not be in trouble after all. Lindenmayer smiled at

Pasha but was no less curious about my background. Younger staffers were so rare that we became a valuable commodity. The zeal and the energy of an up-start could do wonders for bureaucrats who knew how to steer them, and the UN's recruitment system was so averse to hiring anybody who didn't already have years of experience at the UN that when younger staff made their way in, usually through some sort of glitch in the UN's recruitment matrix, they were soon fought over by senior managers. Lindenmayer obviously had her pick, since she was sitting on the thirty-eighth floor, so it was rather flattering that she would take any interest in my profile at all. But my answers must have sounded a bit confused, because, well, I *was* a bit confused. I still didn't know what I was doing up here, and I still worried that the front-company snafu might be about to blow up in my face in a most high-profile manner.

I was about to explain the roots of my last name to Lindenmayer when I saw Nizar Hamdoon, the Iraqi ambassador, walking up the corridor toward us with a delegation of aides. What were *they* doing here?

This was definitely not a good time for me to explain that my last name was Hebrew in origin. The name Soussan traces its roots to the town of Shushan, in ancient Babylon (present-day Iran), and is first mentioned in the Book of Es-ther, in the Old Testament. My father was born in French Morocco, hence the Francophone sound of the name. He had met my Danish Protestant mother in Israel in the 1960s, when it was popular for Northern European hippies to spend summers at kibbutzes, and the result was a child who could best be de-scribed as a Sephardic Viking. In Iraqi, the equivalent to Soussan would be Sas-soon. Yes, like the shampoo. But to most Iraqis, the association would be with the Jewish religion rather than with Vidal's hair products. I knew the Iraqis had refused to give visas to other staff with Jewish names in the past, so I wasn't eager to complicate matters right then by satisfying Lindenmayer's curiosity.

"What's going on? Why's the Iraqi ambassador here?" I asked Pasha, un-tactfully ignoring Lindenmayer.

"I don't know," he said. "They're the ones who called for this meeting. The SG just told me this morning."

"So we don't know what this is about?"

Pasha shook his head. I thought about bringing him up to date on the "can of worms" issue he had asked me to handle, but it was too late. The Iraqis had arrived at our level. After shaking their hands, we all just stood there, as for a moment of silence, occasionally interrupted by an uncomfortable cough.

I caught Ambassador Hamdoon looking at me and shifted position. The man had the strangest curly eyebrows. He looked like a cartoonist's depiction of a vizier; in my previous capacity as a news assistant for CNN, I had ambushed him on several occasions with provocative questions as he walked toward the UN Security Council.

Finally, the door to Annan's office opened, and we were all invited to step inside. His office was sober and immaculate. The mounds of paper that seemed to fill up every corner of the UN building were absent here. The Iraqis sat on the couch, and I found a chair where I sat down and prepared to write up the official notes of the meeting.

I was struck by the fact that the man who always appeared so calm and relaxed when I saw him on TV was actually neither calm nor relaxed. Kofi Annan was controlled, to be sure, but right beneath the surface of his persona I sensed a bubble of nervous energy waiting to burst. His handshake was warm, and the tone of his voice exuded confidence, alertness, and caution. There was a rumor that the man had never lost his temper, ever. Only one person could recollect a time when he nearly lost it, and that was Lindenmayer, now sitting outside. She confided to Philip Gourevitch of *The New Yorker* that Annan had gotten angry once, back in the 1980s, when he was running the UN's human resources. Apparently, he lost his cool at the corrupt way the member states were running the appointment and promotion committee.

"If somebody does not get angry often and suddenly gets very angry, I can tell you it's very powerful," she had told Gourevitch. "He was like a lion roaring, he was so angry at them. . . . I tell you, he's angry with his whole body—with his eyes. His anger comes from every single part of him. His voice goes down. It takes a register, like an organ, which is the lowest one. It's very, very frightening when he gets angry."

My colleagues and I would eventually come to wish that Kofi Annan would get angry more often, either with Saddam Hussein or with the United States (depending on our politics), but it was simply not in his nature. At best, he would flicker his eyes, which was his way of expressing extreme irritation. His eyes seemed able to take in every aspect of the situation at once. Unlike Pasha's, they wouldn't roam around the room, picking up every detail. His gaze was steady, purposefully directed, and unafraid of contact. He addressed people with a humility that immediately put them at ease.

Annan was a likable man. Even the UN's worst enemy on Capitol Hill, Jesse Helms, the former chairman of the Senate Foreign Relations Committee, once admitted to the secretary general that he had taken an extensive look at Annan's background and had not found a single person who disliked him. This was not necessarily meant as a compliment, of course, but there was no question that Annan made a positive impression on the people who met him. An anecdote from his younger days as a student in the United

States has it that he once walked into a barbershop and was told by the shop's white owner, "We don't cut niggers' hair."

Instead of getting angry or simply leaving, Annan replied, "I'm not a nigger, I'm an African."

And the barber said, "Come on, siddown," and proceeded to give him a haircut.

Kofi Annan was more than just a diplomat. He was a black man who was able (and willing) to get a haircut from a white supremacist barber. He did have his detractors within the system, but one could sense a certain jealousy in their criticism. Pasha had been extremely friendly with Annan's predecessor, Boutros Boutros-Ghali, a Coptic Christian from Egypt who managed to become intensely disliked by the Clinton administration. Word had it that Boutros-Ghali saw Annan as a possible successor (and hence a threat) early on, and that this guided his decision to send him to Bosnia, as the failed UN mission there was being taken over by NATO troops. Against all logic, Bosnia proved to be a springboard for Kofi Annan. The U.S. military and diplomatic corps there instantly took a liking to him and put in a good word for the man when it became evident that the United States would not renew Boutros-Ghali's term.

Kofi Annan was the first nominee for the post of secretary general to come from Africa and the first to emerge from within the ranks of the UN Secretariat. He had joined the UN system in 1962, after completing his studies at Macalester College, a small liberal arts school in Minnesota, which he traveled to from his native Ghana on a Ford Foundation grant. At twenty-four, he was unusually young when he got his first UN job with the World Health Organization in Geneva. Like many younger staff, he reportedly predicted that his stint with the UN would be brief: "two years, then I'm out." I had told myself exactly the same thing when I was recruited, at the same age, the previous year. But that morning, as I waited anxiously to hear what the Iraqis had come to say, I prayed that it wouldn't involve any Swiss magistrates. I didn't want to lose this job. In barely a year, my responsibilities had grown exponentially. I had become personally invested in this operation's future.

Unfortunately, the waters for which we were headed were not navigable—not by Kofi Annan or by anyone else. Slowly but surely, the warning signs would accumulate. But much like the incident that was causing me so much anxiety that morning, they would not be acted on. Saddam Hussein was testing the system to see how much fraud he could get away with. The use of front companies had not yet become systematic. We could have nipped this scheme in the bud, but it would have required a number of communications that never took place. The Office of Legal Affairs would have needed to clearly state our own rules. Pasha would have needed to inform Annan of the emerging phenomenon. And Annan would have needed to tell the Iraqi ambassador that we were prepared to go public if the practice didn't stop.

As it stood, I didn't even know if Pasha had briefed Annan on the problem. He would eventually have to, I assumed. But perhaps not quite yet. Surely, the Iraqis were not about to bring up the issue.

As the meeting began, I breathed a huge sigh of relief. Clearly, neither side was interested in the Swiss magistrate's letter. It would be years before I realized that this should have been a cause for concern, not relief. If the UN was not addressing issues of compliance with international law as they related to billions of dollars under its control, then what, if anything, were we doing to exercise "oversight" over this operation?

Well, I suppose we were just trying to keep our jobs, and if anything had become clear to me that morning, it was that doing so involved taking the minimum possible amount of risk.

This would help explain why issues of compliance by the Iraqi regime would be methodically ignored. Merely confirming our own rules to an outside entity had been a complicated affair for us, and the simple fact that I finally decided to act on my own had caused me to fear for my job that morning. Would I take such risks again?

To be sure, with the massive growth of the operation, there would be plenty of occasions to make such calls. Especially in light of what the Iraqis were now telling us.

The Iraqi ambassador had come to complain that his government was unhappy with our proposal to increase the size of the Oil-for-Food program. They wanted an increase, all right, just not of the kind that we had proposed. The humanitarian projects we had presented to the Security Council as part of our pitch to increase the operation were not to their liking. They were, in essence, too humanitarian and did not involve enough industrial projects. The Iraqis did not want to buy as much food and medicine as we had recommended. They wanted more trucks, telecom equipment, and industrial machinery. And they would send a team from Baghdad to New York to negotiate with us on that basis. Only then would they agree to the expanded Oil-for-Food scheme.

Having made his key demand, the ambassador gauged Annan's and Pasha's reactions. Rather than make a commitment, my bosses pledged they would take Iraq's request under consideration. The meeting was kept short. Tensions on the weapons of mass destruction front were still at the forefront of everyone's mind. Iraq's economic future took second place to that conflict.

The Iraqi ambassador had some nerve to criticize us for the way we had handled the expansion of the program. It almost seemed like we, at the UN, were more worried than Saddam Hussein himself about the welfare of the Iraqi people. It almost felt like we were begging him to let us help his country. And now we would have to negotiate down from the terms we had proposed to the Security Council.

Saddam and his cronies were happy to organize parade burials through Baghdad once every couple of months, with little wooden coffins that supposedly contained "children killed by the sanctions," but when it came to actually saving these malnourished kids, there was nobody home. Spooky had fought tooth and nail to make sure the Iraqi government purchased special food for the most malnourished kids. It took them nine months to comply, and they did so only after Spooky threatened to go public with the issue and harm their propaganda campaign.

The fact that Spooky's threat produced a result was proof to me that the Iraqis could in fact be influenced. I would always remain uncertain of what exactly would have happened if we had gone public with the information that Saddam was defrauding the UN humanitarian program as we received it. But here is what would *not* have happened. The UN would never have stood accused of turning a blind eye to Saddam's multibillion-dollar rip-off or of lying to the public when asked about it. And I would certainly not have ended up sitting in this cold little conference room, being interrogated by a team of international investigators, about an e-mail I had long since forgotten, in which a colleague counseled me not to open "that can of worms."

As I sat there being questioned by the Volcker inquiry panel seven years after the start of my UN employment, I could perfectly understand why my interrogator would be frustrated. Especially now that she had this e-mail exchange proving that we knew about Saddam's massive fraud from the very beginning.

"So what happened after this e-mail exchange?" she asked me.

"Nothing," I said.

"What do you mean, nothing?"

"I mean nothing happened. We simply didn't follow up on it. We dropped the ball."

The investigator looked at me strangely, as if it was inconceivable that such an issue would simply vanish from our radar screen. At that point, I recognized the challenge facing the investigators. They were probing a case of massive fraud, yet they were totally unfamiliar with the managerial culture that prevailed within the United Nations. Some kind of guidebook might have helped them, but official papers, even our e-mails, did not contain the most important rules of all: the UN-written rules.

CHAPTER **14**

The Rules of the Game

The investigators who eventually dove into our exclusive little world to try to figure out how billions of dollars could have vanished from right under our noses when the whole point of our operation was to *watch over* this money were deeply baffled by the UN system's inability to enforce even minimal standards of accountability on its members, staff, and agencies.

I tried to explain to them that expecting accountability from the UN system was akin to expecting a blind dog to catch a flying Frisbee.

By design, the UN Security Council is accountable only to itself. There is no proper separation among governing branches on the international stage. All power is concentrated among the five veto-wielding members of the Security Council. If they were to be penalized for their failures, they would have to agree to inflict such punishment as they deem appropriate on themselves.

Alternatively, they can blame the UN Secretariat. As its name indicates, the Secretariat was originally designed to provide conference-support services to its member states, not to manage large and complex multibillion-dollar operations that dwarf its own yearly budget. Of all the operations ever assigned to the UN, ours was the most unusual, grandiose, and unrealistic. But the logic behind asking the Secretariat to manage any new operation is always the same: the great powers don't trust one another. With the UN in charge, they know that they can all maintain control over key managerial decisions. This, in turn, guarantees a high level of inefficiency.

The more the Security Council micromanages, the easier it is for the UN Secretariat to redirect any and all blame right back at that institution's doorstep. It's a simple system, really. The buck can go back and forth between the bodies that share responsibility for a given action and never stop on any one player's desk. That is, if they know how to play by the rules.

The gap that had developed between the UN's high-minded principles and the organization's management culture was a canyon better explored by corporate anthropologists than by law enforcement officials. The investigators would eventually understand this. They came in intending to conduct their probe "by the book," only to realize there really wasn't any book to go by. Theirs was the first large-scale exercise in accountability on the world stage. And the rules that regimented our world could not be found in textbooks.

More often than not, new recruits would encounter these rules in much the same manner as one's forehead encounters a low ceiling. Here are some of the unspoken rules of the game that I banged my head against during my first few months:

Rule #1: The Truth Is Not a Matter of Fact; It Is a Product of Consensus.

One rule that had become clear to me after my numerous blunders in Iraq was that telling the truth as I saw it was *not* (insofar as Pasha and other managers were concerned) my job. Initially, I was forgiven on account of my youth and inexperience. But as I accumulated new responsibilities at a rate that most bureaucrats would consider unwise, I could no longer claim innocence. With greater responsibility came less freedom of speech.

Sir Henry Wotton (1568–1639), a British author and diplomat, once wrote, "An Ambassador is an honest man sent to lie abroad for the good of his country." The endurance of this often-quoted phrase speaks to its resonance. Few experienced diplomats ever challenge the notion that their pursuit of "the greater good" somehow absolves them from having to abide by the Ninth Commandment ("Thou Shalt Not Bear False Witness").

In intelligence circles, this absolution is balanced by what operatives call the Eleventh Commandment: "Don't Get Caught!" Of course, this is an easier rule to follow when one is operating outside the public realm.

Diplomats are occasionally expected to perform before the cameras. Instead of a script they have a policy, which they must defend regardless of its merits or risk incurring the wrath of their government. Hence, when promoting a senseless or immoral policy, a diplomat is better off being caught in a lie than being caught admitting the truth.

I can't say I had a moral problem complying with this rule, especially if it was going to help me become "a player." I just had one question: if it was considered acceptable for a diplomat to lie on behalf of his country, on whose behalf were we, the UN's diplomats, supposed to lie? After all, our allegiance was not supposed to be to any state in particular, not even to the one that issued our passports. To make this extra clear, the UN issued us its own blue passports for use during professional travel.

Was I supposed to lie on behalf of Pasha or Kofi Annan? Or was I supposed to lie on behalf of the Security Council, which was itself composed of ambassadors who were lying to each other?

Some questions were obviously better left unasked. During the process of compiling our first report to the Security Council, I began to understand what kinds of lies were expected of us. In short, our job was to pretend that there was unity of purpose among the members of the Security Council, the UN Secretariat, and Iraq.

The truth, of course, was that no such unity of purpose existed. Competing interests were at work, and everyone involved understood this. But it was felt that the pretense of consensus was a necessary part of keeping the peace. Hence, our job was to pretend that the policies derived from the lowest denominator of common interest among the states in the Security Council were inherently legitimate, moral, and practical.

Just like the oil companies will commission advertisements that exalt their efforts on behalf of "the environment," the Security Council would expect us to report on the humanitarian achievements of a program that, in the big picture, ripped the Iraqi people off. When all expenses were added up, including war reparations (one-third of Iraq's oil revenue) and the cost of arms inspections, UN financial oversight, surcharges, bribes, and kickbacks (more on those later), the Iraqi people received less than fifty cents in humanitarian supplies for every dollar of oil their country sold.

Our charts would show this quite clearly. Yet our words would extol the program's humanitarian achievements. If half-truths make for complete lies, this was a lie that Security Council members could agree to preserve. This did not mean they stopped lying to one another about other things.

Diplomats spend quite a bit of time reading between other diplomats' lies. Official meetings are most tedious in this regard, as each player restates his policies for public consumption. Glimmers of truth are much more likely to emerge during cappuccino breaks, lunches, or, better yet, during diplomatic cocktail parties. *That's* where the real work of diplomacy took place. As Adlai E. Stevenson, the former U.S. ambassador to the UN, once put it, "A diplomat's life is made up of three ingredients: protocol, Geritol and alcohol."

Alcohol is the truth serum, Geritol (a popular multivitamin in Stevenson's day) is for the hangovers, and protocol, I would say, is there to minimize the risk that people whose job it is to lie to one another all day actually end up offending one another.

Inasmuch as I gained a better understanding of why and how diplomats lie, I was struck by the connection between lying and preserving the peace. In a sense, I was back to square one, dealing with the assumption that diplomats were in fact justified in lying as long as their behavior helped maintain peace.

Could peace really be built on blocks of lies? The inescapable answer was yes. Temporarily.

And so we were excused. Temporarily.

Rule #2: Never Get Stuck With the Buck.

There is no more pitiful sight than a bureaucrat who can't find a way to step aside when a hot potato comes flying. Sometimes the inevitable happens, however, and a bureaucrat is given an actual task involving a deadline or, worst of all, a decision.

Making a decision is a dangerous endeavor. Any bureaucrat making a decision runs the very real risk of violating one of the UN's many nonsensical regulations, or offending some country's political sensitivities, and screwing up his career. As servants of the UN Security Council, we had not one boss but fifteen. Any person wishing to gain access to a high-level post in the future needed to keep these fifteen ambassadors with radically opposed worldviews happy. Consequently, the safest decision for a bureaucrat to make was often no decision at all.

The Secretariat was designed to *facilitate* diplomacy, not to manage a country's economy, as we had now been asked to do with the Oil-for-Food program. The challenges we faced were so unusual for us that we were better off ignoring them than dealing with them head-on.

"If you let them sit long enough, most issues go away all on their own," a high-level UN bureaucrat, who shall remain unnamed, once explained at a cocktail party. The official served in the UN's Bosnia operation and may stand as a perfect illustration of the famous Peter Principle, which holds that in hierarchical bureaucracies, each worker rises to the level of his own incompetence. While this man was at a high level of responsibility, a massacre happened in the Bosnian town of Srebrenica. Not surprisingly, the UN took no action, and in one sense, the bureaucrat's theory proved correct. The issue, which was how the UN would protect the population of the town from Serbian forces, went away. Eight thousand Muslim men of Srebrenica were gunned down at point-blank range by Serbian forces while the UN soldiers stood inactive nearby. They had received no clear instructions from New York. This, despite the fact that the town had been declared a "UN safe haven."

One Bosnian once put it plainly: "If you see Blue Helmets, it means you're already fucked."

Well, this may not always be the case. And Blue Helmets have on occasion saved lives. But in this case, how could the organization allow a designated "UN safe haven" to become the site of such a massacre?

Did anybody at the UN take responsibility? Did anybody resign?

No.

By contrast, the entire Dutch government eventually resigned when a report blamed the Dutch peacekeeping troops for having failed in their duties. Now that's accountability.

At the UN, no bureaucrat ever considered stepping down in the aftermath of Srebrenica. As a master's student, I interviewed Gen. Philippe Morillon, who was dispatched to lead the Blue Helmets in Bosnia at the time. The man started crying during our interview. Never had he imagined that he would be asked to lead such a senseless mission as the one that was given to him in the Balkans: to keep a peace that did not exist, with hardly enough authority to keep his own men alive.

Kofi Annan, the head of UN peacekeeping at the time, was poised to become the UN's next secretary general.

If one wants to climb the ladders of the UN bureaucracy, one is far better off dodging responsibility than accepting it. There are plenty of ways one can rationalize such behavior after the fact *as long as one doesn't get stuck with the buck.*

This implies some mastery of the different techniques that allow a bureaucrat to pass along responsibility. Yellow routing stickers are a favorite. If a report comes in to a manager's inbox warning of an imminent debacle requiring a risky decision? Easy: smack a yellow sticker on the memo and pass it along to a colleague with the note "Please advise on credibility of attached report." The colleague will hate the manager, of course, because if disaster strikes while the report is in *his* inbox, he'll be terribly embarrassed. So he'll rush onto the web and print out an article corroborating the report and smack a new yellow sticker right on top of it with the words "See attached— would appear to confirm credibility of report."

What is a manager to do? He could smack a new yellow sticker on it and send it to the Office of Legal Affairs: "Please advise on options for legal action." To doubly protect himself, he could use his URGENT stamp. But he knows that the use of his URGENT stamp may only get the report back into his own inbox faster. So eventually, he decides to call a meeting.

The point of a meeting is to spread out responsibility for decisions—or, better, to find a reason why no decision can be made at all. The meeting agenda is typically made up of pressing issues nobody wants to take action on individually. By the end of the meeting, the youngest person in the room will be asked to summarize what was said, making damned sure he or she doesn't assign work to his seniors. It's a great system. Over time, accountability is diluted to the point where it evaporates completely. In the case of our program, so much vapor would accumulate that it eventually condensed to form what UN leaders would describe as a "dark cloud" hanging over the United Nations. Lucky would be the ones who had taken cover before the storm.

Rule #3: The Assistant of Your Enemy Is Your Friend.

Pasha's distrust of Denis Halliday stemmed from a simple fear, i.e., that Denis would stab him in the back in order to take his post. His fear about Denis was not as irrational as it might appear to the candid eye. Typically, the greatest threat to a bureaucrat's authority would often come from his or her immediate subordinates.

In a hierarchical pyramid, there is only so much room at the top.

UN officials do not normally get to appoint their own deputies. Their seniors—in Pasha's case, Iqbal Riza, Kofi Annan's chief of staff—handpick them.

Did Iqbal Riza not know that he had chosen two people who hated each other's guts to helm the UN's largest humanitarian operation? Of course he did. That was the whole point. Divide and rule.

Having established on the first day of our mission to Iraq that Halliday was indeed "out to get him," Pasha felt justified in depicting his deputy's efforts to challenge the UN policy on Iraq as an attempt to stab him in the back. I don't think that's how Halliday would have described his maneuver, but perceptions seem to have been more relevant than facts. Would Annan back Pasha or would he undermine him only a few months after having appointed him?

Pasha knew the rules would play in his favor. Halliday had exposed himself with decisions and statements that were far more provocative than his own. Pasha's reserve would be rewarded. And his would-be competitor would have no other dignified choice but to resign.

Having gotten rid of the most immediate threat to his authority, Pasha turned all his suspicions on my director, Yohannes Mengesha, the friendly Ethiopian man who had recruited me into the UN. The question in Pasha's mind was not whether Mengesha would undermine him but how and when he would attempt to do so. For an answer, Pasha turned to me. He called me over to his office, which was across the street from our own, and asked me, "So, what are these bozos up to?"

"What bozos?"

"The guys across the street!"

"The Americans?" I asked. The U.S. Embassy lay across the street, too.

Pasha shook his head. "Facking Mengesha and those guys!"

"Oh . . . well, you know, working. . . ."

"Yeah, right . . . working to screw me . . . facking Mengesha and his vacations!"

There we were again. Back to square one. Pasha would never forgive my director for going on vacation while he was in Baghdad. But soon that wouldn't matter, for the Machiavellian Riza had another trick up his sleeve. He would appoint Mengesha to work for Pasha's direct boss, the newly appointed deputy to Kofi Annan, Ms. Louise Fréchette of Canada.

Bureaucratically speaking, it was a beautiful move. Take Pasha's assistant and place him as the assistant to Pasha's boss.

Well, there was never any doubt that Pasha's boss was in fact Kofi Annan. But Annan knew better than to get too involved in the UN's largest and most controversial operation. The very idea that the secretary general should have a deputy was rather recent. Following several instances of gross UN mismanagement, it had occurred to member states that the secretary general could not possibly attend all the receptions and official functions they had lined up for him and be expected to actually *manage* the organization.

The deputy would be given responsibility for management, though not the authority to manage. Decisions would remain firmly controlled by Annan's chief of staff. It made perfect sense, and it reflected the core nature of the UN's management culture in that it ensured that the person with responsibility had no authority; and vice versa, it protected the people with authority from having to take responsibility.

Just as the Security Council arrogates to itself great authority yet bears no responsibility for its actions, the UN Secretariat is given enormous responsibilities yet minimal authority to act on them.

This phenomenon replicated itself at all levels of the UN bureaucracy and naturally fomented suspicions among top managers that their deputies were undermining them behind their back. The system worked brilliantly to sour relations between deputies and assistants all the way down the ladder. Pasha used Halliday's deputy in the field, an Afghan who had betrayed his country and served under the Soviets before joining the UN, to undermine his rival. The alliance between the Afghan and Pasha, an Armenian Cypriot, was a logical one. The Afghan feared that his boss would slam him with responsibility for failures he did not have the authority to address. His alliance with Pasha guaranteed his survival in the long term. And survival was exactly what the game was all about.

Rule #4: Even the Paranoid Have Enemies.

Henry Kissinger, Nixon's secretary of state, knew what he was talking about when he shared this ironic piece of wisdom: indeed, "even the paranoid have some real enemies."

The characters who populated our office certainly acted on this premise. The deputy to my director was a French nobleman of Romanian origin named Gregoire. People in the office told me he was a descendant of the Count of Dracula. Hence his nickname. At first, I thought they were joking. But credible sources eventually assured me that Gregoire did indeed have a distant Transylvanian relative named Dracul. Or something. And then, there was the undeniable fact that Gregoire had fangs. I first saw them at the end of my first week in the office, when I decided to introduce myself to the mysterious man in the large office adjacent to my director's, who always kept his door closed.

With some apprehension, I knocked on Gregoire's door. He yelled for me to "come in!" in a tone signaling that he was in the kind of bad mood only French nobles of Transylvanian descent can get themselves into. I stepped in, interrupting a game of cards he was losing to his computer, and caught him in mid-yawn. That was my first glimpse at his overdeveloped incisors.

"*Oui?*" he said, when he was done yawning. I explained that I had come to introduce myself, when in fact my real agenda was to find out what the hell he was doing all day long behind his closed door.

Gregoire explained that he was quote-unquote deputy director, then grimaced, as if to undermine the statement he had just made, and let silence fill the air. He did not appear eager to chat, even after I nearly split my face smiling, so I decided to ask him straight up what he did when he wasn't playing cards against his PC.

That got his attention. After a moment's hesitation, he smiled and explained that he didn't really do anything at all because "the fellow next door" (my director) didn't give him a chance.

"Aha," I said, flabbergasted at the level of childishness I would have to deal with in this office. I had never worked in a place where someone of relatively high rank would simply admit to doing nothing all day.

For a moment, I tried to figure out if this meant that Dracula and I would have to be enemies. But I couldn't really figure it out. So I asked him what *he* felt should be the nature of our relationship.

The frankness of my question softened him up. After doing a double take to reevaluate me, he told me that I could always come to him if I had any questions. He was, in fact, eager for information himself, because he wasn't necessarily copied on all the correspondence addressed to my director. I promised him that I would send copies his way and seek his advice, and we left on surprisingly good terms. Dracula, it turned out, could be a very warm character once you got on his good side.

Soon after I met him, Dracula suddenly became my direct boss. Mengesha, my first director, accepted the offer to work for Annan's deputy (Pasha's boss). The moment Mengesha packed his things and moved to the thirty-eighth floor, Dracula became the official "officer-in-charge" of the program's Management Division. This meant he had to stop playing cards and start signing faxes, which were mine to draft and submit for his consideration. Much to my surprise, Dracula, whose experience had been in emergency field operations, was eager to do some actual work.

Unfortunately, Pasha had never envisaged that Dracula would become an actual decision-maker. When Pasha intercepted the first fax going from Dracula to Halliday in Baghdad, he officially barred anybody but himself from any official communication with our mission in the field. All faxes going from New York to Baghdad would have to be signed by Pasha personally. This struck me, and everyone else, as incredibly impractical.

Pasha's new "policy" meant I had to run across the street to get his signature every time we needed to send a fax. I ended up having two offices. One on Pasha's side of the street and one on Dracula's. (Eventually our office would take up space in four separate buildings around the United Nations.)

I suppose we could have saved a lot of time simply by using e-mails. But e-mails had yet to gain acceptance as a "formal" method of communication. They did not constitute an "official" exchange and could therefore be ignored by the recipient if he did not feel like dealing with it.

"Our side of the street" was infuriated by the new procedure, and at a meeting Dracula convened, my colleagues decided to appoint me as their emissary to go and persuade Pasha to grant us the authority to send faxes to

Baghdad without his clearance. So off I went across the street in the hope of striking an arrangement with Cindy Spikes, Pasha's special assistant.

Cindy was in her early forties. She had flamboyant TV hair, shiny white teeth, and a reputation as a man-eater. She invited me to sit in her office with a wave of the hand while she continued her phone conversation.

After she hung up, a radiant smile lit up her face, right on cue. It was fake, but still, it had an unapologetic quality that made it convincing at the same time. Clearly, this was a woman in control of her facial expressions. After listening to my argument about the need to let "our side of the street" send faxes to Baghdad, she immediately understood the problem. A mutiny had developed that needed to be crushed, its leader (whom she assumed to be Dracula) castrated.

To emphasize her point, she made an imaginary scissors motion with two fingers, complete with sound effects: "chuck, chuck, chuck!" As my eyes widened, she clarified that such attitudes needed to be nipped in the bud and asked if there was anything else she could help me with.

I tried to speak, but instead I cracked up. Cindy's face immediately became severe. She didn't appreciate being laughed at in her office. Unfortunately, I found it very hard to stop. Her scissors motion had caught me completely off guard. For a moment, it looked like I would get off on the wrong foot with Cindy. I scrambled to think of a reason for my sudden outburst; thankfully, I found one right in front of me.

On Cindy's desk was a small glass jar filled with garlic and labeled "Boutros Boutros Garlic."

"Sorry . . . I just saw this," I said, pointing to the small garlic joke-jar. "Where did you find this thing?" I asked, still snorting. Cindy looked at me strangely. The label on the garlic jar was meant to make people smile, not burst into uncontrollable laughter.

Having narrowly avoided causing great offense to Pasha's "spec ass" (as special assistants are sometimes called behind their backs), I decided to stay off the subject of my visit and make light conversation. I learned that Cindy hated men who "didn't have any balls." In her opinion, this phenomenon applied to most of the males at the United Nations.

Finding an accommodation with Cindy would clearly not be easy, but it would definitely be required if we were going to get both sides of the street to work together rather than against each other. And I did have a few cards in my hands. Since the management arm of the office was on the other side of the street, she saw me as someone who could serve as her eyes and ears there. (The assistant of your enemy is your friend.) I had no intention of playing that role, but I did make it clear that I was tuned in to what was going on in the office. The other thing that I could leverage was that she had never set foot in Iraq and had a limited understanding of the situation on the ground.

So after a bit of polite conversation, I decided to lead a second charge. I whipped out two of the many faxes I had brought with me to get signed by Pasha. One of the faxes was a recommendation to engage the government of Iraq in a discussion of "vulnerable groups," meaning kids without parents and widowed mothers, whom we wished to target with special protein biscuits as a way of improving their health and preventing disease. The government had previously refused to engage in any talks about "vulnerable groups," because it feared that we were interested in helping those it oppressed most severely, like the Shiite Marsh Arabs of southern Iraq. Given the subject's political sensitivity, I explained that I would never let a fax like that go out unless Pasha had signed it.

"I should certainly hope not," Cindy said.

Hoping to have reassured her, I then pointed to the other fax, which was filled with detailed questions about water pumping stations in Ninewah—

"Ninewhat?"

"Ninewah, it's a province of Iraq."

"Right. . . ."

The fax thanked our staff in the field for their report and asked them for tons of additional technical information. You had to be a water engineer just to understand the questions. I handed the fax to her and watched her eyes crease as she tried to decipher what it was all about.

"Tell you what, kiddo," she said, "you can send the routine stuff on your side, but it's *your* ass if there's a fuckup, you hear me? So you better vet it before it goes out or I'll have your head on a stick."

I stood up but stayed in place. Insofar as I could figure this woman out, it was pretty obvious to me that she would not respect anybody who cowered to such threats. So I ventured into the unknown.

"If you want me to send a truckload of faxes like this your way every day, I'll do it. It's your call. Either you trust me to help you or you don't," I said.

"All right, young man, don't take this tone with me," she said. "And sit your ass back down. We're not done."

I sensed she was about to back off her threat, so I sat halfway down on the chair's armrest.

"Look Mikey," she said, using a new nickname for me and suddenly transforming herself into a charming person again. "It's not that I don't trust you, but we need to have control over these guys. They're totally out of control!" I nodded, not because I agreed with her but because I was beginning to understand the world she lived in. It was a world of out-of-control, spineless cowards who were out to undermine her authority. The logic of triangulation would have made her an automatic enemy of Gregoire, and this made me an automatic ally of hers, so her appeal to me was pretty straightforward: "Join me and we shall rule the Oil-for-Food ship together!"

At that point, Pasha walked by in an unusually good mood after a long and probably well-lubricated lunch.

"How are you, Kid?" he said, slapping his hand down on my neck, then feigning to punch me in the stomach.

"Fine, sir . . . "

Pasha turned to Cindy and launched into an imitation of me with a big stupid smile on my face. As usual, Pasha's imitation was great, and I made a mental note not to smile so much all the time.

Pasha then pointed to his signature book, which was fat with faxes, and asked, "What's all this shit?"

"For your signature, sir," I replied.

"Ahrf! Gimme a break!" he said, fleeing the scene unapologetically to take his customary after-lunch siesta.

"Ahrf! Gimme a break!" I repeated, imitating the under secretary general right back at him. Pasha stopped dead in his tracks. Cindy broke the tension first, chuckling, and then Pasha's secretary joined in. Pasha wagged his finger at me and said something about the "facking people across the street" having a bad influence on me. Then he disappeared into his office and closed the door. I turned to Cindy and cringed, realizing I had probably gone too far.

Cindy shook her head and laughed some more. "Ah, Mikey, Mikey, Mikey, what are we going to do with you?"

I sat all the way back down and began the first of many productive meetings with Cindy. She was a very competent woman when she wasn't beset with Paper Flow Paranoia (PFP).

Paper Flow Paranoia is a disease that is proper to large bureaucracies and is especially rampant at the United Nations. A most dramatic form of PFP occurs in individuals who become convinced that every detail of a paper communication is designed with the intent of harming them. The way it works is this: when two people at the United Nations communicate, they have to do so "on paper," because if they merely talk, there's no record of their communication, and if there's no record of their communication, it is as if they had never communicated. For example, if Person A asks Person B to do something and Person B agrees to do it but then doesn't do it, there's nothing Person A can do about it because there's no paper trail, and therefore no accountability.

Sometimes, people are so concerned about getting things on paper that, after a phone conversation with a colleague, they will sit down for an hour and write a "note to the file" about their conversation. The note can be copied to actual human beings, but it took me a while to come around to the notion that one might want to address a note to a file. The idea is to have a record, and the only use one can possibly have for such a record is either to protect oneself or attack another.

Paper Flow Paranoia can be sparked by something as seemingly irrelevant as the order in which staff are copied on a given memo. In the days before personal computers, typewriters were used and copies were made on carbon paper—hence the denomination "cc" for carbon copies. The order in which people's names are listed in any given memo is enormously important and must reflect the hierarchy of the UN. The most important people go first. Only when people are equally important does the alphabetical order kick in, and then it is required. So basically, people at the United Nations know more or less where they stand in the pecking order based on the location of their name on the cc list of a given memo. Even in the UN phone directory, offices were not listed in alphabetical order but in order of (perceived) importance, which made it rather difficult to look up any given division.

The formality of the communication system made it possible for two bureaucrats who did not feel like talking to each other to communicate exclusively through cc's on memos to their boss. In the organization dedicated to world peace, bureaucrats could sit in adjacent offices, separated only by a thin partition wall that allowed each of them to overhear parts of the other's phone conversations, and hate each other's guts as a result of perceived insults contained in memos. In one case, a memo sent by one staff member in 1997 still had another employee royally miffed in 2008. Eleven years had gone by. The issue at stake had lost its relevance ten years ago. For the record, it had to do with food distribution in Iraq.

Memorandums, like bombs, have guidance systems. There are smart memos and dumb memos. A smart memo has a defined target and can navigate its way through the system without causing too much collateral damage. A dumb memo may cause more damage to the sender than to the recipient. Much depends on a bureaucrat's ability to control his or her anger.

Rule #5: Always Be More Polite Than Your Enemy.

"Even in a declaration of war, one observes the rules of politeness."

OTTO VON BISMARCK

One reason interpersonal conflicts at the UN often drag on for years, even decades, is that they are conducted so freaking politely. There are showdowns, of course, but they are rarely conclusive in an absolute sense. Both parties will likely stay at the UN for the rest of their lives. If the UN were to have its own reality show, it would be just like *Survivor*, except nobody would ever get kicked off the island. The show would go on with the same characters even after they conspired to vote one another off the show. It could be called *No Exit*, like the play by Jean-Paul Sartre in which characters who are locked in a room together slowly realize that they are, in fact, in hell and that their punishment is to be stuck together so they can get on one another's nerves forever.

To stay sane, a bureaucrat has to win the occasional showdown. And the yardstick against which performances are judged is simple. In the absence of actual stakes, the bureaucrat who has the last polite word wins.

I once witnessed a scene between two UN staff members that provides an extreme illustration of this point. One rainy morning, I was waiting for an elevator with an Afghan and a Yemenite—both of whom were in their midforties. I was aware that the two characters were avowed enemies, though I did not know exactly why. When the elevator arrived, I stepped in, while the Afghan and the Yemenite stood outside, tensely inviting each other to step in first. Taking turns, they waved the palms of their hands, smiled hypocritically, and said, "Please, I insist," "No, please, *I* insist," until finally, the doors started closing without consulting either of them.

Going the extra mile for politeness, the Afghan tried to hold the door from closing so as to let the Yemenite in first. But the Yemenite retaliated by grabbing on to his own side of the door. I think it must have been impossible for them not to be struck by the absurdity of the situation, but they were now locked in a war of wills. Eventually, the elevator itself went berserk, making a loud buzzing noise and forcing its doors shut. Seized with panic, the Afghan and the Yemenite were both forced to jump in at the same time. The Afghan knocked his head on the door and spilled some coffee on the Yemenite's suit. I immediately asked the Afghan, who had received a substantive blow to the head, if he was OK, but when he saw that I had a smile on my face, he chose not to reply.

"You could at least apologize!" said the Yemenite, tending to the coffee stain on his pants.

"Are you suggesting I did this on purpose?" the Afghan retorted, irritated. Then he caught himself. "If so, please accept my most sincere apologies."

The Afghan was mocking his counterpart, of course, but he had the last polite word. Would the Yemenite be composed enough to retaliate? Not this time. Any word coming out of his mouth would have been a swear word. So he made a serpentlike hissing noise. The Afghan raised his eyebrows and exchanged a smile with the rest of the passengers, savoring his well-earned victory.

I can testify to dozens of tense situations resulting from diplomats having to walk through open doors. What took me some time to understand was why it was so important for them to let the other person go first. Is this not a courtesy normally extended by men to women? Why would two men, or two women, for that matter, be so insistent on having their counterpart take the first step through an open door?

In a world where there is no truth but consensus, where initiative is highly risky, where assistants can turn into enemies, and where paranoia makes practical sense, I suppose it is unfair to blame diplomats for accepting invitations that leave their backs exposed.

CHAPTER 15

Conflict Resolution

"Resistance is futile. You will be assimilated."

THE BORG

Several months after losing his first director, Pasha hired a new one, Bo Asplund. Bo was a competent and morally upright Swede who kept a toothbrush in his breast pocket and liked to run a tight ship. He had made it clear from the outset that he would seek to apply "sound management principles" to the work of the office. Somehow, I had an inkling his lofty goal would meet with some resistance. To begin with, Pasha couldn't get around the fact that someone might be called Bo. And so he called him Boo!, as if he were a ghost.

At the start of his employment, Boo! made every effort to get along with Cindy. For a time it worked reasonably well because Boo! had backbone and Cindy could sense that it would not be wise for her to confront him directly. Instead, she decided to grind him down gradually.

First, Cindy hired one of the most incompetent secretaries available in the entire UN system to work for Boo!: a woman from Haiti who appeared highly cultured and unusually slow to react to urgent demands. She had a knack for transforming a request for her to send a fax into a discussion of nineteenth-century Romantic poetry.

At first, Boo! did his best to appear interested in what his secretary had to say. This could not have been easy for him. Every detail of his body language exuded urgency. He would stand before her cubicle with arms crossed, tapping his foot, and nodding preemptively at every point she made, until such a time that he could cordially remind her that the piece of paper he carried in his hand required her attention.

Bo finally lost his temper with her, one day, after she disappeared for three hours in the middle of the afternoon. After Bo slammed his door shut, his secretary started mumbling to herself in Haitian. She sounded like she was reciting a prayer . . . or maybe a curse? The answer came at the end of the day, when Bo called me into his office and announced, with surprising calm, that he was having an attack of hives. His neckline was red, and itchy plaques were beginning to form on his face. He explained that he needed to rush to an emergency room to get an adrenaline shot.

Bo did not believe in voodoo, he said, when I mentioned how his secretary had been mumbling mysteriously all afternoon. But he never yelled at her again. The search was on for a new secretary. The next candidate Cindy sent him was a nose-ringed, grungy activist type with a history of conflict with her supervisors. After that interview, Bo looked like he was ripe for another attack of hives. "This," he said, "is pure sabotage."

The rapid deterioration in the relationship between Bo and Cindy accelerated as they jostled to determine who was to be the top dog in the office—a conflict Pasha appeared to encourage. Disputes between directors and special assistants are so common at the United Nations that one might think the idea was written into the organization's charter. While the director is of higher rank than the special assistant, the special assistant usually has better access to the big boss and can use that access to undermine the director. The conflict followed a classic triangular pattern. To make matters worse, in this case, Pasha was from the "divide and rule" school of management.

Bo's first order of business was to write a mission statement for the office. So far, our mission statement had been to follow Pasha's wild mood swings, and Pasha himself had an intriguing way of describing his duties.

"I am the Security Council's donkey," he kept saying, before adding, "but even donkeys, sometimes, they kick back!"

Notwithstanding Pasha's intriguing conception of his role, we were not entirely free to do as we pleased. The source of our mission had been inscribed in UN Security Resolution 986 (1995), so it was not as if we were operating without a mandate. The idea of having a mission statement was to adapt our routines and the structure of our daily interactions to maximize the likelihood that we would *fulfill* our mandate.

Bo's mission-statement initiative struck most of my colleagues as a waste of time, because we were constantly running from crisis to crisis. Most of the time, these crises were sparked by Saddam's conflict with the weapons inspectors. There could be armed conflict at a moment's notice. We ran pretty much like an emergency operation, and most of us barely had time to catch our breath. Yet Bo was right. If this operation was going to be effective in the long run, it needed more than a donkey-inspired mission statement.

I suggested a meeting to kick off the effort. We invited Pasha to attend, so that it would be clear to everybody that the big boss was fully behind Bo's initiative. Bo was heading the Division of Program Management. Under his direction, several "chiefs" were supposed to manage the flow of (a) humanitarian reports coming in from Iraq; (b) contracts flowing into the UN system from outside companies; and (c) contracts given by the UN partners working in northern Iraq, where we had responsibility for execution.

Before Bo's arrival we had spent several months without a director, so most of them were used to reporting directly to Pasha, often using me as a conduit when they were proposing ideas Pasha might dislike. Now Bo wanted Pasha's explicit support for instituting more structure. It all made sense. But when Bo explained the point of the mission statement at the meeting, Pasha rolled his eyes for the rest of the staff to see, sparking some awkward chuckles.

I went to see Pasha that night, to see if he had just been joking around or if he was really out to undermine my new director. Over a glass of Chivas, I asked him what he thought of Bo's management style, and he answered me with a question: "You call that *style?*"

His answer made me laugh, even though technically, it was tragic. What Pasha wanted to know was "why Boo needs to hold all these facking meetings all the time." Bo had instituted a weekly management meeting of the senior staff. A note of the meeting was written up (usually by me) and copied to Pasha for his information. Yet Pasha didn't like it one bit when the staff in his office started talking to one another behind his back, and that was precisely what he assumed went on at these meetings.

When I left Pasha's office late that night, I realized it would be an uphill battle to get the Cypriot and the Swede to work together. Deep down, I knew the dice were loaded from the moment Pasha had said "Boo!" And when I realized that Cindy was at work on her own version of a mission statement for the office, for which she had Pasha's backing, it dawned on me that we might be in for a catastrophic clash of egos.

Out of desperation, I enrolled in a conflict-resolution seminar at Columbia University. It was a fascinating class, in which I learned to recognize how easily and unnecessarily people manage to offend one another. The conflict-resolution coaches had the same kind of look in their eyes as people in sects. They spoke like they had "seen the light," and for a time, I thought I had seen the light, too. I became convinced that the problems we had between our senior staff could be resolved if only they would attend a conflict-resolution seminar together. So I raised the idea at our weekly management meeting.

"I think it would be great if all of us could attend this conflict-resolution seminar," I said, with the same honest-to-God round eyes as the gurus who had indoctrinated me.

During the silence that ensued, the tension rose sharply. Cindy became fidgety, and Bo turned into a rigid block of ice.

"I think it would be great if you just took notes and shadap," Pasha replied, releasing the tension by causing an uproar of laughter around the table.

"Just an idea, Sir . . ."

Clearly, I would have to apply the conflict-resolution "techniques" I had learned all on my own.

After a particularly nasty round of Paper Flow Paranoia, Cindy and Bo stopped talking to each other altogether. Bo was not the type of person who would normally refuse to communicate with another staff member, but Cindy was driving him up the wall, and their rivalry was only accentuated by Pasha, who would not rule on the issues that were dividing them.

It got pretty nasty. Bo, with whom I sometimes spoke in French, would refer to Cindy as "*la pouffiasse du bout du couloir*," meaning the "bitch down the hall," and Cindy would refer to Bo as "your boss, that dickhead."

It is in this context that I tried to apply the "de-escalation" procedure I had learned at the training seminar. As I shuttled between "the bitch down the hall" and my boss, "that dickhead," I began by trying to reassure each of them that the other was not, actually, "out to get them." This backfired, because they would then feel I had accused them of being paranoid—an accusation that paranoid people tend to be especially paranoid about. In their defense, they were not wrong to remind me that their nemesis had indeed done a list of things that were offensive. Realizing I was only making matters worse by causing them to concentrate all of their energy on justifying their paranoia, I quickly changed tactics. Rather than deny that wrongs had been committed, I tried to get each of them to understand where the other person was "coming from."

Now, Bo knew exactly where Cindy was coming from. In his opinion, she was coming from the point of view of someone who was a sexually frustrated control freak. As for Cindy, she knew exactly where Boo! was coming from, too: the United Nations Development Program, which, in Cindy's book, was synonymous with the Death Star.

The UNDP and the UN Secretariat competed for managerial control of humanitarian operations every time a new mission was drawn up by the Security Council. Secretariat staff thought themselves more able diplomats, and UNDP staff felt they were better managers. I wish I had been tipped off to that long-running, overarching turf war within the UN system before I tried to intervene between Bo and Cindy. Nonetheless, I plowed ahead with my de-escalation efforts. I tried to explain to Cindy that Bo felt undermined when she issued orders directly to some of his staff and that it would be really helpful if she would just ask him to do so himself. I tried to explain to Bo that Cindy was indeed a very controlling woman but that it would probably be smarter just to ignore some of the awkward things she did and focus on the issues. For a while there, I almost thought I had persuaded them to lay down their arms. Increasingly, I felt that both Cindy and Bo were beginning to listen to me more carefully.

As it turned out, the reason I had their attention was not that I was convincing them. It was that they were growing increasingly suspicious of *me!* The stage was set for a clash that would squeeze the taste for conflict resolution out of me for good.

One afternoon, I walked into Bo's office to bring him some faxes for his signature. He greeted me with an accusatory stare, then held out a piece of paper and declared: "The plot thickens!"

It made me laugh when he said that because he looked like a suspicious Daffy Duck. But Bo wasn't joking. I asked him what he meant, and he sent the memo flying across his desk. I had seen it before, since I saw everything that went into Bo's inbox. It was the memo in which Pasha asked me to draw up a "status sheet" on all the promises we had made in our report to the UN Security Council. The status sheet needed to list who was responsible for following up on each promise and indicate any progress that had (or had not) been made.

The memo was signed by Pasha, but we could tell from its style that Cindy had drafted it. She knew it would cause Bo to blow his top for two reasons. First, the memo was addressed to me, with a cc to Bo, instead of just addressed to Bo, who should have been the person to decide whom he appointed within his own Division of Program Management to do the job.

Second, it suggested Bo should have taken such an initiative himself, that he was behind schedule, and that his office would be the one held accountable for any failure to meet the promises made in our report to the Security Council. The translation from UN-ese read as follows: "If anything goes wrong with the largest operation in UN history, we'll blame it all on *you*."

Bo wanted to know how long I had known about this memo, why I hadn't advised him of it immediately, and why the hell the memo was addressed to me, since I worked for him. I said I didn't know why it was addressed to me. While I hadn't run into his office with it, I had obviously placed it in his inbox so he would see it. I explained that the idea of a status sheet had originally been my own, and that I had no idea, when I shared it with Cindy, that she would use this idea to launch a catty memo to him. But all my explanations were to no avail. Bo was now convinced I was in on the plot to undermine him.

All day long, Cindy walked around like a cat licking the cream off her whiskers, and Bo kept barging into my office and barking orders about how he wanted the status sheet to be prepared, saying he wanted it finished by "close of business today." His anger was compounded when he ran into Cindy on his way out of my office and she asked him how things were going with "Mikey's status sheet." Bo was too angry to answer her. And Cindy couldn't repress a devilish smile.

Cindy's victory was complete. She had put Bo on the defensive with the bureaucratic equivalent of a Panzer division offensive and at the same time sown distrust between Bo and his closest aide. Cindy had played by the unwritten rule handbook: *the assistant of your enemy is your friend.*

Close of business came, and I wasn't done with the status sheet. In fact, I realized that to do it well, I would need to consult with several other offices and that such a process would take days. When I informed Bo of that, he went ape shit. I was in no mood to justify myself. In fact, I felt that if I had to take another second of Bo's abuse, I would start yelling back even louder. So I left the office early and went out for drinks with my pals from the other side of the street, and when I was sufficiently inebriated, I made a decision to call up my director, tell him I wasn't going to "take this shit" anymore, and that he could have my letter of resignation on his desk on Monday.

On Monday morning, Bo called me into his office and apologized. Once again, the management training Bo had undergone at some stage in his career served him well, for he knew exactly how to apologize in a manner that was honest, convincing, and dignified. So I accepted his apology. We talked about how we had gotten to the point of a confrontation, and I realized the extent to which he had begun to question my loyalty. Cindy had really done a masterful job of sowing doubt in Bo's mind. As he retraced the events that had caused him to grow angry, I had to agree that they added up. Bo may have been a tad bit paranoid, but it did not mean Cindy was not out to get him.

In order to put Bo's increasingly Shakespearean mindset into perspective, I laid my cards on the table and explained that I had tried to "de-escalate" the conflict between him and Cindy. He smiled and told me something I had completely overlooked: "That's not your job, Michael."

He was right. It was Pasha's job. Only Pasha had the authority to impose peace between his director and his chief of staff. *My* job was to be loyal to my boss. And yet I had to be careful here too, because my boss could leave for another post any day, and then I would still have to deal with Cindy. I was beginning to understand Spooky's advice: *be your own man.*

Still, there was a problem with this approach: if I started acting on my own agenda rather than just serving the needs of the office, what was to stop me from becoming a turf warrior like the rest of them?

I called up my father for advice. I took great care to explain to him all the intricacies of the current office politics, but at one point, he interrupted me.

"Sounds to me like you need to make yourself some enemies," he said.

"What? How can you say something like that? The whole point here is I'm trying to do my job *without* making enemies!"

"You can't do that. Listen, it's good to have lofty goals. But if you just try to be nice to everybody, nobody's going to respect you. You'll never get anywhere like this."

My father made his point clear by recalling the advice that Talleyrand once gave to Napoleon. Talleyrand was France's top diplomat during the revolutionary wars. Napoleon was considering appointing a young man to a high post, and he asked Talleyrand for his advice. Talleyrand scoffed at Napoleon's choice. The problem was not so much with the candidate's youth. The problem, as Talleyrand put it, was that the man had "not even been capable of making a single enemy yet."

Somehow, that meant something to Napoleon, and the candidate didn't get the job.

"So go ahead," said my father. "Make your enemies. Get into people's faces. But for heaven's sake, do it for the right reasons!"

CHAPTER **16**

Cigars With Criminals

FEBRUARY 25, 1998

"We interrupt this program to bring you live to the United Nations, where Secretary General Kofi Annan is about to address his staff. . . ."

I had stood in the lobby just moments earlier, when Annan made his "triumphant" entrance, but I soon decided to jet up to the third floor to watch the scene on TV and to hear better what he had to say to us. We had received an e-mail earlier that morning urging us to drop whatever we were doing, leave our desks, and descend to the UN lobby. Annan was going to make an entrance shortly after 10:00 a.m., and his aides thought it would create the right message if we showered him with applause and cheers upon his arrival, the way ancient Romans did when Julius Caesar returned from a glorious military campaign.

It was to be Kofi Annan's moment of glory—one that would, as such moments often do, come back to bite him in the ass.

A few months had passed since our first visit to Iraq, and tensions had flared up again. The Clinton administration was once again threatening airstrikes in response to Saddam Hussein's refusal to let UN weapons inspectors into his palaces. Again, CNN began showing footage of F-15 fighters taking off from carriers in the Gulf, followed by images of Iraqi women walking into Saddam's palaces chanting, "We will die for you, Saddam!"

Russia and France were determined to prevent a confrontation. Both countries now had increasing stakes in the expansion of the UN Oil-for-Food operation. Hundreds of hefty contracts had been signed, and a clash easily could have sabotaged their execution. We had just authorized billions of dollars in new oil sales, with more than half of that business going to Russia and France.

Russia and the Arab League had already put forward compromise proposals, but both had been rejected by the United States. Annan would be their man of last resort. A high-profile mission to Baghdad by the world's top diplomat would surely throw a wrench in Washington's countdown to military action.

The United States was dead set against an eleventh-hour round of diplomacy. Tired of letting Saddam Hussein control the crisis agenda, the Clinton administration had hoped to seize the initiative from the Iraqi dictator and bring the crisis to a boil by the end of February. So when word reached the U.S. president that Annan was considering going to Baghdad, Bill Clinton picked up his phone and called the secretary general.

"Don't jam me!" Bill Clinton pleaded, according to a high-level administration official who recounted the phone call to the *New York Times*. But Annan was being pulled in a different direction by his aides, and this was a chance to reach for greatness. Marc Malloch Brown, one of his closest friends, even warned him about the dangers of becoming "a first-year U Thant." U Thant, a Malaysian, served as secretary general from 1961 to 1971; he was generally regarded as a kind but rather irrelevant character who remained "confined by the diplomatic salons of the East River." According to Malloch Brown, going to Iraq could be Annan's "first step out of the box."

Perhaps he had a point. But this crisis was about more than Annan's image. And even if his image was indeed the primary consideration, it was unclear how a trip to Baghdad at this moment would play in the long run. The decision to take center stage in the Iraq conflict would force the secretary general to mediate between Washington and Baghdad, which, aside from being a full-time job, was also a very risky undertaking. First, it risked pitting the UN secretary general against his host nation—a move that had caused his predecessor, Boutros-Ghali, to get sacked after the United States refused to renew his tenure for another term. Second, it meant trying to reach a reliable deal with Saddam Hussein. Others had tried this tactic before, with little success. Gen. Norman Schwarzkopf, who signed the 1991 cease-fire on behalf of the U.S.-led coalition, gives an account in his memoir, *It Doesn't Take a Hero*, of how he was snookered by Saddam. Schwarzkopf had as much leverage as any negotiator could wish for. The tent he was negotiating in, at the Safwan Airbase, was encircled by a dozen U.S. M1 Abrams tanks. Saddam had lost control of his army, and popular uprisings threatened his hold on both the north and south of the country. Yet before signing the cease-fire, Saddam's representative, Lt. Gen.

Sultan Hashim Ahmad, managed to extract one last concession from the American general. Stormin' Norman's account is edifying:

> "We have one point," [Ahmad] said. "You know the situation of our roads and bridges and communications." I nodded, thinking of the overwhelming damage our bombing had done. "We would like to fly helicopters to carry the officials of our government in areas where roads and bridges are out. This has nothing to do with the front line. This is inside Iraq."

Schwarzkopf agreed to the request, but as he recounted the scene in his memoir, he realized he had been hoodwinked:

> Then [Ahmad] said something that should have given me pause:
> "So you mean even helicopters that are armed can fly in Iraqi skies but not the [jet] fighters?"
> "Yeah, I will instruct the Air Force not to shoot down any helicopters flying over the territory of Iraq where our troops are not located."
> In the following weeks, we discovered what the son of a bitch really had in mind: using helicopter gun ships to suppress rebellions in Basra and other cities.

If Saddam could fool Stormin' Norman at a time of war, he could certainly fool the United Nations in peacetime. But what did Saddam have in mind *this* time? Looking narrowly at the weapons inspection game, it was difficult to surmise. But looking at the big picture, including the money his regime stood to make from an expanded Oil-for-Food program, it was evident that the Iraqi dictator had an interest in playing for time, an objective shared by his business partners on the UN Security Council. But what did Kofi Annan stand to gain by aligning himself with those interests? And more important, what did he stand to lose?

Annan, a widely respected figure whose talent as a diplomat was not in question, was at the height of his popularity. But his primary job was not to play world peacemaker. It was to manage UN operations. Offering his "good services" to mediate crises was optional, but the rule of thumb for such forays was to intervene in situations that were actually resolvable through mediation. In this case, the very idea of mediation was strongly opposed by Washington. And it was safe to assume that Saddam never would have invited Annan to visit Baghdad unless he felt such a visit would play to his advantage.

What, then, compelled Annan to go? If Saddam had something to say to the world, he was free to say it. The United States had made it extra clear that the only acceptable outcome would be unconditional cooperation. What difference would a face-to-face meeting make? Shashi Tharoor, Annan's communications adviser, liked to describe his boss as the political version of a yogi. A master of the art of diplomacy was called for. The diplomatically challenged nations of America and Britain simply didn't understand how to talk sense to Saddam. Kofi the Yogi would show them how it was done.

French President Jacques Chirac was elated at the news that Annan would go to Baghdad, and he immediately made his own presidential jet—France's version of Air Force One—available to the secretary general and his staff. With U.S. warships moving into position in the Persian Gulf, time was of the essence.

Having failed to rein in the secretary general, Bill Clinton let his secretary of state, Madeleine Albright, loose on him. As Annan prepared to leave for Baghdad, he was constantly hounded by angry phone calls from Albright, who worried that he was about to get duped by Saddam.

"She's very . . . demanding," Annan confided to an aide after Albright had raised her voice at him on the phone. "You're not going to Baghdad!" she allegedly yelled at the secretary general. But Annan decided to go nonetheless, in defiance of the woman who had sponsored his ascent to the top of the UN hierarchy.

And so, late in the afternoon on February 20, 1998, the secretary general landed at Baghdad airport and declared to the press that he had a "sacred duty" to perform this peace mission.

He was driven to a villa where he and his staff would stay for the remainder of the weekend. But Albright kept calling and insisting that he be woken up in the middle of the night. The world's peacemaker simply could not get a moment of peace from this one.

The next day, a working meeting was planned with Deputy Prime Minister Tariq Aziz to go over a possible deal that might allow UNSCOM inspectors into Saddam's palaces. Annan had only the thinnest margin for maneuver and zero support from Washington, which reserved a right to reject any deal he and Aziz came up with. Working one-on-one for several hours, pens in hand, on a document that would outline the conditions under which palace visits might take place, Annan and Aziz arrived at a text that was substantively no different from Washington's list of conditions, although it read more elegantly. Essentially, Saddam would allow inspectors to search his palaces, but the teams would need to be accompanied by a delegation of diplomats from other countries; in other words, the visits would be formal and the inspectors would not be allowed to run around Saddam's digs without supervision. Aziz submitted this text for review by Saddam.

Shortly before midday on Sunday, February 22, three black Mercedes sedans pulled into the driveway of the Baghdad villa in which Annan and his team had taken residence; Saddam's personal drivers were at the wheels. After several days in Iraq, Annan was finally permitted to see the Iraqi dictator in person.

Annan's spokesman, Ahmad Fawzi, asked one of the drivers where they were going to take the secretary general. Speaking to *New York Times* reporter James Traub shortly thereafter, Fawzi said of Saddam's driver, "He looked at me like I was a cockroach. I think that he wanted to take me out back and have me shot."

The secretary general of the United Nations had gone out on a limb to help Saddam Hussein. Now he was being whisked off by stone-faced drivers to meet with the Iraqi president, whose whereabouts were unknown. After a surprisingly short drive, the three cars entered Saddam's main presidential palace, located on the banks of the Tigris River. It was anyone's guess how Saddam slipped in and out of these palaces. Coalition troops would eventually discover an extensive network of tunnels leading in and out of his quarters. But with the secretary general in the building, the Iraqi president ran no risk of being hit with a Tomahawk cruise missile.

Kofi Annan had made the decision to meet with Saddam Hussein alone, without his aides. His rationale was to avoid a situation in which Saddam might be seen to lose face in front of his staff. It is of course doubtful whether Saddam would have gone through with this whole charade if he had not already made up his mind in favor of a compromise along the lines of the previously negotiated document with Tariq Aziz.

Back at their hotels, reporters were engaged in wild speculations. Shashi Tharoor was estimating the chances of a deal at 51–49. How he came up with those numbers was anyone's guess. Back in Washington, Albright was banging the table for a copy of the tentative agreement. At the Pentagon, images from spy satellites showed Saddam Hussein's palace from every angle, yet nobody was privy to the negotiations going on inside.

Kofi Annan and Saddam Hussein settled down across from each other, over two glasses of orange juice. After a few polite words were exchanged, Saddam offered Annan a nice Havana cigar from his personal stash. It remains unclear whether the secretary general then felt a "sacred duty" to accept this cigar, or whether he was just being polite, or whether he was, in fact, dying for a smoke.

After lighting up, the two men sat back and began exchanging compliments. Annan told Saddam that he was a leader of great scope and courage, a "builder" who had brought Iraq into the modern age.

The secretary general's description of Saddam Hussein's achievements in Iraq did not quite match what we had seen on the ground—the ruins of Kurdish villages that had been destroyed, then mined, then destroyed again during various genocidal campaigns. And though some of the Iraqi dictator's torture techniques were distinctively "modern," others were reminiscent of the Spanish Inquisition. Iraq had missed the modern age because of Saddam; the infrastructure that his people had built up had been destroyed after the Iraqi leader stubbornly refused to relinquish Kuwait in 1991. But Kofi Annan had not come to lecture the Iraqi dictator. He had come to strike a deal with him, to save him from himself. And with very little room to negotiate down from America's demands, Annan was perhaps not wrong to believe that a few compliments might improve Saddam Hussein's disposition.

Annan's pitch to Iraq's dictator was rather simple, in the end. He basically suggested that with everything Saddam had rebuilt since Desert Storm, it would be a pity if his country were to get bombed again. And incredibly, Saddam agreed with him.

Did Annan actually *sway* the Iraqi dictator? The team around Annan publicly described their boss as "the moral conscience of the world," but it is difficult to imagine that Saddam really cared one dime about morality at this stage in his life. In the end, Annan had nothing more to offer the Iraqi dictator than a chance to save face, as the prospect of a heavy bombing campaign loomed. And Saddam Hussein took it.

After he put out his cigar and wished his counterpart the best, the secretary general was whisked out by the same three black Mercedes sedans, and Saddam returned to whatever his hiding place was at the time.

Back at the UN-occupied villa, Annan informed his aides that he believed he had a deal. They could barely contain their joy. The weapons inspectors would be allowed into Saddam's palaces. Not that they would be a very logical place for Saddam to store germ warfare materials. (He had a notorious phobia of germs and sometimes wouldn't even allow small children to kiss him, for fear that their faces may have been smothered with a bio-agent meant to harm him.) But such considerations didn't matter at this stage. Even if there had been something to be found, Saddam would have had ample time to remove it before the inspectors arrived.

The secretary general described Saddam's manners as "very correct, very calm, almost serene." Coming from a yogi, this was quite a compliment for the man who could occasionally be seen shooting his gun into the air from his balcony. Before stepping into his plane in Baghdad, Annan felt it would be important to thank Saddam once again for accepting not to be bombed. "I would like to thank His Excellency President Saddam Hussein and the government of Iraq for the goodwill, cooperation, and courtesy extended to my delegation and myself during the last few days," Annan said. He added that Saddam's regime had been "demonized" by the international community.

Annan then flew back to Paris to give Jacques Chirac his jet back. The French president had ordered that a state dinner be prepared for the secretary general. At a toast that evening, Chirac got up and thanked Annan in front of all the guests for preventing a third world war. Chirac has been known to drink pretty heavily at state dinners, but still, *a world war*? All the Clinton administration had planned was a four-day bombing campaign to destroy suspected Iraqi military and industrial facilities and to try to land a bomb on Saddam's cranium, which was a bit difficult, since the only moment when they knew Saddam's location was when he was meeting with Annan.

Buoyed by his reception in Paris and news reports coming out of Washington saying that the Clinton administration would hold off on a strike to see if Saddam would keep his promise to Annan, the secretary general flew back to New York and made his hero's entrance into the building amid the applause of a staff that had been instructed to stand there by his own aides. As a member of the UN staff involved with Iraq, I had come down more out of curiosity than out of an irrepressible desire to cheer our leader. The lobby was packed, and cameras had been set up to catch the staged hero's entrance. Annan seemed surprised at the sight of all the staff, and perhaps he was. But one thing was clear. New Yorkers had not poured out to meet him at the airport or clap as his car entered the UN's driveway.

Word suddenly got around (nobody could see anything) that Annan was in the building. After shaking hands with some front-row enthusiasts and seeming to downplay the event as only he knew how to, Annan stopped to speak before the cameras. This was his moment of glory. Or as people inside the United Nations liked to put it, his "Hammarskjöld moment," in reference to the first secretary general of the United Nations, who, for lack of a more brilliant successor, remains venerated to this day.

Stepping up to the microphone, Kofi Annan announced that on his journey to Baghdad he had been surrounded by "the world's prayers." I suppose that was his way of sharing the credit for what he had achieved during his "sacred" mission. The UN weapons inspectors, who were clearly the most concerned by Annan's mission, had not even come down to greet him this morning.

Saddam Hussein, he told us, "is a man I can do business with."

Seven months after Kofi Annan had come back from his sacred mission to Baghdad, Saddam Hussein decided to tear up their agreement. Once again, UNSCOM inspectors were barred from doing their work. And again, the United States and Britain went back into countdown mode for military action, and Saddam forced his people back into his palaces to serve as human shields. The buildup to military action lasted from August to November 1998, by which point U.S.-led forces in the Persian Gulf had already received the order to proceed with a strike. They were fifty minutes away from hitting their targets when CNN suddenly announced that Iraq had sent a letter to Kofi Annan saying their deal was back on. The letter, dated November 14, 1998, and signed by Tariq Aziz, informed the secretary general that Saddam Hussein had decided to resume cooperation and allow UN weapons inspectors to "carry out their normal mission."

President Clinton decided to hold off on an airstrike once again. But U.S. forces remained ready to attack on short notice. The decision to use CNN as a diplomatic channel was critical for the Iraqis; if they had waited for their letter to be faxed and re-faxed through the normal channels (i.e., from Baghdad to the thirty-eighth floor of the United Nations, from there to the U.S. mission to the UN, then on to the State Department, and on to the White House), the news might have reached President Clinton a few minutes too late.

Clinton had decided to delay the operation until he had a chance to read the letter. Once he did, the White House was enraged to discover that it contained an annex detailing "conditions" Iraq wanted to impose on the inspections process. Specifically, Iraq insisted that the Security Council start lifting its sanctions as a quid pro quo. This was unacceptable to the White House. Sandy Berger, Clinton's national security adviser, soon made this clear to the media, and before diplomats had a chance to think up new peace initiatives, the airwaves flared up with rumors of an imminent strike. Watching CNN from Baghdad, the Iraqis realized they might be struck because of an annex, so they scrambled to send another letter to Kofi Annan, which they immediately provided to CNN as well, in case the fax machines on the thirty-eighth floor got stuck. Insofar as our role was to facilitate international communications, the UN had been supplanted by a news channel. Once the crisis moved into real time, our main purpose was to serve as a repository for official records.

In their second letter, the Iraqis specified that the annex (which was still attached) did not contain "conditions," merely "views and preferences" of the Iraqi regime. But the White House was in no mood to deal with Saddam Hussein's "views and preferences" at this stage. Saddam had banked that the Monica Lewinsky affair (which got far more coverage than he did on CNN) might interfere with Clinton's ability to act. But in fact it appeared to make Clinton all the more eager to seem "presidential." So Saddam was forced to order a third letter sent to CNN (and the UN) saying that his previous decision to cease cooperation with the weapons inspectors was "null and void." No annexes, no views and preferences, just a full capitulation.

Three days later, on November 17, eighty-six UNSCOM inspectors returned to Iraq. Our Bunny Huggers had watched them leave and come back, then leave again and come back again several times. The cook in the Canal Hotel compound in Baghdad was forced to calibrate his food purchases in relation to the news coming out of CNN, so that he would have enough supplies for lunch the next day, when the Cowboys barged back into the cafeteria and reoccupied their favorite seats.

This time, they would be back at work for less than a month before another crisis erupted. On November 22 the Iraqi government began denouncing "provocative" acts by UNSCOM inspectors, who tried to force their way into certain locations by driving around Iraqi roadblocks and kept leaking videotapes to the media showing Iraqi officials trying to block them. By December 15, UNSCOM reported to the UN Security Council that Iraq was refusing to cooperate with its inspectors, in effect calling Saddam's second promise to Kofi Annan a lie. On December 16, UNSCOM inspectors got back on their C-130 transport plane and headed out of town, which indicated quite clearly that, this time around, the Clinton administration had managed to seize the initiative and act on its own timetable. The submission of UNSCOM's official report to the Security Council had clearly been chosen ahead of time as the spark that would ignite hostilities. Except nobody had bothered to tell *us*.

We were hours away from a military strike. And yet no plan had been made to evacuate our Bunny Huggers—hundreds of humanitarian staff were left behind in Baghdad. I received dozens of calls an hour from panicked staff asking me what they were supposed to do with themselves. My instruction was to tell them to "stay put for now."

"But what's the plan? How are we going to get out of here?"

While Kofi Annan had been playing Peace Messiah, the command structure of the UN's Oil-for-Food operation had collapsed. Denis Halliday had resigned on October 31, more than a month before this crisis, in protest over the sanctions. He left the mission in the hands of his deputy, Farid Zarif, a former minister in the Soviet occupation government in Afghanistan. The man had been forced to flee his country to save his life after the Soviet withdrawal of 1989.

According to the rule whereby "the assistant of your enemy is your friend," Pasha had immediately taken Zarif under his wing. Together, they might have been able to organize an evacuation. But Annan was under pressure to appoint a new head of mission in Iraq, and between two peace initiatives, he chose a German national named Hans von Sponeck, to whom Pasha took an instant dislike.

Pasha soon found reason to be suspicious of his new Number Two. I believe it was a fax in which von Sponeck had copied Iqbal Riza, Kofi Annan's chief of staff, that got the two off on the wrong foot. The contents of the fax were not the problem. The cc sparked Pasha's ire. Why did his Number Two need to copy the thirty-eighth floor? In Pasha's view, only he should have had the privilege of communicating to higher-ups, and the slight to his authority would not be tolerated.

In retaliation, Pasha did a number of things to screw with von Sponeck. First, he allowed Cindy to interfere with von Sponeck's recruitment efforts. Second, he undermined him politically by refusing to let him brief the UN Security Council.

After that, Pasha and von Sponeck no longer spoke to each other. The memos got colder, and each of them got in the habit of sending copies of their communications to Riza, who was starting to get seriously amused. Once again, the thirty-eighth floor did not intervene. And it took the prospect of an all-out military conflict to get von Sponeck to pick up the phone and dial Pasha's number. Pasha was the UN's security coordinator, and von Sponeck could not evacuate his staff from Iraq without his permission.

"*Now* he comes calling again, huh?" Pasha said, when his secretary announced von Sponeck on the line.

Pasha told his secretary to tell von Sponeck he was in a meeting. Von Sponeck would need to call back. This, as a U.S. strike on Baghdad was imminent.

"Don't you guys understand?" a weapons inspector asked me. "This time, it's for real! What are your Bunny Huggers still doing in Baghdad?"

It was unclear how our staff would get out of the country, because unlike the arms inspectors, we no longer had a plane. Saddam Hussein had decided that the staff of the Oil-for-Food operation should no longer be allowed to fly in and out of the country. The Bunny Huggers would have to drive. Although it was illegal for Saddam to impose such a restriction on us, the UN ended up complying without protest. Had von Sponeck and Pasha been on speaking terms, they might have been able to do something about this. But their mutual dislike clearly took priority over the mission, and so the only way our staff could be evacuated was by bus.

The night von Sponeck called to request permission to evacuate, Pasha turned him down. Though he had the authority as UN security coordinator to order the staff to safety, Pasha told von Sponeck that he wanted to consult with Annan first. But Annan was still trying to "exhaust all diplomatic options" to avoid a war, so he was too busy to deal with Pasha and von Sponeck's dispute.

By the night of December 16, 1998, no decision had been made on whether or how to evacuate our Bunny Huggers. We had missed the window of opportunity and could not afford to send our guys on the road without knowing when a strike would commence. I was on the phone with my friend Habibi, who was calling from Baghdad to ask me what the hell was going on, when I heard the first explosions. Some time later (could be minutes, could be hours, our panic skewed our sense of time), CNN brought us live to the White House, where President Clinton was sitting at his desk, on the eve of the impeachment vote in Congress over the Monica Lewinsky affair, to address the American people:

> Good evening. Earlier today, I ordered America's armed forces to strike military and security targets in Iraq. They are joined by British forces. Their mission is to attack Iraq's nuclear, chemical, and biological weapons programs and its military capacity to threaten its neighbors. Their purpose is to protect the national interest of the United States, and indeed the interests of people throughout the Middle East and around the world. Saddam Hussein must not be allowed to threaten his neighbors or the world with nuclear arms, poison gas or biological weapons.

British Prime Minister Tony Blair read out a similar announcement, standing next to a Christmas tree that had just been put up at 10 Downing Street. Neither of them mentioned the fact that hundreds of humanitarian workers had been left behind in Baghdad. Neither they nor Kofi Annan had focused much attention on the Oil-for-Food operation during the past year of the crisis. And yet the massive growth of our program, combined with our increasingly dysfunctional management, may well have played a critical role in Saddam Hussein's decision to trade off the arms inspections for a period of bombing. All year, Saddam had been testing the international community's resolve, studying the impact of his provocations right up to the brink of a showdown. On all three occasions when an acute crisis threatened to escalate, Saddam had observed that the prospect of military action had no impact on the continued expansion of the Oil-for-Food program. If anything, the crises curtailed our ability to oversee the flow of goods into Iraq or track what Saddam did with them once they came in.

Our inability to coordinate so much as a timely evacuation in the midst of a crisis should have served as a warning sign that we simply were not up to the task that had been assigned to us. While the disputes that kept erupting between our leaders may have seemed petty, they were heavy in consequences.

In the middle of the bombing, von Sponeck called once again, to ask Pasha for permission to evacuate the next day. It was feasible because the United States was not in the habit of bombing Iraq during the day, as darkness offered better protection to U.S. pilots. But organizing such a caravan required a swift decision from the UN in New York and reliable communication with the Pentagon to ensure that our convoy of buses was not targeted by mistake. As things stood, we didn't even have reliable communication between Pasha and von Sponeck, much less a line to the Pentagon. And the thirty-eighth floor had yet to make a decision on whether to evacuate our staff.

When Pasha informed von Sponeck that he was still "waiting for a decision from the thirty-eighth floor," von Sponeck went ape shit on the phone. His staff were scared, all huddled inside the basement of the Canal Hotel, and there was no plan to get them out of there. We had no idea how long the bombing would last, and we understood that even the smartest missile technology was not error-proof. A U.S. missile once slammed into a World Food Program warehouse north of Baghdad. And no matter how advanced a bomb's guidance system, human errors could always seep in at the planning stage, as we later learned when a U.S. plane dropped a bomb on the Chinese Embassy in Belgrade.

The journalists staying at the Al-Rasheed Hotel in downtown Baghdad had all volunteered to be in Baghdad in the middle of a bombing. Our staff had never expressed a particular interest in witnessing such fireworks firsthand. They served absolutely no purpose on the ground while bombs were raining down. But the thirty-eighth floor worried that withdrawing them might "send the wrong signal" to Baghdad. The idea was that the humanitarian operation should under no circumstances be affected by developments on the weapons front, and our staff were now hostages to that idea.

Pasha's reaction to von Sponeck's outburst was to hang up, slamming his secure phone down in its box. I was standing at Pasha's doorstep when it happened. My jaw dropped. I had come to support von Sponeck's case for an evacuation at the earliest possible time, and all I could do now was stand there, wide-eyed, as Pasha justified his latest move as UN security coordinator.

"Who does he think he is?" asked Pasha. "Nobody talks to me this way!" With that, Pasha walked out of his office for a trip to the bathroom. I stayed behind for a minute, transfixed by the bombing footage running on CNN. I sat down on the couch and put my face in my hands, trying to think clearly. There was only one logical course of action. A communications link needed to be reestablished between New York and Baghdad.

I ran over to my desk and rang up Habibi, who had been Halliday's assistant and now served under von Sponeck. My first order of business was to clarify what had just happened. Had Pasha really hung up on von Sponeck?

Yes, that certainly seemed to be Habibi's perception. I could hear von Sponeck shouting in the background, and Habibi sounded unsure if he was at liberty to speak.

"Habibi," I said, "does this mean you and I are the only line between New York and Baghdad at the present time?"

"I guess so," said my fellow twenty-five-year-old coworker.

"Shit . . . so what's going to happen now? How will you guys evacuate if they don't talk?"

"No idea. Hans says he's only going to deal directly with the thirty-eighth from now on. I guess at some point we'll just get on the buses and go," said Habibi.

"We should at least put out a press release . . . or something," I said.

The fireworks in the background started getting loud again.

"Listen, I've gotta go," said Habibi. "I'm being ordered down to the basement."

"Yeah. Dude, take care of yourself. . . . Try to get some sleep."

Ba-boom! That was a bomb in the background.

"Are you fucking kidding me?"

"Sorry. . . . Good luck, man. I'll be here if you need to call . . . pass a message or whatever . . ."

"Yeah, well, the message is pretty simple: we'd like to get *out of here!*"

Von Sponeck eventually managed to evacuate his staff from Iraq in a chaotic caravan of buses in which luggage was lost and disputes that nearly degenerated into fistfights, erupted between smoking and nonsmoking staff members. The caravan took to the road right before the end of the four-day U.S. bombing campaign. By the time the buses reached the Jordanian border, Operation Desert Fox was all but over.

Both sides in the conflict declared victory. The United States argued that it had "achieved its objectives," even as Gen. Anthony Zinni kept skirting questions from the media as to what exactly had been hit in Iraq by repeating about a dozen times in the course of one press conference that "battle damage assessment is still ongoing."

Whether any WMDs were actually destroyed was unclear. But those of us who would have to set foot back into Iraq soon thereafter worried about the aftereffects if an actual chemical or biological stockpile had been hit. Wouldn't that endanger the people in the surrounding area? I asked one of the UNSCOM guys. He thought about it and said, "Yeah, I guess there's a chance of that."

The reason I was asking was that a building standing only a few dozen yards from our headquarters had been gutted in a massive explosion that caused windows in our own compound to shatter.

"Oh, don't worry. That's their intelligence building. We don't think they'd stockpile that kind of stuff at their own workplace."

I guess that took some of the wind out of the whole "we need to get into Saddam's palaces" argument, which had been at the center of the many crises that kept interrupting our work for the past year and led Annan to undertake the most high-profile and, ultimately, unsuccessful peace mission of his career. At the onset of Operation Desert Fox, Annan made a somber declaration: "This is a sad day for the United Nations and the world." And then he added, "It is also a very sad day for me, personally."

A colleague wrote a poem for the occasion:

> *Happy in February, sad in December.*
> *Glory has slipped through our boss's fingers.*
> *Smoking cigars, avoiding wars, Kofi tried to reach for the stars.*
> *But all he got, at the end of his trot, was a finger where he would rather not.*
> *Wham, bam, thank you ma'am, that's how business goes with Saddam. . . .*

The rest of the poem got rather dirty. Not that our business with Saddam got any cleaner. Now that he had gotten rid of his greatest headache, or UNSCUM, as our Bunny Huggers called the UN Special Commission, the Iraqi dictator would be able to concentrate his energy on subverting our own mission—or UNSCAM, as the Cowboys would later refer to us. All Saddam had to do was press the right buttons, and a program that was earning him millions in pocket money would soon start earning him billions.

The bombing campaign did not appear to have achieved anything. And while the inspectors were out, the Oil-for-Food program would continue to operate as soon as our staff could get back to their desks. As 1998 drew to a close, Saddam Hussein could be proud of himself. Though President Clinton had signed into law the Iraq Liberation Act, making "regime change" the official policy of the United States, chances were that nothing short of an all-out invasion could destabilize Saddam's hold on power. While Iraq's rebels were promised some $90 million in aid from the U.S. Congress, Saddam could rely on his smuggling and joint venture with the UN to fill Iraq's coffers. The mere fact that he had survived another U.S. strike made him appear all the more invincible to his regional neighbors, who once again began referring to him publicly with a reverence that had been unheard of since the Gulf War. The Arab League and several members of the UN Security Council condemned the Clinton and Blair governments for attacking Iraq. Soon Saddam would be able to throw giant parties again in Baghdad and organize trade fairs that would attract twelve foreign trade ministers and some 18,000 businesspeople from forty-five different countries.

If anybody could claim to be the "desert fox," it was clearly Saddam Hussein.

The UN lobby was deserted on New Year's Eve. Pasha and I were about the last people to leave the building, walking across the dimly lit checkered floor and pausing at the glass doors to zip up before stepping out into the cold. We would be heading to separate parties, and I chose the moment to wish my boss a happy New Year.

"Yeah," he said. "You too."

"So I guess we'll still have a job on the first of January," I added.

Our contracts were subject to renewal every six months, like the Oil-for-Food program itself.

"As long as Saddam is in power," said Pasha, "we'll be working."

We shared an awkward smile. The realization that our job security was dependent on Saddam Hussein staying in power was both comforting and deeply uncomfortable.

I thought about this as we stepped out into the frosty winter night. We split ways at the water fountain nestled at the center of the circular driveway, and I exited the UN grounds near Forty-Second Street to catch a taxi to a fancy restaurant. I had recently been promoted and had purchased a couple of brand-name suits that Pasha approved of. Checks kept filling my bank account every month, earning me as much as staff fifteen years my elder. I denied myself nothing. I was twenty-five, my career was going brilliantly, and I was headed to a great party. So why did I feel like shit?

A yellow cab stopped at the curb. I stepped in, told the driver the address, and took my badge off my neck.

"So," said the cab driver. "You work for Kofi Annan?"

"Yeah," I said. But from the depth of my discomfort a question arose. Weren't we, in fact, working for Saddam?

CHAPTER 17

The Propaganda War

"Hypocrisy is a fashionable vice, and all fashionable vices pass for virtue."

MOLIÈRE

"**U**m . . ." said my intern, popping her head into my office and sounding more worried than usual.

"Yes?" I said, as I continued to type away at my computer.

"There's a priest here to see you," she said.

"A *priest*?"

"Yeah. I mean, he's dressed as a priest. And it's not Halloween, so. . . ."

"What does he want?"

"I think he wants you to lift the sanctions or something."

"Oh. Well, send him in."

It had recently occurred to Pasha that we needed some kind of spokesman for the program, and since recruiting one would take several months, he had appointed me to the task. This meant constant interruptions from journalists, academics, businessmen, and various sorts of activists. So why not a priest?

A few seconds later, a man with a long black gown and a thick gold pendant took a seat across from my desk. He turned down my offer of a coffee with a wise wave of the hand. The devoted smile on his face was not necessarily friendly. And his black, deep-set eyes had a shine that scared me a little bit.

"How can I help you?" I asked.

"It is not I who needs help," said the priest. "It is the children of Iraq."

"Right. . . . Of course."

The priest had come prepared with explicit photographs of children lying wounded in hospitals and a stack of literature detailing horror stories "caused by the sanctions."

"Do you realize what is happening down there?" asked the priest.

"I have some idea, yes."

"The sanctions are killing children, infants, old women. . . . Do you people have no heart?"

"We are working to make things better," I said, adding that we had just massively increased the amount of humanitarian goods that could flow into the country. But the priest just shook his head. He took me through some of the pamphlets he had brought with him and encouraged me to view a videotape a group of activists had shot while on a visit to Iraq.

"Your so-called humanitarian program is just a tool to perpetuate the sanctions," he said. In his view, children would continue to die needlessly until the sanctions on Saddam Hussein were lifted altogether. And until then, UN employees like myself would have the children's deaths "on their conscience."

"I'm sorry," I said. "But it's not in my power to lift the sanctions. I appreciate you coming here and sharing these documents with me. But if you want to lobby for lifting the sanctions, you need to speak to the U.S. or the U.K. . . ."

The priest shook his head for a moment longer, then said, "I will pray for your soul."

"That's all right," I said. "You can save your prayers for the Iraqi children. I'm sure they need them more than I do."

"I will pray for you nonetheless."

He rose, and I stood up to escort him out. As we walked to the elevators, we ran into Spooky in the corridor. Spooky was a devout Anglican, whose first act upon moving to New York had been to set up a shelter for homeless people at his local church. So I thought I'd introduce him to the Catholic priest, to see if two men of deep faith might come to some agreement regarding the dilemma that was facing our collective conscience. But it turned out the two had already met and did not wish to speak to each other again. This was made evident, despite their forced politeness, by the spark of static electricity that hit them both when they came in physical contact.

Dzit!

They both jolted; then, realizing nothing grave had happened, tried to regain composure. We had recently gotten new carpets, and there was static everywhere. Our office had become rather stylish, and we were now proud to receive visitors from the outside world. The iron desks were gone. The secretaries had comfortable booths with blue partition walls, and the electrical wires were tucked safely into discreet rubber conduits that spanned the entire office. The UN, which was normally strapped for cash, had gone on an interior design extravaganza using Iraqi oil money. Since the expansion of the program, we had become the richest operation at the United Nations. We were authorized to spend 2.2 percent of Iraq's oil proceeds, which added up to a total of $1 billion over the course of the program. That was as much as the accumulated dues the United States refused to pay during the Jesse Helms years. In addition, we spent 13 percent of Iraq's revenues through the UN agencies that were responsible for buying goods for Iraqi Kurdistan. This would come to $6 billion ($2 billion more than the entire sum pledged by world nations to provide relief for Asian countries devastated by the tsunami of 2004).

No country on earth had ever paid as high a share of its national wealth to the UN budget as Iraq was doing, and it was far more than we could reasonably spend. So even with all the renovations, there was usually money left over at the end of every budget cycle (as an acting spokesperson, I was quick to point out that the UN poured any leftover funds back into the humanitarian accounts).

After sending the priest off to lobby the U.S. Embassy, I joined Spooky in his office for a cigarette. I resented having a cleric come into my office and accuse me of being a baby killer when all I was doing all day long was trying to help make a humanitarian program work.

"It's getting worse," said Spooky, handing me an article. "Denis Halliday is now going on a tour."

"A *tour*?"

"He's speaking all around England and in colleges in the United States. He's accusing the United Nations of committing genocide in Iraq."

"You're kidding."

After resigning in a hail of glory, Halliday was spending his retirement as an anti-sanctions activist. I had to respect his decision. The guy stood up for his beliefs. But it didn't feel so great to be accused of participating in a genocide. I hadn't joined the UN to commit murder.

During the years when the sanctions had done the most damage to Iraq's civilians (1991 to 1997), few groups had raised their voice to protest what was going on. Ironically, now that the UN was doing something about the situation, anti-sanctions groups were sprouting up all over the world. They ranged from honest, well-meaning, and well-informed organizations such as the Cambridge University student group CASI (Campaign Against Sanctions in Iraq) to far more extreme groups that didn't seem even mildly concerned by Saddam Hussein's massive crimes against his people and that were bent on portraying us as assassins.

The priest who had visited me was associated with a group called Voices in the Wilderness, which staged vivid demonstrations around the world insisting that Saddam should be free to import whatever he wanted. They saw this as the only solution to Iraq's humanitarian crisis. The fact that Saddam did not want to spend as much money on food and medicine as we had recommended did not temper these activists' zeal.

"There's something I don't get, Trevor. The more money flows into this program, the more activist groups sprout up. It's not logical!"

"Of course it's logical," said Spooky.

"How so?"

"Just follow the money. . . ." Spooky liked to let his most intriguing statements hang in the air and watch me try to make sense of them. "Look at who funds them," he finally added.

Well, I didn't have time to do that. I had Reuters calling me about the price of crude oil for next month, a briefing note for Kofi Annan to write up, a weekly press release to send out, and my director's office to manage. Besides, the anti-sanctions activists were not exactly listing the sources of their funding on their websites. Some of them surely had legitimate sources of funding. But how much "grassroots" support money could be raised for this cause by throwing keg parties at campuses? Some groups managed to travel all over the Middle East, put up elaborate websites, and produce a range of documentaries and other media materials. Where was this money coming from?

Years later, it would take sixty international investigators nineteen months to unravel the extensive network of support groups Saddam Hussein was able to set up around the world, using the very same resources we were trying to make available to the Iraqi people.

The story of one priest, Father Jean-Marie Benjamin, certainly shed some light on the question that was preoccupying me that morning. From 1991 to 1994, Father Benjamin worked as an assistant to the Vatican state secretary, Cardinal Agostino Casaroli. In 1997, just as the Oil-for-Food program was getting started, Father Benjamin began to campaign against the sanctions. During his visit to Iraq in 1998, he became friendly with Deputy Prime Minister Tariq Aziz, the sole Christian member of Saddam's cabinet. (Deputy prime minister was a somewhat misleading title for the man whose principal task was to lead Iraq's propaganda war effort.) At the time, Father Benjamin was producing a documentary called *Iraq: The Birth of Time*, which would probably have become a box-office smash hit had the birth of time been traced to 1932, the year a piece of Mesopotamia was carved out of the Ottoman Empire and slapped with the name Iraq.

In 1999, Father Benjamin founded the Benjamin Committee for Iraq. Political campaigning was rather new for a man who had spent most of his extracurricular activities to date composing music and writing lyrical books. Father Benjamin was also a performer, playing the piano, the guitar, and on occasion the electronic keyboards, making spectacular, though brief, forays into the glam world of religious disco.

In April 2000, the flamboyant Father Benjamin decided to risk his life for the Iraqi people by becoming a passenger on an unauthorized (but highly publicized) flight from Rome to Baghdad that purposefully defied the UN embargo. Anti-sanctions activists were multiplying these kinds of publicity stunts even though Iraqi ministers complained in private that they didn't quite know what to do with much of the random supplies these activists brought with them to "save Iraqi lives," since they didn't fit into the normal distribution chain and, again, because Iraq was already receiving more humanitarian goods than Saddam cared to spend money on. In some cases, highly publicized humanitarian flights came in with expired medicine.

But the do-gooders were quite impressed with themselves nonetheless. In 2001 Tariq Aziz expressed his appreciation for Father Benjamin's "prodigious efforts to establish the principles of justice and right." Benjamin even made a public declaration that he had "the Pope's blessing" for going on this trip to Iraq. Did he *really*? One thing is certain. No man of morals would have blessed what happened next.

Meet Alain Bionda, a businessman representing companies seeking to break into the Iraqi crude oil market. After trying several times to approach the Iraqi oil minister to get a contract, Bionda was informed that in order to do business with Iraq, he had to find a man who would introduce him to Tariq Aziz. Bionda looked and looked but found nobody who could make the introduction. But then one night, an Iraqi friend of Bionda's (who requested anonymity when he later testified to investigators) had an idea. He told Bionda that he had once met a priest named Father Benjamin, who in turn had met with Aziz several times and seemed, well, friendly to the government.

At that point, Bionda could have asked his friend, "What are the chances that a priest would intervene on behalf of an oil trader like myself?" But he didn't. Something told him that his luck was about to turn with Father Benjamin, and so he asked his anonymous friend to arrange for a meeting with the ordained priest.

It wouldn't be long before the two men concocted a plan to make some cash off the Oil-for-Food program. Father Benjamin thought that the most proper way to proceed would be to involve Pope Jean Paul II himself in their scheme. In 2001 Father Benjamin asked Bionda to deliver a letter from the Pope to Aziz, the idea being that if Bionda came highly recommended, with a letter from the Pope, Aziz might be impressed. One has to hope that Pope Jean Paul II didn't actually write this letter himself, or at least that he did not know what use Father Benjamin and his new business partner would have for it. Either way, Bionda felt anxious going to Iraq alone with a letter from the Pope. After all, he was an oil trader, not a courier for the Vatican. So he asked Father Benjamin to accompany him to see Aziz. The priest would hand over the letter from the Pope, and, as the investigation later revealed, Bionda would "solicit Mr. Aziz for an oil allocation." All in one fell swoop.

When this odd couple appeared before Tariq Aziz in 2001, with their letter from the Pope and their demand for underpriced Iraqi oil, they tried as best they could *not* to make it look as if they had any business relationship with each other. So when it came time for Bionda to request an oil allocation, Father Benjamin might well have been examining his nails.

Aziz's eyes had a certain Garfield quality to them, especially when he became suspicious of his interlocutors. They'd slide back and forth under half-closed eyelids even as he remained politely silent. Did these jokers think he was born yesterday? Clearly, as far as Aziz was concerned, the two men were in business, and that was how the transaction would be recorded in Iraq's Oil Ministry records.

Following the meeting among Aziz, Bionda, and Father Benjamin, an allocation of two million barrels of oil was granted in Father Benjamin's name and sold to Bionda. Years later, in 2005, Father Benjamin and Bionda would both vehemently deny to investigators that the priest expected anything in return for facilitating this transaction. But investigators found that after he cashed in on his Iraqi oil deal, Bionda transferred $140,000 to Father Benjamin's account at UBS Geneva on December 27, 2001. In defending his action, Bionda explained that he felt a "moral obligation" to pay the priest for his help. The same day, Father Benjamin transferred $90,000 to another account he held at the Vatican Bank; and from that account, he withdrew $20,150 in cash.

I wonder how Father Benjamin felt about himself as he walked around the streets of Rome with twenty grand in his pockets. His cash had been ripped off the humanitarian program illegally, and he understood this. His total commission of $140,000 could buy a lot of Tylenol for Iraq's ailing inpatients. And maybe, just maybe, such a thought eventually occurred to him, because further evidence shows that he may actually have felt some remorse. In January 2002, when he was offered an additional oil allocation to support "his activities in favor of the Iraqi population," Father Benjamin told Aziz, both in person and by letter, that he could not accept any more oil. Investigators found that Oil Ministry records confirmed this new pious stance. Further allocations were made to Father Benjamin for 5.5 million barrels, but the priest never made use of them. His friend Bionda, however, continued his lucrative trade right up to the start of the Iraq War in 2003, graciously accepting the allocation that had been given to Father Benjamin. And no evidence emerged that he continued to feel a "moral obligation" to pay his holy friend further commissions.

After the invasion of Iraq, Father Benjamin sent an "open letter" to his friend Tariq Aziz, who now sat in jail in Baghdad. In his letter (which is very long but very entertaining, and is available at Father Benjamin's website at www.benjaminforiraq.org), the priest recalled "a time when everyone wanted to see" the talented Mr. Aziz.

> From all over the world, politicians, figures from the worlds of science, of culture, of the arts and of the media, leaders of political parties, of associations and others wanted to see you. [Oddly, he doesn't mention oil traders.] Since your arrest, many of them have not spoken a word to defend you, but there remain many others who are ready to do so. The witnesses for your defense will not only be lawyers, but also high-ranking political figures, even several Ministers currently in power, ambassadors, Nobel prize winners, artists, doctors, men of religion, Catholic, Protestant, Muslim and of other faiths, as well as writers and journalists.

Aziz could read the priest's plea between the lines of purple prose: *please don't rat us out, and we'll come to your aid!* But Aziz would talk to investigators, all right. And talk. And talk. And all the influential people Father Benjamin was referring to in his letter would be unable to come to his aid, because they would come under investigation themselves.

Not everyone investigated was guilty, for example, in the late 1990s, George Galloway became an outspoken critic of the sanctions in the British Parliament. But he did more than just follow a fashionable trend. He actually decided to help one very cute little Iraqi child. In 1998 Galloway became chairman of the Mariam Appeal, an organization established with the honorable intention of providing medical treatment to Mariam Hamza, a four-year-old girl who suffered from leukemia, just like the girl we had met at the Baghdad hospital who ended up dying on Christmas Day.

Galloway's organization helped little Mariam by financing a trip for her to a London Hospital, where she received treatment that was unavailable in Iraq. But her treatment cost just a fraction of the money that was raised. The Mariam Appeal used the rest of the money for a much broader political campaign against the sanctions in Iraq. It funded a fancy ten-country bus tour on a London double-decker, which Galloway used as a pro-Iraq publicity stunt. A film was made of this epic voyage. Here's a flier invitation to the film's opening night:

LAUNCH OF THE MARIAM APPEAL BIG BEN TO BAGHDAD BUS FILM
16 NOVEMBER 2000

The Arab Club of Britain is hosting the premiere showing of
the Mariam Appeal film "Big Ben to Baghdad":
the epic journey through three continents, ten countries and 15,000 miles
from London to Baghdad in an antique double-decker London Routemaster bus.

The film will be shown at the Brunei Theatre at the School of Oriental and
African Studies (SOAS), Thornhaugh Street, Russell Square, London WC1 at
6.30 p.m. on Thursday, 16th November, 2000.

Admission free but donations are welcome

FOLLOWING THE PREMIERE, VHS COPIES OF THE 60-MINUTE FILM
WILL BE AVAILABLE AT THE SPECIAL PRICE OF £9.99!!

In all, Galloway's foundation received more than £1 million in donations. One of the contributors, Fawaz Zureikat, a Jordanian businessman, was found by investigators to have funneled money to the Appeal through a complex network of middlemen who profited illegally from Iraq's oil sales.

According to investigators, Zureikat got four oil allocations from Saddam and subsequently deposited £448,000 into the Mariam Appeal foundation. Zureikat was also found to have paid kickbacks into Saddam's bank account in Jordan.

Galloway described the evidence that linked him to Zureikat's oil transactions as fabrications—a "cock and bull story," he wrote in an e-mail to the independent inquiry that investigated his deeds. "I had nothing to do with any oil deals of Mr. Zureikat or anyone else," he said.

Oh, well. At least a little girl got treatment. But how many more kids might have been assisted with the money that was kicked back to Saddam?

Denis Halliday's resignation gave a jolt to the groups lobbying for a lifting of the sanctions. Suddenly, they felt they could achieve their goal. In reality, anti-sanctions activists stood zero chance of lifting the sanctions—which, by then, only really applied to military or "dual-use" hardware. Saddam clearly knew this. So long as he was in power, there would be no circumstance under which the sanctions could be fully lifted. But his propaganda war kept pressure on the United Nations and swayed a lot of honorable people to his cause. People like Denis Halliday were not corrupt. And hundreds of young activists who took time out of their schedules to demonstrate against us were not corrupt either. But ultimately, it came down to this: allowing Saddam Hussein to import new tanks was *not* the way to save Iraqi children.

Saddam's corruption-fueled propaganda machine did manage something important for the Iraqi regime. It put UN workers like me on the defensive. Instead of keeping an eye on Saddam's financial transactions, we spent our time trying to defend ourselves against the charge that we were "committing genocide in Iraq."

Nobody at the United Nations dared to challenge Halliday's statement that the United Nations, and specifically the United States, could "be blamed for crimes against humanity, including possibly genocide." His resignation was not effective immediately. He took the time to do a few victory laps with his friends in the Iraqi regime before leaving the country. The thirty-eighth floor watched Halliday tear away at the UN's reputation without saying a word.

Back when Halliday was on payroll, Pasha had tried to call him back to order, but Halliday treated Pasha's faxes the same way Pasha had treated Halliday's no-smoking signs. Then, on the day that his resignation (finally) took effect, Halliday received a flowery letter from Kofi Annan thanking him for his distinguished service to the United Nations and promising to ask for his assistance again in the future.

This left those among us who had *not* resigned a bit confused as to the nature of our mission. Were we supposed to resign, too? Or were we supposed to carry on with our "genocidal" program?

Annan chickened out when it came to defending our mission in public. And Pasha couldn't articulate his words well enough to get on the air. I figured that before we could have a coherent public relations strategy, we needed to be clear, inside the UN, on where we stood. Either we were doing the right thing or we were doing the wrong thing and should all resign.

The appointment of Hans von Sponeck to replace Halliday had initially given me hope that we might, at a minimum, stop feeding Saddam's propaganda effort against us. Von Sponeck came across as a disciplinarian. Our mission had to be restructured to monitor an increasing flow of oil and goods into Iraq. But the four-day war of 1998, and Pasha's failure to get von Sponeck and his staff out of Baghdad in time, had left the operation deeply divided, once again. At the working level, employees from New York and Baghdad could sometimes manage to collaborate. But such teamwork had to occur under the radar.

Soon after Operation Desert Fox, during which Pasha hung up on von Sponeck, it became clear that the German would probably resign on the Cypriot. What I did not expect from von Sponeck was that he intended to go the same way as Halliday and accuse the UN of conducting a "criminal" policy in Iraq. The resignation of yet another high-level UN official, on February 14, 2000, would completely paralyze our operation once again. Hans von Sponeck announced his decision to resign several months before it would take effect, which essentially meant he remained in a position of management and authority even after his resignation "in protest" over the sanctions had been announced.

Normally, when someone resigns from his post in a foreign ministry, his resignation takes effect immediately, or within a few weeks at most. He does not remain on payroll for several months and use his position to undermine the entire mission while completely desisting from doing his job. Instead of allowing von Sponeck to stay at his post once his intention to resign had been blasted all over the media, Annan should have accepted his resignation, "effective immediately," and replaced him with someone who was interested in managing the thousands of staff we had in Iraq and New York. Instead of taking action, the team around Annan looked on passively as the largest operation under his watch was coming apart at the seams.

At one stage, Pasha managed to recruit a competent spokesperson. John Mills was a former reporter for Australian television and radio, a real newsman, a writer, and a storyteller, who had successfully reconverted his career as a much-sought-after UN spokesperson. John had a beautiful wife who worked for UNICEF, great kids, and a healthy life outside the office—proof, which I sorely needed, that one could pursue an interesting UN career without completely losing one's mind.

Mills arrived at the office like a breath of fresh air. He had all sorts of plans to improve our image. He immediately set out to design a website and a series of media statements that aimed to counter Saddam Hussein's anti-UN propaganda. He made contact with every member of the UN press corps and went for briefings with every senior manager in the office before finally ending up at my doorstep, slightly off balance, asking me if I had time for lunch.

Pasha was refusing to sign the op-ed piece Mills had written for him, people were refusing to feed him information for his website, and the UN field mission in Baghdad had begun calling him a spy.

"Welcome on board," I said.

We sat down at the cafeteria, and I drew him a map of the conflicts (ideological, bureaucratic, and personal) that permeated the operation.

"Shit, where have I landed?" Mills asked, suddenly all depressed.

We were back at square one. In the many months it took Hans von Sponeck to resign, Mills became very ill. He had passed out one day after lunch and had not been seen in the office since. I was not told what ailed him, but I realized it was serious when I was suddenly asked by Pasha to once again serve as the "acting spokesman" for the program.

This time, I had some actual training for the job. Working with John Mills had sharpened my pen, and though we never got to publish much of what we produced, at least we had material available when journalists came knocking on our door. I courted Barbara Crossette of the *New York Times* with graphics and data that showed the various improvements the Oil-for-Food program had brought about, but ultimately she didn't run it. The story lacked that most essential ingredient that makes anything worth publishing: conflict. Unless we actually attacked Halliday or von Sponeck directly, and stirred up the debate that way, the newspeople weren't interested.

Why didn't we? I put the question to Pasha one night. "Why don't you give an interview to CNN and attack von Sponeck? Call him a spokesman for Saddam!" Pasha said it would only make the controversy worse.

"If you want to last in this business," he told me, "you have to fly under the radar."

And unlike Halliday or von Sponeck, who opted to take early retirement and become freewheeling public figures, Pasha intended to last. He didn't want to make waves. Going up against von Sponeck would make him un-popular with France and Russia. And he would wreck his increasingly smooth relationship with Baghdad. I sometimes wondered how Pasha managed to be the only guy in the whole system to stay on the good side of the Americans and the Iraqis at the same time. Even Annan couldn't manage to do this; his statements would inevitably be interpreted as too close to one side in the con-flict and offensive to the other, depending on the day. Pasha played a differ-ent game. He understood the true nature of politics, defined by Ambrose Bierce as a clash "of interests masquerading as a contest of principles."

When the Americans or the Iraqis came to Pasha, it was not to talk poli-tics. It was to talk business. The volume of money that went through our hands was such that a memo from Pasha could hold up billions of dollars. The only real threat to Pasha's survival at the top of the UN food chain came from the thirty-eighth floor.

There were only so many under secretary general posts to go around. Sev-eral career bureaucrats were lurking in the shadows, waiting to be rewarded for their loyal services. And Pasha feared that any excuse would be good enough to designate him as "the weakest link" in the circle around Kofi Annan. He sure wasn't *liked* up there, and he knew it. In fact, he suspected that the reason the thirty-eighth floor refused to rein in von Sponeck was that they enjoyed seeing Pasha's operation undermined. If the controversy boiled over, it might give them an excuse to replace him. They wouldn't even need to fire him. He had reached retirement age and was vulnerable to a smoother type of "coup." So he knew better than to step into an open media squabble. He wouldn't give them any excuse to screw him.

"It's up to the thirty-eighth floor," said Pasha. "If they don't want to rein him in, it's *their* problem. I don't care."

My problem was, *I* cared. I wanted us to be proud of what we were doing. I wanted to publicize it and have the media portray us as the good guys. I didn't want to be associated with a massive failure. First, Halliday had accused us of genocide, and now von Sponeck was accusing us of criminal behavior. *That* got news.

Recent college grads who had come on board were wondering if they had come to work for an evil enterprise. The public's perception of our work had been completely distorted. Protesters were walking around with signs that said, "UN = SS." We, of all people, were now seen as responsible for the plight of Iraq's population, even as we spent our days (and often our evenings and weekends) trying to improve it. The clerk at my gym kept trying to stop me on my way in to talk about "what the UN is doing to Iraq." There had to be a missing piece in this puzzle. Was Kofi Annan even aware of how bad things were? I decided to find out. I had been told about a bright young guy working on the thirty-eighth floor—someone who had experience in Washington and had gone to Harvard. His name was Nader. I had been introduced to him through common friends, and I decided to invite him to lunch.

"So tell me something. Who's *really* in charge here?" I asked him, rather bluntly, after we had spent about fifteen minutes sympathizing.

Nader lay down his fork. "How do you mean?"

"Well, come on. I mean, look at our operation. There's no discipline imposed on anybody. People walk around claiming we're responsible for a genocide! Does nobody on the thirty-eighth floor think that's preoccupying?"

Nader nodded, searching for the right words.

I added, "I'm probably going to do something about this at some point. I don't know what yet—maybe I'll just leave this place, but not before I understand what's going on. So that's why I'm asking. Who's in charge?"

Nader nodded for a few moments longer, then said, "Riza. Riza's in charge." Iqbal Riza was Kofi Annan's chief of staff.

"Well, that's good to know," I said, "because from where I'm sitting, it looks like nobody's in charge."

"Trust me," said Nader. "Nothing happens without Riza knowing about it or approving of it. I've seen him put people back in their place, and trust me, he's capable of doing that."

"So is it *his* decision to tolerate von Sponeck's bullshit?"

Nader didn't answer. You didn't make it to the thirty-eighth floor by biting on this kind of bait.

"Or is it Kofi Annan's decision? Maybe Kofi Annan doesn't believe in the mission either."

"I think he does," said Nader. "It's just hard for him to balance the politics of this. Between Russia and France on one side, the U.S. and the U.K. on the other. . . ."

"All he has to do is appoint competent people to the top posts. I mean, Pasha and von Sponeck don't even *speak to each other!* They're running the UN's largest operation! Does Kofi Annan not realize the risk he is taking by ignoring this situation?"

"I'm only a junior staff, like you. I can't, you know. . . ."

"I know. I just wanted to give someone on the thirty-eighth a piece of my mind before . . . well, whatever I decide to do."

My meeting with Nader was interesting, in that it confirmed to me that the hand on the UN ship's steering wheel was Iqbal Riza's. This was the man who put officials on shortlists for high-level posts and decided on issues as petty as office space allocations within the UN. When the Oil-for-Food scandal eventually broke, Riza would order all his "chronological" files shredded and resign before the investigation could be completed—a smart move for a man who definitely knew a thing or two about flying under the radar. Discreet as a cat, he would show up at official cocktail parties and walk around without speaking to anyone in particular, just observing the crowd. When a staff member spotted him and happened to be of high enough rank to be able to walk up to him and say hello, their conversation rarely lasted very long. Riza wasn't much of a talker. He was a good listener, but one rarely got a sense of what he was thinking or how he would act on given information, if at all. His service to Kofi Annan was loyal, but it was unclear how much of the information that got to Riza filtered through to the UN chief. It was some time after my lunch with Nader that the thirty-eighth floor made a move on the propaganda front. A memo came down.

Annan had come across an article arguing our program was having no impact whatsoever on Iraq's humanitarian situation. It was flat-out wrong, and Annan made a handwritten note on the margin of the news clipping: "We should not let them win this propaganda war."

Iqbal Riza sent a memo with the article attached, and much was made of the fact that the secretary general "himself" had taken pen to paper.

Well, the note landed on my desk, and the problem, of course, was that we had already lost this damn propaganda war. And we had lost it without a fight. We didn't shoot back once. We just kept shooting ourselves in the foot and dodging bullets from our own, self-appointed leaders!

My intern had grown used to hearing me complain about our failure to wage the propaganda war, but there was something she didn't quite understand.

"Michael," she said one day, "you complain and you complain and you complain. But you are a spokesman. . . . Why don't you say something?"

"Because I can't!" I shot back. "Pasha wants to fly under the radar, and Kofi Annan doesn't want to rein in von Sponeck!"

"Why not?" she asked.

"I don't know," I said. "I wish I could ask him that."

"Why don't you?"

I smiled.

"Why are you smiling?" she asked, earnestly confused.

"Because it's a cute question. It doesn't work like that. . . ."

"Don't call me cute!"

"Not you . . . your question . . . agh!"

My intern was definitely not "cute." She was drop-dead gorgeous. Castable in a James Bond movie. Her nickname was Turkish Delight, because she kept bringing delicious Turkish pastries to work and leaving them by the secretaries' desk, thereby ensuring that they would grow fatter and that she would remain the slimmest woman in the office. Not that the secretaries ate all of them. Pasha soon became addicted, too. He would walk by after lunch and pick up a delicate little piece out of the box to take with him into the office. Twenty minutes later, he'd come out again to ask his secretary a question (which he would normally do through the speakerphone) and grab three more pieces. Later in the day, the entire box would lie in his garbage can, and there would be white sugar powder on the carpet next to his chair.

Now Turkish Delight had me on the defensive as I tried to explain why I couldn't simply ask Kofi Annan to rein in von Sponeck.

"You know, I'm not that important in this place. I can't just pick up my phone and call Kofi Annan. There's a difference between being a full-fledged spokesman and just being an *acting* spokesman. I can't take crazy initiatives like attacking another senior official or, you know. . . ."

Turkish Delight was nodding, so I figured she had gotten the point.

"So, like, you see what I mean. . . ."

"Yes," said Turkish Delight. "You are *acting* spokesman but you are afraid to *act* like a spokesman."

CHAPTER 18

Memorandum

FEBRUARY 21, 2000
UNITED NATIONS
OFFICE OF THE IRAQ PROGRAM

MEMORANDUM
FOR INTERNAL DISTRIBUTION ONLY

    TO: Mr. Hans von Sponeck
          UN Humanitarian Coordinator
          UNOHCI, BAGHDAD
  FROM: Michael Soussan
          Program Coordinator, Acting Spokesman
          UN Office of the Iraq Program
          UNHQ New York
SUBJECT: *UN Stance on the Humanitarian Situation in Iraq*

I am writing, in my own capacity and for the record, to inform you that the stance you have adopted publicly does not reflect my views, nor those of a great number of staff.

I understand that it is not customary for a P3 [midlevel staff] to address a senior Assistant Secretary-General in such direct terms as I am about to, but I hope you will appreciate that, like you, I am following my conscience.

The fact that your statements have been left unanswered (even internally), and have brought no disciplinary action, leaves me and others confused about the actual policy of the Secretary-General with respect to our mission. By copy of this interior memorandum, I ask to be informed if the content below is *not* in line with United Nations policy, in which case I will respectfully take the consequence.

I started working at the United Nations almost three years ago. I traveled to Iraq several times and have witnessed, like you have, the plight of the people there. However, I was not blind to the domestic factors that contribute to their suffering, which are described in many human rights reports.

I have also witnessed the dedication of a great number of UN staff, who unlike their successive leaders in the field have stayed on, under difficult circumstances, to help address the problems facing the Iraqi population.

They, sir, have a conscience too. And while they may not be able to just resign in frustration, you have to appreciate that they need to be motivated in their work in order to perform it well. In light of your statements, I have serious doubt about our ability to retain, much less attract, competent and motivated staff to work in Iraq.

Nobody ever told us the task would be easy. And nobody forced us to take on the job in the first place. But having accepted the job, I would have thought that we should do our utmost to ensure that it is done efficiently, and in accordance with our mandate.

Quite frankly, sir, if the UN staff members refuse to implement UN resolutions, who will take them seriously? And if we have no self-respect as an organization, who will respect *us?*

If other staff members were to follow the example set by Mr. Halliday and yourself, they would all resign, and the program, which remains the only way to meet the immediate needs of the Iraqi people right now, would stop functioning.

For the sake of staff morale, I plead with you to stop your media campaign for the time that you remain in the employ of the United Nations, and let us continue our work in a less politicized environment.

On the substance, I understand that you want sanctions lifted as soon as possible. Obviously, you are not the only person to hold that view. Some members of the Security Council share your view, and even a number of legislators in the United Kingdom and the United States have recently expressed such views. The difference is that they are lawmakers, and we are not.

If the international community loses trust in the United Nations to implement its adopted policies, it could have devastating consequences for the future of this organization.

I hope that you will take action to restore the confidence of the staff before you leave, and that a productive handover meeting can take place at headquarters.

CHAPTER 19

A New Wind

When I walked into the office the next day, my colleagues were looking at me strangely—almost as if they were afraid to speak to me. I detected a nervous smile on several people's faces. I had upset the normal order of things by throwing the gauntlet at an assistant secretary general.

In doing so, I had leaned on the laws enacted by the UN Security Council. The assumption, of course, was that the Council was interested in enforcing its own laws, and that the institution hence carried inherent legitimacy as the central recourse in matters of international peace and security. The third act of our collective misadventure would prove this assumption tragically wrong. But in the meantime, it offered me cover to let out some steam and try to re-energize our operation.

I had been purposely provocative in asking the thirty-eighth floor to "inform" me if anything I said was out of line with our mandate—in essence, challenging them to punish me for my insolence.

The truth was that the team around Kofi Annan agreed with Hans von Sponeck's criticism of our mandate. Their attitude toward the sanctions on Iraq had been passive-aggressive from the start. They would not openly oppose the United States and Britain's policy of containment, but their laissez-faire attitude toward von Sponeck and Halliday had been no accident. The UN's leaders had discreetly allied themselves with the positions of the anti-sanctions activists.

My memo reminded them that such an approach clashed with our official mandate and undermined our ability to perform our job. Though I had marked the memo "for internal distribution only," everybody understood that our fax line to Baghdad generated copies for the Iraqis and the Americans alike. Our fax room in Baghdad was manned by local staff, meaning Iraqi intelligence agents, so the Iraqi regime would inevitably learn of its existence. And though we owned a crypto-fax, the only thing that machine achieved was to alert Western interceptors to the importance of a particular transmission. They got copies all the same. (In the lead-up to the Iraq War of 2003, a British intelligence analyst went public with the information that British services eavesdropped on Annan's telephone conversations and shared the transcripts with Washington. The revelation created a mini-scandal but surprised nobody. The UN Secretariat finds various sorts of bugs throughout the building all the time and staff always assume their conversations are monitored.)

I had been careful not to copy Kofi Annan on the memo itself. Doing so would have been amateurish. By copying everybody *except* the secretary general, I had created the perfect hot potato. Only loose cannons sent direct correspondence to the secretary general, and this disqualified them from being taken seriously. Here I had created a problem for his entourage. Would any of them dare react to the memo without consulting the big boss? Of course not.

While I was getting settled at my desk, my director walked into my office with a big smile on his face.

"I want you to know that I'm behind you 100 percent," he said.

"I just sought a clarification on our mandate," I said, playing stupid.

"Come on, Michael. You knew exactly what you were doing," he said, and forced a smile out of me. "But I want you to know, I support you 100 percent. I said so to Pasha yesterday evening."

"Well, thanks. . . ."

"He had tears in his eyes, you know."

"Who, Pasha?"

"Yes. He spoke fondly of you. He said you reminded him of himself when he was your age."

"Oh. . . ."

"And he said von Sponeck fully deserved it. But he also said he would have preferred if you hadn't questioned Kofi Annan's political line. He said *that* went too far."

"But that was the whole point," I said. "I couldn't care less about von Sponeck. He's leaving, anyway. What I want to know is, where does Kofi Annan stand?"

"Well, they called Pasha up for a meeting last night, after you left. Kofi Annan had your memo on his desk. Pasha saw it."

"What did they say?"

"Pasha didn't tell me. He only said they have asked to see your file now. They want to know who you are."

"You think I'm in trouble?"

"No. I think you're about to get promoted."

Suddenly, Cindy appeared at my door, saying, "Yiiiii, there you are!" She literally pushed my director aside, walked over to me, took my head in her hands, and landed a big kiss on my forehead. She then lifted my tie and pinched my, um, pectorals.

"The Kid's growing hair on his chest!" she said, looking at my director. "Aw!"

"Good job, Michael. That was fucking ballsy!" she said.

Cindy had her own turf battle going with von Sponeck, and my memo clearly played to her advantage. Shortly after she left, Pasha appeared at the door, wagging his finger at me, but smiling.

"Careful, you!"

"What?"

"Don't you *ever* send another memo like that without clearing it with me!"

I thought I'd pass on answering that one. I took full responsibility for what I had done and would do so again.

"Anyway," said Pasha, "here's your reply from von Sponeck."

He threw a fax on my desk. Von Sponeck did not address any of the points I had made. He just suggested that we should meet together to discuss them when he came to New York. When we eventually sat down together weeks later, Hans was quite respectful. But he did tell me that my memo had "hurt" him. He told me that the decision to resign had not been taken lightly, after more than twenty years spent in the service of the organization. And I also knew that his final meeting with Kofi Annan had been on the "cold side." That was as far as the secretary general would go to signal his disapproval of von Sponeck's actions. I would have preferred if Annan had reacted by imposing some actual discipline on the operation. But still, it was a clear change of direction from the tacit approval he had offered Halliday when *he* resigned.

I felt bad for the assistant secretary general because I had ruined his resignation. After a long and frustrating career in the UN bureaucracy, a flamboyant resignation was considered something of a perk. One had a right to blow one's top at least once before leaving, and an issue like the Iraq sanctions just seemed too tempting to pass up.

After his resignation, von Sponeck arranged to receive payment for his anti-sanctions activities from a German firm that exported baby-milk powder to Iraq. The firm paid him a fee for writing articles in various low-profile newspapers, in order to gain favor with the Iraqi government. I learned about this when I read the final report on the investigation into the UN Oil-for-Food program, many years later. At that point, I must admit, I felt less sorry for undermining his resignation.

The report noted that, as long as von Sponeck was not employed by the UN when he received a payment from the baby-milk exporter, he had violated no laws. However, the report also suggested that there *should* be a law barring former UN officials from profiting from their prior positions. At least Hans von Sponeck's business inspired a good reform proposal.

All in all, the memo generated very little action. But the "inaction" it generated was positive, as far as I was concerned. High-level UN officials stopped offering blind support for Saddam Hussein's propaganda campaign. Word of Annan's "cold" reception of Hans von Sponeck actually helped clarify that our boss did, in fact, support our mission. Another thing that stopped was the use of my nickname. Nobody called me The Kid again. Well, except for my friend Spooky, but even he upgraded me to Monsieur Le Kid. Pasha no longer told me to "shadap" at meetings. He listened carefully to what I had to say. And I was no longer required to take notes of Pasha's meetings with Iraqi officials. That privilege went to my friend Habibi, who had been imported from our mission in Baghdad for that purpose. The significance of that last change did not hit me until suddenly, one day, I found myself holding the door for the Iraqi ambassador to the UN. I had held the door as a reflex, simply because I had been aware of footsteps behind me, and I was a bit surprised to find myself nose to nose with the Iraqi ambassador. As it happens, so was he. The unintended act of politeness on my part forced us to greet, and the first thing that came out of the Iraqi ambassador's mouth after that was, "What are *you* still doing here?"

"Well, I work here. Remember?"

"I thought you were on your way out," he said with a knowing smile, before walking on.

His remark left me planted with the door in my hand. What the hell did he mean by that? Uh-oh. . . . *Uh-oh!* Had the Iraqis asked Pasha to get rid of me after seeing my memo? I remembered them asking Pasha to get rid of a number of staff, including Spooky, when we first visited Baghdad. And look what had happened to Spooky! Slowly but surely, he had been sidelined. Would the same thing now happen to me? Would I be extricated from Pasha's inner circle?

At the time of my chance meeting with the Iraqi ambassador, months had gone by since I had sent my Tomahawk cruise memo at von Sponeck—months during which I had been walking on air, enjoying a new kind of respect from colleagues. I had been promoted once again, with a commensurate increase in salary. My Swedish director had left and been replaced by another Swedish director. Though they were both very similar in some ways (they'd never attempt to operate any device without first reading the manual), they were very different in others. Bo Asplund had eventually blown his top at Pasha. The latter had been complaining that the operation wasn't running as it should be, and Bo had replied, "Yeah, well, the fish rots from the head!"

I don't think anybody had ever spoken to Pasha like this. But Bo already had plans to return to UNDP, where he had been offered a new post.

My new Swedish director was named Christer Elfverson. Initially, Pasha nicknamed him Smiley Face, but that nickname quickly proved inadequate; the more he learned about the program, the less he smiled. His arrival in the office was greeted with scorn. He would be Pasha's fourth director in three years, and the first thing I said to him when we met was that I would probably be gone soon myself. I was getting ready to move on. We had expanded the program, but we had done nothing to actually quell the fraud that we knew was going on under the surface of public diplomacy. We had failed to stop Iraqis from rewarding political friends by exporting underpriced oil through middlemen, and we had failed even to address the fact that the Iraqis were demanding kickbacks from companies exporting humanitarian goods to Iraq. Finally, our observation mechanism in Iraq had become a big joke, in the sense that it never yielded actionable information about fraud by the Iraqi regime. The resignation of two successive humanitarian coordinators had made it impossible to reform our observation process.

The last few issues fell squarely under the responsibility of the Program Management Division, which I coordinated and which my new director would head. Unless Pasha gave my new director the authority to remedy these failures, I didn't see the point of sticking around. Corruption is like a ball of snow, goes the saying. Once it's set rolling, it must increase. And by the time Smiley Face appeared at my doorstep to announce he had gotten the job of being my director, the ball of snow had long since set rolling. The propaganda war had been my first concern, because as long as the heads of our field mission acted as spokesmen for Saddam Hussein's propaganda, we were politically paralyzed. Now we would have a new head of mission in the field, and I would have a new director in New York.

Would things get better? Would we be able to begin addressing the corruption that seemed to be increasingly plaguing our operation? The signs were everywhere. Even the language we used to communicate on a day-to-day basis had accommodated the corruption as a fact of life. For example, "the 10 percent rule" was UN-speak for the kickbacks demanded by Saddam's government on imported humanitarian goods. By mid-2000 Vice President Taha Yassin Ramadan had even written an official memo to all of Iraq's ministers asking them to inflate the prices of the goods they were importing into Iraq "by as much as possible"—and at a minimum by 10 percent. The result of this policy was quite clear to us and had a direct impact on the quality of the items in Iraq's "food basket." The Iraqi government had enough money available to import the best-quality goods on the market. And it spent enough to do so. But with the kickbacks going to the government, the people ended up with the worst-quality food items: soap that caused skin rashes and so forth.

I briefed Smiley Face thoroughly on the situation during our first meeting together and informed him that if nothing could be done to remedy this situation, I would probably leave soon, so if he took this job, he should probably start looking for a new coordinator.

Smiley Face pledged that he would fight corruption wherever he found it. I warned him that it was not always easy to work with Pasha, but he said he considered himself senior enough to make decisions on his own. I began feeling confident that we would indeed be able to put a dent in the corruption that was affecting the operation. We would now be free from having to fight the propaganda war against our own leadership in the field. Kofi Annan's new appointee as humanitarian coordinator in Iraq was Tun Myat, from Myanmar, and Tun had sworn to the secretary general that he would not resign in protest over the sanctions as his two predecessors had done.

This new element of stability in our field operation, coupled with a director who strongly supported my views, gave me confidence that we would be able to do some good. In addition, Pasha kept saying that he wanted his new director to be more of a "hands-on" manager. "I'm tired of doing everything myself," he kept saying, and I just couldn't believe our luck. Finally, the big boss was ready to delegate responsibility. Had Smiley Face somehow managed to charm him? All in all, it was a golden opportunity to get the operation back on track. All I needed to do was get my new boss up to speed on the issues, and we'd be ready for action.

Well, almost. I would also need to get him off on the right foot with Cindy.

CHAPTER 20

Turf Warriors

"**So, Cindy,**" **I said**, standing confidently outside her office door. "Are you going to be nice to my new boss?"

"You mean the Elf?" she said, referring to his last name, Elfverson. "What kind of a stupid name is that?"

"Cindy. . . ."

"What?" She tried to look innocent, but that devilish smile on her face wouldn't go away.

"I've come to plead with you," I said. "I really think he's a good guy. I'm sure we can find a way for you two to work together. He really seems nice. . . . People even call him Smiley Face!"

Cindy looked at me for a moment, then said that she felt like eating a "slab of red meat."

"Er . . . sure," I said, trying to kick the image of Cindy munching on a raw steak with blood dripping down her chin.

We went to Palm, the Italian restaurant on Second Avenue that is a notorious New York Mafia hangout. Dimly lit, with sawdust on the floor and checkered red-and-white tablecloths, the place felt like it belonged to a different decade. This was the place where the five families had struck deals with one another. And the occasional business dispute had left blood on the floor more than once. In retrospect, the setting was appropriate for the discussion that followed.

Sitting in a booth and chowing down on rare steak, Cindy and I carefully tiptoed around the real subject of our meeting until the last bloody bite. At that point, she took a large gulp of red wine and asked me point-blank: "So, Mikey, what is it you want?"

The waiter, an old Italian fellow who looked like he had witnessed enough dirty deals in his life, decided he would stay away from this one.

"I want you to get along with my new director," I said. "I want a truce."

"Michael, we're talking here. What can I give you? Do you want to join my side of the shop?"

Join me, and we shall rule the empire together!

"No. I want you to get along with my boss. The Program Management Division has certain responsibilities, and I want us to be able to—"

"Michael, the Program Management Division won't exist anymore in six months."

"*What?*"

Cindy just smiled.

"But Pasha said he wanted a hands-on manager! He said—"

"How long have you worked for Pasha now?" asked Cindy.

"About three years."

"So don't you get it yet?"

"Get what?"

"Whatever he says, he means the opposite. There are plans in place."

"Plans?"

"The office will be restructured. And I don't want your boss to interfere."

"Are you getting a promotion?" I asked.

"That's none of your business," said Cindy.

While she was clearly the person who wielded the most power in the office, Cindy's grade level was still quite low. My job description and her own were just one grade apart, and I knew she wanted to establish herself as chief of office, a rather unusual title, which would allow her to yield more power than a traditional special assistant. Clearly, such a change meant that she would pull more office functions under her control, and this would come at the expense of the Program Management Division.

"I promise you he won't interfere," I said. "As long as we can do our work."

"Yeah, right," said Cindy.

"He's my fourth director in less than three years. Does it always have to be this way? Can't you make an effort?"

"You don't expect me to change, do you now?" She said it with a guilty, infectious smile. Cindy, it appeared, was perfectly aware of how I perceived her. She knew she was controlling, scheming, and aggressive with men in positions of power. But it was as if she couldn't help it. She was a fighter—a born turf warrior. She drew her energy from conflict. It wasn't even personal. She just wasn't about to let "that pip-squeak little shit" think he could walk in there and start running the place. Then she repeated, "Just tell me what you want. Maybe you and I can work something out."

"I want a sane working environment! That's why I confronted von Sponeck! I want us to work together and do a job we can be proud of! But maybe he was the wrong person to confront."

Cindy's expression lost its muscle, as her eyes zeroed in on mine.

Are you threatening me, Michael? She didn't say it, but she might as well have.

"All I'm saying is, I don't understand why you always have to—"

"Look, Michael, this isn't Disneyland, OK? Dickheads like your boss are the reason I lost ten years in my career. Male chauvinist . . . cowards!"

"Cindy, come on. . . ."

"No, Michael! You just don't get it." She went on to talk about the number of times guys like my boss had undermined her, causing her to be passed up for promotions. She wanted to promote herself one grade, and to do that, she needed to pump up her job description. If my director took up all of the key responsibilities in the office, her promotion would not go through. It was a zero-sum game, the way she saw it. My director was in her way. The choice she was offering me was to step aside in return for a favor.

"I'm not going to step aside, Cindy. This guy is my director, and we're going to get to work on a number of issues. Whether you like it or not."

Cindy paused to take her third glass of wine. She sipped it with renewed calm, then laid her eyes on my pack of cigarettes.

"Give me one," she said.

"Cindy, you don't smoke."

"*I said give me one!*"

"Hey, OK. . . ."

Cindy took a dragon drag and looked up at the plume of smoke, almost pensive.

"You're a smart kid, Michael. But you're too young. You don't understand what it's like to be stabbed in the back. From one day to the next, you're crushed, you're nothing. You think you're popular, Michael? You think you've got friends? Wait till you're down. You'll see how many of those cowards come to your aid. There's only one way to deal with these spineless bureaucrats. . . ." She made a fist, as if squeezing a ball sack. "It's about control."

I chuckled, laid my napkin on the table, and crossed my arms. She must have read the disdain on my face.

"I guess you'll learn soon enough," she said, cryptically.

"Learn what?"

"What it's like." She looked around for a waiter.

I made a last plea for her goodwill, and Cindy countered by asking me "one last time" if she could do anything for me.

"It's up to you, Cindy," I said, looking at her straight in the eye. "But if you're screwing with my new boss, you're screwing with *me*. And that's not a threat. It's a promise."

With that, her expression turned cold.

The stage was set for a confrontation, and we both knew it. I insisted on paying the bill, as a last gesture of goodwill. She didn't argue over it. She was already deep in thought. We said few words to each other after that. A certain sadness set into both of us as we parted. We rather liked each other, after all. And now we would have to fight.

Initially, I thought myself wise to have drawn a line in the sand with Cindy. What I didn't fully understand was that for me to challenge Cindy to a game of bureaucratic hardball was the equivalent of Kid Rock challenging Garry Kasparov to a game of chess. I could make a ruckus, all right. But I had no experience waging a protracted turf war. I had no actual battle plan to deal with Cindy beyond warning her that I might get mad and hoping she'd back down. She, on the other hand, had planned her attack against my boss twenty moves in advance. And it began with a bureaucratic banana peel.

Shortly after my director took up his post, Cindy arranged for him to brief the Security Council on the "progress the UN had made in improving its observation mechanism in Iraq." Initially, Christer was flattered by the opportunity to brief the Security Council. He popped his head into my office with a big smile and waved the memo. After I read it, I looked up at him and said, "Uh-oh."

"What?" asked Christer, suddenly worried.

"Well, the briefing is about what progress we've made," I said.

"Yes . . . and?" Christer didn't get it.

"Well, the thing is, we haven't made any progress," I said.

"What do you mean?" asked Christer, sitting down. "The invitation mentions a promise we made to the Council over a year ago!"

I knew that only too well, since I was in charge of updating the famous Status Sheet tracking our progress. In this case, we had promised the Council to dramatically improve on our so-called observation mechanism in Iraq, in return for their tripling the money available to Iraq under the program.

Now, to begin with, we hardly had an "observation mechanism" to speak of. What we had was a bunch of guys riding around in cars with their Iraqi minders and reporting whatever the officials were telling them—that is, when these officials were in a mood to answer their questions.

Everybody remembers the footage of the weapons inspectors going out on inspections only to be blocked or stalled by their Iraqi minders. Such incidents, when videotaped, usually led to crises between Iraq and the international community. But our humanitarian observers never made a big deal out of being blocked. As a result, they were blocked all the time. They would simply be told, "Don't go there" or "Don't report on that," and they would comply. So what the world saw on television was weapons inspectors whipping out camcorders to show the Iraqi regime's stalling tactics on the issue of the weapons of mass destruction. What people did not get to see was how the UN system turned a blind eye to the government's mistreatment of its citizens through blatant political discrimination in the distribution of the humanitarian goods it was allowed to buy under our program.

How could we report that the Oil-for-Food program had ensured equitable distribution of medicines when it was clear to everybody that the hospitals in Saddam's hometown of Tikrit had their stocks full and the hospitals in the Shiite south remained chronically underprovisioned? How could we report that food was distributed equitably when we knew full well that entire chunks of Iraq's population, like the Marsh Arabs, were being denied ration cards? We participated in the cover-up because we spent most of our time quibbling among ourselves. In the case of the observers, they were split into three units, and the greatest concern of each unit was to know what the others were observing, in case it contradicted their own findings. In effect, our observers were observing one another instead of observing the Iraqis.

The job of the UN observers was by no means easy. But it did not help that our senior managers in Baghdad basically disagreed with the mandate the Security Council had given them. After working for two successive heads of mission who openly disagreed with the sanctions, our observers had become used to acting as advocates for the lifting of the sanctions instead of actually keeping count of what goods went where. This was made evident to me when I first had the opportunity to meet with the observers in Baghdad in November 1997.

I had expected an orderly briefing on their activities and was treated instead to something akin to an episode of *The Jerry Springer Show*. The observers—about forty of them—were sitting like audience members in a room, and Pasha, Halliday, and I were on a panel. Pasha made a depressing introductory statement about the thankless job they had and then opened the floor for questions. That's when the show started in earnest.

One after the other, the observers took to the microphone and made grand declarations against the United States, the Security Council, and, most important, their rivals within the UN mission itself, whom they referred to as "some people." Each intervention was interrupted with clapping or booing. Most of them talked about the frustrations involved in their work, and some concluded their remarks by calling for a lifting of the sanctions, which inevitably got them a round of applause. This was a far cry from the crack team of expert monitors envisaged by London and Washington when they first drew up their plans for the Oil-for-Food program. Our guys were a mixed bag of humanitarian workers, mostly from Africa and the Middle East, who did their best to adapt to this most unusual mission. Nonetheless, these were the people we had to work with.

When they weren't riding around in cars, our observers were engaged in bitter turf wars that made basic information-sharing between them impossible. Pasha had promised the Security Council we would establish a unified database that would act as a repository for all relevant humanitarian information, but the distrust among the UN agencies made such a project impossible to deliver on. It did not help that two of our observation units—one headed by a Frenchman who spoke no English and the other by an Englishman with a stiff upper lip—hated each other with a vengeance and were, in turn, hated by the UN agency heads in Baghdad, whose observation duties overlapped with their own. They all accused one another of changing their reports. Among the observers themselves, an ethnic rivalry had developed between the "Arabs" and the "Africans"—who together formed a majority of our observer pool. It should perhaps be explained to outside observers that Arab racism toward Africans is generally far less clouded in political correctness than the racism that exists in Western cultures. In Arabic, the word that describes black people is the same word that describes servants. This, in addition to the overlapping responsibilities assigned to different observers and the stress they were under from the Iraqi regime, contributed to making our so-called observation mechanism a gargantuan mess.

After expanding the program, the Security Council had asked us to double the number of our observers on the ground in Iraq. This should have been easy, as it was just a matter of recruitment. Unfortunately, the UN recruitment system was organized in such a way that no single person had responsibility for it. Thus, at each step in the bureaucratic process, a tiny drop of bad will (of which we had bucketloads) would cause the whole system to grind to a complete halt. This meant that it took us up to a year to recruit and deploy an observer to Iraq. The most qualified people would usually not wait that long, which meant that we would have to start all over again with a new, less qualified candidate. Our budgeted posts were never filled, and we never functioned at full capacity. Not for a single day did we have all of our observers deployed on the ground in Iraq. So, while on paper we had promised an increase in the number of our observers, their number had in fact decreased through sheer bureaucratic attrition.

This last fact had caused me to rush into Cindy's office during the week when my new director was still settling in to explain that we needed to get our act together on the recruitment of observers or else look like fools in front of the Security Council. Clearly, this gave her an idea.

According to protocol, briefings to the Security Council were to be delivered by the highest official in charge, which meant that Pasha should have been the one to go and look like a fool. But Pasha was increasingly traveling, and Cindy had managed to arrange the briefing at a time when Pasha would be out of the office, so that Smiley Face would be the one to end up on the hot seat. There was a real risk that Smiley Face would lose all credibility with the UN Security Council on his first appearance, and this would allow Cindy to sideline him (and our whole division) more easily afterward.

"So what am I supposed to tell the Council?" asked Christer, now livid.

"We're going to have to tell them the truth," I said.

"But, I mean . . ." He twitched nervously while looking for words.

"Don't worry. I'll put it in UN-ese for you."

If history were written in UN-ese, the battle of Waterloo might be considered a French military success. UN-ese usually includes a lot of sentences without an active subject: "all efforts must be made, all precautions should be taken, issues must be identified and remedies ought to be found, etc. . . ." *By whom and how?* one might ask. And the answer would usually be "by all concerned" and "in consultation with all relevant authorities."

Nonetheless, there was a limit to how good an impression we could give of the situation. Besides, we had a responsibility to be honest and forthright with the Security Council. The advantage Christer had was that he was new, and so I decided to go easy on the UN-ese and actually send him in with a straightforward briefing. Instead of saying the situation was dandy, we would come in and say it was less than satisfactory. This, I hoped, would reverse the nature of the meeting from one where we got grilled to one where we would do our *mea culpa*. In order to defuse possible criticism, I also called some key aides at some of the missions and made a case for them to go easy on my new director. The aides bought my pitch, and Christer was able to deliver his briefing to a receptive audience.

Christer told them there were serious problems with our observation mechanism and that he would endeavor to fix them as a matter of priority. Above the table, Christer's delivery was good. Below the table, his foot was dancing salsa. He had good reason to be nervous, for at that point he had only a limited understanding of the realities on the ground.

Christer's briefing was a success. He appeared honest, articulate, and committed to doing a better job. The ambassadors did not rip into him, as Cindy had hoped they would. Instead, they wished him good luck.

After the briefing, I passed Cindy in the corridor and thanked her, on my boss's behalf, for the "opportunity" to brief the Security Council. That was UN-ese for "Bring it on, bitch!"

But Cindy knew exactly how to spin the meeting to Pasha. When the big boss returned to the office, she told him that Christer had criticized the operation in front of the Security Council. Pasha's reaction was to block Christer from any further interaction with the Council. The turf war between Smiley Face and Cindy was engaged.

I decided to appeal directly to Pasha, but much to my surprise, I found it really hard to get a meeting with him. His secretary treated me as if I was a stranger all of a sudden, and I had to schedule an appointment like everyone else.

"Forget it," I said. "Just tell him I need to speak with him. That it's important. He'll call me when he has a moment." But Pasha never got in touch. What the hell was going on?

A week later, we received a memo. The entire Program Management Division was ordered to move out of the building at One UN Plaza and over to the Daily News Building on Forty-Second Street. In UN terms, that was like sending us to Antarctica.

With the memo in hand, I walked into Pasha's office without taking an appointment. "What's that?" I asked.

"It wasn't my decision," said Pasha. "We're running out of space, and the Daily News Building was the only place available. It's a temporary thing. . . ."

"Did Cindy talk you into this?"

"Look, give me a facking break with Cindy. At least she comes to me with solutions. With your boss, it's always problems."

Surely, Pasha meant to say "decisions." Christer needed Pasha to make decisions, yes. And the last decision he needed Pasha to make was a pretty important one, too.

Christer had received a call one day from a Swedish company that was negotiating a contract to sell trucks to Iraq. The Iraqis were demanding the

traditional 10 percent kickback payment, but the Swedish CEO hesitated
and called Christer for advice. Christer went into a panic when he received
the call. He wrote Pasha a confidential memo about the incident and advised
that we should inform the Security Council that we had concrete evidence of
Saddam Hussein's fraud.

Pasha exploded.

"Enough with all this hoolabaloo!" That's how he referred to the kickbacks. "We're not facking Sherlock Holmes! We can't investigate every case
we hear about! This is none of your facking business!"

To my director and me, failure to advise the Security Council constituted
a failure to do our job, and we said so very clearly in e-mail communications
to other colleagues. When word of this got back to Pasha, he got even angrier,
and decided to blame Christer for "bad-mouthing" him.

Though Cindy generally agreed with me on the substance and also felt we
should advise the Security Council of the kickback issue, she used Pasha's
anger with Christer to play for advantage in our ongoing turf war. Instead of
helping us persuade Pasha to do the right thing, she confirmed his belief that
we were out to undermine him. And after that, it was only child's play to convince him to move our division to Antarctica.

Pasha seemed increasingly suspicious of just about everyone in the office
and seemed to go along with anything Cindy wanted him to do. He seemed
increasingly aloof, often traveling to Geneva or Lebanon without warning.

"What are you going to Geneva for?" Christer asked him at a staff meeting.

"None of your goddamn business," Pasha said.

It turned out that there was a meeting of OPEC ministers in Geneva.
What was Pasha doing hobnobbing with the world's oil traders? I suppose he
had become sort of an oil producer himself. Take away the UN Oil-for-Food
program, and the oil markets would lose access to the second-largest oil reserves on the planet. This gave Pasha some cachet in the corridors of the oil
conference. He liked being around influential people, and I rationalized, at
the time, that merely networking was reason enough for him to travel around
so much. Had I paused to think about this, I would probably have begun to
ask myself more questions. But my mind was primarily focused on problems
closer to home. I would sometimes wonder if there was really anybody at the
wheel of this gigantic operation we were supposed to be running. Kofi Annan
probably assumed that his deputy, Louise Fréchette, had the situation under
control. And she probably assumed that Pasha was in charge. Or at least that
Annan's chief of staff, Iqbal Riza, had him under control. Pasha, in turn, was
content to let Cindy sit in the control room. We might have done a fine job

together, Cindy and I, had she not felt a compulsive need to eradicate my division from the office map. But the internal battles she was waging (and now winning) were probably the best reason she had to wake up in the morning. And the morning on which we were scheduled to pack up and move out of the main office was a glorious one for her.

As we packed up to move, Cindy walked around the office snickering. She walked into Christer's corner office, even as he was leaving with a box in his hands, and started moving around the furniture. As soon as he was out of earshot, she stepped out and declared, "Good riddance!" loud enough for the rest of the office to hear.

To further ensure that the Program Management Division could no longer function coherently, Cindy sabotaged our e-mail system by ordering the IT guy to provide us with slower-than-dial-up-speed access to our mailboxes. The system she had "approved" for us crashed about four times a day, and for three weeks we couldn't communicate with our mission in the field or with the rest of the UN offices in New York. Finally, she ordered the secretaries who worked for Pasha to bar us from access to the files in his office. I don't know what kind of threats they were under to comply with this order, but one day, after I picked up a report I needed to refer to in a meeting, one of the secretaries literally ran after me.

She was a sweet woman from Madagascar. I had previously helped her son apply to a good high school, and we were on excellent terms. I didn't notice her following me out of the office. I hadn't even imagined that borrowing the file might be an issue, and she was a very small person, so it was difficult for her to catch up with me as I was hurrying to a meeting. She followed me for several blocks, all the way over to the Daily News Building, before I finally noticed someone shouting my name. I turned around and saw her running toward me.

"Hey, darling, what's going on? Are you all right?" I asked after she caught up.

"Cindy said no files should leave the office," she said, still struggling to catch her breath.

"And you *followed* me all the way here?" I asked.

"She'll kill me!" she said, physically begging for the file with her hands.

"But . . . I mean, we still work in the same office, right?" I said. "My office here is still part of 'the office.' It's just two different locations, that's all. I'm sure Cindy didn't mean that only she and Pasha could have access to the files—how are we supposed to work?"

"Please, Michael. . . ." she pleaded, wild-eyed, with sweat dripping from her forehead.

Wow. The poor woman was scared. It was no use arguing with her—she didn't make the rules. She was just a foot soldier in Cindy's growing empire of paranoia. Or perhaps it was Pasha's. It was hard to tell what the power dynamic was between them. Was she manipulating the big boss or was she simply doing his bidding? One way or the other, the department that was officially supposed to "manage" the program in New York was physically and irrevocably cut off from the information flow of Pasha's office.

We wondered how we were supposed to do our work until it became crystal clear that the less we did, the happier Pasha and Cindy were. Pasha never visited our office and never called us over. If he sent us any communication at all, it was to further restrict our responsibilities. Pasha and Cindy's master plan would become clear a year later, when they would request a surprise audit of the Program Management Division.

"What have these bozos done to manage the program?" Pasha would ask the auditors.

This was a classic UN battle plan. Restrict the powers of an office, then attack it for not achieving anything. We would come to the office in the morning, complain all day, and go home at night. People started drinking more than was reasonable at lunch, and there were so many prescription drugs circulating in the office that we could have opened a pharmacy. More than half of the people in the office had some kind of back problem, which was a testament to our collective bad chakra. When my colleagues weren't popping muscle relaxants before meetings, it would be Valium or Xanax. Many of the secretaries were getting high at lunch hour in the UN gardens, then spending afternoons downloading music from the web.

We still held meetings, but I had to point out, at the end of them, that I had nothing of relevance to put down in my meeting notes. The pleading looks in my colleagues' eyes read, *Can't you just pretend?* But no, I could not.

I did my best to stay sane. I went to the gym every day at lunch. I took a night class in screenwriting at New York University. I moved downtown, to the East Village, where there was no shortage of partying going on. But as much as I would have liked to find the answers to my angst in the New York circuit, it mostly just ratcheted up my sense of general panic on hungover mornings.

I tried ignoring my colleagues altogether in order to escape their constant whining, thereby isolating myself further from the people who cared for me the most. Some of my senior colleagues were used to being sidelined at various times in their UN careers. I wasn't. I began to realize that every initiative we took and every problem we tried to resolve wound up being blocked in some way or other.

A UN audit report eventually questioned the wisdom of isolating the Program Management Division from the rest of the office, but that report took several years to emerge. Gradually, I began to malfunction.

I started having bouts of Paper Flow Paranoia that almost rivaled Cindy's. I started snapping at junior colleagues for absurd reasons. Once, I arrived at the office moody from having been inadvertently pushed into the elevator, to find that some denizen of the cubicle prairie in the Contracts Processing Division had posted pictures of an office party on the Internet. I flew into a rage because as "acting spokesman for the program" I hadn't been "consulted," and I sent a nasty e-mail berating the poor kid for treating his workplace like a "summer camp" and holding him personally responsible if the Iraqis decided to use the pictures to accuse us of "partying with Iraq's oil revenues."

My reaction was completely off-the-wall paranoid. When I finally came to my senses, I managed to apologize to him. But there was something about snapping that I enjoyed, for it allowed me to express my hate.

I was fast becoming a real asshole. My social life was equally affected. When people inquired about how my day had gone, they got an earful. My friends worried about me. But there was not much they could do, because whenever they mildly observed that I seemed to be angry all the time, I would snap. My peaceful Norwegian flatmate came home one day and, looking at the remnants of a door I had kicked in half, asked me what had happened. I started talking about my day.

I had come home that evening with the intention of working on a screenplay for my writing class at NYU, but I wasn't able to concentrate because of a memo Cindy had sent to Pasha that afternoon, in which she had cc'd Christer and implied something I felt deeply offended by. As a result, I couldn't concentrate on my screenwriting, because my mind kept going back to the memo we were planning to write in retaliation, which we would cc to Cindi (misspelling her name just to irritate her). After an hour of trying desperately to concentrate, I snapped, karate-kicked my door, and sat down on the sofa to watch the news, only to start fuming about the coverage of Iraq.

It eventually occurred to me that I was well on my way to ruining all aspects of my life if I didn't find a way to shed the extreme frustration that had possessed me in the past few months. I saw two options. I could either leave the UN and let the stupid turf wars continue without me or stay on and make a difference in the world by destroying Cindy.

Everybody wondered why Pasha was letting her have her way around the office. Christer speculated that Cindy was somehow blackmailing Pasha.

"She has to have something on him," he kept saying. But what? We could only speculate, even as she pursued her schemes to render us more irrelevant by the day.

Then, one night, an opportunity to take revenge materialized. It all started with a panicked call to my cellphone.

"AAAHHHHH!" The scream pierced my eardrums, forcing me to hold the receiver away from my head.

"Hello? Who is this?"

"AAAAAAAHHHHHH!"

"Habibi? Is that you?"

"Man! You won't believe what just happened!"

I was at an uptight cocktail party on the Upper East Side. There were people here of princely descent, and they, too, heard the scream coming out of my phone. I stepped out into the corridor and leaned against the coat rack.

"Dude, what's the matter? You OK?"

"No! She tried to . . . AHHHHH!"

"All right, calm down, man. What's going on?"

"She went out of control on me! She wanted me to eat her pussy!"

"Who? Lucy?"

"No!"

"Kim?"

"No!"

It could have been any number of women. Since leaving Baghdad for New York, Habibi had become something of a hipster. He had bought a mountain bike, which he rode through the city every evening in a wild bid to lose weight. And it worked. With his body quickly taking the shape of an Adonis statue, and a redesigned wardrobe to match, he was determined to make up for the three sexually frustrating years he had spent in Baghdad. With his British accent, his smooth Lebanese charm, and a healthy dose of self-effacing humor, Habibi launched out on the New York dating scene with Travolta-like zeal.

"So who was it, then?" I asked.

"Cindy!"

"WHAT?"

"She wanted me to eat her pussy!"

"Habibi, how drunk are you?"

"I'm hammered! But she was even worse! Jesus, I can't go to the office to-morrow. This is totally fucked up!"

"All right, chill out, man. Let me get out of here. I'll meet you for a drink in ten minutes."

We met at Le Bateau Ivre, a discreet French wine bar in the east fifties. A nor-mally calm and composed guy, Habibi looked like he had just come back from running with the bulls in Pamplona. And fallen down. His collar was out of whack, and his tie was hanging out of his coat pocket. Even at the height of the 1998 bombing in Baghdad, when he was hiding down in the basement of the UN compound while the windows above were being shat-tered by the shockwaves, his voice on the phone had remained controlled. But that night, his pitch was bordering on hysterical. Poor Habibi. What had the woman done to him?

Cindy was Habibi's direct supervisor. It was she who had yanked him out of Baghdad. The transfer of Habibi to UN headquarters was part of Cindy's master plan to expand her own power within the office. As chief of office (we called her Queen of Office), she could get her own assistant, which meant she could bypass my director for key jobs that would normally be as-signed to us.

Since Cindy and Christer were in savage competition, Habibi and I were increasingly given similar assignments from our respective bosses. We had a talk about this and swore to each other that no matter how acidic relations got between our supervisors, we would work things out between us. We weren't going to mirror their behavior. We'd stay pals no matter what.

Cindy had made it quite clear that she disliked my visits to his office. Es-pecially when she heard laughter coming out of there, for she assumed (often rightly) that she was the butt of our jokes. Once, she banged on her wall really hard and yelled, "Habibi, get back to work! Michael, stop distracting My Little Habibi!"

"Dude," I whispered. "She calls you My Little Habibi?"

"She calls *you* Mikey!" said Habibi, all defensive.

"Used to," I corrected him. Cindy had stopped calling me Mikey after my memo to von Sponeck. For a period, she addressed me simply as Michael. Then, after I confronted her at the Mafiosi restaurant, I became Mister, a term that had a distinctly negative connotation coming out of her mouth.

"You just sit tight, Mister. We have it under control. My Little Habibi will take care of it."

"I'll make sure to coordinate with you," Habibi would venture, before Cindy had a chance to frown at him. On occasion, she would interrupt him in midsentence with a "Shush!" The room would fill up with discreet smiles. This obviously irritated Habibi, but he was powerless to do much about it. His career was entirely in her hands, and he could not afford to piss her off.

This predicament put him in a bit of a bind on the night of his distress call.

"We were having drinks at this Mexican restaurant," he said, after I had rushed out of my cocktail party to meet up with him. He was drinking water now and looking pale. "We had all these margaritas, and she was getting all rowdy, touching my leg and stuff."

"Well, come on, Habibi, that's no big deal," I said.

"No, you don't understand. She slid her hand all the way up!"

"Oh. . . ."

"She *fondled* me, man! She fondled me right in the middle of the bar! There were all these people looking at us."

"So what did you do?"

"Well, I tried to pay the tab, but then she ordered two more margaritas!"

"Shit. . . ."

"Then . . . then she fell off her chair!"

"Wow. . . ."

"And when I picked her up, she wouldn't let go of me. She tried to kiss me. I was like, 'Cindy, *please!*' But she was, like, licking my face! Everybody was watching. It was horrible."

"Fuck, man."

"Wait, it got worse! I tried to take her to a cab, right?"

"Right. . . ."

"But she blocked the door!"

"What door?"

"The exit door! At the bar! She wouldn't get out! I tried to reason with her, but I sort of had to hold her up. She was kind of unstable, and she started wiggling her ass against my crotch!"

"Holy shit. . . ."

"In front of everybody!"

"Man. . . . Did you manage to get her in a cab?"

"Yeah."

"Phew!"

"No, man, it got worse!"

"How?"

"She made me go with her!"

"Dude . . . she *made* you?"

"She pulled me in! She said I needed to take her home!"

I shook my head, incredulous.

"And I kind of felt worried, too, you know—she could hardly walk."

"OK . . . so you went to her apartment?"

"I tried to leave her at the door, but. . . ."

I had been to Cindy's apartment myself, once, back when we were on good terms. She invited me up one night after work. She lived close to the United Nations, and as we walked home, I mentioned that I was looking for a good air-conditioner. She said I should check out hers, since she lived right up the block. I had barely leaned over the device when the music came on. Seconds later, Cindy was in the act of fixing me a drink. Sensing the onset of a Mrs. Robinson scenario, I came up with a lame pretext and fled in short order. Her Little Habibi had tried to do the same, but with less success.

"She pulled me down on the couch," he said. "She wouldn't let me go before I had a drink." After he managed to fight his way back up, the woman adopted a rather explicit pose and ordered Her Little Habibi to go down on her. Before he was able to get away from this wild sexual advance, poor Habibi was accused, twice, of being a "male coward."

I exploded in laughter, but Habibi didn't think it was funny at all.

"What am I supposed to do?" he asked. "I can't show up at the office tomorrow! It'll be too embarrassing!"

"Dude, *she's* the one who should be embarrassed. Not you."

Habibi thought about it for a bit.

"Do you think this constitutes sexual harassment?" he asked. I don't believe I was able to prevent a diabolical smile from invading my face. Until Habibi uttered the words, it hadn't really occurred to me. Now here was Habibi, a young male fearing for his career after refusing to perform oral sex on his female boss. She had insulted him, too. And he was traumatized to the point that he would not come back to work the next day.

Bingo! Here was an opportunity to crush Cindy. All I needed was Her Little Habibi's cooperation.

"Of course it's sexual harassment, Habibi! You can't let this stand!"

"But what am I supposed to do?"

"You could complain to Human Resources."

"Are you crazy? She'd cut my balls off!"

"No she wouldn't. I'll look into what recourse you have, if you want. There's got to be some kind of UN office that handles this stuff."

There had been many incidences of sexual harassment at UN headquarters. And what happened in New York was nothing compared to what happened in the field missions, where young staffers often have little recourse. Even the head of the United Nations Refugee Agency was being sued for sexual harassment, after he allegedly patted a fifty-year-old coworker on the behind. He denied having done so in a sexual manner and argued that his move had simply been meant affectionately. The guy was from Holland, and it must be said that in Northern Europe, if a woman feels offended at having her behind smacked, she'll generally make it clear right away rather than engage in lengthy lawsuits. Of course, the coworker in question was American and liable to be offended by much less than a pat on the bum, so she pursued her case against him for years, eventually forcing him to resign.

"Wouldn't you want Cindy gone?" I asked Habibi.

"I can't do it," he said.

"You can't do what?"

"The whole sexual harassment thing. It would be too humiliating. Imagine what people would say. . . ."

"You've done nothing wrong, Habibi. You're the victim here!"

"Right," said Habibi, putting his head in his hands. "Shit, man. What if I just ignore it completely—like nothing happened?"

"It's an option," I said. "But what if it happens again? I mean, where does it stop?"

I almost had Habibi convinced, but my eagerness to see him bring down the woman I had come to see as my nemesis caused me to screw it up.

"Here's how we'll do it," I continued. "Tomorrow, I will call up the Human Resources department and ask them what recourse you have. Then, we'll draft an official complaint letter, which we'll copy to the Office of Legal Affairs. Then . . ."

"Look," said Habibi, bringing his head back up. "I really don't want any fuss. Just let me handle it, all right?"

"Sure, man. Whatever . . . maybe she was right to call you a male coward."

It was a mean thing to say, and we left on rather cold terms. Habibi had come to me for help, and as far as he was concerned, I had only offered to make things worse for him with all my talk of legal action. But I was disappointed. We'd never get a better chance to neutralize this pest of a woman.

Habibi didn't exactly "handle it," as promised. Cindy did it for him. She walked into the office at around 11:00 a.m. the next day, sunglasses and all, and casually stopped by his desk.

"How badly do I need to apologize for last night?" she asked. "I don't remember anything after my third margarita."

"It's fine," said Habibi. "Don't worry about it."

At lunch, when he recounted how easily he had let her off the hook, I was boiling inside.

I made a point of visiting Habibi in his office that afternoon. Habibi was so stressed out that he literally couldn't speak to me. All he could do was address me in panicked sign language, pointing to the partition wall that separated his office from Cindy's and urging me to get out of there as soon as I could.

"Are you OK, man?" I asked.

"Yeah, yeah. . . ." And then in sign language *Shush! She's HERE! Go! Get the fuck out of here before she hears you!*

Habibi was dead scared that Cindy might realize he had spoken to me about last night. But I knew that this was exactly the button to press if I wanted to dissuade her from treating Her Little Habibi as a sex poodle in the future.

Instead of leaving, I laughed out loud, not least because Habibi's erratic arm movements were really funny. Habibi rolled his eyes at the ceiling. I can't imagine the expression on Cindy's face next door. But she didn't bang on the partition wall this time. It wasn't as if she had *really* forgotten what had happened the previous night.

I spent some five minutes with Habibi, discussing work, even as he looked at me pleadingly. *Can we do this another time?* He appeared so stressed that I decided to leave him be. But not before stopping by Cindy's office.

"Hello there!" I said. "How are *you* feeling today?"

She would have gladly thrown a machete at my face. She could tell, by my smile, that I had been briefed on her behavior the previous night.

"What do you want?" she asked, stone-faced.

"Oh, nothing! Just saying hi, that's all. . . . I heard the margaritas are pretty stiff at that Mexican bar!"

Her eyes were vibrating with rage.

"I'm busy," she said. "Some people have real jobs around here!"

"Well, you better get cracking!" I said, stepping away, half-expecting Cindy to jump over her desk and attempt a tackle.

Confident that my visit had destabilized her, I walked past Habibi, who was sitting frozen at his desk, sweating beads. Well, at least he wasn't the only one sweating now. His boss deserved to share at least some of the stress she had inflicted on him.

Unfortunately, things did not improve much for Habibi after that. While Cindy never commanded him to give her oral sex again, or called him a male coward, she nonetheless kept treating him like a poodle at the office. Except now he was a poodle she was *angry* with. And that's not a fun position to be in at all.

Habibi eventually fled the office and the city of New York, which he had grown to love so much, for a UN posting in Beirut. Far, far away from Cindy.

But before he had a chance to leave, I began devising a scheme that would bring the Queen of Office down. If Habibi wasn't going to lodge a complaint for sexual harassment, I thought I might bring the matter to the UN personnel office myself. I rationalized that I was out to protect Habibi's career, should Cindy continue to harass him. But the truth was, I was pursuing a personal vendetta. My first gig as a bureaucratic backstabber was well under way when I heard a knock at my door, which I was now in the habit of keeping closed all the time. I flung my research into sexual harassment rules into a drawer and answered with an explicitly angry "Yes?"

At my door was a young, timid kid whose smile had been distorted by fear.

Kid: Um . . . hi.
Me: What is it?
Kid: Well, I . . . we had an appointment?
Me: What appointment? I don't have anything on my schedule. Who are you?

He told me his name, which I instantly forgot. I tried to place him in the context of the ongoing office turf war. We had employed so many new people to process the truckloads of Iraqi contracts being sent to us that I was losing track of new faces.

Me: Who sent you?
Kid: Ah . . . what?
Me: Where are you from?
Kid: Queens?

The kid made every statement sound like a question, adding to my irritation.

Me: What do you mean, Queens?

Kid: That's . . . where I'm from.

Me: I meant what division. What department? What section? Who do you work for?

Kid: Oh, well, nobody, at the moment. . . .

Then I remembered. The kid had e-mailed me a few weeks ago. He was looking for "guidance," meaning he wanted a job at the United Nations. He said he'd found my name on the alumni list of Brown University, and in a moment of generosity I had told him to swing by the office.

"Take a seat," I told him, somewhat angrily. "So, how can I help you?" I asked, looking at my watch. I could tell he was feeling intimidated, and for some reason I was enjoying it. He stumbled on his words and I interrupted him.

"Why do you want to work at the United Nations?" I asked him.

"Well, it would be a dream come true," he said, "to be able to help other people . . . people in need across the world."

I couldn't help but chuckle.

"What if I told you it's actually a nightmare?" I asked. "What if I told you we spend most of our time fighting each other . . . right here in the office? What if I told you we don't *really* give a shit about the starving kids out there? Would you still want to come and work here?"

The poor kid was totally taken aback. He fumbled for words, not knowing whether to take me seriously. Then I felt bad.

"Just kidding," I said. He smiled, visibly relieved. And so was I, because the guilty feeling I got when I thought I was spoiling his innocence was deeply uncomfortable. He would discover the truth soon enough. Why rush it? I guess that's why parents lie to their kids about Santa. They want them to believe the world is good.

Not too long ago, I had been just like the kid sitting in front of me. He was in awe of the institution that was supposed to advance the cause of peace and human dignity. But was that really what we were doing?

I had seen too much hypocrisy—too many battles for the moral high ground conducted by people and nations that had only self-interest in mind. Too many turf wars, too much resentment, too much paranoia, too much cynicism. I felt drained of positive energy. The hate that had grown inside me was eating away at me, transforming me into a man I had never intended to become. What kind of person spends his afternoon trying to nail a colleague for sexual harassment? Without the consent of the person who was harassed? *Jesus,* I thought. *I'm turning into Linda Tripp!*

By allowing myself to hate, I was fast becoming what I despised. Soon, I would probably be no better than Cindy. No better than Pasha. No better than von Sponeck or Halliday. All of us started out naïve and eager, like the young kid now sitting in front of me. The "system" had taken them in and transformed them into angry and paranoid bureaucrats who, unable even to get along with one another, were in no position to promote unity in the larger world. How had it done this to them? The answer now seemed evident. The system promotes hatred. Why? Because the system lacks that essential component of social order: accountability.

As I listened to the young kid talk about his dreams and aspirations, I felt rotten. Where had my own dreams and aspirations gone? We parted with a promise that I would help him get his foot in the door at the UN—preferably into one of the UN agencies like UNICEF, which had a clear mandate and better management than the UN Secretariat. Then I sat back down, emotionally exhausted by the effort it took me *not* to launch into a cynical tirade about the UN. I swiveled around in my chair and looked out the window. I stared into space for a long time before a vision formed in my mind. It was a scary vision—that of a building collapsing, like a house of cards.

I had to get out before it was too late. Notwithstanding my strange visions of buildings collapsing, I was one step away from becoming a bureaucrat's version of Darth Vader. I had the ambition, I had the skill, and I had the anger. What I did not have much left of was perspective. Were it not for that kid, I might have lost it for good.

I turned around and looked at my computer screen. I had never written a letter of resignation before. I fumed at the thought that I was letting Cindy off the hook, that I let her beat me without fighting back. But years later, I would thank heaven for my decision to desist. Cindy was the wrong enemy. We had been set up and manipulated. The person pulling the strings would soon get rid of her, too. If Cindy and I had shared information instead of fighting, we could have connected the dots of a truly rotten scheme. Many years would go by, many people would die, and many buildings would collapse before that final secret could be unearthed.

CHAPTER 21

Exit Strategy

John Mills, our spokesman who had passed out suddenly one day after lunch, eventually returned to the office with a new look and an entirely different personality. The doctors had found a tumor in his brain the size of an orange and had cut open his skull to remove it. As a result, John returned to us with no hair on the left side of his head and a new tendency to speak the truth in all circumstances, without regard for decorum. The New John Mills helped me make my last decisions as a UN employee.

"This is the worst place I've worked in my whole career," he would say. It was not such an original statement. Every one of my directors had said the same thing, except they said it in private, not walking through the corridors. When outside visitors would appear, John would greet them with a "Welcome to the sinking ship!"

He would be out of the office for extended periods of time because of his operations. When he'd return, I would try to bring him up to speed on new developments. But he couldn't really focus anymore. In the middle of a briefing, he interrupted me with a question.

"What are you still doing here, Michael?"

"I don't know," I said. "But how about you? You're still here."

"Forget about me," he said. "You're still young. You're wasting your energy here."

"I guess we all are."

"You know, Pasha has been doing some things he shouldn't be doing."

"I know *that*," I said. John looked at me quizzically. So I pursued. "I mean, some of his management decisions make no—"

"I'm not talking about management decisions, Michael."

"Well what . . . what are you talking about?"

"I'm saying you'd be smart to get the hell out of here. Sooner the better."

I had written a nuclear letter of resignation a few weeks back, right after meeting with the young job seeker. It was a long letter, full of criticisms and grand declarations. I walked around with a copy of it in my pocket, waiting for something, or someone, to make me mad enough, and thus courageous enough, to sign it and slam it down on Pasha's desk.

"Here," I said to John. "Read this."

John took a token look at it and laughed.

"What's funny?" I asked.

"Do you know how many of these letters I've written in my career?" he said. "The longer the letter, the less likely you are to sign it. If you really want to go, it's two lines, and you're out."

"I guess you're right," I said. "I just need some kind of plan."

"John Lennon said it best," said John. "Life is what happens to you while you're busy making other plans."

"Funny you should say that," I said. "Boo used to say the same thing. But I don't agree. I believe in making plans."

"Well," said John, "take it from a dying man. . . ."

"What?"

"Look at me, Michael. I'm dying."

"John, you're *not* dying. . . ."

"Shut up, Michael. I am dying."

I held his gaze for a beat, then looked down, repressing an urge to leap over the desk and hug him as tight as I could.

"I can tell by the look in the doctors' eyes," said John. "The second operation didn't solve anything. Chances are this is it for me."

I was at a complete loss for words. My eyes filled with tears.

"Anyway," he said, as uncomfortable as I was, "get the hell out of here. You might not get another chance, you know. If you stay now, you'll probably stay your whole life. You'll get married, have kids, and you'll be stuck. So go. Get out of here while you're still young."

At twenty-eight, I was still young—but not quite as young as I had been when I started. I now had a secretary who called me old-fashioned when I tried to dissuade her from getting a tongue ring. I now had kids in the office calling me sir. I had a chiropractor telling me to avoid crossing my legs at meetings. I no longer watched MTV and had no clue what artists sang the hits I whistled along to in the shower.

Three and a half years had gone by, yet I felt ten years older. But something was bugging me. Before leaving John's office, I turned around.

"I really thought this was my calling."

"What?"

"You know, working for the UN."

John smiled. "And do you still think so now?"

"I don't know."

"Well, let me put it this way, Michael. There are many things you don't know. There are even things going on right here in this office that you don't know about."

"Like what?"

"Like some people are doing things they shouldn't be doing."

"What are you saying, John?"

"I'm saying you won't regret leaving. Now get out of here. I need to pretend to be working."

I took John's advice and drafted my two-line letter of resignation.

At first, nobody took it seriously. People at the UN write up letters of resignation all the time, as John had said, but few people actually act on them. Pasha didn't reply, hoping I would change my mind. But when it came time for my "goodbye drink," I think everybody realized it was for real. It was December 2000. I had worked for the UN for more than three years.

"You've done it!" said Spooky. "You've actually done it."

"How about you?" I asked. "Are you planning to stick around?"

"The game is not over," said Spooky. "Besides, I kind of enjoy the air of Greek tragedy that surrounds this whole operation."

"Cheers on that," I said.

"To Michael leaving the sinking ship!" said Spooky, raising his glass for a general toast. John Mills had started a trend. Everybody was calling the operation a sinking ship now.

We were having cocktails at an Italian bistro close to the United Nations when a mustached man showed up, sat alone in a corner, and ordered an orange juice. I hadn't noticed him until Spooky came to whisper in my ear that I had the "honor" of being "watched by the Iraqis."

Spooky pointed his eyebrow in the direction of the man. I raised my own eyebrow in disbelief, but Spooky frowned to confirm his claim. So I decided to check out the man for myself. Ignoring Spooky's advice, I turned my gaze directly at the supposed Iraqi operative.

I caught him by surprise, and he immediately looked away. I waited until he did a double take to confirm that I was indeed staring at him. At this point, I smiled and raised my glass to him. He immediately looked away again. *Come on, a little toast. . . .* I kept looking at him provocatively, but he was able to resist the temptation to look back. A normal New Yorker would have asked me what the hell my problem was. Instead, the man glanced around for a bit, then settled firmly on his glass of orange juice, as if he had noticed something truly fascinating about it.

Two options. Either he was indeed an Iraqi operative or he was a freaked-out Middle Eastern tourist who took me for a gay man on the prowl. I settled on the former. Spooky said he knew the man's face from previous occasions. Eventually, before the Iraq War, the man with the orange juice, who worked at the Iraqi Mission, was expelled from the United States for "activities inconsistent" with his diplomatic duties. This was UN-ese for spying.

I felt somewhat proud that the Iraqi regime would be so eager for me to leave that it would send an agent to observe my farewell drinks. I still hadn't resolved the question of whether Pasha had been pressured to sideline me after the Iraqis saw my memo to von Sponeck. But I decided to give him the benefit of the doubt. It was not only I who had been sidelined; it was my whole division. And at that time Cindy remained the person who had the greatest to gain from sidelining the Program Division.

Pasha had never been a role model to me, but as an elder and someone who had, after all, provided quite a bit of entertainment to me, I felt I should say something nice to him before leaving. So I wrote him an e-mail in which I called him a "good soldier with a good heart." There was no way I could call him a great manager with an inspiring vision, but still, my words touched him enough that he invited me to lunch.

At the lunch, he tried to persuade me to come back after a few months. My master plan at the time was to spend all of my savings on a semester of film studies at NYU, the assumption being that I would immediately break into Hollywood and make millions, of course.

"Well," said Pasha, "if you change your mind, give me a call."

I nodded, satisfied that I had managed to leave without burning any bridges.

"When I was your age," said Pasha, with an unusual smile on his face, "I considered going into the theater. But my family told me it was an occupation for homosexuals. So I ended up here, at the theater of the absurd."

CHAPTER **22**

Just When I Thought
I Was Out . . .

At 5:30 in the morning, the phone rang. I was so confused at first that I almost picked it up. Then I remembered I was at my girlfriend's apartment. *Ha!* I ducked under the covers and found a comfortable spot to lay my head while she fumbled with the receiver.

Since leaving the United Nations, my life had improved considerably. It was not always easy living without job security, but freedom from the cynicism that permeated the halls of the United Nations had done me a world of good. I had fallen in love, lost some weight, and was working on acquiring an entirely new set of creative skills at NYU film school. Unfortunately, the bubble of optimism and prosperity that had enveloped New York at the turn of the millennium had recently been pierced by the attacks of 9/11, and living in Manhattan was fast becoming a dark, almost fictional experience.

My girlfriend was still groggy when she answered the phone. Then I felt her tense up. First, she said, "What?" several times. Then she said, "OK, OK," and eased herself out of bed to write something down. Then she said, "All right, I promise, I promise," and hung up.

"Wassgoingon?" I mumbled, eager for her to come back to bed.

"My stepdad says I have to get on Cipro," she said.

"*What?*" My head jumped up.

Cipro was the industrial-strength antibiotic people took when they got infected with anthrax. My girlfriend had recently visited her mother in a New York clinic where traces of anthrax had been found. Apparently, someone from that clinic had gotten sick from it, and every visitor in the past forty-eight hours was asked to get on the medication.

"Is it with a Y or an I?" She was wondering how to spell Cipro.

"I think it's with a Y," I said. "You want me to take you to the doctor?"

"It's 5:30 a.m," she said.

"Right. Do you feel any . . . like, any symptoms or anything?" I was worried. It's not every day the person you love gets exposed to anthrax.

It turned out that she was fine. But that morning, since we couldn't go back to sleep, we each got a bit paranoid about any kind of marks on our skin. Hers was totally clear, but she kept going to the bathroom to inspect herself. And frankly, I spent a few minutes in front of the mirror too. I hadn't dared ask her if anthrax was transmissible, because I didn't want to appear selfish at a time when *she* was the one in danger. But it is impossible not to think about such things.

We watched CNN for about an hour. Paula Zahn was telling us the first symptoms of the disease were similar to those of a "common cold." That was really helpful because we both had a bit of a common cold. The whole thing seemed surreal. Anthrax used to be the name of a rock band, for God's sake!

"You sure it's with a Y?" she asked.

"I don't know, baby. But I'm sure they'll know what you mean." I pressed her in my arms again.

Who the hell was attacking us? The media were as clueless as the rest of us, and they were doubly panicked because they had been the primary victims of this attack. They weren't exactly accusing Saddam Hussein, but his name was bandied around as someone who definitely possessed the bio-agent anthrax. It was a matter of public record that the United States had sold anthrax spores to Iraq in the 1980s, ostensibly for use in preparing animal vaccines.

Warnings of further "spectacular attacks" and government-issued alerts did little to assuage our fears. Most people who live in Manhattan are perfectly capable of experiencing panic attacks without help from the federal government. So with John Ashcroft warning us of "generalized unspecified threats" every time he heard "chatter," we lived in a constant state of alert without ever knowing what that was supposed to entail.

On the morning of September 10, 2001, Saddam Hussein could have been standing in front of his bathroom mirror, humming along to Sinatra's "My Way." He had done it all: confronted the Great Satan, survived Desert

Storm, quelled all the uprisings and coup attempts, weathered the sanctions, kicked out the weapons inspectors, showed Clinton who the Desert Fox was, profited enormously from the Oil-for-Food program, rebuilt his palaces, bribed half the world to lobby on his behalf, and made a dramatic comeback on the Arab political scene by sponsoring suicide bombings against Israeli civilians. While his population was supposed to be suffering, Saddam felt rich enough to announce that he would offer $30,000 to $50,000 to families of bombers who exploded themselves in Israeli cities.

Thanks to the Oil-for-Food program, his policy of eroding the sanctions had shown significant progress. The UN weapons inspectors had been thrown out of the country three years earlier and had still not been allowed back. As of 2001, there was no longer any legal limit on how much oil Iraq could sell, and Iraqi applications for imports varied greatly, from flatbed trucks to Viagra.

Even as anti-sanctions activists continued to claim (falsely) that 5,000 children were dying every month because of the sanctions, Baghdad was holding trade fairs attended by thousands of international companies looking to do business in Iraq. It seemed as if even the government had gotten tired of its own propaganda campaign, and the parades of small coffins through the streets of Baghdad became less frequent. Most serious journalists traveling to Iraq no longer bought the government's lies anyway.

The fact that the Iraqi government could rely on the Oil-for-Food program to cover its civilian needs meant that it could use its own funds, acquired through oil smuggling and illegal back-end bribes, to rebuild its security apparatus and military machine. According to the U.S. General Accounting Office, Saddam Hussein might have accumulated as much as $13 billion from illegal oil sales and smuggling between 1997 and 2003.* Saddam's cronies got fat once again, and the region's leaders were beginning to treat him with the respect they had once shown him before the Gulf War. Proof of that came when the Iraqi vice president and a Saudi royal were caught on camera kissing at an Arab summit.

The chances of a successful coup were as slim as ever, and the only way the regime in Iraq was going to change was if Saddam slipped in the shower and fractured his skull against his golden faucet. If Saddam had died abruptly, it is likely that Iraq would have descended into civil war rather quickly, and the

---

*James J. Barnes, prepared witness testimony, hearing of the House Committee on Energy and Commerce, Subcommittee on Energy and Air Quality, "United Nations Oil for Food Program," May 14, 2003.

international community would have had to face the question of whether to intervene in order to reestablish order or risk losing access to the world's second-largest oil reserves.

The issue of Iraq hardly surfaced in the 2000 campaign. Candidate George Bush had mumbled something about tightening the sanctions. *What sanctions?* The dramatic mushrooming of the UN Oil-for-Food program had all but nullified them. What Saddam could not buy legally through the UN he bought illegally from Russian, Jordanian, and Ukrainian companies.

Richard Perle and Paul Wolfowitz had consistently argued for opposing Saddam Hussein more forcefully. Some inside the Clinton administration, like Kenneth Pollack, agreed, but during the 2000 campaign, their voices were hardly heard; the expression "regime change" had yet to appear on the public's radar screen. In fact, according to Bob Woodward, Bush 43 even said to his national security adviser, Condoleezza Rice, that he thought his father had done the right thing in 1991 by sticking to the UN mandate and stopping short of overthrowing Saddam.

By the time of the September 11 attacks, Saddam had every reason to feel safe. Still, his reaction to the greatest attack on American soil since Pearl Harbor was unwise. When he first heard of the attacks, he rejoiced and declared publicly that they were the result of America's "evil policy," contending that the United States exported corruption and crime through its military forces and its movies.* He was the only national leader in the world to come out publicly in support of the terrorist attacks.

In all fairness, it was difficult to foresee that the aftershocks from the collapse of the World Trade Center towers would soon topple his own statues. The traditional policy of the United States was to react to terrorist attacks by going after the actual perpetrators. In this case, America reacted as it had only twice before in its history, during the world wars of the twentieth century. It reacted by seeking to radically change the world.

The campaign to unseat Saddam Hussein began on 9/12 with a suggestion by U.S. Secretary of Defense Donald Rumsfeld that Iraq be attacked as part of the "first round" of the war on terror.** His proposal, made at an afternoon National Security Council meeting, did not receive much support initially. Secretary of State Colin Powell and the outgoing chairman of the Joint Chiefs of Staff, Hugh Sheldon, both opposed it. The president himself did not question the validity of attacking Iraq as part of the war on terror. But there was

---

*"After the Attacks; Reaction From Around the World," *New York Times,* September 13, 2001.

**Bob Woodward, *Bush at War* (New York: Simon & Shuster, 2002), p. 49.

no provable link between Saddam Hussein and the terror attacks, so the priority remained Afghanistan.

In the months that followed, little evidence emerged to suggest that Saddam had played a role in the September 11 attacks. Yet the argument for attacking America's longtime foe gained ground with every meeting of the president's principals. Powell continued to resist the idea. "What the hell, what are these guys thinking about?" he asked Chairman Sheldon after one meeting. "Can't you get these guys back in the box?" But the split within the administration eventually gave way to a coordinated diplomatic and military strategy to effect regime change in Iraq through war.

What tipped the scales? The anthrax scare was one of several highly stressful post-9/11 events that rattled America's psyche and predisposed the American public toward preventive action to confront threats from weapons of mass destruction.

After that, the notion of acting preventively to disarm Saddam was a much easier sell with the American public. Especially as much of the media fueled suspicion that Saddam had something to do with the anthrax attacks.

Our experience in dealing with Saddam had been rather successful, we thought (mostly because we had completely ignored the harm we had done to the Iraqi people in the process). Operation Desert Storm created very few casualties and had offered images of towering success for the U.S. military. It is doubtful whether public opinion would have supported going back to Vietnam or Somalia for a war "of choice." But Iraq had been a "positive" experience (if war can ever be called that) in the eyes of much of the public. America had gone in, gotten out clean with minimal casualties, and held a parade. The world had paid for much of the war, and in its aftermath, America entered one of the most prosperous decades in its history.

Even though Saddam had not commandeered the 9/11 attacks or the anthrax attacks, the scales had tipped against him. As late as September 2003, seven in ten Americans still believed the Iraqi dictator was likely personally involved in the 9/11 attacks. A majority of Americans had long ago put Saddam's name on the "to do" list. To the hawks of both parties in Washington, getting rid of him was more a question of opportunity than necessity.

The opportunity came in the aftermath of the Afghan war, which in many ways had been anticlimactic. Certainly, it had been nothing like the "big bang" that the head of Fox News Channel, Robert Ailes, had told President Bush the American people wanted. The war in Afghanistan succeeded in toppling the Taliban, but they and Osama bin Laden seemed almost unworthy enemies for the United States. The American military machine had not been designed to go chasing after a "one-eyed man on a motorbike," as Sheikh Omar was described in Pentagon briefings. In President Bush's own words, "The antiseptic notion of launching a cruise missile into some guy's, you know, tent, really is a joke."* After the fiasco at Tora Bora, in which U.S. forces reshaped Afghanistan's mountain range with "daisy cutter" bombs but failed to catch or kill Osama bin Laden, America needed a villain on whom it could land a good, clean punch. And during the summer of 2002, it became clear that Saddam Hussein had gotten the part.

After President Bush's speech to the UN General Assembly in the fall of 2002, I realized an attack on Iraq was inevitable. Back in 1998, I had witnessed the diplomatic circus that preceded any U.S. action against Saddam. It was clear to me that the U.S. would not win Security Council authorization to invade Iraq. It was also clear to me that the United States would act anyway. What was less obvious was how the United States was planning to deal with Iraq *after* an invasion. Did they understand the country they would be charged with running? Did they realize how deeply its economy was revolving around one man? Did they realize how profoundly eroded its basic infrastructure was? And did they understand the consequences of breaking up Saddam's racket?

While New York and Silicon Valley were experiencing something akin to a modern-day gold rush, Baghdad remained frozen in time. Under Saddam had arisen a generation of children who had grown up less educated than their parents. Unemployment levels had risen to an all-time high. Nearly half of Iraq's young had no official job, and criminal gangs were so powerful that even Saddam had trouble controlling them. The Iraqi dictator was unable to stop the pillaging of Iraq's Mesopotamian and Babylonian treasures that occurred during his reign. And he hardly exerted control over the unruly border tribes of western Iraq, which eventually gave allied troops their greatest headache during the occupation. Iraq's frustrated youth, and its growing criminal networks, would present an ideal feeding ground for would-be terrorist leaders.

Invading Iraq would be one thing. Occupying it would be another. With the primary focus on Saddam's WMDs, the United States failed to prepare for the greater challenge of running Iraq's economy and building up a state from scratch in a climate of increasing insecurity.

The only institution that had experience dealing with Iraq's economy in the past seven years was the UN Oil-for-Food program. While we had utterly

*Woodward, *Bush at War*, p. 38.

failed to rein in Saddam's fraud, we did understand how his government managed various sectors of the economy. Whether the U.S.-led invasion force would find WMDs in Iraq hardly solved the problem of how to manage the country after the war. So it seemed logical to me, at a time of such great potential turmoil, that people with our kind of experience should get involved in planning for the post-Saddam era.

Over dinner with my former director (Swede number two) in the fall of 2002, we talked about the idea of me going back to the UN to help with what was likely to be a difficult transition to Iraqi self-rule. A strange change had occurred in the months following my departure. Cindy had been forcibly removed from her position of chief of office within the Oil-for-Food program. Apparently, her power grab had spun completely out of control and led her into confrontation with Pasha himself. In a sense, it was a logical outcome. Cindy was the consummate turf warrior. Once she had won every bureaucratic battle, the only remaining enemy would be Pasha himself.

What issue had been at the heart of their dispute? Nobody knew. And the mystery would last for years. On weekends, Cindy could be seen rummaging through the files in Pasha's office, preparing for what promised to be a major bureaucratic showdown with her own boss. What was she looking for?

Cindy's expulsion had prompted people to speculate that I might come back. Pasha himself had invited me to return. At first, I declined. But the looming war in Iraq changed my mind. The UN would have to face new challenges, and an entirely new operation might see the dawn of day—an operation I hoped would be in support of freedom and democracy in Iraq. Call it an idealistic relapse.

While waiting for my appointment, I watched events unfold in the Security Council with increasing alarm. After thirteen years of jousting for the moral high ground, the Franco-Russian and Anglo-American duos were headed for a theatrical clash on the world stage.

CHAPTER 23

The Clash of Civilized Nations

"Diplomacy is the art of nearly deceiving all your friends,
but not quite deceiving your enemy."

KOFI BUSIA,
writer, former prime minister of Ghana

It was the moment of truth. All lights were on the UN Security Council in New York. The debate would be broadcast live throughout the world and unfold in several parts, like a miniseries. At stake was the fate of twenty-three million Iraqis—though, as usual, the discussions had little to do with *them*. They would focus, as always, on Saddam Hussein's weapons of mass destruction.

The world was divided. Representing the "coalition of the willing" was Secretary of State Colin Powell, a retired four-star general, Vietnam veteran, and the former chairman of the Joint Chiefs of Staff during Operation Desert Storm. He was also considered a credible contender for the presidency of the United States.

Speaking most forcefully for the "peace camp" was a French aristocrat and poet known by his full name as Dominique Galouzeau de Villepin. A product of France's elite *Grandes Ecoles,* de Villepin had risen through the ranks of France's Foreign Service and served several years as the secretary general of

Jacques Chirac's presidential palace. He had never been exposed to the lime-light before his appointment as minister of foreign affairs in May 2002. The author of a book extolling the achievements of Napoleon, he, like his American counterpart, was considered a future presidential contender.

There were good reasons why de Villepin stole the show from the other Security Council members who opposed the war. Unlike Germany, France had a veto and could play a pivotal role in the decision-making process. Unlike Russia, France had participated in the Gulf War and was expected, ultimately, to come on board for this one. Unlike China, France was a democracy that could credibly claim to care about human rights. And unlike all of the above, France had a relationship with the United States that went back to America's birth and included the gift of the Statue of Liberty.

As I watched Powell and de Villepin clash in the UN Security Council in New York, I wondered how a bully from the Iraqi village of Tikrit had managed to cause such a deep rift between two of the world's oldest democracies. Thanks in large part to the financial wealth he had gained from the Oil-for-Food program, Saddam had succeeded in applying the same old "divide and conquer" tactic to the international community as he had applied to tribal Iraq. And, incredibly, it paid off.

The clash between France and the United States had been years in the making. I had seen the resentment between U.S. and French diplomats brew from inside the UN sanctions committee and realized that if it came to an all-out confrontation, it would get very ugly.

For years, France and the United States had waged a battle for the moral high ground in public and a turf war for regional influence in private. The Oil-for-Food program had been a battleground on both fronts. France used to accuse the United States of being insensitive to the plight of Iraq's population. The United States used to clobber France for enriching Saddam Hussein through trade. Both accusations were correct, of course. And that only served to further sour the atmosphere.

France and the United States had led opposite policies toward Iraq for twelve years. While the United States did everything in its power to keep Iraq isolated, France reestablished diplomatic relations with Iraq and did nearly everything it could to gradually rehabilitate Saddam's regime. Iraq rewarded France with big contracts through the Oil-for-Food program, especially when it felt the French government was lobbying sufficiently hard for its cause. France sold about 22 percent of the goods Iraq was buying and received some 15 percent of its underpriced oil allocations, with French Ambassador Jean-Bernard Mérimée receiving about $165,000 in illicit kickbacks. However, when Baghdad decided France had not done enough, it did not hesitate to find other trading partners. Somehow, this worked wonders on French policy-making.

Iraq made its policy of awarding contracts in return for political favors absolutely clear in its public statements. This occasionally caused some embarrassment to France. After one incident in which the Iraqis released a statement berating France for its poor collaboration, I heard a bitter high-level French diplomat vent, "The Iraqis—they treat their friends like dogs!"

Their friends?

Partly as a punishment for insufficient French collaboration, Iraq reduced its wheat imports from France and awarded contracts to Australia instead. Oddly enough, Australia never became a major political backer of Saddam Hussein. They paid the kickbacks, of course: more than $200 million for the wheat alone. But still, usually the policies of a country conformed to Saddam's interests, too. I once asked a man who had helped secure a mother lode of contracts for the Australian Wheat Board if they had come under any pressure to support Iraq politically.

"Sure," he said, with a big smile.

"And?" I asked.

"We just played stupid," he said. "People seem to think Australians are stupid to begin with, you know, because of our accent. Whatever. . . ."

When I repeated the Australian's comment to a junior French diplomat, he shook his head and said, "You see? With us, it is the opposite. We are victims of our intelligence."

One reason the French diplomats allowed themselves to be treated "like dogs" by Saddam's cronies was that, in France, major infrastructure-oriented firms are still partially owned by the state. The CEOs and the ministers work hand in hand. When politicians are out of power, they become consultants for large state-owned companies, and when they come back to power, they return the favor by helping these firms secure contracts. It's rather like Dick Cheney and Halliburton, except for the fact that Halliburton is not technically owned by the U.S. government.

The French oil giant TotalFinaElf began discussions about new oil development contracts with the Iraqi authorities as early as 1992, according to its own general director of production, Christophe de Margerie. In 1997 the company that is generally considered to be a state within the state in France signed exclusive contracts with the Iraqi authorities to develop the Nahr

Omar oilfield in southern Iraq, which holds an estimated ten billion barrels of oil. Such deals were outside the scope of the Oil-for-Food program and were therefore meant to take effect only after the sanctions were lifted. In essence, France was banking on Saddam Hussein for the long term.

The French government often downplayed the importance of its trade with Iraq. But its companies didn't. A spokesman at Alcatel, the French telecom firm that clinched a $75 million deal to rebuild Iraq's phone lines, said it plainly: "These kinds of contracts are our raison d'être."

The greatest contract France got out of the Oil-for-Food program was the one nobody paid attention to at first. It was so big, and so central to the entire operation, that few people realized its importance. It was the very first contract that we awarded—the one that would decide which bank was to hold the *account* into which Iraq's oil revenues were to be deposited. The bank was chosen by the United Nations, in "consultation" with the government of Iraq, but it was clear to all that if the Iraqis didn't like the choice, all they had to do was stop exporting oil and create havoc in the oil market until a new one was chosen.

Surprise, surprise, the Banque Nationale de Paris (BNP) was chosen; $64 billion would travel through its coffers over the span of seven years. Of course, BNP did not get to touch the money, except for the fee it was paid, but for any bank a steady multibillion-dollar yearly stream of cash can do a lot. It can increase the bank's credit rating (which it did), and it can allow the bank to leverage that to merge with other banks. In 2000, BNP merged with Paribas to become the largest financial institution in continental Europe. One of the bank's largest shareholders was Iraqi-born billionaire Nadhmi Auchi, who had extensive dealings with Saddam Hussein's government over the years.

The UN soon worried about the financial risk involved in depositing all of Iraq's oil revenues in a single bank. But when it tried to get Iraq to "diversify" its account, it met a wall of resistance.

By 1998, Suzanne Bishopric, the cheerful UN treasurer, had gotten it into her head that there was a better way to manage Iraq's money. She thought it would be safer for Iraq to spread its accounts across multiple banks. She also wanted to look into how the UN brought cash into the country to pay its staff and whether we were getting a fair exchange rate on our money when we converted it to Iraqi dinars.

Suzanne seemed to be completely oblivious to the notion that some issues were big political no-no's. When one of my colleagues tried to tell her it might not be such a good idea to go nosing around in the financial gutter of the UN's relationship with Baghdad, she simply replied, "Why not? I'm the treasurer. That's my job!"

When Suzanne wanted something done, she simply did it. So she donned a traditional English summer dress and a colonial straw hat and tagged along with Pasha and me on one of our trips to Baghdad. She looked like a character out of an Agatha Christie novel, except for her wide 1970s sunglasses, which were more on the Pink Panther side. The first thing she did in Iraq was visit the "black market" for currency exchange. This caused an electroshock to ripple through the Iraqi secret service chain of command, since senior government officials were personally involved in skimming money off the top of the "special" exchange rate that was offered to the UN. Everyone knew where to exchange dollars for Saddam bills, and the UN got some of the worst rates on the market, from local money changers who had the government's permission to do business. Suzanne, like all of us, was in way over her head. But she had such enthusiasm that nobody at the UN could have stopped her with a subtle hint.

We left her alone for a few days in Baghdad, during which she managed to freak out the Mukhabarat (Iraqi secret service) by asking them highly sensitive questions point-blank. By the time we went to meet with officials from the Iraqi Central Bank, they had been ordered not to say anything in her presence, which made for a very bizarre meeting. We basically sat and looked at one another in the sweltering heat, talking about how good the coffee was at the Iraqi Central Bank. When we insisted on raising the issue of the diversification of Iraqi funds, the sweaty Iraqi Central Bank official simply pointed his finger at the ceiling, signaling that decisions on this matter were made so far above his head that even a wince from him could get him in trouble.

Several years of UN insistence on the subject eventually convinced the Iraqi government that it was in its own best interest to diversify its monetary holdings. Besides, by 2002, the very smart Mr. Auchi had gotten out of the game. He no longer held a stake in BNP Paribas. And as pressure for war mounted in the second half of 2002, Iraq became eager to secure additional political support for its cause from other European countries. The UN suggested Deutsche Bank, which seemed agreeable to the Iraqis, but no deal was ever finalized. Though the management of Iraq's money was generally sub-par given the limitations of the program, the Iraqi dictator did manage to make one financially prophetic call. As of 2002, he insisted on being paid in euros. Even Paul Volcker, the chief investigator of the Oil-for-Food scandal, had to give it to the Iraqi dictator. Saddam's switch to euros was very profitable— and it represented another historical first in the history of oil trading.

France was not the only country to invest heavily in the Iraqi dictator's long-term survival. Russia's efforts dwarfed those of France, and China and Germany were heavily involved in the Oil-for-Food program as well. Russia alone bought about $19.3 billion (or some 30 percent) of Iraq's oil exports and, like France, signed unquantifiable contracts for post-sanctions oil exploration in Iraq's northern and southern regions.

The correlation between Iraq's trade favors and the political protection it received was mathematically unchallengeable.

That said, the correlation could not explain everything. If French officials had acted based purely on economic considerations, the smart thing would have been to imitate Australia: dump Saddam the moment they were sure America was going to attack, and join the coalition. If France had been part of the coalition, it would have been in a much better position to safeguard the contracts it had already signed with Iraq, secure the best possible terms for the repayment of its debt, and get a decent place in line for future contracts with the next Iraqi regime. From an economic standpoint, it only made sense to keep up support for Saddam as long as he had a future. Once he became a losing stock, why expend further political capital to support him?

Yet France went further than any of Iraq's other major trading partners in opposing the United States—so far, in fact, that it jeopardized relations not only with the Bush administration but also with an overwhelming majority of the American public, including many people who were personally opposed to America's "war of choice." It was one thing for France not to support America's war. But it was another thing for France to lure the United States into a diplomatic trap just as it prepared to send its soldiers into battle.

"We are ready!" President Bush had exclaimed in a dramatic address to U.S. troops preparing to leave for the Persian Gulf in early January 2003. His message was not meant for the troops themselves. They were obviously not ready yet, since they were still at their base in Fort Hood, Texas. The message was meant for the American public and the rest of the world: the Bush administration was ready, politically, to go to war with Iraq.

Three days later, Gerard Araud, director of strategic affairs at the Quai d'Orsay (France's foreign ministry), took it on himself to clarify the situation for his foreign minister: "We seem to be acting as though we believe the train has not left the station," he bluntly told Dominique de Villepin. "In fact," he continued, "it has already departed. All we are doing is lying down on the tracks in front of it!"

Araud understood the realities involved in launching a major military invasion of another country—you don't get 400,000 men and women all dressed up for nothing. Accordingly, he explained to de Villepin that France had to choose between two options: it could either find a diplomatic way of supporting the war or prepare for outright opposition.

Neither option appealed to the flamboyant de Villepin. Supporting the war would mean toeing the American line and backtracking on twelve years of French foreign policy, which had banked on Saddam Hussein's revival. On the other hand, if France lay down on the tracks right away, the United States would simply switch away from the UN track and roll into Baghdad unilaterally, leaving France behind in a histrionic but anticlimactic pose.

The only way France could retain any level of influence was if the United States remained on the UN track. And therefore, rather than lay down in protest right away, France opted to lure the United States further down the UN route and organize for acts of sabotage to be committed along the way, in the hope that these could derail or delay the U.S. war effort.

A few days after Araud's poignant briefing, Dominique de Villepin hit the phones to organize a high-level ministerial meeting at the Security Council. In his conversations with other foreign ministers, he said the meeting would not be about Iraq because the issue was "too divisive." As Council president for the month of January, he said France was looking to have a meeting that would strengthen the "fragile unity of the Council," and it should therefore focus exclusively on "terrorism."

The meeting, which much of the media subsequently described as a "diplomatic ambush," was scheduled for January 20, Martin Luther King Day. Colin Powell had a string of speaking engagements planned for that day, all of which he had to cancel in order to go to New York. At the end of the meeting, de Villepin spoke to the media and declared that France would not associate itself "with military action that was not supported by the international community," adding that "military intervention would be the worst possible solution."

The choice of words was interesting. On the one hand, de Villepin did not entirely rule out the possibility that France would support a war *if* that war had the support of the international community, and on the other hand, he was urging the international community not to support the war by calling it the worst possible solution. It was a circular argument: *the international community should not support the war because it does not have the support of the international community, which should not support war.* A beautiful act of diplomatic sabotage—launched at the end of a meeting that was not even supposed to be on the subject of Iraq. Colin Powell was taken completely off guard.

U.S. Deputy Secretary of State Richard Armitage described Powell's reaction upon hearing de Villepin's statement: "He was very amused. . . . When he's amused, he gets pretty cold. . . . He puts the eyes on you and there is no doubt when his jaws are jacked. It's not a pretty sight."

It got worse. On February 5 Powell was sent to the UN Security Council with a multimedia presentation that included a vial of white powder, which he waved around threateningly; computer graphics of trucks he claimed were biological weapons labs; and sound recordings of Iraqi military officers talking about "getting rid of" WMDs before UN inspectors arrived. De Villepin simply shrugged off Powell's presentation, saying it only made the case for giving the inspectors "more time." On February 14, at yet another Security Council meeting, the French foreign minister threw the gauntlet to Powell once more when he declared, emotionally, "We are trying to give peace a chance."

It was positively Lennon-esque, a rallying cry to thousands of people throughout the world who were planning a big peace march the next day.

In a historical first, the public clapped at the end of the French foreign minister's speech. De Villepin was on fire. Powell was jaw-jacked. The humiliation was complete.

In retrospect, and after speaking with French intelligence officials who were active at the time, it became clear to me that France was extremely confident that Saddam had gotten rid of all his WMD programs. How could France be so sure, given the uncertain reports from its own plants inside the UN weapons inspection office? No French (or American or Russian) national working for UNSCOM, then UNMOVIC, could have gotten the job without approval from these countries' respective defense ministries. The UN inspection chiefs (Richard Butler, then Hans Blix) remained uncertain until the very end of this process about what Saddam might have hidden. They had not found anything in 2003 (though they had on many previous occasions, up until 1998, when the inspectors were kicked out); but they knew, from Iraqi records seized after the Gulf War, that some critical WMD-related items that had been imported by Saddam Hussein in the past were still unaccounted for.

So how could France be so sure there was nothing left? It had better contacts with Saddam and his inner circle than the United States did. And some members of the French intelligence community say they made a real effort to share the information they had with their counterparts in the United States. But based on thirteen years of a cat-and-mouse chase that seemed always to prove Saddam a liar, America could no longer be convinced. Saddam's continued pursuit of WMDs had become more than a fact. It had become a policy premise, without which the United States could no longer argue that Iraq was in breach of the 1991 cease-fire (a key component of America's legal argument at the Security Council).

History will recall that Powell's presentation was factually flawed. The vial of white powder he waved before his colleagues would haunt him for a long time to come. No evidence of weapons-grade anthrax production would be found in Iraq after the war. Yet given the information available to Powell at the time, the French foreign minister's unexpected provocation was unpardonable. Following in de Villepin's footsteps, Igor Ivanov of Russia got inspired: "Today is Valentine's Day," he said, "and we should be speaking of love and engagement."

With Saddam Hussein? It didn't work so well for the Iraqi dictator's ex-wife, who had fled Iraq and was now hiding from would-be assassins in Lebanon.

On February 14 Powell had delivered a straightforward speech that had drawn zero applause. Adding insult to injury, de Villepin had gone out for a victory lap with the press outside the Security Council chambers. The meeting was not yet over when journalists were already dictating their headlines into their mobile phones: "Powell's Bad Day."

It had indeed been a very bad day for the U.S. secretary of state. He had been sent to the UN to gather international support, and he was met with humiliation.

Kofi Annan knew better than to get caught in this dispute between France and the United States. His staff overwhelmingly supported France's position, and Annan would not be able to avoid getting cornered on the issue of whether America's planned invasion of Iraq was "legal or not." The secretary general would try his best to say there were several points of view on the question, but when pressed by the BBC, he would have to say that a war that began without Security Council approval was considered illegal by the United Nations. Annan did his best to avoid getting in the way of the United States, despite vocal and persistent pressure from his staff. He knew that with Bush in power and a Republican-controlled Congress, he could not afford to repeat his ill-fated 1998 peace exploit. There would be no eleventh-hour peace initiative this time around. Annan, and the UN system as a whole, could do little more than observe what looked like a pre-twentieth-century classic conflict between the world's great powers.

At stake in the highly dramatic meeting of February 14, 2003, was whether the Security Council should pass "a second resolution" authorizing the use of force against Iraq. The issue of the "second resolution" confused a great many people—including recently assigned reporters who did not have the time to read up on twelve years of bickering in the Security Council over Iraq.

There were opponents of the resolution on both sides of the debate. France thought it was "not yet time" to talk about a new resolution because the UN inspectors needed more time to do their work. It was the same argument France had made before the Gulf War, thirteen years earlier, when President Mitterrand had argued that the sanctions needed more time to persuade Saddam to withdraw from Kuwait.

Back in Washington, the hawks were saying they didn't need a second resolution before they could attack Iraq. There were seventeen resolutions already on the books against Saddam, and the so-called second resolution would in fact be the eighteenth. The twenty-four-hour newspeople were confused, and they, in turn, confused their audience. If Washington didn't feel it needed a second/eighteenth/new resolution, and if France didn't want to pass one, what was the problem? All they had to do was *not pass a resolution!*

The problem, by then, was that Colin Powell and Tony Blair had staked their entire diplomatic strategy on getting explicit UN authorization for going to war. Of course, while Powell made his case for another resolution to the Security Council, his boss, President Bush, was giving interviews from the golf course saying he didn't need UN permission to go to war.

This did little to clarify the issue for ordinary Americans. The message coming out of the White House was: *the UN really needs to pass a second resolution, even though we don't really need it.*

Thankfully, America was not entirely devoid of people who could explain the issue to the public: Senator Joseph Biden, the ranking Democrat on the Senate Foreign Relations Committee, was one of them. Writing on March 10 in the *Washington Post,* he clarified that

> for the United States, a second resolution is not a legal requirement, but it is a strategic one. It would give political cover to key allies such as Tony Blair and Spanish Prime Minister José María Aznar. And it would greatly increase the number of countries willing to join our coalition. This would help spread the risks of military action and the massive burden of putting Iraq back together—something President Bush does not like to talk about.

Those were the reasons Powell and Blair felt it was important for them to do everything they could to win UN authorization before going to war. The only thing they did not understand was that they had already lost the battle at the UN in November 2002, when they signed on to Resolution 1441.

Originally touted as a major diplomatic victory for the United States, Resolution 1441 turned out to be a trap for the Bush administration in general and for Powell in particular. Resolution 1441 gave Saddam one last chance to submit to UN weapons inspections. Of course, neither France nor the United States really cared about the UN weapons inspections. France never had, and the United States no longer did now that it was prepared to go to war. In passing the resolution, the United States thought it was setting a trap for Saddam. Powell thought de Villepin had seen him when he went *wink, wink,* as together they drafted a resolution that was supposed to be Saddam's "last chance to come clean." Powell was clearly counting on France to vote for a "use of force resolution" at the end of that process. What he did not realize was that his "friend" envisaged a road with no end.

Resolution 1441 threatened that if Saddam Hussein failed to get anything less than an A+ from the UN inspectors, there would be "serious consequences." America understood "serious consequences" to mean that Saddam would be deposed. France understood "serious consequences" to mean that the United Nations would pass another resolution. In the end, the "serious consequences" turned out to mean a historic divorce between France and the United States, and a severely devalued UN.

The United States had gone to the United Nations in search of legitimacy and, paradoxically, had ended up with less legitimacy at the end of the process than it had at the beginning. France could have spared its "ally" the humiliation. When Clinton decided to bomb Milosevic to stop him from "cleansing" Kosovo of its Albanian population, he sidestepped the UN altogether. What simplified his choice was the fact that Moscow had been courteous enough to inform him that it would under no circumstance support a UN resolution authorizing force against its "Slavic brothers." Had France been a friend of the United States, it would have made it plain at the beginning of the process that it would oppose any "use of force" resolution. When push came to shove, in March 2003, France asked for another sixty days, then another thirty days. Why? Because "all diplomatic means had to be exhausted." Bush was exhausted already and was complaining of having to sit through the "rerun of a bad movie."

Then, finally, de Villepin said it: "We won't let a resolution that can open the way to war pass in the UN Security Council."

U.S. diplomats simply couldn't believe it. Before de Villepin's diplomatic ambush, most of the U.S. political establishment thought they had France all figured out. Hawks and doves alike believed France would be a pain until the very last minute and then, when the chips were down, come on board—if not with a vote of support for the U.S. intervention, then at a minimum with an abstention. That belief was so deeply rooted in Washington's way of thinking that, at the eleventh hour, the United States felt obliged to repeat its final boarding call. As U.S. Special Operations troops began infiltrating Iraq through Kurdistan, an exasperated President Bush reiterated publicly that the time had come for all countries to "show their cards."

In response, Dominique de Villepin flew to Africa in March 2003 to lobby Angola, Cameroon, and Guinea, all of whom had temporary seats on the fifteen-member Security Council, to vote against the final draft resolution co-sponsored by the United States, Britain, and Spain.

As a permanent member of the Security Council, France had veto power. If it wanted to stop a resolution from passing, all it had to do was use it, and the resolution was dead. So why did de Villepin go thousands of miles out of his way to persuade African nations to vote against it? What was at stake in this battle for world sympathy: the future of the Iraqi people or France's standing in the world?

France's bid to restrain the American Gulliver using UN resolutions as rope was doomed from the outset. The Clinton administration had initiated military action without UN authorization in Kosovo and in Iraq. The U.S. Congress had voted to empower Bush to declare war, and the latter had made it clear that he would proceed without the explicit blessing of the world body.

In the end, the United States and Britain decided not to seek a vote. No vote was better than one against war. Dominique de Villepin had won without a showdown. But what had he really won? His diplomatic zeal did not avert a war. And insofar as France aimed to contend for the title of "champion" on international law, its diplomats would run into a bit of a snag once Iraqi journalists pulled certain files from Saddam's Oil Ministry. The leaders of Angola, Cameroon, and Guinea breathed a sigh of relief. Flattered as they were by all the sudden attention from France and the United States, they didn't have an iota of interest in Iraq and resented being asked to choose sides in a Franco-American divorce.

"You know," said one African diplomat, "this is not a good situation for us. It is not a good situation for France or America either. And clearly, this is not good for the UN. The only winner here is Saddam. He has divided his enemies on the eve of war. He is the greatest diplomat of them all."

CHAPTER **24**

Weapons of Mass Distraction

"There's an old saying in Tennessee—I know it's in Texas, probably [also] in Tennessee—that says, Fool me once, shame on . . . shame on you. Fool me twice . . . ah . . . you can't get fooled again!"

PRESIDENT GEORGE W. BUSH

What pained me most about the diplomatic debacle that preceded the Iraq War was that it did not even occur for the right reasons. The debate about whether to go to war "for disarmament" was simply wrong. There was a real argument to be had about the value of confronting Saddam Hussein as part of the war on terror and the value of transforming enemies into friends by exporting democracy. Unfortunately, that conversation did not begin in earnest until *after* the Iraq War.

Driven by the CIA's forecast of a "slam dunk" on the WMD front, America had failed to prepare its troops and its public for the enormously difficult, bloody, and expensive challenge that lay ahead.

The exclusive focus on Saddam's alleged WMDs was a harmful distraction from the human dimension of the conflict, which should have been at the forefront of the Security Council's agenda right from the beginning in 1991.

Regardless of what the Security Council was doing, I felt that the UN's staff should be hard at work preparing for the aftermath of a possible war. In the late winter of 2003, as the war seemed increasingly inevitable, I was eager to get back to work at the United Nations to help out with Iraq, but the process of my recruitment was taking forever. In early March my former (and perhaps future) director informed me that my recruitment papers were stuck in Pasha's office, so I went to pay the under secretary general a visit to find out what the problem was.

I found Pasha watching CNN behind his desk and puffing on a cigar. He eyed me suspiciously at first as I stood at the door of his office. Then he put on his joking face and invited me in. He knew the reason for my visit, but instead of leveling with me he spent half an hour accusing his director (my former and future boss) of being a two-faced bastard and a liar. Clearly, Cindy's departure hadn't changed much. Pasha and Christer were still not on speaking terms. At some point in his ramble, Pasha noticed that I was getting ready to leave, so he paused for a beat.

"I guess you didn't come here to hear about this," he said, somewhat apologetically.

I seized on this last opportunity to have a relevant conversation.

"This is going to be about nation-building," I said. "What role is the UN going to play? We need to come up with options—a plan. Something the Security Council can use."

I think I lost Pasha there for a minute, because he completely changed the subject.

"Those bozos want a facking TV, can you believe it?" Pasha said. It took me a few seconds to figure out what he was talking about, but I remembered hearing that my director had submitted a request to purchase a TV for his office so that he could follow the latest developments as they happened. It seemed to me a perfectly legitimate request, but Pasha had refused to approve it, arguing that he would not "spend Iraqi money" just so his director could "sit around and watch TV all day."

At that moment I wished my girlfriend had hit me on the head with a frying pan rather than let me go back to the United Nations. The world was going to war, and these guys were fighting over a TV set. I tried to remind myself that the UN would most likely have to start a whole new operation after the war and that it was going to be headed by a different team. A well-informed source in Washington had mentioned to me that Sergio Vieira de Mello was being considered for the job. Sergio had a stellar reputation both as a diplomat and as a manager. My plan was to get back into the system and then join his group as soon as it was set up.

"You're thinking far ahead," Pasha said, nodding pensively. "All right. I'll see what I can do," he said finally.

Then, perhaps because he awoke to the contradiction of having his own TV turned on while blasting his director for wanting one too, Pasha turned off CNN.

"Facking UNMOVIC! This is all a big show! They'll never find any facking smoking guns!" said Pasha.

There I thought he had a point. The whole UN system was paralyzed by the search for weapons of mass destruction. Everything seemed to hinge on whether UNMOVIC stumbled upon some type of evidence that Saddam had kept weapons hidden from the UN. To their credit, the UN arms inspectors did find a few things, like long-range missiles and old shells that could have been used to spread blister agents. To the "coalition of the willing," it was proof that war was necessary. To the "peace camp," it was proof that the "inspections were working" and that there was no need to use force. It was a vicious circle, and a distracting one at that.

An honest debate between France and the United States on the subject of Iraq's weapons of mass destruction ought to have begun with a *mea culpa* from both sides.

Both France and the United States had looked away when Saddam Hussein first used poison gas in the early 1980s, during Iraq's war with Iran. France continued to sell major weapons to Iraq thereafter. As for the United States, it sent Donald Rumsfeld to Baghdad in March 1984 with instructions to deliver a private message to the Iraqi government. According to documents declassified under the Freedom of Information Act, Rumsfeld told the Iraqi dictator that public U.S. criticism of Iraq for using chemical weapons would not derail Washington's attempts to forge a better relationship with Baghdad. Rumsfeld, then President Reagan's special Middle East envoy, was given a brief by Secretary of State George Shultz that urged him to tell Iraqi Foreign Minister Tariq Aziz that previous U.S. statements on chemical weapons "were made strictly out of our strong opposition to the use of . . . chemical weapons, wherever it occurs," and that the U.S. desire "to improve bilateral relations, at a pace of Iraq's choosing," remained "undiminished." "This message bears reinforcing during your discussions," Rumsfeld was instructed. Saddam got the message loud and clear and later used chemical weapons again to exterminate the Kurds.

Of course, the prize for helping Iraq with its WMD programs has to go to France, and to Jacques Chirac in particular. It was he who, in the late 1970s, approved the sale of a seventy-megawatt, uranium-powered nuclear reactor to Saddam.

Experts all concur that, had Israel not destroyed the nuclear reactor in a 1981 air raid, Iraq would have acquired nuclear weapons before 1990. In other words, "Jacques's Iraq" would have been a nuclear power by the time of its invasion of Kuwait. If Saddam had nuclear weapons back then, Kuwait would likely have remained the "nineteenth province of Iraq," as he initially called it, and Saudi Arabia might easily have become its twentieth. Without U.S. military protection, places like the United Arab Emirates, Dubai, and Qatar might easily have fallen under Saddam's control as well. Would the West have risked nuclear war to defend them?

Short of intervening militarily and putting millions of lives at risk of irradiation, the international community would have been forced to contend with a nuclear Iraq controlling a majority of the world's proven oil reserves and headed by a psychopath.

Why did Jacques Chirac sell a nuclear reactor to the Baathist regime of Saddam Hussein?

Trust Christiane Amanpour to get straight to the point, in an exclusive interview with Jacques Chirac:

> **Amanpour:** There have been consistent allegations that Saddam Hussein put money into one of your electoral campaigns. How do you respond to that?
> **Chirac:** [laughter] It's preposterous, really. Anything can be said about anyone. As we say in French, "The taller the tale, the more likely people will believe in it."

Speaking of tall tales: France argued that the "Osirak" nuclear reactor it sold to Saddam was for *civilian* purposes. Even Saddam couldn't keep up that lie.

On September 30, 1980, in the opening days of the Iran-Iraq war, an Iranian aircraft attacked, and lightly damaged, the Osirak facility. In response, the official Iraqi news agency issued the following statement: "The Iranian people should not fear the Iraqi nuclear reactor, which is not intended to be used against Iran, but against the Zionist entity."

The "civilian purposes" of Iraq's nuclear program were clear: massive Israeli civilian casualties. But Chirac never expressed any regrets about the matter. As late as March 2003, when Amanpour gave him the chance to express regret, he couldn't get the word "sorry" out of his mouth.

> **Amanpour:** A lot of people call [Osirak] "O-Chirac," as you know. In retrospect, do you regret that it was destroyed, given that it could have been used to form nuclear weapons?

Chirac: Well, this reactor was a civilian reactor. But in those days, all of the major democracies—all of them, each and every one of them—had contacts and trade and exchanges with Iraq, including on weapons.

No regrets. *Everybody was doing it!* Well, not quite. When President Mitterrand was approached to rebuild the Iraqi reactor, after Israel had destroyed it, he refused.

At the time of the bombing, France's condemnation of Israel was particularly vociferous. Chirac called the Israeli ambassador into his office and told him he was representing a band of "criminals." Even the United States condemned Israel at the time for "violating Iraqi sovereignty," though by the time of the Gulf War, the U.S. government had reversed itself and expressed relief that Israel had destroyed the Iraqi nuclear reactor in 1981.

In subsequent years, Saddam Hussein poured more than $10 billion into rebuilding Iraq's nuclear weapons program, only to miscalculate once again by invading Kuwait before actually acquiring the bomb. According to a report by the London-based International Institute for Strategic Studies, by 1990 Iraq had reached a stage where it could very soon start producing two nuclear bombs per year. Had it not been for Desert Storm, "Iraq could have accumulated a nuclear stockpile of a dozen or more weapons by the end of the decade."

Once they set foot in Iraq in 1991, UN weapons inspectors were able to corroborate that Iraq had been far more advanced than Western intelligence agencies had thought. Saddam had successfully disseminated his nuclear facilities throughout the country and cobbled together a program that could have produced a nuclear device sometime in the 1990s. This finding was not based on iffy intelligence reports. It was based on firsthand inspections conducted in the initial months after Desert Storm, when Saddam's regime was at its most fragile. During that time, the UN weapons inspectors destroyed more Iraqi WMDs than had been destroyed by bombings during the war itself. As late as 2005, UN reports reconfirmed this. In report S/1005/351, UNSCOM's successor, UNMOVIC, confirmed that

in 1991, Iraq declared that it had carried out laboratory research on [the chemical nerve agent] VX gas. By 1995, UNSCOM uncovered evidence that the scope of Iraq's activities on VX was much broader. Consequently, in 1996 Iraq declared the production of 3.9 metric tons of VX, the production of 60 metric tons of key VX precursors and the acquisition of some 650 metric tons of other precursors for the production of VX. Iraq also acknowledged that it had decided to conceal various aspects of its VX activities from UNSCOM.

Saddam's earlier subterfuges were not in question. Ironically, he may have been so efficient in his pursuit of the ultimate weapon that the intelligence community would never again underestimate his ability to reconstitute his WMD program. If anything, the community ended up overestimating it in the run-up to the Iraq War. Regardless of intelligence estimates (which are uncertain by nature), it was a mistake for the United States to present the war against Saddam as one waged for "disarmament."

Washington's main objective was always regime change, defined as the temporary administration of Iraq by the United States, the reconstruction of its economy, and the stabilization of its tribal feuds with a view to building a democratic and secure Iraq. The case for doing all that may not have sold well in sound bites, but it would have been honest. And it would have forced a discussion of the future management of Iraq's transition—something the UN Security Council should have been seized with long before the beginning of hostilities.

Though it came late, Bush did eventually lay out a positive vision for the liberation and reconstruction of Iraq, in a speech at the American Enterprise Institute on February 27, 2003. "The nation of Iraq," said Bush, "with its proud heritage, abundant resources, and skilled and educated people, is fully capable of moving toward democracy and living in freedom." He added that America was preparing for such a transition by making plans to meet basic humanitarian needs. "We will provide medicine for the sick," he said. And he promised to keep running the 50,000 food distribution centers set up under the Oil-for-Food program.

But this was just one month before the war. By that time the argument for disarmament had already taken hold in the minds of so many people that Bush's "vision speech" left many observers deeply skeptical of his administration's ability to make good on its promises. Besides, the UN Security Council completely ignored Bush's words, because the UN Charter does not consider freedom and human rights relevant to authorizing the use of force. According to the UN Charter, force can be used only in situations of legitimate defense or as authorized by the UN Security Council under Article 42, to confront threats to international peace and security.

If the UN Charter were applied domestically—say, to a village—then every head of household in that village would have the right to beat his wife (assuming a male dominates the household) and starve his children, and the society would *not* have the right to intervene. Only if a person attacked another family's house could he be restrained, and even then he might be left in charge of his own family—as was the case in 1991, when Saddam was left as the ruler of Iraq.

Knowing they stood no chance of selling the war to other members of the UN Security Council merely on the merits of overthrowing the Iraqi dictator, the United States and Britain went ahead and made a case for intervention based on the need to "disarm Saddam Hussein."

The case for disarmament was a tough one to make because most experts agreed that Iraq had fewer WMDs in 2003—if any—than it had in 1991. To complicate matters, there were no indications that Iraq was about to attack any of its neighbors (or the United States, for that matter). Arguing "legitimate defense" was out of the question. It was therefore crucial for the United States that Saddam still possessed WMDs.

Since it would be very difficult without invading to prove that Saddam possessed WMDs, the United States and its allies found themselves in the awkward rhetorical position of having to invade Iraq to prove why it was necessary to invade Iraq (only to demonstrate that the invasion had, in fact, been unnecessary according to its own rationale). Such was the cost of making a case that didn't make intuitive sense.

The UN Security Council found itself transformed into a strange version of a "world court" with fifteen divided judges. Nobody could agree on what would actually constitute a smoking gun. When Colin Powell played an intercept of an Iraqi military leader ordering chemical weapons destroyed, he felt confident he had provided solid evidence for his case. In the intercept, two Iraqi commanders had the following exchange:

Commander 1: Remove, Remove!
Commander 2: Got it.
Commander 1: Nerve agents! Nerve agents! Wherever it comes up. . . .
Commander 2: Got it!
Commander 1: Wherever it comes up! . . .
Commander 2: Got it!

Was this proof that Saddam's military possessed nerve agents? Not quite. But it showed that if it did possess nerve agents, it was clearly trying to get rid of them.

Meanwhile, the news channels, always in need of images to match their words, kept showing footage of Saddam dressed (fittingly) as Al Capone and shooting a gun in the air from the balcony of one of his palaces. I thought the news editors made an important point by superimposing that image on the smoking gun debate. The problem was not with Iraq's guns but with the madman in charge of them—a man who had done far more damage using conventional weapons than with WMDs.

What should have been a moral debate about whether to go to war to topple the Iraqi regime was replaced by an idiotic reality show—featuring weapons experts driving around Iraq in convoys of Toyota Land Cruisers looking for hidden weapons. This led to a number of awkward situations. In one instance, the inspectors were stalled at the entrance to a warehouse because nobody could find the key to the front door. Panic ensued. *Were the Iraqis failing to collaborate?* Since there was a camera crew along for the ride, the inspectors had to look tough—so they broke down the door and stepped into the little warehouse, a few minutes before the Iraqi chicken farmer who owned it arrived with the key. "What have you done to my door?" he asked. The inspectors found nothing.

The incident I found most revealing did not involve weapons of mass destruction in any way. It involved an Iraqi civilian. On January 25, 2003, an Iraqi man stopped a UN-marked Land Cruiser right outside the UN compound in Baghdad, pleading, "Save me! Save me!" According to a CNN report of the incident, the unarmed man then boarded the UN car and refused to get out.

"Appearing agitated and frightened, the young man, with a closely trimmed beard and a mustache, sat inside the white UN-marked SUV for 10 minutes," the Associated Press reported. Then, according to CNN, "an Iraqi guard struggled to pull him out, while an unfazed UN inspector watched from the passenger seat."

As the Iraqi guard struggled to pull him out, the man shouted, "I am unjustly treated! I am unjustly treated!"

Clearly, the Iraqi man was assuming that the UN cared.

CNN had no idea how to spin the incident. Why would a random Iraqi who was being unjustly treated seek refuge with the United Nations? What did it have to do with Iraq's WMDs? Correspondent Nic Robertson tried to tie the incident in with the story of the day, involving the (non-happening) interviews with Iraqi scientists. It didn't occur to anybody that the drama we got to watch on the nightly news was far more relevant to Iraq's condition than any development on the weapons inspections front.

"Then," according to the CNN report, "UN security men arrived, and they and the Iraqi police carried the man by his feet and arms into the fenced compound . . . and turned him over to Iraqi authorities." And the report went on about the hunt for weapons of mass destruction.

The man was never heard from again. This, in a nutshell, was the story of Iraq and the international community. We were so self-centered, so concerned with threats against our own security, that we had become completely desensitized to the fate of ordinary Iraqis. All we cared about was the weapons. While I disliked this narrow focus, I also resented those who dismissed the existence of such weapons to begin with. After watching the inspectors work from up close for all these years, I was pretty convinced Saddam was hiding *something* from the UN.

In his first postwar visit to a U.S. base outside Doha, Qatar, President Bush skipped quickly past the niceties and went straight to his chief political obsession: where are the weapons of mass destruction? According to *Time* magazine, he first turned to his Baghdad proconsul, Paul Bremer, and asked, "Are you in charge of finding WMD?" Bremer said no, he was not. Bush then asked the question to his military commander, Gen. Tommy Franks. But Franks said it wasn't his job either. A little exasperated, Bush asked, "So who is in charge of finding WMD?" After aides conferred for a moment, someone volunteered the name of Stephen Cambone, a little-known deputy to Donald Rumsfeld, back in Washington.

"Who?" asked Bush.

The lack of WMDs had become a political hot potato, and nobody in the administration wanted to be the one to break the bad news to the commander in chief.

One of the many mistakes the Bush administration made in the run-up to the war was to attack the chief UN weapons inspector, Hans Blix, as a means to pressure him into strengthening the case for war. Blix was a straight shooter. He reported to the UN Security Council exactly what he saw. I had met him at a dinner once before he was thrown into the limelight, and he had come across as a very reasonable man who, unlike some of our colleagues at the UN, had no illusions about the regime of Saddam Hussein. Iraq's cooperation was imperfect, and that is how he presented it to the Security Council. When asked if the United States would find WMDs in Iraq, Blix responded, "That is the $64 billion question," noting also that the inspections had cost merely $64 *million.*

Of course, that wasn't counting the cost of positioning troops on Iraq's borders, which was why the inspectors were allowed back into Iraq in the first place. But still, if the war was really about disarmament, the Swede had a point. Then, when it grew increasingly clear that the United States had not found any WMDs in Iraq, Blix cracked: "It is somewhat fascinating to me that you can have 100 percent certainty about the weapons of mass destruction [being in Iraq] and zero percent certainty about where they are."

Ultimately, President Bush was forced to call on former UN weapons inspector David Kay to continue the search where Hans Blix left off. (Blix, an old man who loves his wife more than the spotlight, retired without controversy in June 2003.) Kay eventually reported that Iraq had indeed been in violation of the cease-fire resolution but that he could find no stockpiles of chemical or biological weapons in Iraq. It was a total, unmitigated fiasco.

The French, the Russians, and the Germans were laughing now. But they wouldn't be laughing for long.

The CIA report that finally admitted finding no WMDs in Iraq also unearthed another interesting fact—evidence of major corruption in the UN Oil-for-Food program. The effort to divert the public's attention was shamelessly transparent. But at least the United States and Britain would not run out of "smoking guns" this time. Saddam Hussein had left plenty of evidence around to implicate his former business partners.

Part Three

CHAPTER **25**

There Will Be Blood

In a document that would become known as the Downing Street Memo, which contained the minutes of a top-secret briefing, Richard Dearlove, the head of British intelligence, had warned Prime Minister Tony Blair that the United States was ill prepared for the aftermath of the invasion of Iraq. He decried the absence of a coherent plan of action for the post-Saddam transition. While the United States had prepared for humanitarian emergencies that might require an influx of food or medicine, the wider, forward-looking planning process had fallen hostage to a bitter turf war between the Pentagon, on the one hand, and a loose alliance including the State Department and the CIA, on the other. While each side wrestled for budgets and power, the first victims, as usual, would be the Iraqi people.

During the war itself, France's Dominique de Villepin refused to comment when a journalist from the *Telegraph* asked him whether he hoped American and British forces would win. "I'm not going to answer," he replied angrily, saying he had already expressed himself on the subject. He had previously said that he hoped for "a swift conclusion" to the war, but that did not exactly answer the question of which side he hoped would win. De Villepin was not the only one in France reluctant to support the coalition. A poll conducted for the daily *Le Monde* found that one-third of the French people surveyed answered no when asked whether "deep down" they wished for a victory of the U.S. and British forces. Only half of the French people surveyed hoped the coalition would win.

On the other side of the Atlantic, Fox News kept showing footage of average Joe Americans pouring French wine down the gutter. One Congressman decreed that the fries sold in Capitol Hill cafeterias should be renamed Freedom Fries (which didn't matter much to the French, since French fries were actually invented by Belgians, and it was probably a testament to some Americans' poor sense of geography that the fries ended up being called French in the first place). Another grandstanding Congressional bill would let families of veterans killed in action on French soil in the course of the twentieth century have their relatives repatriated and reburied in the United States.

Amid all this bitterness, the international community had a nation to rebuild. And the brawl that preceded the war left the international community too divided to put together a coherent mandate for the UN after the fall of Saddam Hussein in April 2003.

All sides initially urged the UN to return to Iraq, but for radically opposite reasons. France wanted a speedy end to the U.S. occupation. The United States wanted the UN to legitimize its occupation. The Sunnis of Iraq hoped that a UN intervention would offset the growing power of Shiite and Kurdish leaders. And the latter hoped that a token UN presence might persuade France, Germany, and others to join the reconstruction effort.

Without a coherent mandate, the UN found itself projected into a conflict where it would take hits from all sides.

The first blow would come from the Sunni terrorists, the second blow would come from Shiites and Kurds on the Iraqi Governing Council, and the third blow would come from powerful lawmakers and opinion-makers in the United States. The third act of this collective tragedy would force me into a role I had never envisaged for myself.

CHAPTER 26

The Road to Hell

"I cannot conceive of any vital disaster happening to
this vessel."

CAPTAIN SMITH, commander of the *Titanic*

On the afternoon of August 19, 2003, Pasha stepped out of his office
at the United Nations headquarters in Baghdad to light up a Cohiba. He had
recently pledged to lay off the puffers, but the sound of distant gunfire, low-
flying helicopters, and the general sense of chaos that prevailed in Baghdad
after the U.S.-led invasion chipped away at everyone's nerves nonstop. Pasha
could use a little nicotine break.

A few hundred yards away, a flatbed truck packed with more than 2,000
pounds of high-grade explosives was rolling toward the UN building.

It was a sunny afternoon. Reporters were trickling in from the parking lot
to attend a press briefing on the humanitarian situation in Iraq. A few days
earlier, on August 14, the UN Security Council had passed Resolution 1500,
establishing the UN Assistance Mission for Iraq (UNAMI) under the leadership of Kofi Annan's special representative, Sergio Vieira de Mello.

While Pasha stepped out for a smoke, Vieira de Mello was in his office
meeting with a human rights lawyer. A native of Brazil, Vieira de Mello had
a stellar reputation for navigating delicate UN missions successfully and for
putting the interests of civilians first. He had helped manage East Timor's
transition to democracy after it emerged from decades of brutal rule by In-

donesia. As the man in charge of mine clearance in Cambodia and in the Balkans in the early 1990s, and as a leader in handling central Africa's refugee crises later in that decade, he had set new standards for UN management. In 2002 he was named UN High Commissioner for Human Rights. By the time of the Iraq War, he appeared to be the UN's most able and widely respected manager; so when it came time to pick a leader who would help Iraq get back on its feet, all eyes naturally turned to him.

Vieira de Mello had been reluctant to take the job. In e-mail exchanges with colleagues, he had complained that the UN's mission was unclear. But pleas from President Bush and Condoleezza Rice, and Kofi Annan's promise to limit his tour of duty to four months, finally persuaded him to take the job, ill defined as it was.

The mandate had been written in haste. Christer, my former director, had asked me for input at the time. I had suggested we propose focused objectives we knew we could deliver on. The key, as I saw it, was to help oversee upcoming elections—something the UN (and Vieira de Mello in particular) had experience with. Apart from that, I thought we'd be busy enough coordinating international aid efforts while Iraq underwent what looked like an increasingly violent transition.

The Security Council saw things differently. These were the days when President Bush was declaring "mission accomplished," even as it was becoming clear to America's military commanders that Iraq was growing increasingly unstable by the day. For France and Russia, the solution to Iraq's ills, including the spread of terrorism throughout that country, lay in ending the occupation immediately. With this objective in mind they piled a wide range of responsibilities on Vieira de Mello's shoulders, hoping this would encourage the United States to disengage. They knew they would have far more influence over Iraqi politics if the UN took center stage in managing postwar Iraq. They had signed billions of dollars' worth of contracts through the Oil-for-Food program and didn't want to lose those. Ironically, therefore, they were suddenly not as keen to lift the sanctions, as that move might put their business at risk. Russia was arguing that Iraq had to be "certified" clear of WMDs before sanctions could be lifted. This pushed the Bush administration into a corner. As long as inspectors were roaming the country, the United States didn't have to admit how flawed its prewar intelligence had been.

In addition, Saddam's government had incurred astronomical debt. Iraq owed France and Germany $5 billion each and Russia $12 billion. Much of these loans had been granted in return for future oil exploration rights.

France and Russia didn't want Paul Bremer and the newly established Coalition Provisional Authority messing with the business they had lined up during the Saddam era.

The State Department saw no harm in piling up a range of unrealistic mission objectives on the United Nations. If anything, one diplomat confided, they would have somewhere to lay blame if things went wrong.

As I went about the process of reenlisting with the UN, I had the familiar feeling that the international community once again saw Iraq as a cake to be divided among the great powers. I received e-mails about international conferences where contractors advertised the opportunity to "make a killing" in Iraq.

A killing would indeed be made, only in a far more literal sense than most outsiders had imagined. A number of observers had warned about the possible spread of terrorism in postwar Iraq. But the violence that stood to be unleashed would dwarf their worst predictions.

As the United Nations reentered Iraq, the organization's members had yet to agree on an official definition for "terrorism." That fact alone should have dissuaded me from going back to Iraq with the UN. Yet I could not get myself to stop caring about the country that had defined much of my academic and professional life thus far. I had written about Iraq for my honors thesis at Brown University, assisted in covering Security Council decisions on Iraq while at CNN, and worked for more than three years for the UN operation that was Iraq's main lifeline to the outside world. I had since written about the conflict for a variety of newspapers, often warning of the difficulties we might face if the international community set out to address Iraq's deep-rooted fault lines before tending to its own stark divisions.

In many ways, I had come of age with the Iraq conflict, and it seemed only natural that I should contribute my services at this most critical stage. Despite Vieira de Mello's vast and muddy mandate (which included everything from promoting economic reconstruction, human rights, judicial reform, and the return of refugees to reestablishing Iraq's looted cultural sites), he was able to articulate the essence of his mission in words that resonated with me. Speaking to reporters on the day of his nomination in May, he said, "Iraqi society is rich, and that richness has been suppressed brutally for the past twenty-four years." Vieira de Mello had not been a supporter of the war; but unlike many others within the UN, he saw the need to take the situation from there and felt confident that he would be able to liaise with American and Iraqi leaders and bring in more support from European powers. He had

a proven ability to interact productively with the military. All sides trusted
him to put his heart into the task of unifying the international community
and defending the interests of Iraq's civilians.

Pasha and Vieira de Mello held equal rank as under secretary generals, but
their roles were quite distinct. Pasha was there to close down the Oil-for-Food
operation, to clean up the remnants of the UN's controversial past. Vieira de
Mello was there to help prepare the country for a better future.

Even as I was placing call after call to the UN bureaucracy to speed up the
process of my deployment to Iraq, Al Qaeda was wrapping up plans for the
destruction of the UN's new operation. Exploiting the Pentagon's failure to
control the vast arms caches contained in Saddam's former military bases, terrorist operatives had acquired a 500-pound Soviet-made bomb. Such a large
bomb would have been sufficient to destroy our UN headquarters completely, but to minimize the UN leaders' chance of survival, the terrorists
packed in another 1,500 pounds of high-grade explosives. The truck they
used had been purchased through the UN's Oil-for-Food program the previous year. It had a brown driver's cabin and a bright-orange cargo container.
Many such trucks had been stolen from the government's fleet during the
looting rampage that followed the invasion. An Algerian national named Fah-
dal Nassim, who had come to Iraq to enlist as a warrior in this new jihad, was
chosen as the driver. The only challenge remaining was how to get the truck
bomb close enough to the UN building to ensure its destruction.

That part of their job was greatly facilitated by the UN's deep-seated incompetence in caring for the security of its staff. Pasha's past performance as UN security coordinator had been lax, owing in part to his double posting as head of
the Oil-for-Food program. In May 2002, Kofi Annan finally decided to appoint a full-time head of security. For that job he picked Tun Myat, who had
served as Pasha's humanitarian coordinator in Iraq but had no formal experience as a security manager. The bureaucrat from Myanmar had started his career as an insurance officer for the World Food Program and worked his way up
to director of external relations. The press release announcing his appointment
as security coordinator sought to boost the man's credentials in the field of security by saying he had "traveled extensively" in some "hazardous" areas.

Well, so had Angelina Jolie (in her capacity as a goodwill ambassador for
UNHCR, the UN's refugee agency, the actress actually traveled to more "hazardous" conflict zones than Myat). Myat was no more qualified for the post
than countless other humanitarian workers. He had never served as a commander in the police or in the military. And his analysis of the security situation in Iraq was downright disconcerting.

Before the war, I had developed an obsession with the UN's evacuation plan. Compared with the 1998 campaign, the 2003 war would be a far more protracted and dangerous affair for the humanitarian community, and I did not want to see my friends trapped in Baghdad at the onset of hostilities once again. During the run-up to the war, when I was doing some pro bono work for Christer, I suggested that we make preparations for a common evacuation with the weapons inspectors before the start of hostilities. He agreed and took the matter up with the new UN security coordinator.

"Don't you worry," Tun Myat told him. "My friend al-Sahaf will *never* let anything happen to us."

Sahaf was the Iraqi information minister at the time of the war, also known as Baghdad Bob. He was the first Iraqi official Pasha and I had met, back in 1997, when he was minister of foreign affairs. At the time, we had feared a bombing campaign was about to start even as we sat in his office.

The thought that any UN official might call this guy a "friend" was absolutely bewildering to me. Had Myat not watched television in 1990, when Saddam took all foreign workers in Iraq hostage? And did he not understand that Saddam's information minister had no sway over matters of security? In Angelina Jolie's action films, we at least know who the "bad guys" are. In the very real and dangerous environment that was postwar Iraq, the same could not be said of the UN's security chief. In fact, under Myat's leadership, it sometimes appeared as if the U.S.-led coalition was perceived as a graver threat to the UN than elements of the former regime or the terrorists.

When the UN returned to Baghdad in May 2003, the compound was occupied by the U.S. forces' Second Armored Cavalry Regiment. After a good amount of looting, the coalition decided to secure the premises awaiting the UN's return. The first thing the security coordinator's office did was to ask U.S. forces to vacate the building and move to the compound's "outside perimeter." Fiercely protective of its office space, the UN also insisted that U.S. forces had no authority to search vehicles or people coming into or out of the complex. Myat thought the job would be done far better by the UN's old local Iraqi security guards, who, under Saddam, had reported all UN movements to the Iraqi secret service. Most of the UN's former guards were in fact security agents themselves, handpicked by the Iraqi government.

While Myat felt safer under the protection of Saddam Hussein's former spies than under that of coalition troops, the staff on the ground were growing increasingly alarmed. As John Burnett, a journalist with National Public Radio, wrote in the *New York Times,* many UN staff were a lot more worried about their security than the UN security coordinator was:

At a barbecue in the parking lot in late June, conversation among United Nations staffers focused on how easy it would be for a determined terrorist to drive a truck into the compound. The heavy steel door that opened onto the street had finally fallen off its hinges, and the entrance to the compound had become an open thoroughfare. The guards at the gate seemed to be more for show than for effectiveness.*

If only they had been just for show. Odds are inside information was passed on to those who commandeered the attack, which coincided with a time when both UN leaders were scheduled to be on the premises.

Fiona Watson, a young British woman who served as Vieira de Mello's assistant on mission, was particularly worried. Spooky told me she had called colleagues in New York and shared her growing fears. She wanted to come home as soon as possible.

Attacks against humanitarian and diplomatic personnel had increased significantly in recent weeks. On August 7 a car bomb detonated outside the Jordanian Embassy in Baghdad, killing eighteen people. On August 10 and 11, security briefings noted that "information became available to the UN security team of an imminent bomb attack in the Canal Road area of Baghdad."** The UN was the only conceivable international target in that zone.

Despite warnings from the coalition that the security environment was "hostile" for humanitarian workers, the UN did not raise the alertness level. Several humanitarian workers from NGOs had been kidnapped, some killed. Yet in the assessment of the UN security coordinator, who completely ignored the warnings from his team in Baghdad, the threat to UN personnel remained "low." As defined by his written evaluation, the main risk for UN personnel in Iraq was to find themselves in the "wrong place at the wrong time."

Given the UN's security posture, one might wonder why the terrorist didn't simply drive straight through the broken front gate and ram the UN building head-on. But the attack was well planned. The location had been scouted out. And the prime objective of the mission was to target the UN's top leaders, whose offices faced the back of the building.

Running right behind the UN compound was an access road that led to a training school for hotel workers. A U.S. Avenger platoon had blocked the

*John Burnett, "Waiting for the Inevitable in Baghdad," *New York Times,* August 20, 2003.
**Report of the Independent Panel on the Safety and Security of UN Personnel in Iraq, October 20, 2003.

road for security reasons using a five-ton truck, in part because the road ran in close proximity and parallel to Vieira de Mello's and Pasha's offices. In addition, the platoon set up an observation post on the roof of the UN building in order to see any suspicious oncoming vehicles from a distance. The UN leadership felt "uneasy" and "uncomfortable" with this highly visible U.S. presence and asked coalition forces to withdraw their heavy equipment and dismantle the rooftop observation post.

No alternative security measures were requested by the UN. Worried U.S. soldiers later laid down concertina wire on the access road, but the UN requested that it be removed as well. Fearing a diplomatic incident, U.S. forces complied. The access road was therefore unchecked and open for traffic on August 19, the day Al Qaeda decided to strike.

The driver of the bomb-laden truck advanced slowly at first, until he reached the west side of the UN compound. There, he turned left onto the access road that ran parallel to the UN building. He then cranked up his engine and floored the gas pedal, accelerating down the passageway, sending pebbles flying at office windows that lined his path. If his information was correct, his two principal targets—Pasha and Sergio—would be at their desks. He slammed on the brakes right below their office windows.

Vieira de Mello was meeting with Gilbert Loescher, a professor from the University of Notre Dame and an expert in human rights and refugee issues. They were trying to work out how to help the weakest elements of Iraqi society, many of whom were being forced into exile by religious violence and terror.

They heard the spray of gravel from down below, the sound of screeching tires, the tearing of metal from the truck's brakes . . . then nothing.

The blast ripped right through the façade, spreading shrapnel and flying glass on the building's occupants and causing half of the structure to collapse. Buildings located a kilometer away had their windows shattered by the shockwaves. Arriving at the scene shortly after the explosion, Bernard Kerik, the former New York Police Department commissioner, was dumbfounded by the "enormous amount of explosives" used by the bomber and by the precision of the attack.

Twenty-two people died and more than 150 sustained injuries, some very serious. The masonry buckled, leaving Vieira de Mello trapped under rubble several floors down from where his office had been. His legs were crushed under a cement block, and he was treated with morphine to dull the pain. His military adviser kept talking to him, trying to keep him conscious for as long as possible. But the bleeding was heavy, and rescue workers lacked the equipment to dig him out fast enough. For hours, the media reported that he was alive and that he had even spoken on his cellphone. But as the blood slowly drained from his body, Vieira de Mello became unconscious. When he died, so did all hope that the humanitarian community would be able to operate in postwar Iraq.

It was early in the morning in New York when all news channels interrupted their programs to show live footage from the scene. In the past few days, I had banged my head against the UN bureaucracy. My recruitment had been cleared by the interview panel, and if everything had gone according to plan I would have been on the ground in Iraq. Spooky and I were both mad as hell that we hadn't been able to join Vieira de Mello and Pasha in Baghdad. Spooky was a lot more knowledgeable about Iraq than many of those who had been sent in. He, too, was going ballistic over the slow pace of the bureaucracy. We both suspected interference, perhaps even from our good old foe Cindy, who, after being booted out by Pasha, had finally landed a job at UN Human Resources (of all places). We had no proof that she was delaying our paperwork, but old paranoid reflexes die hard. It would eventually occur to me that the UN's dysfunctional bureaucracy might have saved my life by preventing me from being at the scene at the time of the bombing.

When I first saw the carnage, I worried about Pasha. I flipped the channels nervously as I scoured the web for information and called everyone I knew at the UN to inquire. Spooky finally got word that Pasha was alive. Miraculously, he had survived with only minor injuries. His decision to step out of his office seconds before the blast had saved him. It had to be the best-timed cigar break of his life.

Fiona Watson, who had grown increasingly fearful in previous days, was killed. Loescher, who was in Vieira de Mello's office, lost both of his legs and stayed in a coma for days but ultimately survived.

Many of the survivors had pierced eardrums. They could not hear their own voices. Nonetheless, they quickly gathered themselves, sometimes using sign language, and started organizing the rescue as best they could, digging into the rubble with their bare hands and trying to take care of the injured. There was blood everywhere. One hundred yards from the explosion, a pair of severed hands and feet were recovered. It was assumed they belonged to the suicide bomber.

The report following the incident praised the courage of UN staff and U.S. troops alike in reacting to the tragedy. But it also stated that the lack of contingency planning by the United Nations for an attack with a large number of casualties had hurt the rescue mission. There were no organized command posts or points of assembly, no method to track casualties as they left the site either by their own means or by medical evacuation. One female staff member was listed as killed even though she was, in fact, alive. She was left without UN contact or support for several days in an Iraqi hospital. Her family was in mourning when they received a phone call from her a week later, when she was finally able to speak.

Flying glass shards caused most of the injuries and disfigured a good number of people. Back in 2000, Christer had submitted a mission report in which he specifically advised that the UN urgently install anti-fragmentation film on the windows of its Baghdad headquarters. The proposal was ignored by the security coordinator's office. In 2003 the World Food Program offered to buy anti-fragmentation film for the UN and pay for installation itself. The UN Secretariat declined, saying it would finally procure the anti-fragmentation film on its own. By the time of the blast, the large windows of the UN cafeteria were still unprotected.

Following the attack, Myat declared at a press conference that "never," in his "wildest dreams or nightmares," had he imagined that the United Nations could be the target of terrorism. That statement alone should have caused Kofi Annan to pick up his phone and fire him on the spot. Myat refused to resign despite ample calls from UN staff. It took until March of the following year, and the publication of a detailed independent investigation, which found Myat to be "oblivious" and grossly negligent, before Annan finally demanded his security coordinator's resignation. In other words, UN staff security remained under dangerously incompetent management for another six months after the August 19 attack, which put the UN on Al Qaeda's official list of targets.

Several Iraqi groups claimed responsibility for the attack, but ultimately, one of Abu Musab al-Zarqawi's chief bomb-makers, a man known as Al-Kurdi, was arrested and charged with organizing the operation.

Zarqawi, a Jordanian petty criminal turned terrorist mastermind in the battlefield of Iraq, had leveraged the attacks on the Jordanian Embassy and the UN headquarters to claim leadership of the newly formed Al Qaeda in Iraq umbrella group. In a video acquired by PBS *Frontline*, he declared, "We destroyed the UN building, the protectors of the Jews, the friends of the oppressors and aggressors. The UN has recognized the Americans as the masters of Iraq. Before that, they gave Palestine as a gift to the Jews so they can rape the land and humiliate our people. Do not forget Bosnia, Kashmir, Afghanistan and Chechnya."

In Bosnia, the UN had sought to help Muslims. In Afghanistan, the United States had helped free the country of Soviet occupation. The international community had widely condemned the Soviet carpet-bombing of Chechnya. And the UN had long since relegated Israel to the status of a pariah state in the General Assembly. Finally, the UN had opposed the invasion of Iraq. And according to the UN's communication director in Baghdad, Salim Lone, the UN's aim was to help "end the occupation" as soon as possible.

But such facts mattered little to terrorists like Zarqawi, for whom any entity that sought to help Iraq rebuild was a fair target. Much to my dismay, however, Zarqawi's irrational accusations against the UN actually found resonance among a large part of the UN community.

Denis Halliday, then retired, spoke for many of them when he appeared in the media and said that the reason the United Nations had been attacked was that the UN had been in "collusion" with the United States. In his view, the UN had been taken over by the United States and turned into a "dark joke," a "malignant force" in the eyes of much of the world.* In his remarks he referenced the Israeli-Palestinian conflict, blaming the United States for using the Security Council to defend Israel unfairly and fomenting additional Arab anger at the United Nations. Though expressed differently, these points were in fact very similar to those made by Zarqawi himself.

While Annan and his inner circle initially thought it right to lay at least some blame on the United States (which had refused to let the UN in on its military security briefings in Baghdad), it soon became clear that U.S. forces had offered more protection than the UN had been willing to accept. Still, in the aftermath of the attack, the organization redoubled its efforts to distance itself even further from the United States. Mark Malloch Brown, then the head of the United Nations Development Program, summed up the prevailing lesson the UN had learned after the attack by stating that the organization should seek to "regain its position of neutrality" in the world.

Perhaps there was a case to be made that UN agencies like UNICEF and the World Food Program would benefit from an image of neutrality in certain conflicts. But would neutrality save the United Nations from further harm in Iraq? Would the terrorists really care about the UN's effort to distance itself from the United States? And would it even be possible, or warranted, for the United Nations to remain neutral in the fight against terrorism?

---

*Neil MacKay, "Former UN Chief: Bomb Was Payback for Collusion with US," *Sunday Herald*, August 24, 2003.

In my own view, such talk of "neutrality" ultimately made no sense in the context of this war. The UN's own Charter, and the Universal Declaration of Human Rights, made it an automatic enemy of groups like Al Qaeda. Even if the UN remained unable to adopt an official definition of terrorism, it could no longer ignore that it was a target of it and would remain so as long as it purported to defend values of human dignity and tolerance that are anachronistic to the aims of violent fundamentalist groups.

Terrorism against the UN and other humanitarian agencies would continue. In Afghanistan, Iraq, southern Lebanon, and Sudan, UN staff would remain prime targets for months and years to come. Unfortunately, the United Nations would remain unable to adopt an official definition for terrorism.

Thankfully, there are dictionaries. Here's one definition from the *Encyclopedia Britannica*: "the systematic use of violence to create a general climate of fear in a population and bring about a particular political objective."

Why couldn't the United Nations adopt this simple definition? The states that voted against adoption did so mostly because they did not wish to condemn Palestinian terror actions against Israel. More generally, they would argue that terrorism could be justified in circumstances of occupation.

Obviously, attacks against an occupying army cannot be lumped together with attacks against civilians and noncombatants. But this distinction can be accommodated easily in a definition. One UN panel, led by Alex P. Schmid, a Dutch scholar, proposed the following formulation: "any act intended to cause death or serious bodily harm to civilians or noncombatants, with the purpose of intimidating a population or compelling a government or an international organization."

Unfortunately, the United Nations could not adopt that definition either. The argument against adoption was ultimately summed up with the following slogan: "One man's terrorist is another man's freedom fighter."

That slogan never made any sense to me. In my reading, the people who attacked us in Iraq were not freedom fighters. Nor, in fact, did they claim to be.

Zarqawi, who stood behind this and many other attacks, made it very clear in a letter to Osama bin Laden, in February 2004, that he feared the progress of democracy in Iraq. Specifically, he worried that it might take some steam out of his efforts to foment a civil war. "A gap will emerge between us and the people of the land," he wrote. "How can we fight their cousins and their sons, and under what pretext, after the Americans, who hold the reins of power from their rear bases, pull back?"

THE ROAD TO HELL   263

"Democracy is coming," he added, "and there will be no excuse thereafter." Hence his advice to bin Laden to try everything to foment a civil war, which would sabotage the establishment of democracy: "The only solution is for us to strike the religious, military, and other cadres among the Shi'a with blow after blow until they bend to the Sunnis. Someone may say that, in this matter, we are being hasty and rash and leading the Islamic nation into a battle for which it is not ready, a battle that will be revolting and in which blood will be spilled. [But] this is exactly what we want, since right and wrong no longer have any place in our current situation."

Were these the words of a freedom fighter? Not by any stretch of the imagination. What Zarqawi's words illustrate is how easy it can be to justify blind violence against civilians once one no longer feels a duty to distinguish between right and wrong on a basic human level.

As I witnessed Iraq descend into an inferno of violence in the months following the destruction of our compound, I noticed how some diplomats and journalists were careful to avoid using the word "terrorist" when describing attacks that clearly qualified as such. Terrorists were often referred to as "militants" or "insurgents," even when the targets were clearly civilian and the intent was clearly to spread terror.

I wondered how the bombings of weddings, of mosques, of markets, and even of funerals could be described as acts of insurgency. What were those "militants" rebelling against? The institution of marriage? The right to sell and buy food? The right to pray? The right to bury one's kin with dignity?

Whether the victims of such acts were in New York, Baghdad, London, Amman, Sharm el-Sheikh, Istanbul, Tel Aviv, Algiers, Casablanca, Tunis, Madrid, Paris, Bali, Amsterdam, or Mecca, they had one thing in common. They were victims of a crime against humanity called terrorism. The ones who commandeered and perpetrated such crimes did not achieve freedom for anybody. They merely sullied whatever causes they claimed to be acting for.

There are only so many ways of responding to acts of terror. One way is to hold the perpetrators responsible and seek to eliminate the threat they pose. Another way is to cower. The UN did claim, officially at least, that it would never bow to terror, that it was active in the "fight against terrorism." But what did this mean, concretely, if the organization could not even adopt an official definition for the phenomenon it was supposed to fight against?

In the months following the tragic bombing that forced the United Nations and most of the humanitarian community to flee from Iraq, Zarqawi's terror network used brutality against Iraqi civilians to take control of several cities. One of them was Fallujah, in Anbar province, which would become the scene of one of the most bloody battles between Al Qaeda and Iraqi and U.S. forces.

During the counterattack against terrorists holed up in Fallujah, in March 2004, Kofi Annan wrote a letter to Iraq's interim prime minister, Iyad Allawi, in which he asserted that the "use of force" against insurgents only risked "deepening" the Iraqi people's "sense of alienation." To which the Iraqi minister replied, "I was surprised by the lack of mention in your letter of any of the atrocities" committed by the terrorists.

I attended a memorial concert for Fiona Watson, at the Cavalry Church in Manhattan's Gramercy Park, a few weeks after the bombing. Spooky had decided to play the harpsichord. All my former colleagues were there to honor Fiona's life and sacrifice. It was difficult to understand how such a positive and lively woman could be taken from us.

As Spooky performed the encore—an aria from Handel's *Great Oratorio*—I let my gaze rest on a candle.

> *Descend, kind pity, heav'nly guest,*
> *Descend, and fill each human breast*
> *With sympathizing woe.*
> *That liberty, and peace of mind,*
> *May sweetly harmonize mankind,*
> *And bless the world below.*

To which I added a personal prayer: *may the perpetrators of this attack be found and taken out.*

Insofar as the United Nations reacted to this bombing by seeking to rekindle its "position of neutrality in the world," it was clear to me that I could not afford to rejoin the UN in Iraq. Neutrality was simply not a cause I was willing to die for.

CHAPTER 27

Saddam's Secret List

"When I get a hold of the son of a bitch who leaked this,
I'm gonna tear his eyeballs out, and I'm gonna suck his
fucking skull!"

GORDON GEKKO, *Wall Street*

On January 25, 2004, beepers and cellphones began ringing at intelligence headquarters and chanceries around the world. The reason was an article published by *Al-Mada*, an independent newspaper in Baghdad, which contained a secret list of names compiled by Saddam's personal accountants.

**"Presidents, Journalists, and Political Parties
Received Millions of Oil Barrels From Saddam"**
[translated from Arabic]
BAGHDAD—*Al-Mada* has obtained a list of the individuals and firms to whom Saddam Hussein allocated crude oil during the various stages of the UN "oil-for-food" program. The list includes the names of individuals, companies, political parties, groups, and organizations from all over the world.

Interestingly most of the recipients of Iraqi oil had nothing to do with the oil business. They were neither involved in oil distribution nor in its storage or its sale and were not known to be interested in oil before they received these allocations. They include, among others, the Russian Orthodox Church . . . the Russian Communist Party . . . French politicians . . . the president of Indonesia . . . a British member of Parliament

. . . Jordanian, Syrian, and Egyptian politicians . . . and the list goes on. Two hundred and seventy people in all.

[The list shows that] the defunct regime of Saddam Hussein had turned the UN program into a dirty business and a political game to fund his secret purchases of armament, expensive construction materials for the presidential palaces, and luxury items for extravagance. It also turned the contract for selling oil into the biggest operation in modern history for buying loyalty and influence around the world. . . .

Foreign journalists jammed inside the U.S.-occupied "Green Zone" of Baghdad scrambled for copies of the article. *Al-Mada*, owned by Fakhri Kareem, a Kurdish opponent to Saddam Hussein, made a name for itself that day. It was not a scoop; it was a bomb. The list of 270 bribe-takers was picked up by the newswires, and within hours bloggers in the United States had pounced on the story, running independent searches to confirm the identities of the people it named.

The list had been found in the archives of the Iraqi Oil Ministry and, according to the article, had been leaked by former Baathists to members of Iraq's Governing Council. In September 2003 I had been warned, by an old college friend whose father now sat on the Iraqi Governing Council, that extremely sensitive documents had been retrieved from Saddam's files, one of which implicated the UN Oil-for-Food program in massive international fraud.

I had immediately called the United Nations to warn them and advise them to launch an internal investigation into fraud under the program. I spoke to Christer, my second Swedish director, who told me he knew for certain that Pasha would not permit such an investigation. So I called Spooky. The latter told me to meet him for lunch. He set a rendezvous point at "the clock, by the information desk, in the middle of Grand Central Station."

"Why not meet directly at a restaurant?" I asked.

Then I remembered. It is a standard security precaution, when one wants to make sure a conversation stays private, to set a meeting point that is not the ultimate place where the talking takes place. We would meet by the clock at Grand Central and pick a restaurant at random from there.

Trevor asked me for the source of my information. My friend from Brown University was called Tamara Chalabi. Her father, Ahmad Chalabi, had been the Pentagon's candidate of choice to lead the "new Iraq." The CIA and the State Department opposed the man and gave preference to Iyad Allawi. Chalabi had been accused in the media of defrauding the Petra Bank in Jordan in the 1980s. He personally argued that he was forced to flee Jordan because Saddam had sent assassins to kill him. I had no idea which version was true, but I knew Tamara well. She had worked for *The Brown Journal of World Affairs*, which I had cofounded and edited, and she had gone on to get a PhD in history at Harvard. She had followed her father to Baghdad during the war and visited the old home from which her family had been ejected before she was born. The Chalabis are an old, well-known Iraqi family whose prominence dates back further than the creation of the modern Iraqi state itself, in 1924. Her forefathers had participated in the creation of Iraq at the time when Gertrude Bell, Lawrence of Arabia, and Winston Churchill were involved in transforming that piece of the Ottoman Empire into a kingdom that would ultimately achieve independence from British rule. Her father was now working with Paul Bremer, the CIA veteran President Bush had appointed as proconsul in Iraq. The finance committee of the Iraqi Governing Council, which included Chalabi and other Iraqi leaders, had discovered Saddam's secret list months before it was leaked to *Al-Mada*.

Back when I met with Spooky, I had no idea what shape or form the document would take, or what it included, but if Tamara said it was incriminating for the United Nations, I trusted she had it from a good source. She had heard that I was considering rejoining the United Nations and was telling me to be careful because a scandal might break out. She was not at liberty to give me further details, and I would not reveal her as my source to Spooky. But I repeated my advice that the UN should investigate itself before it was too late.

Spooky smiled, the way he always did when he thought I was being naïve. "They're going to shove it all under the carpet," he said, as he ordered another glass of wine. Then he shared the story of another UN colleague named Rehan Mullick, a bright Pakistani-American database manager, who had joined the UN right after I left. Rehan had sought to alert New York to the Iraqi government's massive diversion of goods bought under the Oil-for-Food program. His report was ignored. No action was taken—except for the fact that Rehan's contract was not renewed.

I asked why the man had not sought protection as a whistleblower. Spooky reminded me there was no such law protecting UN employees.

"They simply got rid of him. Just like they got rid of you."

"I resigned," I reminded him.

"Well, one way or the other," Spooky said. "They sidelined our office. Now my own contract is up for renewal. They're delaying it. I don't know if I'll have a job next month."

We parted rather depressed. Spooky seemed resigned. All he wanted was a chance to put his skills and knowledge to good use in Iraq, but in the aftermath of the bombing, the UN had evacuated all personnel and everything was on hold (pending the revamping of the UN's security office, a process that would take several years). In any case, Spooky was in no position to push for an investigation either.

Several months passed, and still no scandal erupted. Pasha had been thanked profusely by all members of the United Nations Security Council as the Oil-for-Food operation officially closed down in November 2003. Was it possible that the Iraqis had been persuaded not to make public the documents they had found? By mid-January, I was beginning to think that history would simply roll forward and that the story of how the international community defrauded the Iraqi people for years, in collaboration with Saddam Hussein, would never fully come to light. Hundreds of cardboard boxes filled with UN files would simply be hoarded off to a huge depot, never to be opened again.

Then *Al-Mada* dropped the bombshell. A wave of panic spread through the thousands of companies that had traded under the program, and a great number of international oil traders and other power brokers were awakened by calls from reporters trying to establish whether Saddam's secret list of bribe-takers was genuine. Soon, they would receive visits from law enforcement officers as well.

Upon reading the news, I picked up my phone.

"Did you see it?" I asked Spooky.

"Yes."

"That's it. The endgame has begun," I ventured.

"I suppose you're right," he said. "God only knows where this will end."

It took time to decipher Saddam's secret list. But right off the bat there were some interesting surprises. Few delegations on the UN Security Council would be spared embarrassment. Spooky had predicted a bloodbath in which only the most agile political backstabbers would survive. Another veteran of political investigations in Washington had made it even plainer to me: "Sharpen your knife, young man. There's only two ways these things can go. Either the blame is put on people at the bottom of the pyramid or it's laid on people at the top. Where do *you* think it belongs?"

I'd have to think about that one. In the meantime, I tried to focus on understanding who did what and when, how it all related to my own experience and decisions, and how it might reflect on my former office.

The case that most shocked the Iraqi newspaper's editors was that of British Parliamentarian George Galloway. "The case of George Galloway is truly tragic," the paper wrote. "This man defended many just Arab causes. But as soon as he got closer to the Iraqi regime, he was corrupted. . . ."

Galloway was never charged with corruption. His Mariam Appeal charity was criticized by the British charity commission for not screening its funders and for losing its records. But the Iraqis were hardly surprised to find out the UN operation in general had been corrupted. They knew they weren't getting their money's worth. Seeing the newspaper name people who appeared to have lobbied on their behalf in the past was just another piece of bad news, in another bad news week, crowning a bad news decade.

The new Iraqi government was the first to launch an investigation, hiring the consulting firm KPMG to track down the sales records of people and firms listed as Saddam's secret bribe-takers. The U.S. Congress, then dominated by Republicans, raised the stakes even further, launching *five* separate investigations. Committee chairmen in the House and Senate were falling over one another to shed light on the brewing scandal. Soon France, Britain, New Zealand, India, South Africa, Australia, Spain, Italy, Germany, Denmark, and just about every accountable state on the planet (note the absence of Russia) would launch probes of their own.

Bloggers went into overdrive, digging up all sorts of connections between people on the list and posting them on the web for journalists to feed on. Soon stories began to surface linking companies named on UN and U.S. terror watch lists for funding Al Qaeda as having benefited from Oil-for-Food contracts. Unnamed U.S. government officials would be quoted as saying, "It seems very plausible that [Iraq's] oil money went to terrorism financing."

To some conservatives, it suddenly looked like the long-sought "smoking gun" linking Saddam to international terrorism might finally have surfaced. Saddam's secret list allowed intelligence analysts to establish a connection between the Iraqi dictator and specific companies, such as Delta Oil, a Saudi oil company that supported the Taliban during the time Osama bin Laden was active in Afghanistan. But Pakistan, a nominal U.S. ally, had provided similar support to the Taliban. Not to speak of Congress itself, which, while it did not support the Taliban per se, was, thanks to the spectacular yet covert efforts of Congressman Charlie Wilson, the primary underwriter of weapons flowing into Afghanistan up to 1989.

Other companies that traded under the UN relief program were linked to Al Taqwa, a cluster of financial entities spanning the globe, from the Bahamas to Italy, and controlled by members of the Muslim Brotherhood, which the United States and even the UN had placed on the terrorism watch list. Ayman al-Zawahiri, Osama bin Laden's number two, was an early member of the organization, which essentially pioneered modern Islamist terrorism.

Some columnists who had supported the war similarly decided this was the long-sought "smoking gun" linking Saddam to 9/11. But it was a tenuous link, and the public didn't really bite. The links that reporters had established between companies doing business under the UN program and Al Qaeda did not prove that actual Oil-for-Food money had landed in bin Laden's hands. Short of the name Osama bin Laden appearing directly on the list, the Oil-for-Food program could not legitimately be linked to the 9/11 attacks.

This did not mean Saddam did not use the UN program to support other terrorist organizations more directly. Right there on the list of corrupt purchasers was the Popular Front for the Liberation of Palestine. (PFLP should not be confused with the Palestine Liberation Organization, or PLO, formerly led by Yasser Arafat and now by Mahmoud Abbas, who has abandoned terrorism and recognized the State of Israel, and is actively trying to achieve peace.) The PFLP is a Syria-based terrorist organization that has claimed responsibility for suicide bombings in Israel. Usually, it acts when Israel and the PLO are getting closer to a deal, and it often succeeds in derailing all progress made with a spectacularly bloody attack against civilian targets. There on the list, in black and white, was proof that Saddam had used the humanitarian program to support an international terrorist organization.

I felt nauseous. Upon learning this news, I expected a statement to come out from the UN, a pledge finally to investigate this new evidence and get to the bottom of it. But nothing came.

So I continued my own investigation, using all the information I could get my hands on. It soon became clear that the UN would be too embarrassed to shed light on some of the other names on the list as well, as they had been intimately linked with UN activities for years.

One such person was France's former ambassador to the United Nations, Jean-Bernard Mérimée. Ambassador Mérimée had sat on the UN Security Council when the Oil-for-Food scheme was first negotiated, at times presiding on the UN Security Council. One year after he retired from the French Ministry of Foreign Affairs, in 1998, he was appointed by Kofi Annan to serve as his special adviser on European affairs. His tenure in that position was extended until February 14, 2002, and he continued to work for Annan right up to the 2003 Iraq War. He was a known advocate within Annan's team of advisers for lifting the sanctions. Even as he was working in Annan's inner circle, he was profiting from Saddam's bribes.

Tariq Aziz would later confirm from prison that Mérimée had made a request for an oil allocation after he retired as France's ambassador to the UN. Mérimée was included for the first time in the list in a table dated August 4,

2002. He would ultimately receive oil allocations totaling approximately six million barrels. While still in the position of special adviser, Mérimée arranged to resell two million barrels of oil for a net profit of $165,725. Nice little commission.

Another key French official was Charles Pasqua, the former minister of the interior, who received eleven million barrels of oil from the government of Iraq. According to Iraqi officials and records, the oil allocations were handled on Pasqua's behalf by his diplomatic adviser, Bernard Guillet. According to Guillet, Tariq Aziz conveyed through him an offer of underpriced Iraqi crude to Pasqua to thank him for his "support for Iraq." The oil allocated to Pasqua was resold to Genmar Resources GMBH, a company based in Switzerland. The resale was handled by Guillet, who received at least $234,000 in cash payments as commission. His accounting of the distribution of that money was rather vague.

Pasqua had met with Aziz twice, in 1993 and in 1995, and he also facilitated a visit to France for Aziz at a time when the two countries had no official diplomatic relations. In addition, Pasqua's diplomatic adviser traveled to Baghdad on two more occasions, including in June 1999, when an Iraqi Oil Ministry official wrote a memo certifying to the Iraqi leadership that Guillet was indeed there to represent Pasqua and was authorized to handle his eleven-million-barrel oil allocation for him. Again, Aziz told Guillet that "the leadership [i.e., Saddam Hussein] would like to thank Mr. Pasqua for what he did for Iraq." Guillet would later tell investigators he was worried that a man of Pasqua's stature might not be able to take in this kind of bribe. But Aziz must have said something reassuring, because Guillet then went straight to the Oil Ministry to discuss the details of the Iraqi offer.

Upon returning to France, Guillet said he provided Pasqua with an oral briefing, during which he told him about Aziz's generous offer. According to Guillet, Pasqua exclaimed, "*Je serai le roi du pétrole!*" ("I'll be the king of oil!").

Guillet explained that this was meant as a joke and that Pasqua then added, "I hope you did not accept this offer."

Pasqua, who by then was a French member of parliament, denied ever shouting that he'd be the king of oil, and said he never received a briefing from Guillet as he returned from Iraq and never heard about Aziz's offer. But documents prove that the firm Genmar did purchase Iraqi oil that was allocated to Pasqua. And an internal memo from the executive director of Iraq's oil marketing organization to Iraq's minister of oil specified that "the Swiss company Genmar is confirmed as the company nominated by Charles Pasqua to lift" (meaning, pick up) the eleven million barrels of oil from the Iraqi port. And a third man, Elias Firzli—a consultant for Total, a large French oil conglomerate closely linked to the French government—confirmed to investigators that he helped Guillet (who had never traded oil before in his life) resell the under-priced Iraqi crude to Genmar. In return for his help, Firzli would collect the profits from the oil sale and pay Guillet a commission. Guillet traveled to Switzerland on eight occasions to collect the cash from Firzli's account there. This lucrative business eventually yielded Guillet a total profit of $1,111,874—money that should have gone to Iraq's most needy.

Investigators left open the possibility that Guillet acted on his own, using Pasqua's name to make money behind his back. Whether it was Pasqua or his diplomatic adviser who in fact became the "king of oil" would be investigated by a French anticorruption judge. In April 2005, Guillet was arrested in his home and questioned by a French magistrate. The affair would hang over Pasqua for years to come as court proceedings dragged on. As with all the members of Sad-dam's secret list, no final conclusions can be drawn about their guilt outside of a court of law. Even as he claimed his own innocence, Pasqua speculated that it was quite likely that other French officials had taken part in the illicit scheme.

Russia's parliament was well oiled as well (as previously mentioned), with Vladimir Putin's oil minister distributing underpriced oil allocations to the rest of Russia's political parties and favored oligarchs directly. Just as Saddam had used the program to strengthen his hold on power, Putin had used it to solidify his control over the Russian parliament and prepare his post-presidential power shift to the post of prime minister. Of course, the informa-tion contained in Saddam's list would take time to confirm. In the case of Russia, where the justice system was not free to do its job, it would take until 2008 to find a firsthand witness to corroborate key information.

In January 2008, a former Russian top spy confirmed that he personally set up a network of agents who helped the Russian government steal nearly $500 million from the United Nations' Oil-for-Food program in Iraq before the fall of Saddam Hussein. Sergei Tretyakov, who defected to the United States in 2000 as a double agent, revealed in a book that he oversaw an oper-ation that helped Saddam's regime manipulate the price of Iraqi oil and allow Russia to skim profits. Tretyakov, a former deputy head of intelligence at Rus-sia's UN mission from 1995 to 2000, revealed that he recruited a senior Rus-sian official in the Oil-for-Food program. Though he speaks of the person in code name, I recognized the description of our Russian "oil overseer"—one of those we used to refer to as Double O's.

It was interesting to find out what kind of work our former colleague actually did all day long. He basically helped "fix" Iraq's oil prices in a way that facilitated fraud. And to think I suspected him of merely picking his nose all day long.

As the governments and diplomatic establishments of Britain, France, and Russia, three key members of the Security Council, had now been implicated, I wondered if they would retaliate with information involving wrongdoing by the United States.

Once again, Saddam's secret list provided ample ammunition for competing intelligence services to sling mud at one another. Judging from the vigor with which the U.S. Senate engaged in the investigative process, I found it interesting that the White House seemed to be taking a step back from the whole scandal. Why the sudden silence from the Bush administration? As both houses of Congress and think tanks like the Heritage Foundation and the American Enterprise Institute (where President Bush had made his "vision" speech about a new Iraq and a new Middle East) were banging on about the scandal, how could the White House stay aloof?

It turned out that U.S. firms, some of which had strong White House connections, had been in on the illegal and deeply immoral feeding frenzy as well. This, despite the fact that the Iraqi government followed an explicit policy of favoring companies and individuals based in France, Russia, and the Middle East as recipients of its underpriced oil bribes.

To circumvent this policy, some British and American oil-trading companies attempted to disguise themselves as French to fool the Iraqi regime. In October 1998, an official in the French government's Sanctions Department— that is, the arm of the French government that was supposed to *enforce* the sanctions on Iraq rather than *break* them—wrote to an Iraqi official in Paris about his own "concerns, and his government's concerns . . . regarding the increase in British and American companies who exploit the decision of the Iraqi leadership to provide priority to French companies, by signing contracts with Iraq through their offices in France."

The French official referred to these as "hoax" companies. An interesting word choice given the general setup France itself was involved in. Nonetheless, after being notified of the official French complaint in November 1998, Iraqi Vice President Taha Yassin Ramadan wrote a letter titled "Dealing with French Companies." In his letter, Ramadan made it clear to all ministries that Iraq needed to prevent American and British companies from exploiting Iraq's preferential treatment of French companies. Clearly, they didn't like being conned at their own game. Texans with French berets on their heads would no longer be tolerated.

On one occasion, in order to obtain more oil, a beneficiary named on the list—the French diplomat Serge Boidevaix—emphasized to Iraqi officials a position taken by the French government that was supportive of Iraq at the UN, thereby going on the record to establish a clear link between France's voting record at the United Nations and Saddam's preferential oil sales policy.

"We were happy to see the decision of the Security Council to increase the total amount for exports to $8.3 billion," wrote Boidevaix in a letter to the Iraqi government, "and as you may know, on the French side we proposed an increase without limits or restrictions. As I mentioned in my last letter, we would be grateful for an increase to our [read: my own] current allocation of 5 million barrels, and could lift at Basra [port] anytime in October or November if you had additional volumes to allocate."

French officials would later deny that their policy was guided by economic interests. France had acted to "uphold international law," explained Dominique de Villepin, even as French diplomats were being investigated for *breaking* international law and had themselves gone on record linking their country's UN policy to their thirst for more Iraqi oil. The most respected French newspaper, *Le Monde,* eventually published an editorial that openly questioned France's claim to have acted purely in the interest of international law, given the undeniable profits made by its diplomatic and political elites.

At least France's justice system, and its press, saved the country's honor by pursuing wrongdoers. The same could be said for the United States. But the mere fact that Texas oil companies had tried to disguise themselves as French was not the most embarrassing part for the Bush administration. Two stories in particular had the White House concerned. The first was the fact that Chevron had been one of the U.S. companies buying Iraqi oil and allowing for kickbacks of more than $20 million to find their way back into Saddam's pocket. As it turned out, Condoleezza Rice was a member of Chevron's board at the time. Specifically, she led Chevron's public policy committee, which oversaw areas of potential political concern for the company. In 2007 Chevron was brought to court and forced to settle for a large fine after admitting it "should have known" in 2000 that kickbacks would be going to Saddam.

Correction: it knew. And the woman who would soon be named secretary of state after serving on the board's policy committee was probably aware of this dirty business as well.

The other awkward "link" that had the White House concerned was a tad more complex. It started with a rather banal crooked deal but ended up causing possible embarrassment for Vice President Dick Cheney, because it involved a client previously represented by one of his aides, I. Lewis "Scooter" Libby.

Here's how that twisted entanglement of interests came into existence. In 1998, after several unsuccessful attempts to participate in the UN Oil-for-Food program by trading pharmaceuticals and cosmetic goods, a French businessman named Claude Kaspereit, the son of a French parliamentarian, decided to get into the oil business and established a company called EOTC. The question was: how could he get an underpriced oil allocation from the Iraqi government? Word of mouth had it that one had to be recognized as one of Saddam's little helpers in order to gain entry to the den of thieves.

Kaspereit found a rather creative solution. In June 2000 he arranged to charter a flight to Iraq, without UN authorization and in violation of the embargo, to generate publicity against the sanctions. His plane included a number of anti-sanctions activists, including, bizarrely, Jany Le Pen, the wife of the notoriously racist and Arab immigrant–bashing French politician Jean-Marie Le Pen, who came in second in France's 2002 presidential election. Jany Le Pen had started a "nonprofit" organization called SOS Enfants Iraq (SOS Iraqi Children).

This embargo-breaking visit attracted the attention of Saddam Hussein, who sent a delegation out to the airport to receive them. Kaspereit later sent letters to a number of senior Iraqi officials, including Tariq Aziz, to thank them for their warm reception. He requested that Aziz and Amer Rashid, Iraq's oil minister, convey directly to Saddam the group's solidarity with the Iraqi people and their "support for Saddam Hussein's political action."

Such shameless statements had a way of turning out profits. Following Kaspereit's publicized flight to Baghdad, the government of Iraq began granting him oil allocations, for a total of 9.5 million barrels. The problem was, Kaspereit's EOTC was a shell company that had no means of financing such large purchases of crude oil.

Enter Marc Rich and Company. Remember Marc Rich? The Jewish-American multimillionaire was convicted in U.S. federal court of tax evasion, racketeering, and other charges related to his oil deals with Iran during the U.S. embargo on *that* country. Rich had fled to Switzerland, where he received asylum, but his ex-wife, Denise Rich, continued to live in the United States, where she was an active supporter of the Democratic Party; she contributed money to Bill Clinton's presidential library fund and to Hillary Clinton's 2000 Senate campaign. On top of giving $450,000 to the Clinton Library, Denise Rich gave upwards of $1 million to the Democratic Party and $109,000 to Hillary Clinton's 2000 Senate campaign.

The Riches' generosity paid off when Marc made the list of more than 100 people President Clinton pardoned just before leaving office in January 2001. Rich's pardon prompted a public outcry and Congressional investigations into whether it had been granted in return for Denise Rich's political contributions. Clinton regretted his decision but tried to defend it partially by saying that Marc Rich had received a lot of letters of support from Jewish leaders and had been an active supporter of Israel.

Well, he was certainly also a supporter of Iran in the 1980s, and he had no scruples about making a profit by trading with Saddam Hussein under the UN Oil-for-Food program.

Still, Rich had to act discreetly. Following the media frenzy that followed his pardon, he could not be seen to help finance purchases of underpriced Iraqi crude oil by Saddam's political friends, especially not people like Kaspereit, who had gone on paper supporting Saddam's "political action." It wouldn't look good for Marc Rich to support the political action of a funder of Palestinian terrorism while he was cultivating an image as a strong supporter of Israel. . . . In any case, "Moses is Moses, business is business," goes the saying. Clearly, Rich had not gotten rich by letting scruples keep him up at night. He was quite prepared to finance Kaspereit's deal, as long as his name was not revealed to the United Nations. So, in his instructions to the French bank BNP, which held the UN's Oil-for-Food account, Rich specified that the letters of credit for the purchase of Iraqi crude should *not*, under any circumstance, be under the name of his own company (even though he was underwriting the deal); instead, it was attributed directly to Kaspereit's company, EOTC.

This meant that the French bank had to lie to the UN about the real source of funding for the oil purchase, thereby breaching the terms of its contract with the world organization, which obliged it to disclose the identity of buyers. The request even violated the BNP's internal rules. But the BNP had no problem with Rich's request.

The oil would go to a "do-gooder." Kaspereit's self-anointed title was chairman of the Society for Support of Iraqi Children. Thanks to his help, Iraq's children saw $1.83 million that might have gone to humanitarian aid vanish into the pockets of Saddam Hussein, via a Jordanian bank account. It is perhaps ironic that it also made Rich, a pro-Israel financier, and Kaspereit richer at these same children's expense.

Given Clinton's involvement in pardoning, I began to wonder why the Bush administration didn't jump on this opportunity to discredit the Clintons and the Democrats. Claudia Rosett, the first and best-informed investigative reporter working the Oil-for-Food scandal, had revealed the full extent of the link and given the White House a clear opening to score points in the run-up to the 2004 presidential election. But soon it became clear that the story involving Rich could not be exploited for political gain against the Democrats without boomeranging on the White House itself. Rich's former lawyer in the United States had been none other than Scooter Libby—Dick Cheney's chief of staff—who was by then being investigated for having leaked the name of CIA official Valerie Plame, whose husband had criticized the administration's WMD claims before the war.

The more Saddam's secret list was studied, the more power brokers from all sides of the political spectrum feared becoming entangled. And for good reason. The threads that spread from Saddam's secret list seemed endless.

Soon it was revealed that during the sanctions years, Cheney, the former CEO of Halliburton, America's supersized oil and war-effort contractor, had also been involved with Iraq's oil industry. Halliburton wasn't named on the *Al-Mada* list. But as reporters dug deeper, they realized there had already been news coverage of the company's dealings with Iraq under the Oil-for-Food program. A 2001 *Washington Post* article by Colum Lynch cited confidential UN records and oil-industry executives saying Halliburton held stakes in two firms that signed contracts for more than $73 million to provide Iraq with oil-industry spare parts. Employees at Halliburton confirmed to Lynch that they were "certain Cheney knew about these Iraqi contracts."

In 1998 Halliburton bought Dresser Industries, which exported equipment to Iraq through French affiliates from 1997 to 2000. There was nothing illegal about trading with Iraq under the Oil-for-Food program. But had the contracts included the usual kickbacks for Saddam? Or had Halliburton been holier than the 2,400 companies found guilty of participating in the illegal kickback scheme?

To be sure, the vice president was not interested in finding out the answer. Such kickbacks are routine, and it is doubtful that Cheney had any direct involvement in such a minor transaction. But increasingly, the Oil-for-Food debacle became less and less popular with the Bush administration. The U.S. coalition raided Ahmad Chalabi's house in Baghdad and made off with records that he claimed were related to his Oil-for-Food investigation. Paul Bremer, the U.S. proconsul in Baghdad, also stopped funding for the KPMG investigation.

But it was too late. Too many reporters, Congressmen, and justice officials around the world had started dipping their noses into the affair. The lid was off—well, almost.

All the key documents that could confirm the information in the *Al-Mada* list and help trace those who had violated international law were locked up at the United Nations, about to be sent off to a humongous storage facility in Queens. The U.S. government, which should have had copies of all Iraqi contracts that went through the UN, was claiming to journalists that these had not been kept on file at either the State or Defense department. This, to me, sounded inconceivable. We had held meetings at the UN with the D.C.-based government analysts who reviewed Iraq's contracts. Did these people throw the contracts in the trash after making a decision to block or clear them for export? Not likely. The whole point, from the Pentagon's point of view, was to have specific records of everything Saddam purchased, in particular for those items that could potentially have "dual use" as weapons components.

The whole point of Security Council oversight was to make these contracts available to members of the Council. How could the U.S. government claim it no longer had these documents?

It soon became clear that neither the United States nor Britain nor France nor Russia nor China would open up their files. The United Nations was the official repository for all the records that might confirm the veracity of Saddam's secret list and allow investigators to check the amount of money that had been stolen from Iraq's most vulnerable civilians by the very same people and governments that had claimed to be out to help them.

I felt I had to do something. In fact, I felt it was long overdue for me to take decisive action. I had failed to persuade the bureaucracy to follow up on clues to wrongdoing internally, and my multiple attempts to spark an investigation even after I had left were ignored. I had resigned, and insofar as I had decided not to rejoin the UN in the aftermath of the Baghdad bombing, I could now afford to break my rule about never burning bridges. I wouldn't do it for pleasure. In fact, it would be a serious risk for me to step into what looked like a potential political bloodbath. For several days, I hesitated. Each day, new allegations would make headlines. The media was clamoring for the UN to open its records, but with no member of the Security Council wishing for it, the UN could claim confidentiality for another fifty years. What could I possibly do to change that?

On February 29, 2004, I saw an opportunity to act. I came across an article by Susan Sachs in the *New York Times,* which quoted Ali Allawi, a former World Bank official now working as Iraqi trade minister, recalling how part of the corruption worked.

"You had cartels that were willing to pay kickbacks but would also bid up the price of goods," Allawi said. "You had rings involved in supplying shoddy goods. You had a system of payoffs to the bourgeoisie and royalty of nearby countries. Everybody was feeding off the carcass of what was Iraq."

I thought his description was exactly right. And then, a few paragraphs later, I found the opening I needed to intervene effectively in the unfolding scandal.

According to Sachs, "United Nations overseers say they were unaware of the systematic skimming of oil-for-food revenues. . . . The director of the Office of Iraq Programs, Benon V. Sevan [Pasha] declined to be interviewed about the oil-for-food program. In written responses to questions sent by e-mail, his office said he learned of the 10 percent kickback scheme from the occupation authority only after the end of major combat operations."

Wrong answer!

We had ample proof that kickbacks were being extorted. Sometimes they were even put into the contracts as blatantly unjustified "surcharges." The practice was clearly illegal. But Pasha refused to make a fuss about them. At the time I blamed his failure to react on mere incompetence. I knew he wanted the program to stay away from the spotlight, to "fly under the radar," and that he thought more goods would get into the country if we stayed away from controversy. But now that the operation was over and the truth was coming out in Iraq, I felt certain that the UN would do better to admit what had happened than to try to cover it up by lying to the *New York Times.* So I banged out a furious op-ed.

> The cat is out of the bag. Documents recently discovered by the Coalition Provisional Authority, and corroborated by interviews with former Iraqi officials, confirm that Saddam Hussein extorted cash kickbacks from companies trading with Iraq under the U.N. Oil-for-Food Program. The most damning document is a memo dated Aug. 3, 2000, by Iraqi Vice President Taha Yassin Ramadan (now in U.S. custody) instructing his ministers to tell their suppliers to inflate their prices by the "biggest percentage possible." As a former employee of the program, I cannot say I was surprised by this news. What surprised me was the U.N.'s response to it.
>
> U.N. officials claim they were unaware of such fraudulent practices by the Iraqi regime until after the Iraq War. They would be better off telling the truth. By winter 2000, serious concerns had been raised about the use of front companies by the regime. We had heard allegations of a 10% kickback scheme, and were exceptionally well positioned to investigate the matter. Why did the U.N. fail to investigate?

U.N. officials claim it was not their responsibility to hold the Iraqi regime accountable. False again. The whole point of putting the U.N. in charge of overseeing Iraq's trade was to ensure that the country's oil revenues were used exclusively to help its ailing population, not to fill Saddam's personal coffers. And according to Security Council resolutions, the U.N. had a legal responsibility to report on any issue affecting the "adequacy, equitability and effectiveness" of the Oil-for-Food Program. Saddam's kickbacks affected all three aspects. There were many instances in the time I was there when the U.N. preferred to look the other way rather than address obvious signs of what was going wrong.

Take the medical sector. The regime's decision to use kickback-friendly front companies to purchase drugs meant that hospitals often received medicines that were nearly expired or otherwise damaged from unscrupulous suppliers. Iraqi doctors would complain about the quality of the drug supply to our U.N. observers. Kurdish leaders raised similar concerns directly with high-level U.N. officials. We knew exactly how much the Iraqi government paid for any contract, and we had the authority to inspect each shipment when it crossed into Iraq. We had all the elements necessary to piece together a clear picture of what was going on and alert the Security Council to the fact that Saddam and his cronies were buying poor quality products at inflated prices and cashing in the difference. While the U.N. likes to claim this was the most audited program in its history, I never once read an audit report that raised questions about these practices—even though they were an open secret to anyone involved in the program. . . .

As long as Saddam was in control, it was perhaps inevitable that he would have profited from any attempt to feed his population. But the least the U.N. could have done was denounce his practices. . . .

The U.N. should not have been in the business of covering up for Saddam; and it should not now stonewall efforts to have an independent investigation look into which companies broke the law in their dealings with the regime and who profited from schemes to get around the restrictions set out under Oil-for-Food. If the U.N. fails to become a partner in the investigative process, it may end up as co-defendant in a scandal that has yet to reach its full-blown proportion.

I sent the piece out to several editors. It was picked up by the *Wall Street Journal* and published on March 8, 2004. CNN, Fox News, ABC News, and the BBC packed my voicemail with messages asking me to come on the air. I declined most requests for interviews and spoke only on background to reporters I trusted, because the scandal had become intertwined with the election cycle in Washington. Republicans sought to use it to discredit the United Nations (which had opposed the war), and Democrats initially sought to dismiss the scandal as an attempt by Republicans to bring attention away from the failure to find WMDs in Iraq. Ultimately, the truth of this story would not reflect well on either party.

A few days after my piece was published, I received a panicked call from my former Swedish director, who, though he had also left the UN, was now helping Kofi Annan manage the crisis on a pro bono basis. Annan's major problem in dealing with the unfolding scandal was that he simply didn't have enough helpers to work the spin cycle. His "war room" was filled with bureaucrats who were coming up with press releases that made sense only to insiders and had no impact on the wider public debate that was starting to take shape. The only two people who could put together compelling arguments in Annan's defense were Shashi Tharoor, the head of public information, and Edward Mortimer, Annan's chief speechwriter. But these people hadn't been intimately involved with the Oil-for-Food program. They were playing catch-up with the facts. And two people hammering out replies to hundreds of articles and TV reports, not to speak of radio and Internet stories, hardly put a dent in the growing public perception of a massive cover-up. It would take Annan nine months to bring an additional qualified PR professional on board, in the person of Marc Malloch Brown. In the meantime, as the scandal edged toward a climax, public perception of the UN plummeted. Less than half of the U.S. public told pollsters they had a favorable view of the United Nations. This was down from 77 percent favorable opinions four years earlier.

Things got significantly worse when Annan came under direct attack for letting the UN award a major contract under the Oil-for-Food program to a company that employed his son, Kojo Annan. I remembered receiving press queries about the incident back in 1998. The company in question was called Cotecna, and it was awarded a contract worth $4.87 million to inspect relief supplies going into Iraq. The company employed Kojo Annan as a consultant. The kid was twenty-four years old at the time, and Cotecna, which works in many countries that need help keeping track of their customs, said Kojo was working in the company's Africa division. At the time of the initial press queries, I realized there was the appearance of a conflict of interest. But given the thousands of companies that contracted with the UN under the Oil-for-Food scandal, I didn't think it would be fair, in principle, for Kojo to be barred from working for all of them. The key question was whether Annan had pressed the UN's procurement division to give the contract to Cotecna, and I just didn't think of Kofi Annan as that type of a guy.

Well, there was a lot more to this story than I initially realized, but suffice it to say that my call for an independent investigation came at a very bad time for Annan and his team. Christer, one of my former directors, was asked to try to rein me in to avoid further damage. I was walking in noisy Midtown when I answered his call.

"What the hell are you doing, Michael?"

"What do you mean?"

"Your article was very damaging!"

"I'm not out to damage anybody. I advised an investigation for months! Nobody listened, so now I made the advice public. I figured it was the only way to get anyone's attention over there." I heard a sigh on the other end of the line, so I added, "If anything I said was untrue, let the UN respond publicly."

"But Michael, this is very embarrassing for the secretary general. He's just finished dealing with the investigation into the bombing of UN headquarters. It's difficult for him to order another investigation right now. And all that stuff with Kojo. He's being dragged through the mud!"

I hadn't mentioned Kojo and Cotecna in my piece. But if anything, an investigation would help the secretary general establish his innocence.

"I think an investigation is Annan's only way out," I said. "If he still thinks he has a choice, then he is being very, very badly advised."

"But why did you have to go public? Don't you see it helps those who hate the UN?"

Ah, yes. The famous "Conspiracy to Undermine the United Nations." The way I saw it, the UN was doing a fine job of undermining itself all on its own.

"Either the UN is transparent or it's not. Either it's accountable or it's not. You know as well as I do that we tried to raise compliance issues internally many times. It never went anywhere, and now there's a scandal, and the UN is lying to the *New York Times*. I won't be part of a cover-up!"

"There is no *cover-up*, Michael. . . ."

"Yes, there is. . . . Either the UN opens up its files, or it's a cover-up."

"Well," said Christer, "Kofi Annan asked me to tell you that he would have much preferred if you had sent him a memo about this. . . ."

"*A memo?*" I thought I heard him wrong. I was no longer working for the UN. And Rehan Mullick, the last person who had written a memo that rocked the boat, had been ignored, then fired.

"Yes, a memo. . . ."

"I'm sorry," I said. "I'm no longer in the business of writing memos."

The conversation ended on a cold note. I suddenly felt very alone. Christer and I had been very good friends. How many friends might I lose in this process? How many enemies would I make?

Soon after I spoke to Christer, I got a call from his former secretary. She told me people had been asking for my personnel file.

"They're going to attack you, Michael." She sounded panicked.

"What kind of attack are they planning?" I asked. "Do I need to wear a helmet?"

She laughed but soon became serious again.

"Aren't you worried?" she asked.

Actually, I felt like I had just gotten a big load off my chest. A load of lies that had been building up for years. Until recently, I had managed to convince myself that our operation had actually been successful overall and that the compromises we had made were necessary evils. Even if that were true, the time had come to admit everything we knew. I was glad I was no longer working for an organization that valued its employees most dearly for their ability to hide their eyes, cover their ears, and shut their mouths in the face of gross incompetence and corruption.

"Just remember," said my former colleague, "not everyone has the option of doing what you are doing. Most people can't afford to leave this place. They have nowhere else to go."

She was right. And I was grateful for the reminder. Most UN employees had come to the organization filled with passion for making a positive difference in the world, just like I had. I realized some of them might feel betrayed by my criticism of the organization, just like I had felt betrayed when Denis Halliday and Hans von Sponeck, our former humanitarian coordinators, had left the organization to speak their own minds. In an odd twist of fate, I had ended up following the same path as the people I had denounced most vehemently in the early days of my UN career.

I suppose each of us hotheads could find justification in the words of Mark Twain: "Loyalty to petrified opinion never yet broke a chain or freed a human soul."

CHAPTER 28

Boomerang

"In this town, you're considered innocent until investigated."

From the 2005 film *Syriana*

CRUNCH GYM, EAST VILLAGE,
NEW YORK CITY, APRIL 2004

I was pedaling on a bicycle specifically designed to go nowhere. To compensate for the extremely uneventful nature of this activity, I was, like the rest of my pedaling neighbors, looking up at a large TV screen to see what else was going on in the world.

A week or so after my *Wall Street Journal* op-ed, Kofi Annan had given in to reason and ordered an independent investigation of the Oil-for-Food corruption scandal. Surprising even his most ardent critics, he had appointed Paul Volcker, a highly credible personality, to head a panel of inquiry. Volcker was the former chairman of the U.S. Federal Reserve and a veteran of high-level political investigations (Enron, the Nazi gold/Swiss banking scandal, among many others). He would lead a team of sixty international investigators, who would be given broad access to Iraqi and UN files.

I felt somewhat vindicated by this turn of events, especially vis-à-vis those who had called me a traitor. After all, Annan had gone along with what I had advocated for. Others, including Congressmen and news editors, had made similar calls. But as the first UN insider to join the chorus, I may have helped tip the scale against continued stonewalling by the thirty-eighth floor. Also, former U.S.

Ambassador to the United Nations Richard Holbrooke had specifically warned the secretary general, in a secret meeting aimed at keeping Annan's tenure afloat, that even people who were not traditional enemies of the UN were quickly becoming its harshest critics. Annan concluded that "a dark cloud" hung over the UN and decided that his only way out was to let the light shine in.

My prediction had been that the onset of an investigation would keep the story out of the headlines for at least a few months, until Volcker's findings were made public. I was wrong.

Suddenly, as I was pedaling at the gym, Pasha's face appeared on the TV screen above my head.

I gasped. *Pasha? What are you doing on the news?* The Oil-for-Food program had shut down months ago. Pasha was getting ready to retire. Now he was being followed in the street by a Fox News camera crew. At one point, he stopped, faced the journalist, and took off his sunglasses. For a moment, it looked like he was going to head-butt the man with the microphone. What the hell was going on?

News ticker: ". . . high-level UN official accused of taking bribes from Saddam . . ."

What?

After a few brief words with the Fox News reporter, which I couldn't hear because I didn't have freaking earphones to plug into the bloody bike, Pasha briskly walked away. The unsteady camera followed him.

I started pedaling again, but only because the bike had Internet access. I Googled Pasha's name and came across news reports citing Claude Hankes-Drielsma, a KPMG private investigator hired by the Iraqi authorities, saying he believed one of the names on Saddam's secret list referred to the former under secretary general. Buried at the deep end of the list was a certain Mr. Sifan, which the Iraqis now alleged was a misspelled transliteration of Pasha's last name: Sevan.

Mr. Sifan was listed in association with a Panamanian trading company owned by a Lebanese individual. Millions of barrels of oil had been allocated to this murky Panamanian entity in the name of Mr. Sifan.

Could Mr. Sifan really be Mr. Sevan?

The names Sifan and Sevan had only three out of five letters in common. What if this Mr. Sifan was someone else? I Googled "Sifan" to check if that was an actual name, but little came up except articles alleging Mr. Sevan's corruption. And the deeply uncomfortable fact of the matter was, "Mr. Sifan" was exactly how our Arabic counterparts used to address Mr. Sevan.

Had *my own boss* been on Saddam's payroll?

No way. I knew the guy. He wouldn't. . . .

I called up Spooky. "Do you believe this shit?" I asked.

"No," he said. "I think some people are out to discredit the UN. I know things you don't. Can't talk now. . . ."

Spooky had never been wrong before.

I called up Christer: "What do you think?"

"Nah. Pasha was a lot of things, but I don't believe he was a crook. Kofi Annan can't believe it either. Nobody's buying this."

I dialed Pasha, but nobody picked up. I finally looked at my BlackBerry and feared it might short-circuit if it absorbed any more of my sweat. It showed five voicemails. Reporters and news producers, no doubt. A text message from a friend who worked in finance: "Dude, saw your boss on my Bloomberg screen. Think he did it?"

Feeling a physical pinch of panic in my heart, I finally concluded that this stationary bike was not an ideal location for multimedia crisis management. Besides, I needed to think.

As I showered, memories crept into my mind, fighting one another for my attention. I remembered Pasha quelling the agency rebellion on our first visit to Baghdad. Pasha had never been an open advocate of lifting the sanctions. He had flown under the radar, tried to make the program work. He had cried at the Baghdad hospital, in front of that little girl. Would he be able to do that and participate in a scheme to rip off Iraq's civilians at the same time?

It just didn't make any sense.

Pasha had made many enemies over the years. The Kurds, in particular, who now held prominent roles in the Iraqi government. The Shiites had grown resentful of the UN as well. The former Baathists had it in for us, too. I was pretty certain some of them had helped Al Qaeda engineer the bombing of our headquarters. If the list had indeed come from Saddam's people, could it really be trusted? Or had the list been "adapted" to fit vengeful agendas?

All scenarios were possible. A lot of money had flowed through the operation under Pasha's control. Only the investigation that was now under way could deliver real answers. But it would take months before Volcker would reveal his findings. In the meantime, the media played judge, jury, and executioner. They would insert a small quote by Pasha at the end of a given article, saying he denied the charges against him, but by the time one got to that part, Pasha looked guilty as a raccoon atop a trash can. An increasing number of such reports surfaced every day.

And yet nothing had been proven.

Instead of facing reporters and answering their questions straight up, Pasha often tried to walk away, and then, when the reporters managed to corner him, he issued moody outbursts of gobbledygook, which were then spliced into semi-understandable sound bites by news editors and organized into a news sequence that made him look like a crook on the run.

It was painful to watch. Pasha flew to the other end of the world to escape the spotlight, but when he arrived in Australia, he found reporters waiting for him in the lobby of his five-star hotel and casino resort. The media smelled blood. Pasha's defensive statements, and the UN's previous stonewalling, had only made the situation worse. When Pasha decided to return to New York, I felt somewhat relieved. He enjoyed diplomatic immunity, and Kofi Annan had made no threat to lift it. Annan confirmed his belief that Pasha was innocent. They had known each other for decades. And nobody I spoke to at the UN, including some of Pasha's avowed enemies, believed in his guilt.

I hoped they were right. For Pasha's sake, for the UN's sake, and for the sake of all of us who had worked for this operation, I hoped Pasha was innocent. If he wasn't, chances were I might have been at his side when the man got himself into trouble. And the last thing I wanted to do was testify against Pasha in court.

From now until the investigation was completed, everything I had ever said or done while working for Pasha could be subject to scrutiny. Every e-mail, every memo, every note would come under the microscope, as Pasha became the main target of Volcker's $30 million probe.

When I shared my concerns with my flatmate, he laughed, then observed, "So I guess this whole investigation thing might boomerang back in your face."

It was one way to put it.

CHAPTER 29

The Man Who Could Have Been a Millionaire

HELMSLEY HOTEL, NEW YORK CITY, AUGUST 8, 2005

It was a chaotic media circus. Some thirty camera crews and more than a hundred journalists stepping over one another, arguing over seating arrangements and microphone spots, in a conference room at the Helmsley Hotel, on Forty-Second Street, a few blocks from the United Nations. Paul Volcker had chosen a site outside the UN for his press conference to emphasize his independence from the organization.

Volcker was a giant in reputation and stature. When Kofi Annan called him, he took a quick glance at the Oil-for-Food fiasco and asked the secretary general what part of that mess he was supposed to investigate. Annan was eager to have the allegations against his own person cleared as a matter of priority, and he very much hoped the bribery accusation against Pasha was baseless. But the big question was how the UN had allowed Saddam Hussein to get away with a multibillion-dollar heist at a time when that money was meant to alleviate the "urgent humanitarian needs of the Iraqi people."

Volcker quickly figured out the political implications of the probe. In his previous investigation of the Swiss banking scandal, he had shown no hesitation about accusing the Vatican itself of financial fraud. He was not afraid to dive into this challenge. But he understood that he would need a clear mandate, and legal authority, before proceeding.

He told Annan he would do it, but only if he was appointed by an official Security Council resolution.

The nerve. . . . It's not anybody who can just walk into the UN and demand a Security Council resolution before getting to work.

This put the UN Security Council in somewhat of a bind. All members understood that if a man of Volcker's caliber stuck his nose into the secret proceedings of their sanctions committee, where all the wheeling and dealing had occurred, he'd find evidence that would make all of them look very bad.

Russia, the country that did the most business with Saddam, denounced the effort publicly. "This is the first time that the American media is imposing such a thing on the UN," said the Russian ambassador.

Well, yes, it was. And now members of the Security Council had to contend with Volcker himself. The new sheriff in town had the diplomats backed into a corner. If they turned down his request for a resolution, it would be the PR equivalent of O.J. Simpson fleeing justice in his white Bronco.

France calculated that it had better get behind this probe. French diplomats were in the process of doing damage control after Foreign Minister Dominique de Villepin had sparked a wave of anti-French sentiment in the United States in the lead-up to the war. France knew that if it refused to back the investigation, it would be in for another public flogging in the U.S. media. France's public enthusiasm for the probe was almost comical, in that it was a 180-degree reversal from its long-standing efforts to loosen UN oversight of the Oil-for-Food program. But it was also a critical, defining decision, as it left Russia cornered. Finally, in April 2004, Russia caved under pressure from the media. Resolution 1538 was adopted unanimously. However, as was tradition when it came to Iraq issues, it would not be *complied* with unanimously.

After getting his way in the Security Council, Volcker gave its members an ominous warning. He said he wanted to make sure they understood what they were "getting into" here. He had ambassadors from the most powerful nations on earth looking down at their feet.

Thirty million dollars and sixty investigators. Those were Volcker's next demands. Where would the money come from? As usual, Iraqis were asked to foot the bill. Actually, they weren't even asked; they were forced. There was money left over from the Oil-for-Food accounts. Without waiting for the Iraqis to consent, the Security Council allocated this money to the investigation. None of the countries on the Council would dip into their own pocket for funding.

The Iraqis had paid the UN to oversee the Oil-for-Food program, and now they were going to pay the UN to investigate itself for having screwed it up. Some Iraqi politicians were outraged by this development. But they had no voice, no seat at the table.

It took Volcker a long time to get his shop up and running. After experiencing firsthand the frustrations of dealing with the UN, he assembled a team of people from outside the organization and went to work.

The day of the press conference, he was scheduled to brief the press on his initial findings. By then, I had made a transition to journalism. I attended the briefing as a freelancer.

I should have arrived earlier. There was no place to sit. Among the early birds were familiar faces—members of the UN press corps and some journalists who had made it to New York from around the world especially for the occasion, from countries where indictments had started to fly. In Australia, Prime Minister John Howard had come under investigation for the role the Australian Wheat Board—a governmental body—had played in sending kickbacks to Saddam. Germans were interested in the fate of companies like Siemens and Mercedes-Benz, which had clearly also gone along with the kickback scheme. Swedish carmaker Volvo had been cited as well, as had Danish water and sanitation companies, Jordanian pharmaceutical traders, South African construction firms . . . the scheme seemed to have reached every corner of the globe.

I trusted Paul Volcker to get to the bottom of this affair. Others, however, did not.

The independent panel Volcker headed was seen by many conservatives to be too soft on Annan. Lawmakers in Congress had set up their own investigations to bring extra pressure to bear on the secretary general. Several Republican lawmakers had already called for Annan's resignation. In addition, investigations had been launched by the FBI, the CIA, the District Attorney's offices in New York and Texas, as well as a string of international judges—a total of twelve were up and running, all competing to scoop one another as reporters were racing for the ultimate prize.

Calls for Annan to step down were getting louder with every one of Volcker's interim reports. But the UN secretary general was determined to hang on. When CNN's Richard Roth asked him point-blank if the time had come for him to resign, Annan replied, "Hell no!"

Of all the corruption charges that had been brought against the United Nations, the ones against Annan were the most speculative. He had neither taken a bribe from Saddam nor given him a kickback, which made him less guilty than more than 2,300 companies worldwide and hundreds of international power brokers.

Yes, he had mismanaged—or, rather, refused to get personally involved in—the Oil-for-Food operation, despite the fact that it was the largest financial scheme the organization was asked to manage under his tenure.

As the UN's official CEO, he had presided over the most corrupt enterprise in the organization's history without once moving a finger to set it right before it was too late. And the political forces that the secretary general had enraged by calling the invasion of Iraq "illegal" were not about to let him off the hook. The presidential campaign was in full swing, and the Bush administration was subject to intense public scrutiny. The absence of significant stockpiles of WMDs in Iraq, the Abu Ghraib debacle, the Scooter Libby investigation into the outing of CIA agent Valerie Plame—all were dogging the White House. The scandal at the UN provided a welcome reprieve.

The problem with the Oil-for-Food affair, from Annan's point of view, was that as revelations gradually trickled out over time, they would not necessarily grab the front page. But they would appear frequently enough to stay in the public eye and require mainstream news editors to assign reporters to the "UN scandal beat" for extended periods of time. Once journalists started digging into the gutter of the UN's relationship with Iraq, they came across a wealth of material, including an old story involving a possible conflict of interest by Annan himself. In 1998 the *London Telegraph* had reported that the UN had wrongly awarded a contract to Cotecna, the company that employed Kofi Annan's twenty-four-year-old son Kojo. The company was in charge of certifying the arrival of humanitarian supplies at the Iraqi border. The story had been leaked to the *Telegraph* by Lloyd's Register of London, which lost the bidding war to Cotecna.

Had Kofi Annan intervened in favor of the company that employed his son? It was a legitimate question to ask. Kojo had indeed been roaming around the UN's procurement department (where secret bids are accepted on all UN contracts), and there were rumors describing him as something of a "player" who liked to use his father's name to get ahead. But that in itself is not a crime, and ultimately, no solid proof emerged that Kofi Annan had tried to influence the procurement process in favor of his son. Perhaps some people, including Pasha, helped Cotecna along to gain favor with the secretary general, but that would assume they knew Kojo was employed at Cotecna, which was not a proven fact.

Nonetheless, some of the Volcker Committee investigators believed Annan had lied to them during one of his interviews. Confidential documents from the Volcker Committee were leaked to Congress, then to Fox News. They included a transcript of a conversation between Volcker and Robert Parton, one of his investigators. When the discussion turned to how truthful Kofi Annan had been under questioning, Volcker said, "Well, my general feeling about the report is that *if* you accuse him of lying, he is *gone*"—meaning Annan would be forced to resign. "I don't know if we have the evidence to make that accusation. But we have a lot of unexplained business. The facts will speak for themselves. We can't conclude he lied. But other people may conclude that."

Volcker had spoken. But Parton, the investigator who had questioned Annan, saw the situation from a reverse angle: "You start adding up a collection of individual points—maybe none of them is sufficient alone, but when you add them together I don't believe him on our standard of proof."

"What is our standard of proof?" asked Volcker, to which Parton replied, "More likely than not."

Volcker argued that this was not a standard to which the committee agreed. "I am not prepared to hang Kofi Annan on that," he said. Volcker said he required "reasonably sufficient evidence."

Following the release of the first report, Kofi Annan made an appearance in the UN press room to announce he had been vindicated. Now *that* was certainly not true either. But the fact was, the accusation that might have toppled him was *not* related to the heart of the Oil-for-Food bribery scandal. Annan had not taken a bribe, nor had he put undue pressure on colleagues to approve a contract for the firm that employed his son.

Did Annan receive special treatment from Volcker? Parton believed so. In his testimony behind closed doors to the House panel, Parton argued that "reasonably sufficient evidence" was not a legally accepted term because it was too subjective and that Volcker's committee had previously agreed to judge each of the other individuals under investigation on the commonly used "more likely than not" standard of proof. After he failed to get his way, Parton resigned from the investigation in protest. (At least *someone* had the guts to resign in this whole affair.) But ultimately, whether one agrees with Volcker or Parton on the credibility of Kofi Annan's testimony, both men had to agree they lacked solid proof to reach a definitive conclusion about Annan's guilt. Conflict of interest there was. But a case for legal prosecution there was not.

Still, the image of Kofi Annan had been thoroughly ruined. The average man in the street thought there was something fishy going on. The *New York Post* published a cartoon of a Kofi Annan statue (looking ominously like a Saddam Hussein statue) being toppled, about to fall into barrels of oil. The vagaries of his son Kojo provided plenty of mud for the media to sling at

Kofi. They portrayed Kojo as a flashy playboy who had tried to get into all sorts of shady business deals. And there was no question that Kojo had lied to investigators about the length of his employment with Cotecna or that he had used his father's name to get a good deal on a Mercedes-Benz sedan, which he imported to Ghana without paying tax duties.

My answer to journalists who focused on such questions was, "Who cares? This is about what the international community did to the Iraqi people, not about what Kojo did using his father's name!"

It was quite obvious that the secretary general was learning about Kojo's screw-ups at the same time as the public did. This, of course, was all the more fun for the press. UN officials were telling journalists, "Don't blame the father for the sins of the son," only to see the media exploit the potential for a family feud reality show.

Short of resigning, all Annan could do to salvage what was left of his image was submit to what Volcker called "a good scrubbing" in full view of the public.

The name of the game had changed. The challenge for the secretary general was no longer merely to keep the UN's member states happy. The challenge was to fight a media war for which the UN was thoroughly unprepared. Until the scandal broke, Annan had applied every one of the cardinal rules that normally kept bureaucrats out of trouble. He had not made it to the top of the UN bureaucracy by taking risks. Annan put a perfect potential scapegoat in charge of the Oil-for-Food program (Pasha) and built an extra layer of protection by delegating all oversight responsibility to his deputy, Louise Fréchette.

As Donald Rumsfeld, the perennial political survivor, once put it, "Move decisions out to the cabinet and agencies. Strengthen them by moving responsibility, authority, and accountability in *their* direction." Yet even *he* submitted his resignation twice to President Bush after the Abu Ghraib fiasco.

Of course, in the case of Kofi Annan, who was he to submit his resignation to? The Security Council, members of which had made millions in illegal revenues in defiance of their own resolutions? Certainly, none of the Security Council's veto-yielding members were in a position to throw Annan the "first stone." Annan asked for a vote of confidence in the Security Council for his continued stewardship. The United States abstained. Russia, China, Britain, and France backed him up.

With Annan barely out of the woods, the investigation had turned to the allegations against other UN officials, the most important of which concerned Pasha. Had the head of the UN operation been on Saddam's payroll?

In my various testimonies—to Congress, the New York District Attorney's office, the Volcker Committee, and even in some articles I wrote for *The New Republic* and *Salon*—I had been protective of Pasha, occasionally insisting that the charges against him were "highly unlikely" and most often concentrating my fire on the UN's larger systemic flaws. I had gone back and researched the original vision that gave birth to the UN and previous institutions like the League of Nations, and even the Concert of Europe (which followed the Napoleonic wars). I ultimately ended up studying Immanuel Kant's "Philosophical Sketch" on "Perpetual Peace." Back in 1795, this Prussian philosopher had outlined a vision for an international institution that might be trusted to perpetuate peace among its members. In Kant's vision, all members of such an institution would need to be democratic republics in order for it to work reliably as a conduit for the peaceful resolution of conflicts. The United Nations aspired to universalism and aimed to include every state in the world as a member, irrespective of whether a given state could be trusted to play by the rules outlined in its Charter and Declaration of Human Rights. As a result of this widespread lack of accountability in the system, few states, including the democracies, were inclined to respect the institution's rules when these were not convenient to their interests. In this conclusion I found a core explanation for what had happened.

Now, in a historical first, the UN's highest officials had become subject to real public scrutiny and accountability. Would Pasha survive this process?

While we waited for Volcker to step up to the microphone, the tension in the packed room rose sharply, as a strange mix of reporters from diverse backgrounds angled for position. A fight broke out between a Korean camera crew and a French sound guy as we were waiting for Volcker to appear.

"*Merde alors, quel bordel!*" said the Frenchman, replying to what must have been an insult in Korean. And it was, indeed, a bit of a *bordel*. Well-groomed, UN-accredited, diplomatic correspondents were pitted against loud and pushy paparazzi types. Reporters who might find it bold to ask an ambassador to "please elaborate on the substance" of his discussions were wrestling for position with hacks from the "Hey Jacko! Lose the umbrella!" school of journalism.

Enter the giant.

The room fell silent, except for the camera flashes, as Paul Volcker strode toward the podium. He seemed relaxed, almost aloof to the excitement that permeated the room. He had just wrapped up an investigation of the Enron scandal. That firm had tanked after it suddenly revealed losses of some $600 million. In this case Volcker was not even sure how many *billions* of dollars had gone missing, but he had discovered enough fraud by Saddam that we could safely add another zero to the Enron figure.

Volcker's towering presence (six feet eight inches!) made us look like a bunch of Lilliputians. He'd seen audiences like this before. He smiled calmly at us as he adjusted his glasses before lowering his tortoiselike head to read his statement.

"Some principal findings based on evidence presented in the report are . . ."

I sat on the edge of my seat, as Volcker cleared his throat.

"One: that Mr. Sevan corruptly derived personal pecuniary benefit from the program through cash receipts from the sale of oil allocated by Iraq to Mr. Sevan and bought by African Middle East Petroleum Company Limited. Two: the participants had knowledge that some of the oil was purchased by paying an illegal surcharge to Iraq in violation of United Nations sanctions. . . ."

As Volcker laid out his case, connecting events I had experienced firsthand with events I could not have imagined, vivid memories flashed to life inside my head.

Volcker spoke too slowly to respond to all the questions that tumbled around in my mind. Copies of the report had been distributed at the press conference, and as I was racing through it, one sentence caught my eye: "During one of his meetings with Oil Minister Rashid, the Executive Director of the Oil-for-Food program asked him for an allocation of oil."

Wait a minute. . . . I was *there* during Pasha's meetings with the oil minister . . . and something relevant to the investigation had indeed taken place during one of those meetings, something I had failed to mention to Congress or even to the investigators, for fear that I might have to testify against Pasha in court. The report said Pasha asked for an oil gift from the Iraqis in "one of his meetings." Well, that's not exactly how it happened.

Cut to Baghdad, summer of 1998. It was our second visit to Iraq. Pasha had been invited to lunch by the Iraqi minister of oil, Amir Mohammed Rashid, at the Baghdad Hunting Club—a members-only club used by Saddam Hussein to throw parties for the Baathist elite. In later years, it had been one of Uday Hussein's hangouts; I had read various anecdotes that testified to the kind of festive mood that kid could get into. On one occasion, Uday had apparently barged into a wedding and kidnapped and raped the bride. The groom was left to close down the party by putting a bullet through his own head. A charming little anecdote to give one an appetite for lunch.

The red-carpeted stairway led into a plush dining room, where Rashid treated Pasha, Bo, and me (plus three Iraqi oil technocrats) to a four-course meal. I was surprised by this development, because the last time we had met him, near the northern city of Kirkuk, he had gotten so angry that he all but spat in Pasha's face. My notes from that meeting stopped suddenly, with these last scribbled words: "Wow—minister royally pissed off!!! Telling us to go back to New York!"

What had prompted Rashid's outburst had been a suggestion, by Pasha, about how the UN should monitor the oil-industry spare parts that the UN Security Council had recently approved for Iraq.

After the UN raised the ceiling on how much oil Iraq was allowed to export, earlier that year, the Iraqi government had asked for the permission to import more spare parts to maintain its oil industry. The problem was that Iraq had started construction on an oil pipeline to Syria, which everybody knew would be used to export oil illegally for the sole profit of Saddam Hussein. So before the Security Council could agree to the request for oil-industry spare parts, we needed to set up a new "monitoring" system, to make sure the equipment wouldn't be used to bust the sanctions. This required fielding monitors on location to Iraq's oilfields. But the oil minister would allow us to position monitors only in Baghdad, where there were no oil facilities. From there, our inspectors would not be in a position to monitor much except their own fingernails. So Pasha had to insist, causing the minister to lash out in anger and call us spies.

Then something strange happened. Pasha had said something about "a friend" who was interested in buying Iraqi oil. He first mentioned his "friend" in a conversation with the Iraqi foreign minister, Mohammed Said al-Sahaf, during a visit to the Foreign Ministry. This question by Pasha had somehow provoked a dramatic change in atmosphere in our relations with the Iraqi government.

"How does it work," Pasha had asked the foreign minister, right in front of me, "if someone wants to buy Iraqi oil?" It was a good question, though perhaps a strange one coming from the head of the UN Oil-for-Food program. *Shouldn't Pasha know this?*

The minister's eyes creased. "I'm sorry?"

"Well, I have this friend who wants to buy Iraqi oil, and he was asking me how to do it, you know. . . ."

"Aha. . . ." Sahaf nodded, adding, after a brief pause, that he would get back to us on the matter.

It was soon thereafter that we received this invitation to lunch from the Iraqi oil minister—a dramatic change in approach by the Iraqis, who had, until then, treated Pasha with glaring contempt. I felt rather uncomfortable at the prospect of sitting down for lunch at the Baghdad Hunting Club. Having coffee with these criminals was part of our job. Having lunch was not.

As we got out of the car, Pasha told me to leave my bag inside. He would not need me to take notes. We were served fancy salads and fish from the Tigris River by a staff of older men dressed in traditional black-and-white bistro attire. Pasha strayed away from official business, commenting on how good the food was. Rashid boasted that all ingredients were local, at which point my stomach said, *Oh, really?*

Or some such sound. Pasha and Rashid got along brilliantly, as far as I could tell, between my various excursions to the men's room. Every time I returned, Pasha would grimace at me discreetly, as if berating me for offending our host. Then he would encourage me to eat more, even though it had to be clear to anyone present that I had lost complete control over my digestive process.

Years later, when investigators would grill me about the substance of the discussions that took place at that lunch, I would be hard-pressed to come up with anything useful to them. But now that Volcker was putting the pieces together, I suddenly realized what all these investigators were fishing for—an indication that a deal had been struck between Pasha and Iraq's oil minister.

In fact, the oral transaction the investigators were looking to corroborate happened right after lunch. We were walking down the red-carpeted staircase with the Iraqi oil minister when Pasha again mentioned his "friend." He said his "friend" had tried to buy Iraqi oil and had sent a faxed inquiry to the Iraqi government but had not heard back from the ministry.

Rashid turned his head to look at Pasha, then at me, and then said nothing until we stepped out of the building. "What is your . . . friend's name?" asked the minister, once outside.

Pasha said something incomprehensible. The man's name was Fakhry Abdelnour, but with Pasha's elocution, such a name stood no chance at being communicated.

"Tell your friend to contact us again," said the oil minister. It was the first time I had seen the man smile.

And that was it, the beginning of another beautiful relationship. Before everyone started hugging, I went back to the car, where I had left my bag containing my Imodium pills. After swallowing a few I looked back at the crowd of jovial dignitaries shaking hands like old friends. Bo, my director, left the lunch party and walked back to the car briskly and sat beside me in silence for a few beats.

"Who's this friend he keeps talking about?" he asked.

"I don't know," I said. "Fackrablanour, or something."

"This is *not* the proper way to conduct official business," said Bo before the driver got back into the car.

That much seemed obvious. But since neither of us was yet aware of the specific practices that surrounded the oil trade, we couldn't imagine that Pasha might stand to profit from this introduction. Besides, even after I found out more about the corruption involved in that trade, I figured Pasha wouldn't do something so blatant as to put his foot in it right in front of *me!*

As it happens, the Iraqi oil minister did not catch the name of Pasha's "friend" any more than we did. So he instructed Iraq's deputy ambassador in New York, Muwafaq Ayoub, to check with Pasha. Pasha had nicknamed Muwafaq "Bumblebee" because he was always buzzing around our office, uninvited, in search of information. He would ask for advance copies of reports, and he rather disliked me because I regularly declined his requests. Bumblebee would then buzz on, to see if someone else in the office would slip him a copy or if he could simply pick up documents that were lying around.

"Keep an eye on Bumblebee," Spooky had told me. "He's spying on us right under our nose." Increasingly, Pasha would agree to meet with Bumblebee alone. The proper counterpart for Pasha would have been the Iraqi ambassador himself, and protocol would have demanded the presence of a note-taker. But on more and more occasions, Bumblebee would show up unannounced, and Pasha would let him into his office, telling me, "No, it's OK," as I instinctively rushed over with a notepad in my hand. I was a bit surprised by this development, but again, I could not conceive of Pasha engaging in corruption so openly.

What happened next would take place in great secrecy but would be detailed in carefully preserved Iraqi Oil Ministry files and eventually would be reconstructed by Volcker.

In a letter dated August 10, 1998, the oil minister was informed by his marketing manager that a company called Africa Middle East Petroleum (AMEP) had asked to buy Iraqi oil. The company was owned by Fakhry Abdelnour, Pasha's "friend." Here's how this information was communicated to Iraq's oil minister by one of his aides:

> *Dear Minister [. . .]*
> *Mr. Muwafaq Ayoub of the Iraqi mission in New York informed us by telephone that the abovementioned company [AMEP] is the company that Mr.*

Sevan, director of the Iraq Program at the United Nations, mentioned to you during his last trip to Baghdad.

For your consideration and proportioning.

In his own handwriting, the Iraqi oil minister then added that, following consultation with Saddam Hussein, "the permission of the Vice President of the Republic was received in a meeting of the Command Council on the morning of 15.8.1998. for the sale of 1.8 million barrels of oil" in the name of Mr. Sevan.

It was a done deal.

Pasha had probably hoped that all communications between himself and the Iraqi minister had stayed oral, *en passant,* and free of note-taking. But his poor elocution forced at least two additional communications, one by telephone and one by letter, to be inscribed into the meticulous records of the Oil Ministry before his friend could be helped.

In a telex dated August 18, 1998 (eight days after the Iraqis confirmed that Abdelnour was indeed Pasha's "friend"), Abdelnour was invited to visit Baghdad "to discuss matters related to the crude oil supply."

Abdelnour received Pasha's allocation for 1.8 million barrels of crude oil. He immediately resold that voucher to Shell and pocketed a net profit of $300,000. Shell would take care of sending a ship to pick up the barrels. Abdelnour had made a quick (though illegal) killing. And it would be the first of many deals to come, as Pasha would repeatedly solicit the Iraqis for oil allocations on his behalf.

In total, Abdelnour was given vouchers for 7.3 million barrels of Iraqi oil, which he swiftly resold for an estimated total profit of $1.5 million— money he could never have made without Pasha's intervention. Between 1999 and 2003, Pasha repeatedly solicited oil allocations from the Iraqis, even demanding increases for his friend Abdelnour. The Oil Ministry's records left no doubt. In their eyes, the recipient of these allocations was Pasha. And AMEP, the Panama-registered company owned by Abdelnour, was merely a front.

This was the same period in which Pasha isolated our Program Management Division, as we kept trying to blow the whistle on other types of Iraqi fraud. The same period during which he made a great push for the United States to allow more contracts through the system. The same period in which he undertook sudden trips abroad, to Geneva, Vienna, Lebanon, and Cyprus—even flying in for "consultations" with the Iraqi oil minister without note-takers. Pasha, who never used to take a single day of vacation, was now traveling the world and acting increasingly paranoid with his colleagues at the office upon his return.

According to Volcker, Pasha might have received money through various intermediaries, possibly including his aunt, who lived in Cyprus. He was supposedly given $160,000 in cash from his aunt, a retired government employee in Cyprus, who lived a modest life and was not reported to have had access to such sums. Interviews with friends, neighbors, and employees at her bank suggested that this money could not have come from her own government-issued retirement checks, which barely allowed her to get by. She had no other known sources of revenue.

Pasha reported these cash payments from his aunt as "reimbursement" for letting her stay with him at his New York apartment for a few months. Who makes his aunt pay for staying with him? Pasha's relationship with his aunt was a close one, too. She had taken care of him like a mother when he was a child. According to a relative who spoke with a journalist from the *Times* of London, Pasha was an illegitimate son whose father had apparently refused to recognize him. His mother was shunned by his father's family and was forced to leave little Pasha in the care of his aunt.

In April 2004, just as the Volcker Committee started investigating the Oil-for-Food program, Pasha's eighty-four-year-old aunt fell down an elevator shaft. She went into a coma. The same month, Pasha closed a bank account they had held jointly. She died in June in a hospital, having never emerged from her coma. Her tragic death prevented the investigators from interviewing her and prompted speculation about whether the old woman had in fact been pushed down that elevator shaft.

It looked really, really bad. The suggestion, made by some observers, that Pasha's aunt's death might not have been so accidental, given her unique role as a witness in this affair, was never substantiated. But this didn't stop journalists from speculating or even joking about the tragic event. One particularly acerbic journalist declared that the United Nations' credibility was plummeting "as fast as" Pasha's aunt "down the elevator shaft."

A rather distasteful image.

While Pasha's aunt's untimely death prevented Volcker from proving that Pasha used her to funnel money from Abdelnour, investigators found other evidence to corroborate the bribery charge. In fact, the Volcker Committee proved that he had made use of a secret bank account in Switzerland held by Abdelnour (who also happened to be Boutros Boutros-Ghali's cousin). Together with another influential Egyptian businessman named Fred Nadler (who happened to be Boutros-Ghali's brother-in-law), they formed a trio that allegedly split the profits derived from Iraq's underpriced oil allocations to Pasha.

Boutros-Ghali was the UN's chief back in 1996, when the Oil-for-Food program was adopted. An extensive examination of his bank accounts revealed no evidence that he had ever taken a bribe. Then again, the $10 million in cash that Saddam had given Korean lobbyist Tongsun Park to create "goodwill" at the UN for an Oil-for-Food program might never have entered the banking system.

We would probably never know if Boutros-Ghali ever touched any of the money allocated to bribes by Saddam at the outset of the program. But Pasha's fate was now sealed.

Through his lawyer, Pasha denied having received "a cent" from Abdelnour's oil transactions. But Pasha did not help his case by lying to Volcker about the nature of his relationship with the man.

At first, Pasha denied having met with the Egyptian oil trader more than once. Their only meeting was supposed to have occurred in March 1999 at an OPEC conference in Vienna. When confronted with his own mobile phone records, which showed multiple calls between the two men, Pasha's story changed, and he admitted they had a second "chance" meeting in Geneva (that would explain the second business card for Abdelnour, which investigators found in Pasha's cigar box when they searched his office). The second business card had a different address for Abdelnour's company, following a relocation of his business to Monaco. This suggested at least two separate meetings. Eventually, when pressed by investigators, Pasha admitted to having developed an "acquaintance" with the oil trader, and later admitted to a "friendship" that had lasted several years.

"I came to like the guy," said Pasha. "He is an interesting character, you know, he's been around the world." A minute before, he had never heard of the guy. His story was falling apart fast.

Then came the question of what Pasha was doing at the March 1999 OPEC meeting, since he had no official business being there. According to Volcker, Pasha had gone there to ask the Iraqi oil minister for an increase in Abdelnour's oil allocation. This was according to the Iraqi minister himself, who was now in U.S. custody. When pressed on this question by the Volcker team, Pasha contradicted himself again:

Investigator: In the meeting in Vienna, did you ever have any discussions with the oil minister about lifts for this particular company [AMEP]?

Pasha: No.

Investigator: Or the amount of lifts that this particular company would get?

Pasha: Well, like I said, the guy wants more oil.

Investigator: You would have said that?

Pasha: I might have said, yeah. I don't know. I don't remember.

Unfortunately, the Iraqi oil minister remembered. It's incredible how much people remember when they sit in jail. And records showed an increase in the allocation to AMEP after this crucial meeting.

The facts were in. Pasha had solicited and gotten a total of five allocations, for millions of barrels of oil, for his friend. And each time, these allocations would be duly noted in the Iraqi Oil Ministry's records and approved personally by Saddam. The Iraqi oil minister explained that they had given these allocations to Pasha because he was "a person of influence." The oil minister even boasted about having Pasha in his pocket to his associates in the Iraqi government, whom the Volcker Committee also interviewed.

Suddenly, the many pieces of my Kafkaesque UN experience started falling into place. For example, one day in 1999, we received a call from a Swedish company that wanted to export trucks to Iraq.

"The Iraqis are demanding 10 percent in kickbacks on the contract," the company's representative said to Christer, my newly appointed Swedish director. "Is that . . . ehh . . . *legal?*"

Christer stormed into my office to inquire.

"No, of course it's not legal," I said.

"So what do we do?" he asked.

"We tell the Security Council!"

"But we're no longer allowed to communicate with the Security Council," said Christer.

"Damn Cindy!" I said.

This was during my own paranoid phase, when I was blaming Cindy for manipulating Pasha into isolating our office.

I had it all wrong. Pasha was always firmly in control. Cindy was only his tool, and he knew exactly how to use her. The reason he didn't want our office communicating with the Security Council was that we were constantly raising issues of noncompliance by the Iraqi regime.

After the Swedish manufacturer was informed that it would need to pay a 10 percent kickback to the Iraqi regime, the company had, naturally, sought help from the UN. But after an absurd exchange of memos between my director and Pasha's office, the company was told it had come to the wrong window.

Pasha had squashed an attempt to denounce Saddam's fraud. And yet none of us held Pasha directly responsible. The ongoing turf war in the office allowed him to cover his tracks and kept us busy blaming each other, every step of the way.

"Don't underestimate me!" Pasha used to say. He repeated that warning to the journalists who hounded him following the publication of his name on the list of Saddam's bribe recipients. And indeed, how could one underestimate a man who had managed to fool everyone around him for years, even as he skimmed money off the fund he had been charged with safekeeping?

Had it not been for the war, Pasha would never have been caught. He had not made a single obvious mistake. No money had been transferred directly to his account. He had withdrawn the money in cash from Switzerland, then fed it into his bank account in New York in smaller sums of less than $10,000, which triggered no alarm bells at the Treasury Department. And his political maneuvers in the UN Security Council had not even gotten the United States or Britain angry, or even suspicious of him. He had not taken any political stance in favor of lifting the sanctions, as others had. (Of course, this would have been bad for his little business.) He had flown under the radar and had everybody around him, including me, convinced of his innocence right up to the day of Volcker's briefing, which found him guilty of fraud that presented "a grave conflict of interest and . . . seriously undermined the integrity of the United Nations."

When Volcker was done with his account, he was assaulted with questions from the press. I had a million questions for him myself, but I just sat there, in the middle of the media frenzy, emotionally knocked out.

As I looked around the room, the whole situation seemed unreal, almost fictional.

"Would you say that Mr. Sevan took a bribe?" came the question from CNN's Richard Roth (for whom I had worked right after college, before I joined the UN). It was much worse than that. Pasha had actually *asked* for a bribe. Many bribes. . . .

Why, Pasha?

I recalled an evening in the fall of 2000. An impending storm had kept me in the office late. It was one of those massive New York tempests that gather steam all day long and wait until people leave the office to wreak havoc on the city.

As I waited for the tempest to break, I decided to visit with some colleagues in the office. Cindy had recently sent a memo around reminding all staff that it was "against UN rules" to accept any gifts from contractors doing business under the program. Since Cindy never sent out memos without a reason, I was trying to find out whom she might be suspecting. She had sent the memo right before going on extended leave, so I didn't have the luxury of asking her directly. At the time, I assumed she was probably setting the stage for another one of her power grabs. But in retrospect, there was only one explanation: she knew what Pasha was up to. And this was her way of letting him know.

Had her memo been a subtle way of blackmailing him? Or was she simply trying to do what she could with the means that she had? Memos were our only tools. We were in business with one of the most corrupt regimes on earth, and we were expected to enforce international law with memos.

It didn't help, of course, that the man who ultimately controlled the flow of these memos was on Saddam's payroll. And I can only imagine how stressed Cindy would have felt if she had indeed come across clues that Pasha was dipping in the pot. Whom could she confide in? Her drive to consolidate her power in the office had been successful, but it had left her all alone in a position of enormous responsibility. Pasha had let her have her way. *You want control? Take it. It'll keep you busy while I run my little business on the side.*

Cindy eventually had a breakdown, which explained why she was away from the office that stormy night. Officially, the problem was with her lower back. She functioned on double doses of Valium, painkillers, and muscle relaxants, and had gained a lot of weight before finally throwing up her arms and going on sick leave. What I didn't realize at the time was that she, too, was going through hell in this office. Everybody who worked for Pasha eventually went the same route. And rarely did they realize that he was the source of what ailed them. They would blame other colleagues but never Pasha. He played stupid all along, even as he was sowing division around his shop.

In retrospect, I'd say nobody played stupid better than Pasha. He had elevated it to an art form. His outbursts of anger, irrational as they seemed, were never improvised. Even his incomprehensible elocution often worked in his favor. He could sound clear when he wanted to. But occasionally his blurry words allowed him to remain noncommittal when it suited him, to be evasive when necessary, and to bait his interlocutors. He would sometimes say just one word, without bothering to make a sentence, just to see one's reaction. And that was what he did that night, when he surprised me in a colleague's office as I was conducting my little investigation into the reasons for Cindy's memo.

"Happy now?" Pasha said, after slapping me on the neck by surprise.

"Oh, hello, sir."

"Happy now, huh?"

"Why should I be happy?"

"Your friend Cindy is in the hospital!"

"She is? Why? What's wrong?"

"Her back's facked ap!"

"Shit. . . ."

"So your director is officer-in-charge!"

"Why, you leaving?"

"Yeah, I have to go to this . . ." (didn't bother to finish the sentence). "But keep an eye on your boss, eh? I don't want no shit while I'm gone. It's not because Cindy's in the hospital that he can do whatever he wants! These two, really, they're like cats and dogs!" Pasha continued, as if he had no role in setting his underlings up for a permanent conflict. "You should see the shit I have on my desk. Back and forth, back and forth, they never stop with the facking memos."

I followed him to his office to see what he was on about, but when we arrived, Pasha's mind had flipped the channel.

"Scotch?" asked Pasha.

The storm was now pounding the building. A thousand little red lights down on First Avenue told me traffic was hell. So I slipped into the leather chair facing Pasha's desk and took a burning sip of scotch. It had been a long time since we had sat down one-on-one like this. Since isolating our side of the shop, he had kept interactions to a minimum. But the moment he had said "scotch" that night, I got the feeling he had something to tell me.

"Look at all this shit," said Pasha, pointing to a bunch of bills on his table. "I spend all my time on this facking program," he complained. "Everybody's making millions, and me, I don't even have time to pay my bills!"

I had heard him say this before. But that night, he seemed more stressed than usual. His daughter was applying to college—Boston University. Thirty thousand bucks a year. And the thirty-eighth floor was sitting on his contract renewal, raising the prospect that he might soon have to retire. Pasha, of course, had no desire to leave his throne.

"I spent my whole life for this organization and this is how they thank me!" he said, relighting his cigar. The guy was worried about his financial future. He made a respectable $186,000 a year, tax-free, owned an apartment in

New York and a house in the Hamptons, but his social status was linked to his job. In retirement, he wouldn't have a diplomatic passport, nor would he be able to expense his travels.

"If I had wanted to, I could have been a millionaire," he said. "With all the people I know . . . trust me . . . it would not have been a problem!"

"I'm sure," I said.

"You don't believe me?"

"No, I do."

"You better believe it! *Millions!*"

The man who could have been a millionaire looked around his office, contemplating the remains of his career—native artwork from the Pacific islands, a picture of Pasha in his thirties with a naked cannibal from Papua New Guinea, a political cartoon by Plantu of *Le Monde* from his days in Afghanistan. He had served as the top UN envoy there during the fall of the Communist regime in Kabul. On the floor was a Shisha pipe from his days in Lebanon. Though his office was larger than the apartments of most of his employees, he didn't have enough room on the wall for all his paintings. Gifts, for the most part.

For an Armenian kid from Cyprus, whose father rejected him at birth, he had come very far in life. He had enjoyed a fascinating UN career and had reached the top of the pyramid with his appointment as under secretary general, now in charge of the largest operation in UN history.

"Ah, yeah. . . ." said Pasha, nodding at the past.

"You've had some great experiences," I said.

"Ha!" said Pasha, reminiscing.

During his stint in Afghanistan, the Pakistani government had lent him a luxury jet plane with a mini-bar and all the amenities. Those were the days. UN officials used to get respect in this world. . . .

"It used to be good money, too," said Pasha. "Now? Forget it!"

UN officials could still travel the world without putting their hand in their pocket, but the bubble of prosperity that had enveloped New York in the 1990s had sent prices skyward and left the world's civil servants relatively poorer. They used to be able to afford large apartments in the city and lavish dinners at the hottest nightspots. The system was now populated by top managers who hated one another. Pasha could hardly mention the name of another high-level official without disgust. His enemies were numerous, and soon, they would band together to force him into retirement. Or so he feared.

"I bet the secretary general will renew your contract," I said.

"Oh, really?" said Pasha, his eyes getting smaller. "Why? Who are you talking to on the thirty-eighth floor?" Pasha made his suspicious face.

"It's not about the thirty-eighth floor. You have enemies there—they may be delaying your contract. But ultimately, it would be a headache to replace you. There's too much money at stake now. Every member of the UN Security Council would want their own man at the wheel. Kofi Annan doesn't need the headache."

Pasha puffed on his cigar for a beat, taking in the logic. "But Riza is up to something," he said, mentioning his main enemy, Kofi Annan's chief of staff, by name.

"Maybe," I said. "But Kofi Annan needs to pick his battles. He'll get rid of you only if Council members press for it. And nobody's pressing for it."

The Americans had issues with Pasha, but at least he wasn't an anti-sanctions activist, like other high-level UN officials. The French and the Russians would have preferred someone more outspoken in this post. But Pasha was good for business. He never fussed about front companies or kickback allegations. *Obviously.* And you never knew with political hotheads like Halliday. They might just get incensed one day and denounce the corruption of a well-oiled business.

"You're irreplaceable," I said to Pasha.

"Nobody's irreplaceable!" said Pasha, holding up his cigar as he repeated the old bureaucratic mantra. "But I don't care, anyway," he lied. "If they want this mess they can have it. I've worked my ass off to make this facking program work! Billions of dollars! And I don't even have time to pay my bills!"

The bills again. . . .

"And you think anybody's going to thank me? Huh?" Pasha asked.

"I guess not. But that's the system. . . ."

"The system? What system?" Pasha shouted. "They don't give a shit about me or you or anybody! It's every man for himself, Kid. . . . Every man for himself!"

And so it was.

After thirty years in the UN system, Pasha had seen it all: member states violating their own resolutions over and over, vast sums of money changing hands, political favors rewarded with hard currency. Why should everybody be getting rich except him?

He had spent hours at meetings of the Security Council sanctions committee. That was where the Iraqi contracts were approved—where the real haggling took place. It was a multibillion-dollar diplomatic bazaar. A typical trade might involve the Russian representative agreeing to certain language in a given UN resolution, in exchange for the United States and Britain approving $300 million worth of (overpriced) Russian contracts. The United States and Britain would then play good cop/bad cop to get further concessions out of the Russians. The latter would then seek help from the French or the Chinese, who would raise new issues and complicate the equation further, until finally, a deal would be struck. The United States and Britain would get their tough language reprimanding Saddam, and the Russians, the Chinese, and/or the French would get their contracts approved.

As the man in charge of this bazaar, Pasha felt he deserved a cut. The money he declared as gifts from his spinster aunt would just about pay for four years of college plus expenses for his daughter (the rest of his profits were likely kept abroad, according to the Volcker Committee). Pasha knew his days at the UN were numbered. So he raked in what he could, using the influence of his office, and went into retirement a richer man.

I don't think his little business stopped him from sleeping at night. But I do believe he felt the need to justify himself that evening. The man who had shed tears in front of a dying kid at an Iraqi hospital had to know it was wrong to dip in the pot of money that was specifically designed to help such children. But the man who could have been a millionaire felt cheated by the system—a system in which he had long since stopped believing, yet which he had figured out how to play better than anybody, to the point where he became truly difficult to replace.

Pasha had played his cards with great skill. As he sat there talking to me that evening, he had already pocketed a nice cash prize. And he felt confident enough to go ask for more. He could not possibly have foreseen, back then, that his business partners in Iraq would be toppled; that the Kurdish and Shiite rebels, whom he had treated so arrogantly, would end up in power; that they would find his name on a bribe-takers list; that they would publish it in a free Iraqi newspaper, sparking a scandal, which the kid now sitting in front of him would react to by calling for an investigation that would nail him.

Back to The Edge

I was back at The Edge, the bar I had discovered during my first visit to northern Iraq. The place still deserved its name, and once again it adequately reflected the state I was in when I arrived.

I had traveled back to Iraq as a journalist, contributing articles to the *International Herald Tribune* and my old college-town paper, the *Providence Journal.* I was also gathering footage for a documentary on the UN Oil-for-Food experience, to be produced by Denis Poncet, an Academy Award–winning filmmaker who had taken an interest in our most unusual experience.

I was traveling with my friend Amir, a Persian-American doctor of history and psychiatry. Together, we had visited refugee camps, hospitals, and even a mental ward, where every patient had a shaved head and was dressed in a sweat suit. In our group photo with them, Amir and I looked like the coaches of a rather unlikely soccer team. The mental institutions had strange names, which made one worry about the type of people who got locked up in there. One place was called the center for the "deaf and dumb." Apparently, that was a widely used expression across the world before the advent of sign language.

In Iraqi sign language, I learned, the gesture for "American" involved making a gun with one's fingers and imitating the act of shooting. This came from old cowboy movies, but one could clearly understand why it was still in use.

Though the Americans were disliked in many parts of Iraq, they were extremely popular with the Kurds up north. People here liked foreigners in general, and we were warmly welcomed regardless of where we showed up. During an early visit to a hospital, we met a group of friendly young Iraqi psychiatrists, who took us under their wing and helped us travel long distances without resorting to following military convoys or hiring protection.

The Edge was located in the Christian neighborhood of Erbil, the largest city in Iraqi Kurdistan. Protected by cement walls, the enclave housed the only non-hotel bar in the city. It looked smaller than I remembered it. And the population that packed the room was very different as well. Standing at the bar were a group of rugged-looking white men, whom we recognized as "Blackwater types," meaning security contractors. The dance floor looked completely out of place. A group of young Filipina girls were dancing provocatively under the ogling eyes of the sex-deprived men getting drunk at the bar.

There was something of a Wild West saloon feel to the place. So I decided to order a whiskey. We sorely needed a drink. We had spent the afternoon visiting hospitals, assessing the needs of the region's health facilities. These were far better equipped than the ones I had visited during my first trip. They also benefited from an influx of Sunni Arab doctors who had been forced to flee the chaos in the south of Iraq, where the Health Ministry and the main hospitals had come under control of the Shiite militias and were often no longer safe for Sunnis. Arab Iraqis with friends in the Kurdish north could buy their way to relative safety in that region.

Unfortunately, the hospitals were also very busy operating on men who had been wounded in fighting around Mosul and Kirkuk, two cities right to the south of the Kurdish mountain range, which still harbored significant terrorist networks and remained a powder keg of ethnic rivalry between Arabs and Kurds. I was not used to seeing so much blood and so many wounded patients.

Based on my expression as we left the busy hospital, Amir recommended we go get a drink. The change of scenery was welcome. As we entered the bar we were surprised at the sight of the dancing Filipina girls. In a land where many women wore veils (though far less so in the north than in southern parts of the country), the sudden appearance of skimpily clad women shaking their booties to hip-hop music was rather bewildering. What in the world were they doing here?

As I sipped my drink, one of the girls came up to me. "What hotel are you staying at?" she soon asked.

It didn't take me long to figure out she was a hooker. In fact, she even introduced me to her pimp, a middle-aged English bloke with white hair tied in a ponytail. He wore a Manchester United soccer jersey, a black leather vest, and a fat gold chain around his neck. Though there was a sign at the entrance of the bar asking people to leave their weapons outside (these signs were as common as nonsmoking signs might be in New York), I noticed this rule did not seem to apply to the pimp.

Instead of asking him how much he charged for the Filipina girl, I asked him if he had friends in the security business who could fly us to Baghdad. We had flown directly into northern Iraq with a company called Zozik Airlines. It wasn't British Airways, but the plane was in good shape and tickets were relatively affordable. The flight was packed with Kurdish emigrants and their children, who now lived in Europe and were going back to their homeland to visit their families. Most of them clapped, and many had tears in their eyes upon landing in Sulaymaniyah. They were greeted with glee at the airport, and the joy of these reunions almost made us forget that we had landed mighty close to an active war zone.

The drive down to Baghdad was a dangerous one. Security contractors charged exorbitant prices for protection. We had met a group of South Africans a few nights ago. After we bought them more drinks than I could recount, they were ready to cut us a deal.

When I asked them how they had managed to stay alive on Iraq's dangerous roads, their answer was simple: "We shoot first, and never stop to ask questions."

Countless Iraqis had been harmed by trigger-happy security contractors. In September, a Blackwater convoy would come under criticism for killing seventeen civilians in one fell swoop, at a traffic junction in Baghdad. The Iraqi government sought to expel the company from the country, but it turned out many of its own officials, as well as the State Department, benefited from these mercenaries' protection.

In the case of the South African guns for hire, we decided to drop any plans to ride with them after one of their crew revealed himself to be a bitter racist. He was a veteran of South Africa's war in Rhodesia, and when he talked about that experience, it soon became clear to Amir and me that we were dealing with a war criminal.

Another event dissuaded us from driving to Baghdad from the north altogether. One night, as we came back to our hotel, we found that the front door was locked. There were no staff at the front desk, and we were effectively locked out for the night. After sleeping on the couches of a nearby hotel, we returned the next morning to complain to the hotel owner. The owner apologized before explaining the tragedy that had befallen his staff the previous night. Two of his employees had traveled down to visit their families further south. On their way back, they had been captured by terrorists and tortured for three hours. One of them, a Kurd, was killed. The other one, an Arab, was released after his family paid a ransom.

"This is your 'new Iraq,'" said the hotel owner. He was an Arab who had fled the violence in Baghdad, leaving behind his home and all his possessions, to take refuge in the Kurdish north. He was one of the lucky ones. More than two million Iraqi refugees had lost everything they owned. Iraqi women were forced to work as prostitutes in Syria and Jordan. Entire families were confined to refugee camps, with scant hope of ever finding their way back home. Terrorism and ethnic or religious violence had ravaged the country in the four years since the U.S. invasion. Nobody knew how long this senseless violence would go on.

After spending an hour with me, drinking coffee and smoking cigarettes as he reminisced about the events that had brought him into exile in his own country, the hotel owner slapped his knees with both hands. He needed to get back to work. In a country where even funeral processions had become targets, mourning had become a privilege few people could afford.

The British pimp at The Edge advised us to forget about catching a ride to Baghdad. Just getting a lift with a secure convoy from the airport into the Green Zone would cost us $600 each. Clearly, most of Iraq had become impenetrable to all but men who were prepared to shoot their way through. Neither Amir nor I was interested in taking more risks than necessary to do our job. We scratched our plan to visit Baghdad on the spot and ordered another drink.

One of the girls tried once again to lure me onto the dance floor. The thought of how many contractors she must have been with was enough to make me cling to the bar.

After my second shot of whiskey, I suddenly started to feel nostalgic. The eclectic and diverse humanitarian community that used to call this place home had all but vanished from Iraq. I remembered how Pasha had launched into a wild Greek dance extravaganza on the same dance floor.

Ah, Pasha. . . . People still remembered him in these parts. Many Kurds had developed an intense dislike for him, and I was wise enough not to introduce myself to local politicians as a former Oil-for-Food employee. During one visit to a TV station, where I got to look through old video footage of Pasha cutting ribbons and visiting local dignitaries, one producer told me that Pasha would probably not be safe if he ever came back to the region.

"Rest assured, he has no such plans," I said.

Since his demise at the hands of the Volcker Committee, Pasha had been forced to flee New York, where he no longer enjoyed diplomatic immunity. He had settled into retirement in his native Cyprus, where the local government had pledged not to extradite him for trial in the United States. On January 16, 2007, the Southern District Court of Manhattan had indicted him on charges of bribery and conspiracy to commit wire fraud.

In March 2006, Claudia Rosett, the freelance reporter who had broken most of the scoops in the Oil-for-Food affair, showed up at Pasha's doorstep in the Cypriot capital of Nicosia. In the short time it took him to open the door and shut it back in her face, Pasha said, "I am not running away!" Then he added, "I am not ashamed to look into the mirror when I shave."

Pasha being Pasha, he eventually invited Rosett in for coffee. As a rule, he liked to "keep his enemies close," even if this meant having coffee with someone who had hounded him for the past couple of years and played a significant role in causing his downfall.

In his last letter to the staff, Pasha had argued that he had been made a scapegoat. While he was found guilty of corruption by Volcker, there was something to be said for the fact that he was far from the only one involved who had profited at the expense of Iraq's civilians. In a sense, Volcker's investigation reminded me of Hercule Poirot's inquiry in Agatha Christie's *Murder on the Orient Express.*

This was a whodunit in which most parties involved had "done it." A truly "multilateral" heist. The entire international community had been involved in the fleecing of Iraq.

At the end of *Murder on the Orient Express,* Poirot assembled the passengers in the train's main dining room to present them with the results of his investigation. Poirot had two theories about how the murder went down, and he asked the assembly to decide which one was correct. His first theory was that a single individual, who had since escaped, was guilty of the crime. It was a perfectly plausible theory, of course, but not one that could answer all his questions. And thus Poirot exposed his second theory: namely, that every passenger in the compartment had participated in the crime. Poirot was not surprised to see the assembly enthusiastically endorse his first theory.

Volcker approached his task in much the same manner as Poirot. The Security Council was perfectly content with his first line of inquiry into the petty corruption of a retired UN bureaucrat who had since escaped to Cyprus. But when he started to dig deeper, revealing how systematically the member states of the Security Council had participated in the fraud by violating their own laws, his investigation began to run out of cash.

Council members weren't about to pay Volcker to cause them further em-barrassment. Even the U.S. government stonewalled some of his requests, es-pecially after he started calling for the investigation of the staggering levels of corruption that had followed the war itself.

While some people were outraged that Pasha had managed to escape the law, personally I could not help but feel relieved to know that the man who had taken me under his wing when I was an absolute beginner in the world of international diplomacy would be spared the prospect of spending his re-tirement years in jail.

Had I connected the dots earlier and talked to the authorities about Pasha's efforts to introduce his "friend" the oil trader to the Iraqi government during our lunch at the Baghdad Hunting Club back in 1998, it is possible that the District Attorney's office might have moved against him much faster and ar-rested him while he was still in New York. But if Pasha's guilt could have been proved before a wider investigation got under way, chances are we never would have found out about the true extent of the corruption that plagued our international system.

After one interview, in which I had refused to speculate about Pasha's guilt, an assistant DA asked me, point-blank, whether I was protecting Pasha out of a sense of loyalty. *Was I?* I pondered the question as I walked out of the Federal Building in downtown New York. I suppose there was a difference be-tween *wishing* that Pasha was innocent and *hoping* for the same. In truth, I had scant reasons on which to base real hope. How could I have missed the obvious signs that Pasha's behavior toward the Iraqi government had changed dramatically after our fateful lunch with the oil minister? How could I not have concluded that Pasha's effort to plug his "friend" Abdelnour constituted a gross conflict of interest that would likely land him a cash commission? How could I have been so naïve?

Perhaps I had found it convenient to lie to myself, as so many of us had done, in order to rationalize the cynical realities that permeated our world. The news of Pasha's guilt had burst the last illusion I maintained about my former employer and cast new light on the meaning of my work in the ser-vice of the United Nations.

And yet I could not afford to become cynical about this journey. If any-thing, I had seen where cynicism led people. Pasha had been corrupted by cynicism long before he had been tempted by greed.

My colleagues and I had paid a steep price for our experience. But it was not without value. The Oil-for-Food debacle had sparked the most meaningful push for reforms since the UN's creation. And it exposed the true nature of the organization's core institution: the Security Council itself.

The black elixir that fueled the world economy enticed most members of the Security Council to violate the laws they had adopted together, completely discrediting the institution's claim to legitimacy and moral authority.

Sad as this discovery was, it would have been far worse if it had never been made. While no amount of reforms would transform the United Nations into a perfectly accountable body, we had witnessed a historic first with the imposition of previously unimaginable demands for transparency on the world body.

If transparency, or *glasnost*, as Mikhail Gorbachev used to call it, could bring the Soviet empire to its knees, surely it could be trusted to provoke real change in the ossified structures that govern international affairs.

The demise of our operation marked the end of an era. Radical new ideas were emerging about how to reshape the world organization. One former adviser to Kofi Annan, who also resigned, argued for a dissolution of the Security Council and its Secretariat in favor of an agency-driven approach to solving global challenges. In a *New York Times* op-ed published in September 2005, Nader Mousavizadeh, a fellow Danish national of Persian origin, challenged the forces of the status quo, which had opposed reforms even in the aftermath of the Oil-for-Food debacle. "At this stage," he wrote, "the burden surely falls on the proponents of the status quo—those who cannot imagine a world without a Security Council, a General Assembly or Secretariat—to explain what value these structures add that outweighs the profound damage they have done to the very idea of multilateral action."

The forces of complacency were being rattled. People who could hardly be described as right-wing UN bashers or left-wing radicals were starting to make their voices heard.

Instead of rattling my faith in the need for international governance, my experience had strengthened it. As much as I researched the history of UN reform, however, I never found a better blueprint for healthy international organization than that originally offered by Immanuel Kant in his 1795 essay "On Perpetual Peace." Unfortunately, neither the United Nations nor its predecessor, the League of Nations, sought to abide by Kant's guidelines, which foresaw an organization of democratic, independent republics that would apply to the international realm the laws and values that the Enlightenment had brought to bear on the domestic realm.

The financial corruption I had witnessed had its roots in the corruption of a great vision, an attempt to apply international laws to governments that considered themselves above their own domestic laws and whose actions had a spillover effect that tainted the entire system.

"Corruption is nature's way of restoring our faith in Democracy," wrote Peter Ustinov. The Security Council was indeed coming under mounting criticism for failing to adhere to the basic principles of the democratic process and for concentrating all power in the hands of a few states. The lack of separation between the legislative, judicial, and executive branches of governance on the world stage would eventually need to be addressed. A legal body whose members violated their own laws with impunity would not prove sustainable in the long run. Change was inevitable.

Perhaps I was fooling myself once again. But insofar as delusions go, optimistic ones are far healthier than pessimistic ones. The lies we tell ourselves, for better or worse, often end up defining the way we act. Greater transparency was a cause in which I felt comfortable placing my faith. And our debacle, while tragic in many ways, had given this cause momentum. Never before had so many corrupt individuals and companies been exposed on the world stage. Under pressure from NGOs like the Government Accountability Project, UN whistleblowers were offered new protections. A steady progression toward greater transparency was in motion, and, to the best of my ability, I would contribute to this process in the future.

After returning from Iraq, I took up a teaching job at New York University's Center for Global Affairs. In the spring semester of 2008, after one lecture in which I had spoken of my misadventures working for the United Nations, a student came up to me and asked me for advice. She had an opportunity to join the United Nations and was wondering, in light of my experience, whether I thought it was a good idea.

Spooky's old words of advice came to mind: *be your own man.*

It had been the best advice I received throughout this whole journey. It ultimately led me into a confrontation with the "system," and I can't say that made for only good times. I realized that Pasha had felt betrayed by my decision to call for an investigation. And surely, he realized that I felt equally betrayed by his corruption, too. I suppose our trajectories had been on a collision course from the start.

The system tends to transform young idealists into old realists. Both outlooks have their inherent flaws (idealists can be alarmingly naïve, just as realists can be dangerously cynical), but both offer necessary, even complementary, contributions to the process. In fact, the idealism/realism dichotomy is at the center of most debates in the field of international affairs. In the real world of diplomacy, the clash between these two worldviews often translates into a clash between generations.

Ours was a game in which most players ended up feeling stabbed in the back at some point or another, either on the level of their ideals or on the level of their raw personal interests. The key to surviving in such an environment was to try to be true to oneself. And so, in answer to the young student, I found myself repeating the advice that I had received at the outset of my own journey.

"I can't advise you against joining the UN," I said. "In fact, I hope that my own experience doesn't dissuade you from joining. I do feel I made a difference. And if that's what you want to do at this stage in your career, nothing should hold you back."

She nodded.

"But if the going gets tough, as surely it will, just remember: be your own . . . woman. Your own person. Think for yourself. And if you see something rotten, don't be afraid to speak out."

Seeing signs of confusion in her expression, I remembered how confused I had felt myself, some ten years ago, when Spooky first welcomed me to the game. And it made me smile.

INDEX

A.V.M. Air, 73
ABC News Channel, 3
Abdelnour, Fakhry, 297–299
Abdel-Rahman, Omar ("Sheikh Omar"), 224
Abramoff, Jack, 12–13, 37
  lobbyist extraordinaire, 9–10
Abu Ghraib, 293
Accountability
  Government Accountability Project, 316
  UN system lacking, 133–137, 214
  UN's lack of, internationally, 282, 294
Adnan, 57, 59, 61
Afghan v. Yemenite, 146–147
Afghanistan, 223–224, 261, 262, 269
African Middle East Petroleum (AMEP), 295, 298
Afsane, 35
Ahmad, Sultan Hashim, 157
Ailes, Robert, 223
AK-47 rifle, 39, 81, 101
Albright, Madeleine, 28–29, 44, 158
Alcatel telecom firm, 229
Algeria, 255
Allawi, Ali, 278
Allawi, Iyad, 264, 266
Allies (World War I), 77
Al-Mada, 265–266, 268, 278
Al-Rasheed Hotel, 39, 49, 166
Amanpour, Christiane, 241–242
AMEP. *See* African Middle East Petroleum
American Enterprise Institute, 273
American oil companies, 84
  Chevron, 274

Delta, 269
Shell, 299
  See also United States
Amnesty International report (2001), 56–57
Angola, 237
Annan, Kofi, 23, 33, 40, 46
  on anti-UN propaganda, 184–185
  background of, 129–130
  Baghdad mission by, 156–161
  buck passing by, 137
  called upon to step down, 290–291
  "Hammarskjöld moment," 161–162
  ordering investigation, 284–285
  weapons inspection deal by, 70
Annan, Kojo, 118, 282, 291
Anthrax, 220, 234
Anti-sanctions activities, 41–42, 51, 172, 175–177, 221
  in Baghdad, 132
  Halliday's, 173–174, 183
Arab Club of Britain, 178
Arab League, 156
Arabs
  Kurds' ethnic rivalry with, 310
  Lawrence of Arabia, 267
  Shiite Marsh Arabs, 143, 198
  Sunni Arab doctors, 310
  Sunni Muslims, 77
  Sunni terrorists, 251
  See also specific Arab nations/persons
Araud, Gerard, 231–232
Armitage, Richard, 233
Arnett, Peter, 39